EAP Foundation

# Academic Writing Genres: Essays, Reports & Other Genres

Sheldon Smith

Academic Writing Genres:
Essays, Reports & Other Genres
*Part of the EAP Foundation series*

Copyright © 2019 by Sheldon Smith

All rights reserved. No part of this publication may be reproduced, stored in a retrieval system, or transmitted, in any form or in any means – by electronic, mechanical, photocopying, recording or otherwise – without prior written permission.

ISBN 978-1-912579-02-0

First Edition

This book is published by Evident Press.

Acknowledgements
Academic collocations listed at the start of each unit are derived from the Academic Collocation List (ACL), developed by Kirsten Ackermann and Yu-Hua Chen using the Pearson International Corpus of Academic English (PICAE). The lists were generated using the online ACL highlighter of the EAPFoundation.com website. See: http://www.eapfoundation.com/vocab/academic/acl/highlighter/.

All texts from external sources are licensed under Creative Commons CC BY. Attribution to the original source is given wherever those texts occur.

EAP Foundation Series
The following titles form part of the *EAP Foundation series*.

Writing
- Academic Writing Genres

Speaking
- Academic Presentations

Other titles will be released soon. For more information visit www.evidentpress.com/publications/.

# About the EAP Foundation series

The *EAP Foundation* series is written for students who are preparing for, or currently studying at, a Western university, including students on foundation or pre-sessional courses. In contrast to many English language textbooks, which offer fragments of information scattered around a series of exercises, books in the *EAP Foundation* series focus on presenting practical information in a straightforward and readable manner, with exercises coming at the end of each unit as a way to check understanding and deepen comprehension. This straightforward presentation of material makes the books ideal not only for classroom use, but for independent study or review after class. There are checklists for each unit, which serve to foster self reflection and peer feedback, which are important principles behind the *EAP Foundation* series of books. All books have additional resources which can be downloaded, including worksheets, copies of checklists, teaching tips, lesson plans and mp3 recordings (for books in the speaking and listening series). This is ideal for personal use (if you are a student) or classroom use (if you are a teacher). These resources are available free of charge, using the access code available in *Appendix 1: Accessing online resources*. A full answer key is provided at the end of the book, meaning there is no need for a separate teacher's manual.

# About the author

Sheldon Smith has been teaching English for Academic Purposes (EAP) since 2002, working in the UK, Indonesia and China. Since 2005 he has been working on pathway programmes which prepare students for university study at Western universities, chiefly in the USA, UK and Australia. In addition to textbooks for academic English, he is the author of several novels, as well as textbooks for Chinese language learning. He is the founder and chief developer of the EAPFoundation.com website. He currently resides in Guangzhou, Guangdong province, China.

# Contents

Introduction .................................................................................. 7

## Part I: Essays ........................................................................ 11
Unit 1: About the Essay Genre ............................................................ 13
Unit 2: Compare & Contrast Essays ....................................................... 33
Unit 3: Cause & Effect Essays ............................................................ 51
Unit 4: Problem-Solution Essays .......................................................... 67
Unit 5: Classification Essays ............................................................ 79
Unit 6: Argument Essays .................................................................. 95
Unit 7: Discussion Essays ................................................................ 109
Unit 8: Definition Essays ................................................................ 119
Unit 9: Process Essays ................................................................... 129
Unit 10: Exemplification Essays .......................................................... 139
Unit 11: Description Essays .............................................................. 149

## Part II: Reports .................................................................... 159
Unit 12: About the Report Genre .......................................................... 161
Unit 13: Laboratory Reports .............................................................. 179
Unit 14: Business Reports ................................................................ 199
Unit 15: Other Report Types .............................................................. 219

## Part III: Other Genres ............................................................. 229
Unit 16: Posters ......................................................................... 231
Unit 17: Reflective Writing .............................................................. 247
Unit 18: Book Reviews .................................................................... 259
Unit 19: Research Proposals .............................................................. 271
Unit 20: Theses/Dissertations ............................................................ 281

## Part IV: Genre Elements ............................................................ 293
Unit 21: Abstracts ....................................................................... 295
Unit 22: Literature Reviews .............................................................. 305

# Appendices .................................................................... 317
- Appendix 1: Accessing online resources ................................. 318
- Appendix 2: Answers to exercises ......................................... 319
- Appendix 3: Transition signals .............................................. 411
- Appendix 4: Essay titles ....................................................... 417
- Appendix 5: Essay Grid ........................................................ 421

# Index ............................................................................. 424

# Introduction

## Contents of this section

**INTRODUCTION** ..................................................................7

    Overview .........................................................................................7
    What are academic writing genres?..................................................7
    Features of the book.......................................................................8
    Structure of the book......................................................................8
    Internal/external links ...................................................................10
    Key to language phrases ..............................................................10

## Overview

Students at university are expected to write in a range of genres. This book examines frequently used academic writing genres, identifying common features such as structure and language, and providing clear models, in order to scaffold learning and provide a way for students to master each one.

## What are academic writing genres?

Genres are social actions used to achieve a particular purpose, for a particular audience and context. The ability to understand and use genres is part of becoming a member of a given community. Academic English has spoken genres, including lectures, seminars, presentations and dissertation defences, as well as written genres, such as essays and reports. **EAP Foundation: Academic Writing Genres** focuses on those in the written form.

The most common genre for undergraduate study is the essay, which can be sub-divided into many different types, such as comparison and contrast, cause and effect, argument and classification. Because of the many types, and their importance for student writing, the essays section is the largest section in the book, with detailed exercises for each unit. Reports are also very common, especially in the sciences, and are looked at in detail. Other genres (and genre elements), such as posters, research proposals, theses/dissertations and abstracts, are also covered.

# Features of the book

Each unit begins with a clear list of learning outcomes, along with key vocabulary. As with all books in the *EAP Foundation* series, information is presented in a straightforward and readable manner. The main text is accompanied by additional tips to help improve performance, as well as numerous 'In short' boxes, which give a summary of the main points covered (an example is given to the right). These are useful for previewing the unit before reading and reviewing later. Each unit contains a checklist to give feedback on writing (to yourself or a peer). There are full examples of essays of each type, reports, posters, abstracts and so on, to provide clear models. Each unit concludes with a range of exercises to check comprehension and deepen understanding. Appendices give information on accessing online resources, full answers to the exercises, and other information.

| In short |
|---|
| The book contains:<br>• learning outcomes;<br>• key vocabulary;<br>• practical information;<br>• additional tips;<br>• 'In short' summaries;<br>• checklists;<br>• example texts;<br>• exercises;<br>• additional resources. |

# Structure of the book

The first section of the book considers **essay** writing. It begins by looking at the content and structure of a typical essay (*Unit 1: About the Essay Genre*), then looks at different essay types, namely *Comparison & Contrast (Unit 2), Cause & Effect (Unit 3), Problem-Solution (Unit 4), Classification (Unit 5), Argument (Unit 6), Discussion (Unit 7), Definition (Unit 8), Process (Unit 9), Exemplification (Unit 10)* and *Description (Unit 11)*.

The second section of the book looks at **report** writing, beginning with an overview of report writing (*Unit 12: About the Report Genre*), followed by a detailed look at the two most common report types, namely *Laboratory Reports (Unit 13)* and *Business Reports (Unit 14)*. Other report types are also covered (*Unit 15: Other Report Types*).

The third section covers **other genres** which do not fit into the essay or report category. They are *Posters (Unit 16), Reflective Writing (Unit 17), Book Reviews (Unit 18), Research Proposals (Unit 19),* and *Theses/Dissertations (Unit 20)*.

The fourth and final section considers **genre elements**. These are types of writing which can form part of other genres, but can also be stand-alone pieces of writing, and need looking at in detail. They are *Abstracts (Unit 21)* and *Literature Reviews (Unit 22)*.

The graphic on the following page summarises the structure of the book.

# Introduction

**Overview of units and sections**

## Part I — Essays

Types:
- About Essays [Unit 1]
- Comparison & Contrast [Unit 2]
- Cause & Effect [Unit 3]
- Problem-Solution [Unit 4]
- Classification [Unit 5]
- Argument [Unit 6]
- Discussion [Unit 7]
- Definition [Unit 8]
- Process [Unit 9]
- Exemplification [Unit 10]
- Description [Unit 11]

## Part II — Reports

- About Reports [Unit 12]

Types:
- Laboratory [Unit 13]
- Business [Unit 14]
- Other types [Unit 15]

## Part III — Other Genres

- Theses/Dissertations [Unit 20]
- Research Proposals [Unit 19]
- Book Reviews [Unit 18]
- Reflective Writing [Unit 17]
- Posters [Unit 16]

## Part IV — Genre Elements

- Abstracts [Unit 21]
- Literature Reviews [Unit 22]

# Internal/external links

Some internal links are included in the book. These point backwards or forwards to other units related to the area under discussion, which will help you make connections between different aspects of writing. Two examples are given here. The first is an example of an internal link to an *earlier* section of the book; note the arrows pointing *backwards* (i.e. to the left), and the left-aligned text. The second is an example of an internal link to a *later* section of the book; note the arrows pointing *forwards* (i.e. to the right), and the right-aligned text.

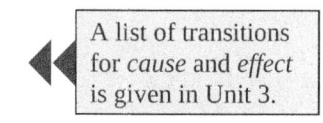

◀◀ A list of transitions for *cause* and *effect* is given in Unit 3.

*Abstracts* and *executive summaries* are covered in more detail in Unit 21. ▶▶

Some content may be closely related to another aspect of EAP. In this case, there may be an external link to another book in the *EAP Foundation* series. The following is an example of an external link; note the arrows pointing *forwards* and *backwards* (i.e. out of the book), and the centred text. The colouring is also different for clarity (dark background, white lettering).

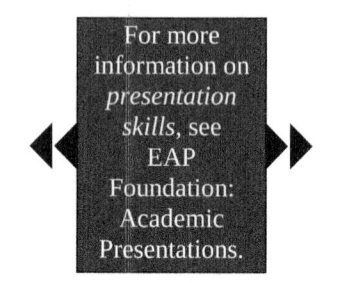

◀◀ For more information on *presentation skills*, see EAP Foundation: Academic Presentations. ▶▶

# Key to language phrases

Language phrases are generally shown in a way which minimises space and shows how the parts of the phrase can be combined. See the following examples, from Unit 5.

| [X] | can be<br>may be<br>is/are | classified<br>grouped | into…<br>as… |

These parts can be combined in a total of 12 ways (3 x 2 x 2 = 12). For example:
- [X] can be classified into…
- [X] can be classified as…
- [X] can be grouped into…
- [X] may be classified into…
- [X] is grouped as…

# Part I:
## Essays

# Unit 1 | About the Essay Genre

## Learning Outcomes

By the end of this unit, you should:
- understand the general structure of an essay;
- know what elements an introduction contains;
- know how to write a clear thesis statement;
- know how to write a topic sentence;
- know different types of support which can be used in a paragraph;
- know what elements a typical conclusion contains;
- be aware of some common phrases to introduce a concluding sentence.

By completing the exercises, you will also:
- study an example essay for structure and support;
- study the structure of sample introductions;
- identify topic and supporting sentences;
- study how transitions link sentences of a paragraph together;
- identify parts of a topic sentence;
- practise writing thesis, topic sentences and summary of an essay.

## Key Vocabulary

*Nouns*
- introduction
- main body
- conclusion
- background
- thesis statement
- topic sentence
- topic
- controlling idea
- supporting sentence
- summary
- final comment

## Additional Vocabulary

*Academic Collocations (in the unit)*
- future research (adj + n)
- general statement (adj + n)
- overall structure (adj + n)
- strongly suggest (adv + v)

*Academic Collocations (in the essay)*
- negative effects (adj + n)
- public transport (adj + n)

## Contents of this section

### Unit 1: About the Essay Genre ..................... 13
Overview ..................... 14
Introduction ..................... 15
Main Body ..................... 17
Conclusion ..................... 20
Structure of an essay ..................... 21
Checklist ..................... 22
Example essay #1 ..................... 23
Example essay #2 ..................... 24
Exercises ..................... 25

# Overview

Although essays vary in length and content, most essays have the same overall structure. The general structure of an academic essay is shown in the diagram below. Each area is discussed in more detail later in the unit.

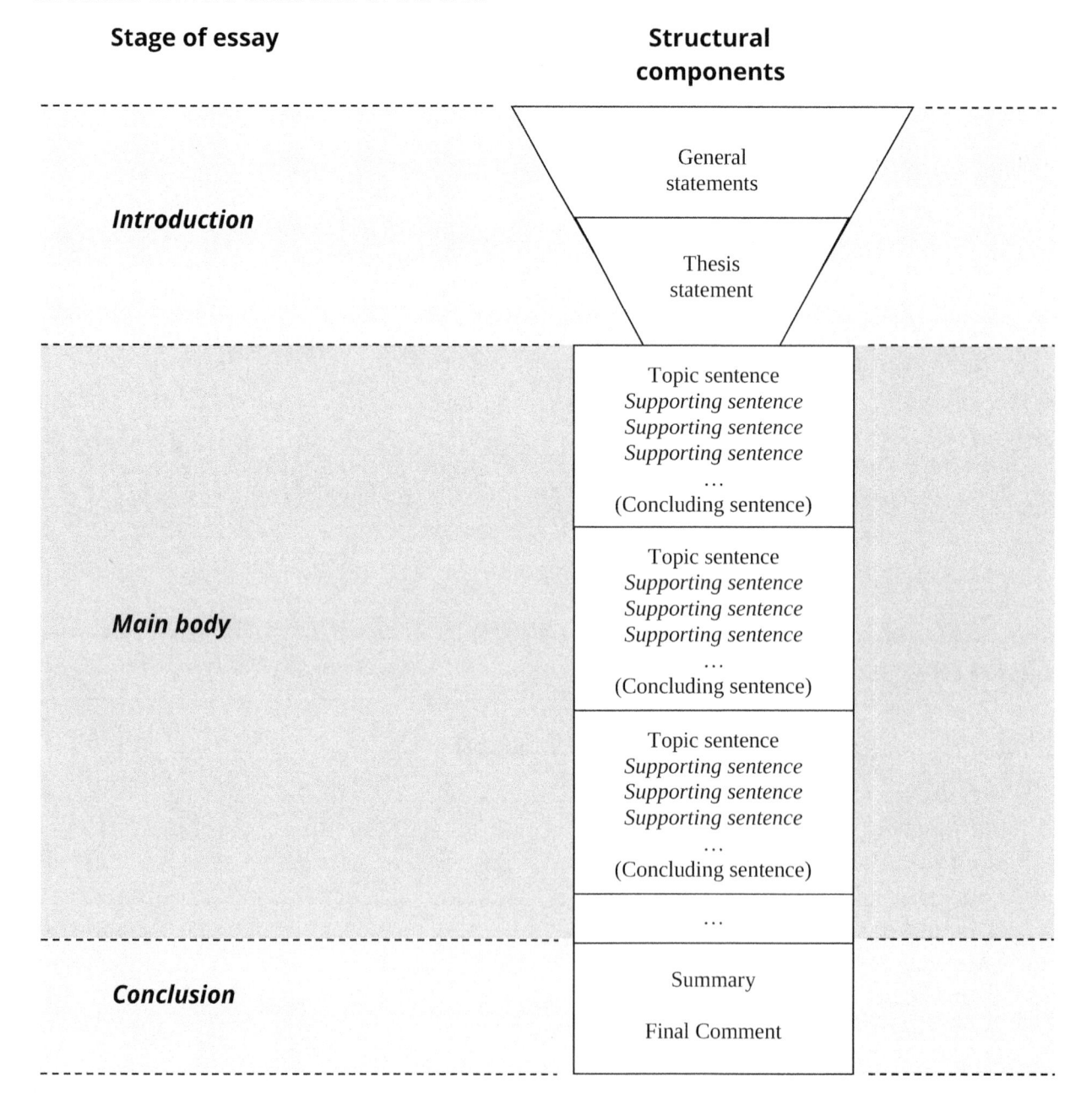

| Stage of essay | Structural components |
|---|---|
| **Introduction** | General statements |
|  | Thesis statement |
| **Main body** | Topic sentence<br>*Supporting sentence*<br>*Supporting sentence*<br>*Supporting sentence*<br>…<br>(Concluding sentence) |
|  | Topic sentence<br>*Supporting sentence*<br>*Supporting sentence*<br>*Supporting sentence*<br>…<br>(Concluding sentence) |
|  | Topic sentence<br>*Supporting sentence*<br>*Supporting sentence*<br>*Supporting sentence*<br>…<br>(Concluding sentence) |
|  | … |
| **Conclusion** | Summary<br>Final Comment |

# Unit 1: **About Essays**

# Introduction

Getting started can often be difficult. Even professional writers say that the hardest part of writing is the beginning. Writing an introduction to an essay can therefore seem a daunting task, though it need not be so difficult, as long as you understand what an introduction needs to contain. It will begin with some **general statements** which make clear what the topic is and give some background information. This will help the reader to understand what you are writing about and show why the topic is important. It will also contain an overall plan of the essay, which is called the **thesis statement**. Many writers choose to write the introduction last, after they have written the main body, because they need to know what the essay will contain before they can give a clear plan.

| In short |
|---|
| The main purpose of the introduction is to:<br>• introduce the topic of the essay;<br>• give background information on the topic;<br>• indicate the overall plan of the essay. |

## *General statements*

The general statements will introduce the topic of the essay and give background information. The general statements should become more and more specific as the introduction progresses, leading the reader into the essay. For a short essay, the general statements may be just one or two sentences. For longer essays, the general statements could include one or more definitions (see *Unit 8: Definition*), or could classify the topic (see *Unit 5: Classification*), and may cover more than one paragraph.

The following is an example of background statements for a short essay.

> *Although they were invented almost a hundred years ago, for decades cars were only owned by the rich. Since the 60s and 70s they have become increasingly affordable, and now most families in developed nations, and a growing number in developing countries, own a car.*

These sentences introduce the topic of the essay (cars) and give some background to this topic (situation in the past, the situation now). These sentences lead into the thesis statement (see below).

## Thesis statement

The thesis statement (also just called the 'thesis') is the most important part of the introduction. It gives the reader clear information about the content of the essay, which will help them to understand the essay more easily. The thesis states the specific topic, and often lists the main (controlling) ideas that will be discussed in the main body. It will usually indicate how the essay will be organised, for example cause and effect, comparison and contrast, classification, order of importance and so on. It is usually at the end of the introduction, and is usually (but not always) one sentence long.

> **In short**
> The thesis statement:
> - states the specific topic of the essay;
> - often lists the main (controlling) ideas;
> - usually indicates the method of essay organisation;
> - is usually at the end of the introduction;
> - is usually one sentence.

Here is an example of a thesis statement with no subtopics mentioned:

> *While cars have undoubted advantages, they also have significant drawbacks.*

This thesis statement tells us the specific topic of the essay (advantages and disadvantages of cars) and the method of organisation (advantages should come first, disadvantages second). It is, however, quite general, and may have been written before the writer had completed the essay.

> **Tip: Writing the thesis**
> It may be better to write the thesis *after* the main body, as you will know what the main ideas are.

In the following thesis statement, the subtopics are explicitly stated:

> *While cars have undoubted advantages, of which their convenience is the most apparent, they have significant drawbacks, most notably pollution and traffic problems.*

This thesis gives us more detail, telling us not just the topic (advantages and disadvantages of cars) and the method of organisation (advantages first, disadvantages second), but also tells us the main ideas in the essay (convenience, pollution, traffic problems). This essay will probably have three paragraphs in the main body.

> **Open vs. closed thesis**
> A thesis statement which does not specify the content of the main body is called an 'open' thesis. In contrast, a 'closed' thesis is one which specifies the main body content.

# Unit 1: About Essays

# Main Body

As the name suggests, the main body is the main part of your essay. It is a collection of paragraphs related to your topic, and in order to understand how to write a good main body, you need to understand how to write good paragraphs. To do this, you need to understand the three main structural components of any good paragraph: the **topic sentence**, **supporting sentences**, and the **concluding sentence** (optional).

> **In short**
>
> The main body is a collection of paragraphs, each of which should contain:
> - a clear topic sentence;
> - supporting sentences, giving reasons, facts, examples, statistics, or citations;
> - a concluding sentence (optional).

## *The topic sentence*

The topic sentence is the most important sentence in a paragraph. It is usually the first sentence, though may sometimes also be placed at the end, and in fact can be positioned anywhere in the paragraph. It indicates what the paragraph is going to discuss, and thus serves as a useful guide both for the writer and the reader; the writer can have a clear idea what information to include (and what information to exclude), while the reader will have a clear idea of what the paragraph will discuss, which will aid in understanding. As it presents the main idea, without supporting information, the topic sentence is the most general sentence in the paragraph.

The topic sentence comprises two separate parts: the **topic** of the paragraph, and the **controlling idea**, which limits the topic to one or two areas that can be discussed fully in one paragraph.

> **Tip: Topic sentence**
>
> Although the topic sentence can appear anywhere in the sentence (which can make reading difficult), for clarity you should always try to make it the *first* sentence.

Consider the following topic sentence, from the same example essay as before.

> *The most striking advantage of the car is its convenience.*

The topic of this short essay is the advantages and disadvantages of cars, as a result of which each paragraph has either advantage or disadvantage of cars as its topic. In this case, the topic is *advantage of cars*. The controlling idea is *convenience*, which limits the discussion of advantages of cars to this one idea. This paragraph will therefore give supporting ideas (reasons, facts, etc.) to show why convenience is an advantage of cars.

Here is another topic sentence from the same example essay:

> *Despite this advantage, cars have many significant disadvantages, the most important of which is the pollution they cause.*

The topic of this paragraph is the *disadvantage of cars*. The controlling idea is *pollution*. This paragraph will therefore give supporting ideas (reasons, facts, etc.) to show why pollution is a disadvantage of cars.

Here is the final topic sentence from the same example essay:

> *A further disadvantage is the traffic problems that they cause in many cities and towns of the world.*

The topic of this paragraph is again the *disadvantage of cars*. The controlling idea this time is *traffic problems*. This paragraph will therefore give supporting ideas (reasons, facts, etc.) to show why traffic congestion is a disadvantage of cars.

**In short**
The following are key points to remember about the topic sentence:
- it should be a complete sentence;
- it should contain both a *topic* and a *controlling idea*;
- it is the most general sentence in the paragraph, because it gives the main idea without supporting details.

## Supporting sentences

Supporting sentences develop the topic sentence. They are more specific than the topic sentence, giving **reasons**, **examples**, **facts**, **statistics**, and **citations** in support of the main idea of the paragraph.

Below is the whole paragraph for the second topic sentence above.

> *Despite this advantage, cars have many significant disadvantages, the most important of which is the pollution they cause. Almost all cars run either on petrol or diesel fuel, both of which are fossil fuels. Burning these fuels causes the car to emit serious pollutants, such as carbon dioxide, carbon monoxide, and nitrous oxide. Not only are these gases harmful for health, causing respiratory disease and other illnesses, they also contribute to global warming, an increasing problem in the modern world. According to the Union of Concerned Scientists (2018), transportation in the US accounts for 30% of all carbon dioxide production in that country, with 60% of these emissions coming from cars and small trucks. In short, the harm to our health and to the environment means that pollution from cars is a major drawback.*

# Unit 1: About Essays

The paragraph above has the following support:
- burning fuels (petrol and diesel) in car engines emits pollutants – **fact**;
- cars emit carbon dioxide, carbon monoxide, nitrous oxide - **examples** (of pollutants);
- the pollutants are harmful for health – **fact**;
- the pollutants cause respiratory disease - **example** (of how they harm health);
- the pollutants contribute to global warming – **fact**;
- 30% of carbon dioxide in the US comes from transport – **statistic**;
- 60% of these emissions come from cars and small trucks – **statistic**;
- this information comes from Union of Concerned Scientists (2018) - **citation**.

## *The concluding sentence*

The concluding sentence is an *optional* component of a paragraph. In other words, it is not absolutely necessary. It is most useful for especially long paragraphs, as it will help the reader to remember of the main ideas of the paragraph.

Below is the concluding sentence from the paragraph above:

> *In short, the harm to our health and to the environment means that pollution from cars is a major drawback.*

Here the concluding sentence not only repeats the controlling idea of the topic sentence, that cars cause pollution, but also summarises the information of the paragraph, which is that the pollution from cars is harmful to both our health and the environment.

The following are useful transition signals to use for the concluding sentence.

- In conclusion...
- In summary...
- In brief...
- Therefore...
- Thus...
- In short...
- These examples show that...
- This evidence strongly suggests that...

# Conclusion

While getting started can be very difficult, finishing an essay is usually quite straightforward. By the time you reach the end you will already know what the main points of the essay are, so it will be easy for you to write a **summary** of the essay and finish with some kind of **final comment**, which are the two components of a good conclusion.

> **In short**
> The concluding paragraph consists of the following two parts:
> - a summary of the main points;
> - your final comment on the subject.

## *Summary*

It is important, at the end of the essay, to summarise the main points. If your thesis statement is detailed enough, then your summary can just be a restatement of your thesis using different words. The summary should include all the main points of the essay, and should begin with a suitable transition signal. You should not add any new information at this point.

The following is an example of a summary for the essay on advantages and disadvantages cars used in this unit:

> *In conclusion, while the car is advantageous for its convenience, it has some important disadvantages, in particular the pollution it causes and the rise of traffic jams.*

Although this summary is only one sentence long, it contains the main (controlling) ideas from all three paragraphs in the main body. It also has a clear transition signal ('In conclusion') to show that this is the end of the essay.

## *Final comment*

Once the essay is finished and the writer has given a summary, there should be some kind of final comment on the topic. This should be related to the ideas in the main body. Your final comment might:

- offer solutions to any problems mentioned in the body;
- offer recommendations for future action;
- give suggestions for future research.

Unit 1: **About Essays**

Here is an example of a final comment for the essay on cars:

*If countries can invest in the development of technology for green fuels, and if car owners can think of alternatives such as car sharing, then some of these problems can be lessened.*

This final comment offers solutions, and is related to the ideas in the main body. One of the disadvantages in the body was pollution, so the writer suggests developing 'green fuels' to help tackle this problem. The second disadvantage was traffic congestion, and the writer again suggests a solution, 'car sharing'. By giving these suggestions related to the ideas in the main body, the writer has brought the essay to a successful close.

# Structure of an essay

The following chart summarises the structure of an essay.

| Stage of essay | Structural component | Purpose(s) |
|---|---|---|
| **Introduction** | General statements | • To introduce the reader to the subject of the essay. |
| | Thesis | • To inform the reader of the organization of the essay and what will be included. |
| **Main body** | Topic sentence | • To indicate what the paragraph will discuss.<br>• To guide the writer (who will have a clear idea what information to include).<br>• To guide the reader (who will have a clear idea of what the paragraph will discuss). |
| | Supporting sentences | • To develop the topic sentence, using reasons, examples, facts, statistics, and citations. |
| | Concluding sentence | • To remind the reader of the main ideas of the paragraph (optional, most useful for long paragraphs). |
| **Conclusion** | Summary | • To give the reader a brief reminder of the main ideas. |
| | Final comment | • To bring the essay to a satisfactory close. |

# Checklist

Below is a checklist for essays. Use it to check your own writing, or get a peer (another student) to help you.

| Stage of essay | Item | OK? | Comments |
| --- | --- | --- | --- |
| **Introduction** | The essay begins with *general statements*, which introduce the topic. | | |
| | The introduction ends with a *thesis statement*. | | |
| | The *thesis statement* shows the essay type/organisation (e.g. comparison and contrast, advantages and disadvantages). | | |
| | The *thesis statement* shows the main ideas of the essay. | | |
| **Main body** | Each paragraph has a *topic sentence*. | | |
| | Each topic sentence has a suitable *topic* and *controlling idea*. | | |
| | Each paragraph has detailed *supporting ideas* (facts, reasons, examples, statistics, citations). | | |
| | Long paragraphs have a *concluding sentence* for clarity. | | |
| | Any concluding sentences are introduced using a clear *transition signal* (e.g. 'In short'). | | |
| **Conclusion** | The conclusion begins with a suitable *transition signal* (e.g. 'In conclusion...', 'To summarise...'). | | |
| | The conclusion has a *summary* of the main ideas. | | |
| | The conclusion ends with a *final comment* (the writer's idea or a recommendation). | | |

# Unit 1: About Essays

# Example essay #1

Below is the example essay used throughout Unit 1 (above).

*Title: Consider whether the advantages of the car outweigh the drawbacks.*

Although they were invented almost a hundred years ago, for decades cars were only owned by the rich. Since the 60s and 70s they have become increasingly affordable, and now most families in developed nations, and a growing number in developing countries, own a car. While cars have undoubted advantages, of which their convenience is the most apparent, they have significant drawbacks, most notably pollution and traffic problems.

The most striking advantage of the car is its convenience. When travelling long distance, there may be only one choice of bus or train per day, which may be at an unsuitable time. The car, however, allows people to travel at any time they wish, and to almost any destination they choose.

Despite this advantage, cars have many significant disadvantages, the most important of which is the pollution they cause. Almost all cars run either on petrol or diesel fuel, both of which are fossil fuels. Burning these fuels causes the car to emit serious pollutants, such as carbon dioxide, carbon monoxide, and nitrous oxide. Not only are these gases harmful for health, causing respiratory disease and other illnesses, they also contribute to global warming, an increasing problem in the modern world. According to the Union of Concerned Scientists (2018), transportation in the US accounts for 30% of all carbon dioxide production in that country, with 60% of these emissions coming from cars and small trucks. In short, the harm to our health and to the environment means that pollution from cars is a major drawback.

A further disadvantage is the traffic problems that they cause in many cities and towns of the world. While car ownership is increasing in almost all countries, especially in developing countries, the amount of available roadway in cities is not increasing at an equal pace. This can lead to traffic congestion, in particular during the morning and evening rush hour. In some cities, this congestion can be severe, and delays of several hours can be a common occurrence. Such congestion can also affect those people who travel out of cities at the weekend. Spending hours sitting in an idle car means that this form of transport can in fact be less convenient than trains or aeroplanes or other forms of public transport.

In conclusion, while the car is advantageous for its convenience, it has some important disadvantages, in particular the pollution it causes and the rise of traffic jams. If countries can invest in the development of technology for green fuels, and if car owners can think of alternatives such as car sharing, then some of these problems can be lessened.

References
Union of Concerned Scientists (2018) *Car Emissions and Global Warming*. Available at: https://www.ucsusa.org/clean-vehicles/car-emissions-and-global-warming (Accessed 8 May 2018).

# Example essay #2

Below is a second (new) example essay. It is used in one of the exercises later.

> *Title*: In the past people were more careful with money and did not buy until they had saved their money. Nowadays, an increasing number of people are buying on credit. What are the short- and long-term effects of this?

Society is becoming increasingly materialistic. There is an ever-increasing array of new products which advertising makes us desire. To help consumers meet this desire, it is becoming easier to buy goods on credit. While there are some obvious, positive short-term benefits of this, most notably an improved quality of life, there are also many long-term, mainly negative effects, such as the possibility of life-long debt.

One of the most obvious short-term effects of buying on credit is that quality of life will be improved. In the past, only the rich could afford luxury items such as cars, washing machines, or computers. Now, however, these items can be purchased by almost anyone. This has many obvious benefits. If, for example, parents want to help their child's education by purchasing a computer, then they can do so regardless of how much money they have in the bank.

Despite this positive short-term effect, there are also some more negative long-term effects, the most important of which is that buying on credit can lead people into a life of debt. Although some people may claim that credit gives much convenience to the consumer, it must be remembered that they pay for this convenience in the form of high interest rates. They will consequently pay much more for the products than if they had saved up and bought them, and it will thus take them much longer to pay for them. Furthermore, the ease with which credit cards can be obtained and used may lead to reckless spending. Credit card users will later be faced with monthly bills, which will use up much of their income and take them years or even a whole lifetime to pay off.

In conclusion, although buying on credit has positive short-term benefits such as improved quality of life, it also has many negative long-term effects, the most important of which is the possibility of a life of debt. While advertising makes us all want to buy the newest, fastest, smallest product, it would be wise for consumers who plan to buy on credit to consider the long-term consequences before they purchase.

# Unit 1: **About Essays**

## Exercises

### Exercise 1: **Comprehension**

Answer the following questions about this unit. Either do this after reading the unit, or make notes first then use your notes to answer the questions.

**1** What are the three parts of a typical *essay*?

- _____
- _____
- _____

**2** What is the main purpose of the introduction?

_____

_____

_____

**3** In the diagram at the start of the unit, the introduction has a 'funnel' shape (right). Why?

_____

_____

**4** List some features of the *thesis statement*.

- _____
- _____
- _____
- _____
- _____

**5** What are the three components of a typical *paragraph*?

- _____
- _____
- _____

# Academic Writing Genres — Sheldon Smith

**6** Why might the final component of a paragraph be missing?

_____
_____

**7** What is the *controlling idea*? Where would you find it?

_____
_____

**8** Why is the topic sentence important to:
- the writer  _____
- the reader  _____

**9** Is the following statement true or false: *The topic sentence is the most specific sentence in the paragraph.* Justify your answer.

_____
_____

**10** Give examples of types of support that a paragraph might contain.
- _____
- _____
- _____
- _____
- _____

**11** What are the two components of a typical conclusion?
- _____
- _____

# Unit 1: About Essays

## Exercise 2: **Example essay**

Study the example essay #2 earlier in the unit (on the topic of *buying on credit*) and answer these questions.

a) Highlight the following aspects of the essay:
- background;
- thesis statement;
- topic sentences;
- summary;
- final comment.

b) What method of organisation has been used? I.e. what type of essay is this?

_____

c) Use the following table to record the *controlling ideas* as they appear in the *thesis*, the *topic sentences* and the *summary*.

| Thesis | Topic sentences | Summary |
|--------|-----------------|---------|
|        |                 |         |
|        |                 |         |

d) What do you notice about the language in b) above? Are the *exact* same phrases used each time? If not, how are they different? Why do you think that is?

_____

_____

_____

e) Study the following paragraph again. Identify the different types of *support* which are used.

> One of the most obvious short-term effects of buying on credit is that quality of life will be improved. In the past, only the rich could afford luxury items such as cars, washing machines, or computers. Now, however, these items can be purchased by almost anyone. This has many obvious benefits. If, for example, parents want to help their child's education by purchasing a computer, then they can do so regardless of how much money they have in the bank.

# Academic Writing Genres        Sheldon Smith

## Exercise 3: **Introductions**

Study the following three essay introductions (from essays later in the book). For each one:
- identify which part is the *background*;
- identify which part is the *thesis statement*;
- decide how many paragraphs the main body is likely to have;
- identify the controlling ideas of the paragraphs;
- identify the method of organisation of the essay (i.e. the essay type).

---

**1**

Number of paragraphs:_____
Controlling ideas:
_____
_____
_____

Method of organisation:
_____

Most people spend around fifteen years of their life in education, from primary school to university study. In the past, students only had the opportunity to study in their own country. Nowadays, however, it is increasingly easy to study overseas, especially at tertiary level. Tertiary education, also called post-secondary education, is the period of study spent at university. As the final aspect of schooling before a person begins their working life, it is arguably the most important stage of their education. While there are some undoubted benefits of this trend, such as the language environment and improved employment prospects, there is also a significant disadvantage, namely the high cost.

---

**2**

Number of paragraphs:_____
Controlling ideas:
_____
_____
_____

Method of organisation:
_____

Products that are bought by the end user are called consumer products. They include electric razors, sandwiches, cars, stereos, magazines, and houses. Marketers must know how consumers view the types of consumer product their companies sell so that they can design the marketing mix to appeal to the selected target market. To help them define target markets, marketers classify consumer products by the amount of effort needed to acquire them. The four major categories under this classification are unsought products, convenience products, shopping products, and specialty products.

---

**3**

Number of paragraphs:_____
Controlling ideas:
_____
_____
_____

Method of organisation:
_____

Before the advent of computers and modern technology, people communicating over long distances used traditional means such as letters and the telephone. Nowadays there is a vast array of communication tools which can complete this task, ranging from email to instant messaging and video calls. While the present and previous means of communication are similar in their general form, they differ in regard to their speed and the range of tools available.

# Unit 1: About Essays

## Exercise 4: Identifying topic and supporting sentences

Study the following paragraphs. The sentences need to be rearranged into the correct order to form the completed paragraph. In each case, you should:
- decide which sentence is the *topic sentence* and label it **TS**;
- decide on the order of the supporting sentences, and label them **1, 2**, etc.;
- highlight any transition words or phrases which helped you to order the sentences.

### Paragraph 1

|   |   |
|---|---|
|   | Some organisms, like sea sponges, lack a true nervous system. |
|   | The insect nervous system is more complex but also fairly decentralized |
|   | Nervous systems throughout the animal kingdom vary in structure and complexity, as illustrated by the variety of animals shown in Figure 35.2. |
|   | Others, like jellyfish, lack a true brain and instead have a system of separate but connected nerve cells (neurons) called a nerve net. |
|   | Octopi may have the most complicated of invertebrate nervous systems—they have neurons that are organized in specialized lobes and eyes that are structurally similar to vertebrate species. |

### Paragraph 2

|   |   |
|---|---|
|   | In this case, although exclusivity can provide an initial motivation for going global, managers must realize that competitors will eventually catch up. |
|   | Perhaps the most urgent reason is to earn additional profits. |
|   | In other situations, management may have exclusive market information about foreign customers, marketplaces, or market situations. |
|   | Companies decide to go global for a number of reasons. |
|   | If a firm has a unique product or technological advantage not available to other international competitors, this advantage should result in major financial success abroad. |
|   | Finally, saturated domestic markets, excess capacity, and potential for cost savings can also be motivators to expand into international markets. |

### Paragraph 3

|   |   |
|---|---|
|   | Taiwan and South Korea have long had an embargo against Japanese cars for political reasons and to help domestic automakers. |
|   | In another example, when the environmentally conscious Green movement challenged the biotechnology research conducted by BASF, a major German chemical and drug manufacturer, BASF moved its cancer and immune-system research to Cambridge, Massachusetts. |
|   | Large multinationals have several advantages over other companies. |
|   | For instance, multinationals can often overcome trade problems. |
|   | Despite this fact, Honda USA, a Japanese-owned company based in the United States, sends Accords to Taiwan and South Korea. |

Paragraph 1 adapted from *Biology 2e* by OpenStax. Download for free at https://openstax.org/details/books/biology-2e. Paragraphs 2 and 3 are adapted from *Introduction to Business Studies* by OpenStax. Download for free at https://openstax.org/details/books/Introduction-to-Business.

# Academic Writing Genres — Sheldon Smith

## Exercise 5: Identifying the parts of a topic sentence

a) Study the following topic sentences. For each one, identify:
- the **topic** (underline it and label it **t.**);
- the **controlling idea** (highlight it and label it **c.i.**).

b) Do you notice any pattern in the order of topic and controlling idea?

**Example**

                     *t.*                  *c.i.*

The most striking <u>advantage of the car</u> is its ==convenience==.

i) There are several important reasons for the collapse of the Roman Empire.

ii) Obtaining nutrition and energy from food is a multistep process.[*]

iii) The final step in digestion is the elimination of undigested food content and waste products.[*]

iv) The amount of sleep we get varies across the lifespan.[**]

v) One similarity between current and previous methods of communication relates to the form.[**]

vi) There are a number of factors which affect our body weight.[**]

vii) Sleep debt has significant negative psychological and physiological consequences.[**]

viii) Other theorists believe that intelligence should be defined in more practical terms.[**]

ix) In order for a memory to go into long-term memory, it has to pass through three distinct stages.[**]

x) The second distortion error is suggestibility.[**]

   \*    From *Concepts of Biology* by OpenStax. Download free at https://openstax.org/details/books/concepts-biology.
  \*\*   From *Psychology* by OpenStax. This OpenStax book is available for free at https://cnx.org/content/col11629/1.5.

## Unit 1: **About Essays**

### Exercise 6: **Writing thesis, topics sentences, and summary**

a) Brainstorm ideas for the following essay title, then write the **thesis, topic sentences** and **summary** for an essay, using the grid below. Make sure these are *complete sentences*.

*Title*: What are the advantages of being able to speak a second language?

*Use this space to brainstorm ideas*

*Thesis statement:* _____

Topic sentence #1: _____

Topic sentence #2: _____

Topic sentence #3: _____

Summary: _____

b) Below is a modified version of the checklist for essays from earlier in the unit. It has been modified so that it can be used with an essay outline like the one above. Use it to check your own writing, or get a peer (another student) to help you.

| Stage of essay | Item | OK? | Comments |
|---|---|---|---|
| Introduction | The *thesis statement* shows the essay type/organisation (i.e. advantages). | | |
| | The *thesis statement* shows the main ideas of the essay. | | |
| Main body | Each topic sentence has a suitable *topic* and *controlling idea*. | | |
| Conclusion | The conclusion begins with a suitable *transition signal* (e.g. 'In conclusion...', 'To summarise...'). | | |
| | The conclusion has a *summary* of the main ideas. | | |

## Exercise 7: Learning outcomes check

a) The following are the learning outcomes for this unit. Decide how well you have mastered each one by giving it a score, as follows.

    3 = I understand/can do this well.
    2 = I understand/can do this fairly well, but I can improve with more practice.
    1 = I understand/can do this, but not well enough yet. I need to practise more.
    0 = I do not understand/cannot do this yet. I need more time.

| Score | Learning Outcome |
|---|---|
| _____ | I understand the general structure of an essay. |
| _____ | I know what elements an introduction contains. |
| _____ | I know how to write a clear thesis statement. |
| _____ | I know how to write a topic sentence. |
| _____ | I know how to write a summary. |
| _____ | I know different types of support which can be used in a paragraph. |
| _____ | I know what elements a typical conclusion contains. |
| _____ | I know some common phrases to introduce a concluding sentence. |
| _____ | I can identify topic sentences and supporting sentences. |
| _____ | I understand how transitions link sentences in a paragraph together. |
| _____ | I can identify parts of a topic sentence. |

b) Use this information to review the unit and improve.

# UNIT 2 | Comparison & Contrast Essays

## Learning Outcomes

By the end of this unit, you should:
- know what a comparison and contrast essay is;
- understand ways to structure a comparison and contrast essay;
- be able to use language for showing comparison and contrast;
- understand how to apply criteria to make appropriate comparisons and contrasts.

By completing the exercises, you will also:
- study an example essay for structure, language and content;
- practise using language for comparison and contrast;
- use a Venn diagram to complete a comparison and contrast essay;
- use a Venn diagram to brainstorm ideas for an essay;
- write a comparison and contrast essay;
- peer edit a comparison and contrast essay, using a checklist.

## Key Vocabulary

*Nouns*
- comparison
- contrast (also *verb*)
- block
- point-by-point
- similarity
- difference

*Adjectives*
- similar
- different

*Verbs*
- compare

## Additional Vocabulary

*Academic Collocations (in the unit)*
- close proximity (adj + n)
- historical periods (adj + n)
- human behaviour (adj + n)
- natural world (adj + n)
- stress levels (n + n)
- cause stress (v + n)

*Academic Collocations (in the essay)*
- modern technology (adj + n)
- significant difference (adj + n)
- vast array (adj + n)
- frequently used (adv + past)
- complete this task (v + n)

## Contents of this section

### Unit 2: Compare & Contrast Essays .................. 33

    Overview ........................................................................................................ 34
    Structure of comparison and contrast essays............................................. 35
    Language for comparison and contrast ...................................................... 36
    Criteria for comparison/contrast................................................................. 40
    Checklist ....................................................................................................... 40
    Example essay.............................................................................................. 41
    Exercises....................................................................................................... 42

## Overview

To compare is to examine how things are similar, while to contrast is to see how they differ. A *comparison and contrast* essay therefore looks at the similarities of two or more things, and the differences. This essay type is one of the most common at university, where lecturers frequently test your understanding by asking you to compare and contrast two theories, two methods, two historical periods, and so on. Sometimes the whole essay will compare and contrast, though sometimes the comparison or contrast may be limited to one or two paragraphs. It is also possible, especially for short exam essays, that only the similarities or the differences, not both, will be discussed. See the examples below.

- What are the structural and functional similarities and differences between mitochondria and chloroplasts? [*comparison and contrast* essay]
- Examine how the economies of Spain and China are similar. [*comparison* only essay]
- What is the difference between a reflex and a learned behaviour? [*contrast* only essay]

# Unit 2: **Comparison & Contrast**

# Structure of comparison and contrast essays

There are two main ways to structure a comparison and contrast essay, namely using **block** or **point-by-point** structure. For the *block* structure, also called *subject-by-subject* structure, all of the information about one of the subjects being compared or contrasted is given first, and all of the information about the other subject is listed afterwards. This type of structure is similar to the *block* structure used for cause and effect and problem-solution essays. For the *point-by-point* structure, each similarity (or difference) for one subject is followed immediately by the similarity (or difference) for the other.

| In short |
|---|
| A compare and contrast essay looks at *similarities* (comparisons) and *differences* (contrasts), and can be structured in two ways:<br>• block (also called subject-by-subject);<br>• point-by-point. |

Both types of structure have their merits. The *block* structure is easier to write, and might be suitable for short essays. For longer essays, it can be difficult to remember the earlier points, and the use of 'reminder' phrases, referring back to the earlier points, is often necessary. The *point-by-point* structure is generally clearer as it ensures that the similarities and differences are stated immediately, making them easier to follow.

> Block structure is also used in *Cause & Effect essays* (Unit 3) and *Problem-Solution essays* (Unit 4). ▶▶

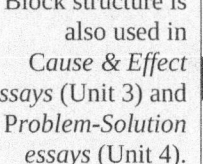

The two types of structure, block and point-by-point, are shown in the diagram below.

**Block**

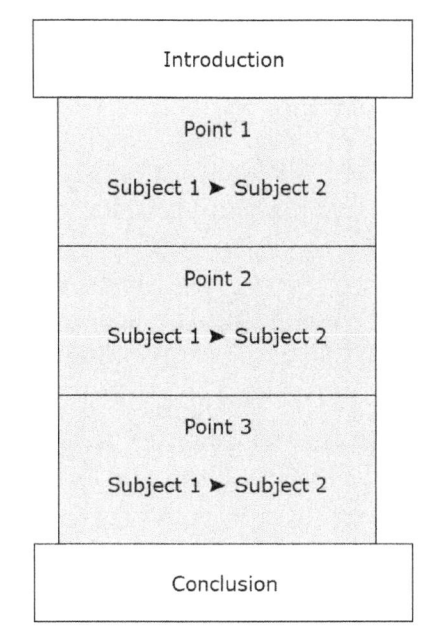

- Introduction
  - Subject 1 - Point 1
  - Subject 1 - Point 2
  - Subject 1 - Point 3
- Transition sentence/paragraph
  - Subject 2 - Point 1
  - Subject 2 - Point 2
  - Subject 2 - Point 3
- Conclusion

**Point-by-point**

- Introduction
  - Point 1
    - Subject 1 ▶ Subject 2
  - Point 2
    - Subject 1 ▶ Subject 2
  - Point 3
    - Subject 1 ▶ Subject 2
- Conclusion

# Language for comparison and contrast

Comparison and contrast transitions are words and phrases which show similarities or differences. Below are some common examples for *comparison*.

> More information on types of *transition signal* is given in Appendix 3.

## Comparison

*Sentence connectors*
- Similarly
- Likewise
- Also
- In the same way

*Clause connectors*
- as
- just as
- both... and...
- not only... but also...
- neither... nor...
- in the same way as

*Other*
- like
- just like
- to be similar to
- to be similar in (+ *similarity*)
- to be comparable to
- to be the same as
- alike
- to be alike in (+ *similarity*)
- to compare (to/with)

**Vocabulary in use: *compare/similar***

It is important to know and use different forms of words in order to vary your writing.

The following are word forms (and language notes) for **compare**.
- (v) to **compare** to/with
- (n) a **comparison** of
  in **comparison** to
- (adj) **comparative**
- (adv) **comparatively**

The following are word forms (and language notes) for **similar**.
- (v) to be **similar** to
- (n) **similarity**
- (adj) **similar** to/in
- (adv) **similarly**

If using the words in speaking, note the shifting stress.

○ ○ ○      ○ ○**○**○○
**similar** (adj)    **similarity** (n)

The following are examples of these in use.
- Anyone who has studied economics knows the law of demand: a higher price will lead to a lower quantity demanded. **Similarly**, the law of supply shows that a higher price will lead to a higher quantity supplied.[***]
- We feel a burst of pleasure following such things as a marriage proposal, birth of a child, acceptance to law school or a lottery win (Lutter, 2007). **Likewise**, we experience a surge of misery following widowhood, a divorce, or a layoff from work.[*]
- Whales have slow-growing populations and are at risk of extinction through hunting. **Also**, there are some species of sharks that are at risk of extinction.[**]

# Unit 2: **Comparison & Contrast**

- An increase in the price of some product signals to consumers that there is a shortage and the product should perhaps be economized on. **In the same way**, price changes give a useful signal to producers.[***]
- Organelles, which means "little organs", have specialized cellular functions, **just as** the organs of your body have specialized functions.[**]
- Heterotrophs are organisms that obtain energy and carbon by consuming other organisms. Humans are heterotrophs, **as** are all animals.[**]
- Scientists have long noticed that bacteria, mitochondria, and chloroplasts **are similar in** size. We also know that mitochondria and chloroplasts have DNA and ribosomes, **just as** bacteria do.[**]
- **Both** non-REM sleep **and** REM sleep appear to play important roles in learning and memory.[*]
- The spinal cord **not only** routes messages to and from the brain, **but also** has its own system of automatic processes, called reflexes.[*]
- **Neither** stimulus-based **nor** response-based definitions provide a complete definition of stress.[*]
- **In the same way as** Earth revolves around the sun, the negative electron in the hydrogen atom can revolve around the positive nucleus.[**]
- **Like** geology, physics, and chemistry, biology is a science that gathers knowledge about the natural world.[**]
- Watson's ideas were influenced by Pavlov's work. According to Watson, human behaviour, **just like** animal behaviour, is primarily the result of conditioned responses.[*]
- By about 1980, however, the unemployment rate for women **was the same as** that for men.[***]
- Lampreys **are similar to** hagfishes in size and shape.[**]
- Without this information, it becomes difficult for everyone—buyers and sellers **alike**—to react in a flexible and appropriate manner as changes occur throughout the economy.[***]
- Lampreys and hagfishes **are alike in** size and shape.[**]
- In a more detailed review, Allen, Eby, Poteet, Lentz, & Lima (2004) found that mentoring positively affected a person's compensation and number of promotions **compared with** non-mentored employees.[*]
- Because stress weakens the immune system, people with high stress levels are more likely to develop an illness **compared to** those under little stress.[*]

[*] From *Psychology* by OpenStax. This OpenStax book is available for free at https://cnx.org/content/col11629/1.5.
[**] From *Concepts of Biology* by OpenStax. Download free at https://openstax.org/details/books/concepts-biology.
[***] From *Principles of Economics* by OpenStax. Download free at https://openstax.org/details/books/principles-economics.

Below are some common examples of transitions for *contrast*.

## Contrast

*Sentence connectors*
- However
- In contrast
- In comparison
- By comparison
- On the other hand

*Clause connectors*
- while
- whereas
- but

*Other*
- to differ from
- to be different (from/to)
- to be dissimilar to
- (to be) unlike
- in contrast to

> **Vocabulary in use:** *contrast/differ*
>
> The following are word forms (and language notes) for **contrast**.
> (v)    to **contrast** with
> (n)    in **contrast** to
> (adj)  **contrasting**
> (adv)  **contrastingly**
>
> If using the words in speaking, note the shifting stress.
>
> ○ o                o ○
> **contrast** (n)    **contrast** (v)
>
> The following are word forms (and language notes) for **different**.
> (v)    to **differ** from/in
> (n)    **difference**
> (adj)  **different** from/to/than[+]
> (adv)  **differently**
>
> [+] *different than* is US English

The following are some examples of these in use.
- Chimpanzees and humans are very similar genetically, sharing 99 percent of their genes. **However**, chimpanzees and humans show considerable anatomical differences, including the relative lengths of arms and legs.[**]
- Hostile aggression is often motivated by anger. **In contrast**, instrumental aggression is not motivated by anger or the intention to cause pain. Instrumental aggression serves as a means to reach a goal.[*]
- Martin Seligman conducted a series of experiments in which dogs were placed in a chamber where they received electric shocks from which they could not escape. Later, when these dogs were given the opportunity to escape the shocks by jumping across a partition, most failed to even try. **In comparison**, dogs who were previously allowed to escape the shocks tended to jump the partition and escape the pain.[*]
- The World Bank sets the poverty line for low-income countries around the world at $2/day. **By comparison**, the U.S. 2015 poverty line of $20,090 annually for a family of three works out to $18.35 per person per day.[***]
- If we are under-aroused, we become bored and will seek out some sort of stimulation. **On the other hand**, if we are over-aroused, we will engage in behaviours to reduce our arousal (Berlyne, 1960).[*]

# Unit 2: **Comparison & Contrast**

- **While** some populations are fairly stable, others experience more flux.**
- Extroverts are sociable and outgoing, and readily connect with others, **whereas** introverts have a higher need to be alone, engage in solitary behaviours, and limit their interactions with others.*
- Evolution led to changes in the shapes and sizes of these bones in different species, **but** they have maintained the same overall layout.**
- Lizards **differ from** snakes by having four limbs, eyelids, and external ears, which are lacking in snakes.**
- Asexual reproduction produces genetically identical offspring (clones), **whereas** in sexual reproduction, the genetic material of two individuals combines to produce offspring that **are** genetically **different from** their parents.**
- Concession transitions **are dissimilar to** contrast transition in that they show an unexpected result, rather than a dissimilarity.
- **Unlike** neurotransmitters, which are released in close proximity to cells with their receptors, hormones are secreted into the bloodstream and travel throughout the body, affecting any cells that contain receptors for them. Thus, **whereas** neurotransmitters' effects are localized, the effects of hormones are widespread.*
- **In contrast to** psychoanalysis, humanistic therapists focus on conscious rather than unconscious thoughts.*

> **Concession transitions**
>
> *Concession* transitions show an unexpected result. They are similar to but not the same as *contrast* transitions. Although some sources include these transitions in the list of contrast transitions, this is inaccurate and can lead to error.
>
> The following are concession transitions.
> **Sentence connectors:** however[+], nevertheless, nonetheless, still
> **Clause connectors:** although, even though, though, but[+], yet
> **Other:** despite, in spite of
> [+] These are also contrast transitions.
>
> For example:
> - *Although the sun was shining, he took an umbrella to work.* [The sun shining means taking an umbrella is *unexpected*.]

> **Vocabulary in use:** *On the contrary*
>
> The phrase *on the contrary* is used for contrast, but has a special meaning, and cannot be used interchangeably with other contrast transitions. It is used to contrast what was said or expected with the real situation, which is the opposite or very different. E.g.
> - *They expected the exam to be easy. On the contrary, it was extremely difficult.* [They thought the exam would be easy; the reality was that it was *not* easy.]

---

\* From *Psychology* by OpenStax. This OpenStax book is available for free at https://cnx.org/content/col11629/1.5.
\** From *Concepts of Biology* by OpenStax. Download free at https://openstax.org/details/books/concepts-biology.
\*** From *Principles of Economics* by OpenStax. Download free at https://openstax.org/details/books/principles-economics.

# Criteria for comparison/contrast

When making comparisons or contrasts, it is important to be clear what criteria you are using, in other words what aspects are being compared or contrasted (also called the *basis for comparison*). Study the following (unclear) example, contrasting two people.

- Aaron is tall and strong. **In contrast**, Bruce is handsome and very intelligent.

Although this sentence has a contrast transition, the criteria for contrasting are not the same. The criteria used for Aaron are height (tall) and strength (strong). We would expect similar criteria to be used for Bruce (maybe he is short and weak), but instead we have new criteria, namely appearance (handsome) and intelligence (intelligent). This is a common mistake for students when writing this type of paragraph or essay. Compare the following (criteria are shown in italics, transition signals are in bold).

- Aaron and Bruce **differ** in four ways. The first difference is *height*. Aaron is tall, **while** Bruce is short. A second difference is *strength*. Aaron is strong. **In contrast**, Bruce is weak. A third difference is *appearance*. Aaron, who is average looking, **differs from** Bruce, who is handsome. The final difference is *intelligence*. Aaron is of average intelligence. Bruce, **on the other hand**, is very intelligent.

# Checklist

Below is a checklist for comparison and contrast essays. Check your writing, or ask a peer.

| Area | Item | OK? | Comments |
|---|---|---|---|
| Comparison & contrast | The essay is a comparison and/or contrast essay. | | |
| | An appropriate structure is used, either *block* or *point-by-point*. | | |
| | Comparison and contrast transitions are used accurately. | | |
| | The criteria for comparison/contrast are clear. | | |
| General essay skills | The essay has a clear thesis statement. | | |
| | Each paragraph has a clear topic sentence. | | |
| | Each paragraph has enough support (facts, reasons, examples, etc.). | | |
| | The conclusion includes a summary of the main points. | | |

# Unit 2: **Comparison & Contrast**

# Example essay

Below is an example *comparison and contrast* essay. It is used in one of the exercises later.

*Title*: *There have been many advances in technology over the past fifty years. These have revolutionised the way we communicate with people who are far away. Compare and contrast methods of communication used today with those which were used in the past.*

Before the advent of computers and modern technology, people communicating over long distances used traditional means such as letters and the telephone. Nowadays there is a vast array of communication tools which can complete this task, ranging from email to instant messaging and video calls. While the present and previous means of communication are similar in their general form, they differ in regard to their speed and the range of tools available.

One similarity between current and previous methods of communication relates to the form of communication. In the past, both written forms such as letters were frequently used, in addition to oral forms such as telephone calls. Similarly, people nowadays use both of these forms. Just as in the past, written forms of communication are prevalent, for example via email and text messaging. In addition, oral forms are still used, including the telephone, mobile phone, and voice messages via instant messaging services.

However, there are clearly many differences in the way we communicate over long distances, the most notable of which is speed. This is most evident in relation to written forms of communication. In the past, letters would take days to arrive at their destination. In contrast, an email arrives almost instantaneously and can be read seconds after it was sent. In the past, if it was necessary to send a short message, for example at work, a memo could be passed around the office, which would take some time to circulate. This is different from the current situation, in which a text message can be sent immediately.

Another significant difference is the range of communication methods. Fifty years ago, the tools available for communicating over long distances were primarily the telephone and the letter. By comparison, there is a vast array of communication methods available today. These include not only the telephone, letter, email and text messages already mentioned, but also video conferences via software such as Skype or mobile phone apps such as WeChat and WhatsApp, and social media such as Facebook and Twitter.

In conclusion, methods of communication have greatly advanced over the past fifty years, and while there are some similarities, such as the forms of communication, there are significant differences, chiefly in relation to the speed of communication and the range of communication tools available. There is no doubt that technology will continue to progress in future, and the advanced tools which we use today may one day also become outdated.

# Academic Writing Genres                                Sheldon Smith

# Exercises

## Exercise 1: **Comprehension**

Answer the following questions about this unit. Either do this after reading the unit, or make notes first then use the notes to answer the questions.

1  What are the two types of comparison and contrast essay structure?

   • _____                • _____

2  What is the difference between the two types of structure? What are the advantages of each?

   _____
   _____
   _____

3  What are *criteria* for comparison and contrast? Why it is important to be clear about the criteria which are used?

   _____
   _____

4  Study the following transitions. Place them correctly in the table. An example is done.

   - ~~similarly~~
   - in comparison
   - whereas
   - likewise
   - however
   - just as
   - both... and...
   - not only... but also...
   - to be dissimilar to
   - to be the same as
   - in the same way
   - while
   - but
   - in contrast to
   - to be different from
   - just like
   - to be similar to
   - in contrast

|  | Comparison | Contrast |
|---|---|---|
| **Sentence connectors** | similarly | |
| **Clause connectors** | | |
| **Other** | | |

42

# Unit 2: Comparison & Contrast

## Exercise 2: Example essay

Study the example essay on *communication methods* (earlier in the unit) and answer these questions.

a) What type of structure has been used? _____

b) Complete the following diagram, summarising the main ideas of the essay.

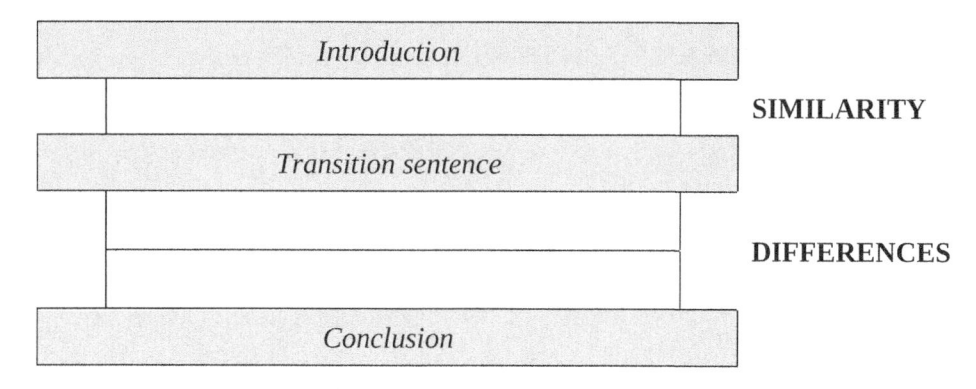

```
          Introduction
                                    SIMILARITY
         Transition sentence

                                    DIFFERENCES

           Conclusion
```

c) Study the example essay and highlight the following:
- language for comparison and contrast;
- the main ideas listed in: (a) the *thesis*; (b) the *topic sentences*; (c) the *summary*.

d) The following is the *main body* of the same essay. However, this has been rewritten so that it uses the other type of structure. Study this main body and highlight the following:
- transition phrases for comparison and contrast;
- the 'reminder' phrases used in the second paragraph, i.e. phases which refer back to ideas in the first paragraph.

In the past, written forms such as letters were frequently used, in addition to oral forms such as telephone calls. Communication, especially written communication, could be very slow. Letters could take days to arrive at their destination, while memos passed around the office could take some time to circulate. The tools available for communicating over long distances were primarily the telephone and the letter.

Just as in the past, written forms of communication are prevalent today, for example email and text messaging. In addition, oral forms are still used, including the telephone, mobile phone, and voice messages via instant messaging services. In contrast to the past, however, when written communication could take several days to arrive, an email arrives almost instantaneously and can be read seconds after it is sent. In comparison to the limited forms of communication in the past, nowadays there is a vast array of communication methods available. These include not only the telephone, letter, email and text messages already mentioned, but also video conferences via software such as Skype or mobile phone Apps such as WeChat and WhatsApp, and social media such as Facebook and Twitter.

# Academic Writing Genres                              Sheldon Smith

## Exercise 3: Language for comparison and contrast #1

Study the following sentences. Complete each one by choosing the correct comparison and contrast transitions to fill the gaps, based on the structure and meaning of the sentence.

**1)** Mainland China _____ Hong Kong in the Confucian aspects of its culture.
   a) compares to        b) is similar to        c) is alike

**2)** Mainland China _____ Hong Kong in the form of written Chinese, as it uses simplified rather than complex characters.
   a) differs from        b) different from        c) whereas

**3)** The UK has important trade relations with the USA. _____, trade is an important part of the relationship between China and the USA.
   a) The same as        b) Just like        c) Likewise

**4)** _____ to the UK, China does not have close military ties to the USA.
   a) In contrast        b) Dissimilar        c) On the other hand

**5)** France and the UK _____ in their reliance on nuclear energy as a clean energy source.
   a) also        b) both        c) are alike

**6)** Nuclear energy accounts for almost 40% of the energy produced in France. _____, it is only around 20% of the energy produced in the UK.
   a) In contrast        b) While        c) On the contrary

**7)** China is _____ a Communist country _____ a rapidly developing country with many free market principles.
   a) both… but also        b) neither… and        c) not only… but also

**8)** Although China operates under some free market principles, it _____ true free market economies in many aspects.
   a) is unlike        b) be different from        c) dissimilar to

**9)** _____ Mexico, Chile is a Spanish-speaking country.
   a) The same as        b) Just like        c) Similarly

**10)** Mexico _____ Chile in the size of its population, which is almost ten times as large.
   a) dissimilar to        b) is different from        c) while

# Unit 2: **Comparison & Contrast**

## Exercise 4: **Language for comparison and contrast #2**

Study the following pairs of sentences. Each pair either demonstrates difference or similarity. Join the sentences using the transition signal which is given. Some sentences may need to be rewritten to fit the grammar of the word.

Example: **While**
- A presentation has aims.
- An essay has a thesis statement.

A presentation has aims, **while** an essay has a thesis statement.

**1. Likewise**
- A presentation has a clear structure, with introduction, main body and conclusion.
- An essay has a clear structure, with introduction, main body and conclusion.

_____

_____

**2. To differ from**
- A presentation uses semi-formal language.
- An essay uses formal language.

_____

_____

**3. Both... and...**
- A presentation uses transition phrases.
- An essay uses transition phrases.

_____

_____

**4. In contrast to**
- A presentation uses text and visuals.
- An essay uses only text.

_____

_____

**5. In contrast**
- A presentation concludes with a Q&A section.
- An essay concludes with a reference section.

_____

_____

45

# Academic Writing Genres          Sheldon Smith

## Exercise 5: **Criteria for comparison and contrast**

a) Read the following passage. Identify the *criteria* used to make comparisons and contrasts.

*Topic: What are the structural and functional similarities and differences between mitochondria and chloroplasts?*

Mitochondria (singular = mitochondrion) are oval-shaped, double membrane organelles that have their own ribosomes and DNA. They are often called the "powerhouses" or "energy factories" of a cell because they are responsible for making adenosine triphosphate (ATP), the cell's main energy-carrying molecule. ATP represents the short-term stored energy of the cell.

Like the mitochondria, chloroplasts have their own DNA and ribosomes, but chloroplasts have an entirely different function. Chloroplasts are plant cell organelles that carry out photosynthesis. Photosynthesis is the series of reactions that use carbon dioxide, water, and light energy to make glucose and oxygen. This is a major difference between plants and animals; plants (autotrophs) are able to make their own food, like sugars, while animals (heterotrophs) must ingest their food.

Like mitochondria, chloroplasts have a double membrane. The contents of the inner membrane, however, are quite different. Within the space enclosed by a chloroplast's inner membrane is a set of interconnected and stacked fluid-filled membrane sacs called thylakoids. Each stack of thylakoids is called a granum (plural = grana). The fluid enclosed by the inner membrane that surrounds the grana is called the stroma.

Adapted from *Biology 2e* by OpenStax. Download for free at https://openstax.org/details/books/biology-2e.

b) Study the following similarities and differences. Complete the gaps by identifying appropriate *criteria*.

    i. Dogs and cats differ in terms of their _____. Dogs rely very much on their owners, for example to feed them and take them for a walk. In contrast, cats can be let out to wander the neighbourhood and can even catch food such as mice or small birds.

    ii. One difference between alligators and crocodiles is the _____ of their snout. An alligator's snout is shorter and wider than that of a crocodile.

    iii. A second difference between alligators and crocodiles relates to the _____ of their teeth with the mouth closed. A crocodile's teeth can be seen protruding from their bottom jaw when its mouth is closed. In contrast, when an alligator's mouth is shut, none of its teeth are visible.

    iv. One similarity between China and India is _____. China had 1.39 billion people in 2018. Likewise, India had over 1 billion people in 2018, totalling 1.34 billion. By contrast, the USA, in third place, had only 300,000 in the same year.

    v. One difference between China and India, however, is _____. The population in China is increasing by 1.5% per year, while that of China is only increasing by 0.7% per year, which is only half as much.

## Unit 2: **Comparison & Contrast**

### Exercise 6: **Using a Venn Diagram**

Below is a Venn diagram, which shows features of an essay, features of a presentation, and features of both (the overlapping portion). Use the diagram to complete the summary below. Note that not all ideas in the diagram are used.

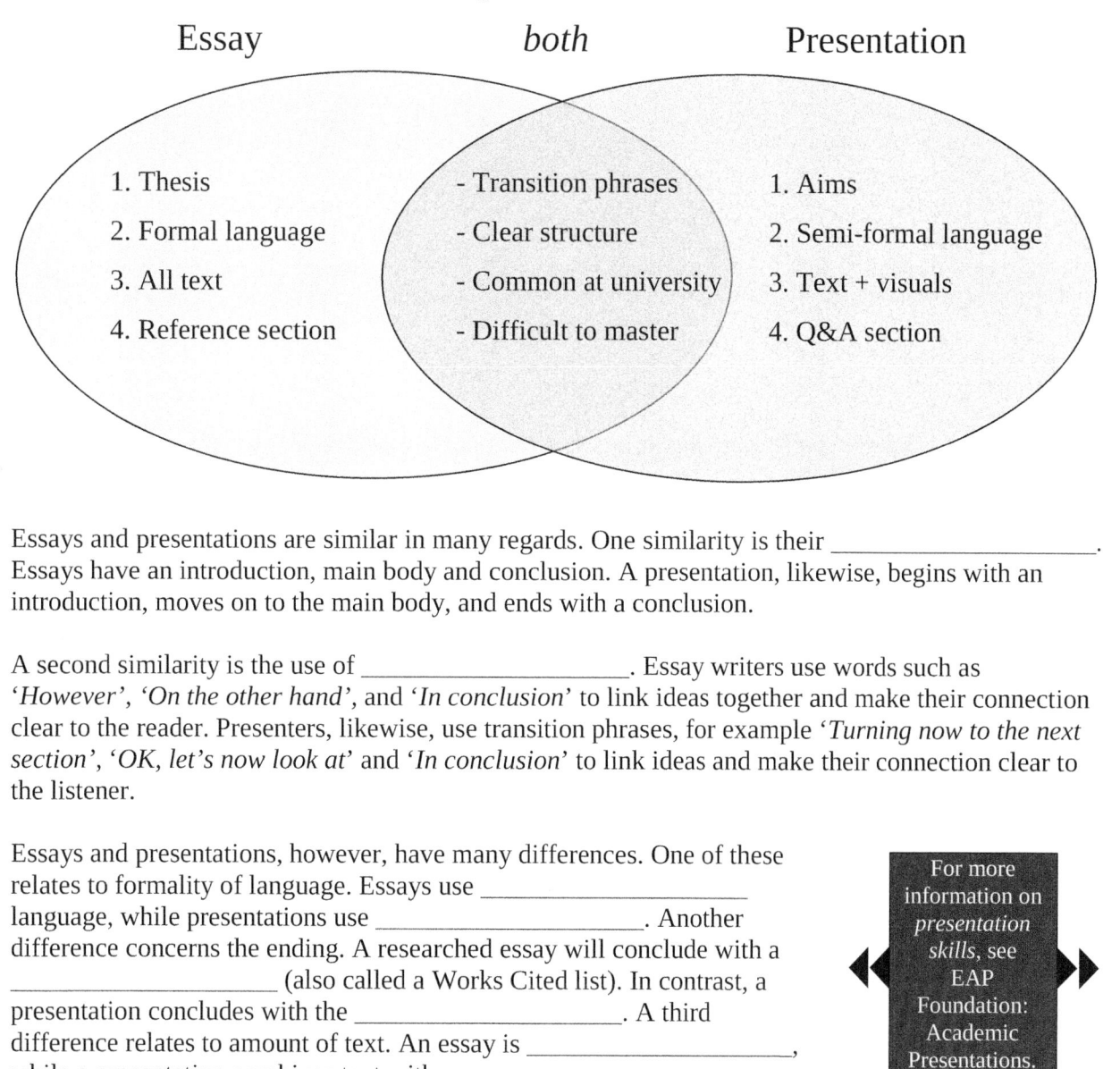

*Essay* — *both* — *Presentation*

- 1. Thesis
- 2. Formal language
- 3. All text
- 4. Reference section

- Transition phrases
- Clear structure
- Common at university
- Difficult to master

- 1. Aims
- 2. Semi-formal language
- 3. Text + visuals
- 4. Q&A section

Essays and presentations are similar in many regards. One similarity is their _____. Essays have an introduction, main body and conclusion. A presentation, likewise, begins with an introduction, moves on to the main body, and ends with a conclusion.

A second similarity is the use of _____. Essay writers use words such as '*However*', '*On the other hand*', and '*In conclusion*' to link ideas together and make their connection clear to the reader. Presenters, likewise, use transition phrases, for example '*Turning now to the next section*', '*OK, let's now look at*' and '*In conclusion*' to link ideas and make their connection clear to the listener.

Essays and presentations, however, have many differences. One of these relates to formality of language. Essays use _____ language, while presentations use _____. Another difference concerns the ending. A researched essay will conclude with a _____ (also called a Works Cited list). In contrast, a presentation concludes with the _____. A third difference relates to amount of text. An essay is _____, while a presentation combines text with _____.

For more information on *presentation skills*, see EAP Foundation: Academic Presentations.

## Exercise 7: **Writing a comparison and contrast essay**

a) Choose *one* of the following topics to write a *comparison and contrast* essay, using either *block* or *point-by-point* structure.

1. One aspect of two cultures (e.g. education, family life, entertainment).
2. One aspect of your country today compared to 20 years ago (e.g. education, family life, technology).
3. Two historical periods or events (e.g. Roman Empire vs. Egyptian Empire, World War I vs. World War II).
4. Two religions.
5. Two forms of government (or governments in two different countries).
6. Online learning vs. traditional classroom-based learning.
7. Secondary (i.e. high school) education and education at tertiary (i.e. university) level.
8. One aspect of two languages (e.g. vocabulary, grammar, writing).
9. Two famous people from the same field (e.g. two writers, two actors).
10. Two famous creative works (e.g. two paintings, two novels, two films).

Use the following Venn diagram to brainstorm some ideas.

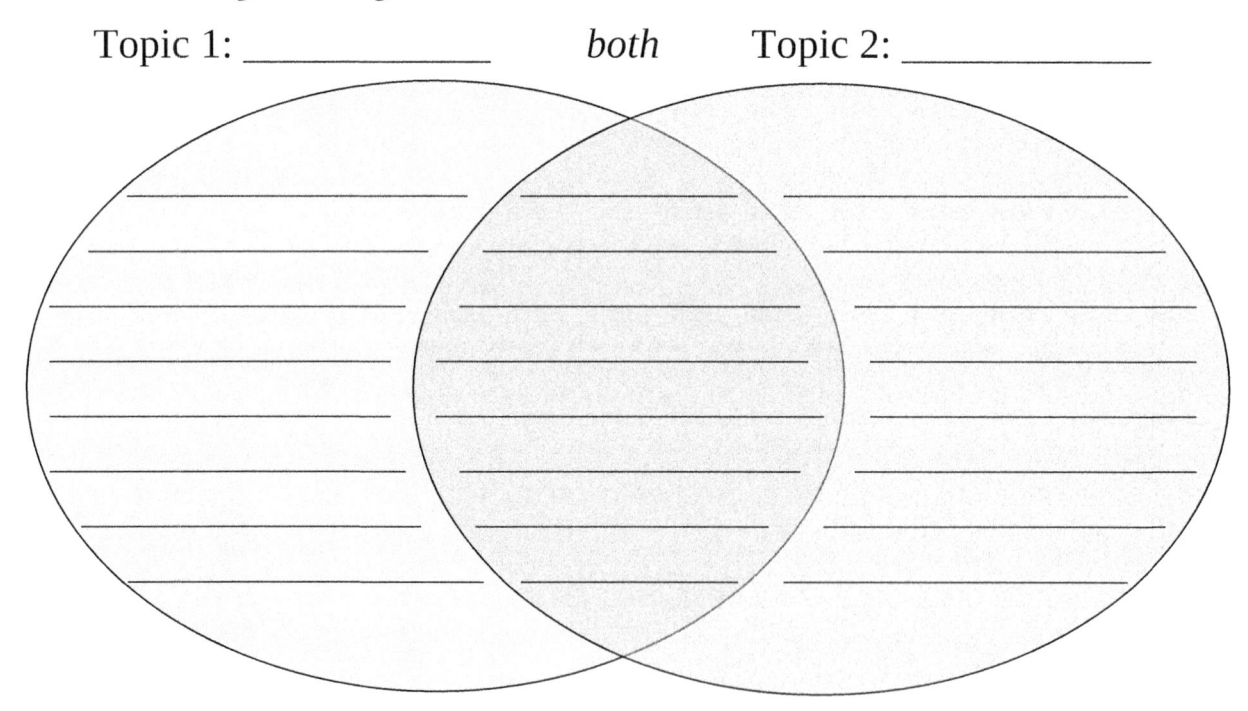

Topic 1: _____    *both*    Topic 2: _____

b) When you have finished, get a peer to check your essay, using the checklist earlier in the unit. You should also check another student's writing.

# Unit 2: **Comparison & Contrast**

## Exercise 8: **Learning outcomes check**

a) The following are the learning outcomes for this unit. Decide how well you have mastered each one by giving it a score, as follows.

    3 = I understand/can do this well.
    2 = I understand/can do this fairly well, but I can improve with more practice.
    1 = I understand/can do this, but not well enough yet. I need to practise more.
    0 = I cannot do this yet. I need more time.

| Score | Learning Outcome |
|---|---|
| _____ | I know what a comparison and contrast essay is. |
| _____ | I understand ways to structure a comparison and contrast essay. |
| _____ | I can use language for showing comparison and contrast. |
| _____ | I understand how to apply criteria to make appropriate comparisons/contrasts. |
| _____ | I can use a Venn diagram to complete a comparison and contrast essay. |
| _____ | I can use a Venn diagram to brainstorm ideas for an essay. |
| _____ | I can write a comparison and contrast essay. |
| _____ | I can peer edit a comparison and contrast essay, using a checklist. |

b) Use this information to review the unit and improve.

# Unit 3 | Cause & Effect Essays

## Learning Outcomes

By the end of this unit, you should:
- know what a cause and effect essay is;
- understand different types of cause (main, contributing, immediate, remote);
- understand different types of effect (short-term, long-term, primary, secondary);
- understand ways to structure a cause and effect essay;
- be able to use language for showing cause and effect.

By completing the exercises, you will also:
- study an example essay for structure, language and content;
- practise using language for cause and effect;
- write a cause and effect essay;
- peer edit a cause and effect essay, using a checklist.

## Key Vocabulary

**Nouns**
- block
- chain
- reason
- result
- cause (also *verb*)
- effect
- consequence

**Adjectives**
- main
- contributing
- immediate
- remote
- short-term
- long-term
- primary
- secondary

**Verbs**
- affect

## Additional Vocabulary

*Academic Collocations (in the unit)*
- academic writing (adj + n)
- close proximity (adj + n)
- increased demand (adj + n)
- lower income (adj + n)
- major reason (adj + n)
- previous paragraph (adj + n)
- equally important (adv + adj)

*Academic Collocations (in the essay)*
- contemporary society (adj + n)
- domestic violence (adj + n)
- greater equality (adj + n)
- legal rights (adj + n)
- purchasing power (adj + n)
- significant contribution (adj + n)
- significant effects (adj + n)
- significant impact (adj + n)
- gender equality (n + n)

# Contents of this section

## Unit 3: Cause & Effect Essays.................................. 51

Overview .................................................................................................... 52
Types of cause and effect ......................................................................... 53
Structure of cause and effect essays ....................................................... 54
Language for cause and effect ................................................................. 55
Checklist .................................................................................................... 57
Example essay .......................................................................................... 58
Exercises ................................................................................................... 59

# Overview

A cause and effect essay looks at the reasons (or causes) for something, then discusses the results (or effects). For this reason, *cause and effect* essays are sometimes referred to as *reason and result* essays. They are one of the most common forms of academic writing. Sometimes the whole essay will be cause and effect, though sometimes this may be only part of the essay. It is also possible that only the causes or effects, not both, are discussed.

The following are examples of cause and effect essay titles.
- Discuss the causes and effects of global warming. [*cause and effect* essay]
- Explain the high birth rate in India. [*causes* only essay]
- Discuss the WTO and its effects on the Chinese economy. [*effects* only essay]

Sometimes one cause leads directly to one effect (e.g. boiling water creates steam). Often, however, many different causes will lead to an effect (or phenomenon). See this example.

| Causes | Effect |
|---|---|
| • Burning of fossil fuels<br>• Methane emissions from farming<br>• Deforestation<br>• Use of fertilisers | **Global warming** |

Likewise, a single cause (or phenomenon) can result in many different effects. E.g.

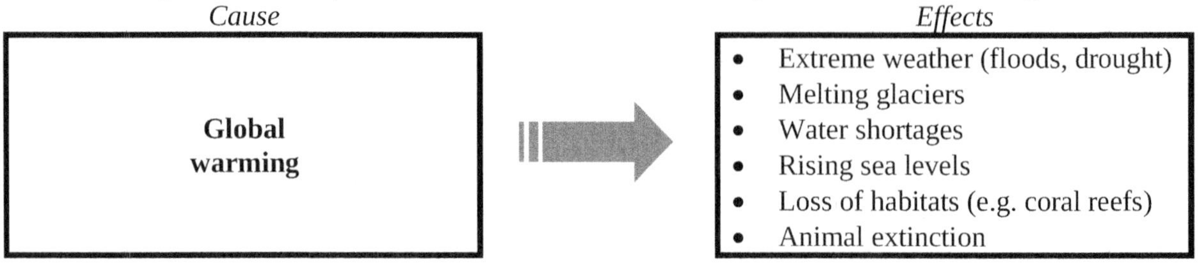

| Cause | Effects |
|---|---|
| **Global warming** | • Extreme weather (floods, drought)<br>• Melting glaciers<br>• Water shortages<br>• Rising sea levels<br>• Loss of habitats (e.g. coral reefs)<br>• Animal extinction |

# Unit 3: Cause & Effect

## Types of cause and effect

Causes can be classified in different ways. It is often important to distinguish between the **main cause** (or *main causes* if there are several equally important ones) and a **contributing cause** (also called a *contributing factor*), in other words a cause which added to the effect, but is not the main reason for it. For example, someone who smokes, is obese and does not get regular exercise might suffer a heart attack. The *main causes* of the heart attack are likely to be the person's obesity and lack of fitness. The fact that the person smokes, however, is likely to be a *contributing factor*, as while this is a less direct cause of the heart attack, smoking nonetheless affects the condition of the heart.

| In short |
|---|
| Causes can be:
• main or contributing;
• immediate or remote.

Effects can be:
• short-term or long-term;
• immediate or delayed;
• primary or secondary. |

It may also be important to distinguish between the **immediate cause** or causes (also called *proximate cause*) and the **remote causes**. The immediate cause is the one closest in time to the effect, which led to it happening. To use the example above again, an obese, unfit smoker may climb twenty flights of stairs and suffer a heart attack. The *immediate cause* of the heart attack, i.e. the closest event which led to it, is climbing twenty flights of stairs. Without this event, the person would not have suffered a heart attack at that exact moment. The *remote causes* in this case are the obesity, lack of fitness and smoking.

Effects likewise can be divided into different types. The main way to classify effects is according to how long they last. This leads to **short-term effects**, which last for a relatively short time, and **long-term effects**, which last for much longer. For example, the *short-term* effects of smoking include a feeling of relaxation, increased heart rate and decreased appetite. *Long-term effects* of smoking include damaged lining of the lungs (which can lead to cancer) and narrowing of blood vessels (which can lead to heart attack and stroke).

Another way of classifying effects is according to when they happen. There are **immediate effects**, which happen straight away, and **delayed effects**, which happen later. The long-term effects of smoking, listed above, are also examples of *delayed effects*.

Sometimes there may also be **primary effects** and **secondary effects**. *Secondary effects* are ones which happen as a result of the *primary effects*, i.e. the effects of the effects. For example, after a strong earthquake, *primary effects* include landslides, building collapse and burst water and sewage pipes. *Secondary effects* include homelessness (a result of the landslides and collapsed buildings) and disease (a result of burst water and sewage pipes).

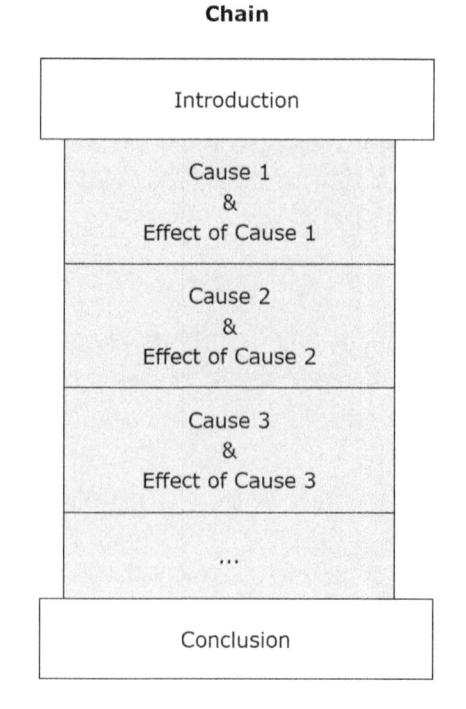

# Structure of cause and effect essays

There are two main ways to structure a cause and effect essay, namely using a **block** or a **chain** structure. For the *block* structure, all of the causes are listed first, and all of the effects are listed afterwards. Usually, there will be a transition paragraph in the middle, to link causes to effects. With the *chain* structure, each cause is followed immediately by its effect. Often the effect will then be the cause of the next effect, which is why this structure is called 'chain'.

> Block and chain structures are also used in *Problem-Solution essays* (Unit 4).

Both types of structure have their merits. The *block* structure is generally clearer, especially for shorter essays, while the *chain* structure ensures that any effects you present relate directly to the causes you have given. The *chain* structure is not always possible, however. For the global warming example given earlier, only the *block* structure can be used, as the individual causes of global warming do not link directly to individual effects (the causes collectively lead to global warming, which in turn leads to the collective effects).

> **In short**
> There are two ways to structure a cause and effect essay:
> - *block* (all causes first, then all effects);
> - *chain* (cause 1 => effect 1, cause 2 => effect 2).

The two types of structure, *block* and *chain*, are shown in the diagram below.

**Block**

- Introduction
- Cause 1
- Cause 2
- ...
- Transition sentence/paragraph
- Effect 1
- Effect 2
- ...
- Conclusion

**Chain**

- Introduction
- Cause 1 & Effect of Cause 1
- Cause 2 & Effect of Cause 2
- Cause 3 & Effect of Cause 3
- ...
- Conclusion

# Unit 3: **Cause & Effect**

## Language for cause and effect

Cause and effect transitions are words and phrases which show the cause and effect relationships. It is important to be clear which is the cause (or reason) and which is the effect (or result), and to use the correct transition word or phrase. Remember that a cause happens first, and the effect happens later.

Below are some common cause and effect transition signals. The symbol [C] is used to indicate a cause, while [E] indicates the effect. They are organised by type (sentence connectors, clause connectors, and other). Those in the 'other' group are sub-divided according to the main word used in the transition signal (e.g. *reason, cause, result, effect*).

| Sentence connectors | |
|---|---|
| [C]. | As a result,<br>As a consequence,<br>Consequently,<br>Therefore,<br>Thus,<br>Hence,    [E] |

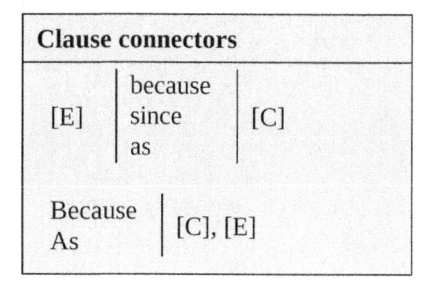

| Clause connectors | |
|---|---|
| [E] | because<br>since    [C]<br>as |
| Because<br>As | [C], [E] |

**Other**

*reason (n)*
- [C] is the reason for [E]
- [E]. The reason is [C]

*cause (n)*
- [C] is the cause of [E]
- [C] is one of the causes of [E]
- The cause of [E] is [C]

*cause (v)*
- [C] causes [E]
- [E] is caused by [C]

*lead to (v)*
- [C] leads to [E]

*because of (conj)*
- Because of [C], [E]
- [E] is because of [C]

*due to (conj)*
- Due to [C], [E]
- [E] is due to [C]

*owing to (conj)*
- Owing to [C], [E]
- [E] is owing to [C]

*explain (v)*
- [C] explains why [E]

*explanation (n)*
- [C] is the explanation for [E]

*result (n)*
- [C]. The result is [E]
- As a result of [C], [E]
- The result of [C] is [E]
- [E] is the result of [C]

*result (v)*
- [C] results in [E]
- [E] results from [C]

*effect (n)*
- The effect of [C] is [E]
- [C] has an effect on [E]
- [E] is the effect of [C]
- [E] is one of the effects of [C]

*affect (v)*
- [C] affects [E]
- [E] is affected by [C]

*consequence (n)*
- As a consequence of [C], [E]
- The consequence of [C] is [E]
- [E] is a consequence of [C]
- [E] is the consequence of [C]

The following are some examples of cause and effect transition phrases.
- Each year, heart disease **causes** approximately one in three deaths in the United States, and it is the leading **cause of** death in the developed world (Centers for Disease Control and Prevention [CDC], 2011; Shapiro, 2005).*
- If you look at a straight rod partially submerged in water, it appears to bend at the surface. **The reason behind this effect is** that the image of the rod inside the water forms a little closer to the surface than the actual position of the rod, so it does not line up with the part of the rod that is above the water. The same phenomenon **explains why** a fish in water appears to be closer to the surface than it actually is.**
- **A major reason for** Amazon's success is its production model and cost structure, which has enabled it to undercut the prices of its competitors.***
- Freud's theories are widely taught in introductory psychology texts **because of** their historical significance for personality psychology and psychotherapy.*
- **Because of** the relationship of rest energy to mass, we now consider mass to be a form of energy rather than something separate.**
- The amount consumers buy falls for two **reasons**: first **because of** the higher price and second **because of** the lower income.***
- Many students are taking longer (five or six years) to complete a college degree **as a result of** working and going to school at the same time.*
- A Cooper pair can form **as a result of** the displacement of positive atomic nuclei.**
- Jet lag is a collection of symptoms that **results from** the mismatch between our internal circadian cycles and our environment. These symptoms include fatigue, sluggishness, irritability, and insomnia (Roth, 2007).*
- Learning is a relatively permanent change in behaviour or knowledge **that results from** experience.*
- Prolonged stress ultimately **results in** exhaustion.*
- Soap bubbles are blown from clear fluid into very thin films. The colours we see **are** not **due to** any pigmentation but **are the result of** light interference, which enhances specific wavelengths for a given thickness of the film.**
- If exposure to a stressor continues over a longer period of time, exhaustion ensues, and the body's ability to resist becomes depleted. **As a result**, illness, disease, and other permanent damage to the body—even death—may occur.*

> **Vocabulary in use:** *effect*
> Remember that *effect* is usually a noun, while *affect* is a usually verb (usually, because *effect* can also be a verb, meaning 'to produce', while *affect* is a noun used in psychology).
>
> Also note that the word *effect* does not always show effect. For example, the phrase *In effect* means 'essentially', while *take effect* means 'begin to be effective', i.e begin to work.

# Unit 3: **Cause & Effect**

Examples (continued)
- Unlike neurotransmitters, which are released in close proximity to cells, hormones are secreted into the bloodstream and travel throughout the body. **Thus**, whereas neurotransmitters' effects are localized, the effects of hormones are widespread.[*]
- The theory of rational ignorance says voters will recognize that their single vote is extremely unlikely to influence the outcome of an election. **As a consequence**, they choose to remain uninformed about issues. This theory helps **explain why** voter turnout is so low in the United States.[***]
- A recent increased demand for ethanol has **caused** the demand for corn to increase. **Consequently**, many farmers switched from growing wheat to growing corn.[***]
- Parenting styles were found to **have an effect on** childhood well-being.[*]
- While it is clear that the price of a good **affects** the quantity demanded, it is also true that expectations about the future price can **affect** demand.[***]
- Anything the mother is exposed to in the environment **affects** the foetus; if the mother is exposed to something harmful, the child can show life-long **effects**.[*]

[*] From *Psychology* by OpenStax. This OpenStax book is available for free at https://cnx.org/content/col11629/1.5.
[**] From *University Physics* by OpenStax. Download free at https://openstax.org/details/books/university-physics-volume-3.
[***] From *Principles of Economics* by OpenStax. Download free at https://openstax.org/details/books/principles-economics.

# Checklist

Below is a checklist for cause and effect essays. Use it to check your writing, or ask a peer.

| Area | Item | OK? | Comments |
|---|---|---|---|
| Cause & Effect | The essay is a cause and/or effect essay. | | |
| | An appropriate structure is used, either *block* or *chain*. | | |
| | If necessary, the essay shows the type of cause (*main/contributing, immediate/remote*). | | |
| | If necessary, the essay shows the type of effect (*short-term/long-term, immediate/delayed, primary/secondary*). | | |
| | Cause and effect language is used accurately. | | |
| General essay skills | The essay has a clear thesis statement. | | |
| | Each paragraph has a clear topic sentence. | | |
| | Each paragraph has enough support (facts, reasons, examples, etc.). | | |
| | The conclusion includes a summary of the main points. | | |

# Academic Writing Genres — Sheldon Smith

# Example essay

Below is an example *cause and effect* essay. It is used in one of the exercises later.

> *Title*: More and more women are now going out to work and some women are now the major salary earner in the family. What are the causes of this, and what effect is this having on families and society?

In the past, most women stayed at home to take care of domestic chores such as cooking or cleaning. Women's liberation and feminism have meant that this situation has been transformed and in contemporary society women are playing an almost equal role to men in terms of work. This has had significant consequences, both in terms of the family, for example by improving quality of life and increasing children's sense of independence, and also for society itself with greater gender equality.

The main reasons behind the increase of women in the workplace are women's liberation and feminism. The women's liberation movement originated in the 1960s and was popularised by authors such as Simone de Beauvoir. As a consequence of this, new legislation emerged, granting women equal rights to men in many fields, in particular employment. Because of feminist ideas, men have taken up roles which were previously seen as being for women only, most importantly those related to child rearing. As a result of this, women have more time to pursue their own careers and interests.

These have led to some significant effects, both to family life and to society as a whole.

Although the earning capacity of a woman in her lifetime is generally much less than that of a man, she can nevertheless make a significant contribution to the family income. The most important consequence of this is an improved quality of life. By helping to maintain a steady income for the family, the pressure on the husband is considerably reduced, hence improving both the husband's and the wife's emotional wellbeing. Additionally, the purchasing power of the family will also be raised. This means that the family can afford more luxuries such as foreign travel and a family car.

A further effect on the family is the promotion of independence in the children. Some might argue that having both parents working might be damaging to the children because of a lack of parental attention. However, such children have to learn to look after themselves at an earlier age, and their parents often rely on them to help with the housework. This therefore teaches them important life skills.

As regards society, the most significant impact of women going to work is greater gender equality. There are an increasing number of women who are becoming politicians, lawyers, and even CEOs and company managers. This in turn has led to greater equality for women in all areas of life, not just employment. For example, women today have much stronger legal rights to protect themselves against domestic violence and sexual discrimination in the workplace.

In conclusion, women's liberation and feminism have led to an increasing number of women at work, which in turn has brought about some important changes to family life, including improved quality of life and increased independence for children, as well as affecting society itself. It is clear that the sexes are still a long way from being equal in all areas of life, however, and perhaps the challenge for the present century is to ensure that this takes place.

# Unit 3: **Cause & Effect**

# Exercises

## Exercise 1: **Comprehension**

Answer the following questions about this unit. Either do this after reading the unit, or make notes first then use the notes to answer the questions.

**1** What are the two types of cause and effect essay structure?

- _____
- _____

**2** What is the difference between the two structure types? What are the advantages of each?

_____

_____

_____

_____

**3** Match each word on the left with a word on the right, and decide whether they are types of *cause* or *effect*. [Note: *immediate* is included twice, as it is both a type of cause and effect.]

- primary
- delayed
- short-term
- contributing
- immediate

- immediate
- long-term
- secondary
- remote
- main

**4** Study the paragraph below. Try to identify *at least one* example of each of the cause and effect types given in Q3 above. [Note: Each cause and effect could be more than one type.]

*The individual had spent the evening drinking with friends, and was over the legal alcohol limit when he drove his car home. The individual received a text message and was checking the message on his phone, which caused him to be distracted. As a result, he did not see the oncoming vehicle. He was unable to stop in time and crashed into the other vehicle. Both vehicles were severely damaged. The individual sustained a broken wrist in the accident. Initially he seemed otherwise unharmed and spoke to police officers. However, after 10 minutes he began to speak in a confused manner, and later fell into a coma. Surgeons operated on him and removed a blood clot from his brain. Although the individual recovered from the coma, he was subsequently paralysed and will spend the remainder of his life in a wheelchair.*

# Academic Writing Genres  Sheldon Smith

## Exercise 2: **Example essay**

Study the example essay on *women at work* (earlier in this unit) and answer these questions.

a) What type of structure has been used? _____

b) Complete the following diagram, summarising the main ideas of the essay.

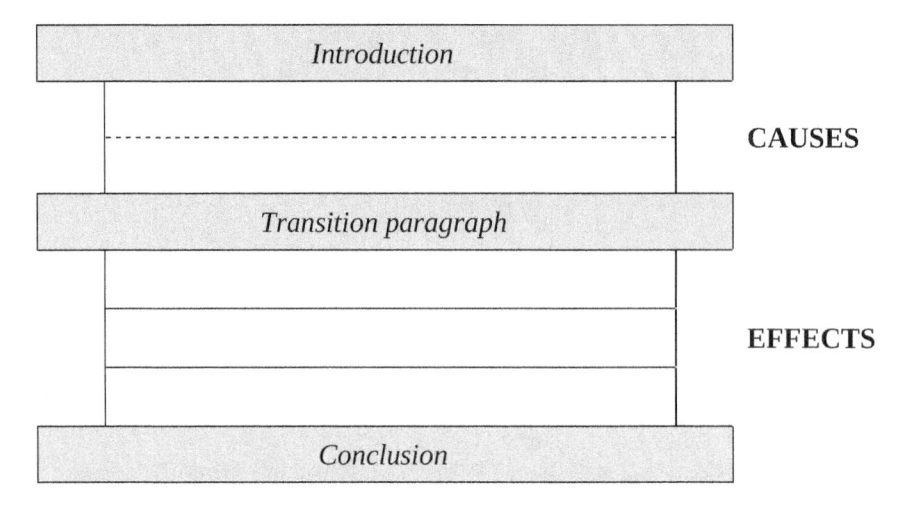

```
┌─────────────────────────────────┐
│         Introduction            │
└─────────────────────────────────┘
        │
        ├─────────────────────────────────  CAUSES
        │
┌─────────────────────────────────┐
│      Transition paragraph       │
└─────────────────────────────────┘
        │
        │                              EFFECTS
        │
┌─────────────────────────────────┐
│          Conclusion             │
└─────────────────────────────────┘
```

c) The first *effect* paragraph from the essay shows a 'chain' structure (twice), as one effect becomes the cause for the next effect. Complete the missing words in the flowchart below to show the chain of cause-effect in this paragraph.

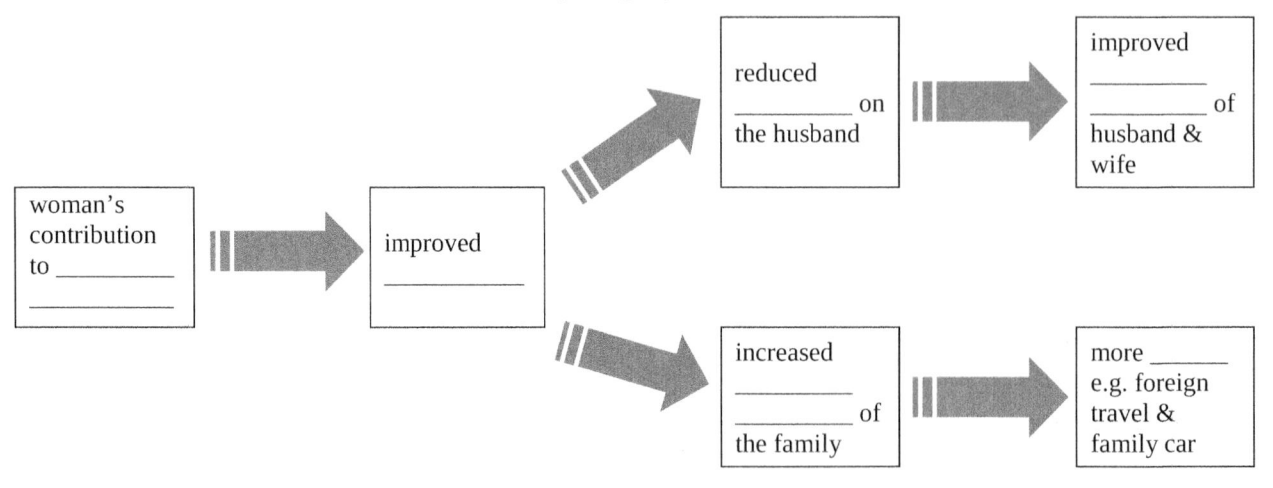

woman's contribution to _____ → improved _____ → 

- reduced _____ on the husband → improved _____ of husband & wife
- increased _____ of the family → more _____ e.g. foreign travel & family car

d) Study the example essay and highlight the following:
 - language for cause and effect;
 - the main ideas listed in: (a) the *thesis*; (b) the *topic sentences*; (c) the *summary*.

# Unit 3: Cause & Effect

## Exercise 3: Language for cause and effect #1

Study the following sentences. Complete each one by choosing the correct cause and effect transitions to fill the gaps, based on the structure and meaning of the sentence.

1) _____ increased emissions of pollutants, the Green House effect is accelerating.
   a) As a result of    b) As a result    c) Since

2) _____, extreme weather incidents are increasing.
   a) As a result of    b) As a result    c) Since

3) _____ her hard work, her spoken English made great improvement.
   a) As a consequence of    b) As a consequence    c) Causes

4) She also worked extremely hard on her writing. _____, her grades for her assignments went up considerably.
   a) As a consequence of    b) As a consequence    c) Results in

5) A lack of understanding of referencing conventions can _____ plagiarism.
   a) result from    b) be the result of    c) result in

6) _____ a lack of funding, the research department had to close down.
   a) Results from    b) Consequently    c) Owing to

7) The sharp increase in immigrants since January _____ the violent unrest in a neighbouring country.
   a) results in    b) is due to    c) affects

8) Stimulants such as caffeine are substances which _____ the body, leading to increased alertness and difficulty in getting to sleep.
   a) have an effect on    b) cause    c) result from

9) The increased use of stimulants _____ sleep disorders such as insomnia.
   a) is a consequence of    b) is one of the causes of    c) effects

10) Although free trade provides overall benefits, increasing imports can hurt domestic industries. _____, barriers to trade continue to exist.
    a) Because    b) Consequently    c) Consequence

# Exercise 4: Language for cause and effect #2

Study the following sentences. Complete each one by choosing the correct word (mostly prepositions) in the box.

i) Urbanisation has increased in many countries as a result [in / from / of] industrialisation.

ii) The increased use of green energy results [in / from / of] a reduction of carbon dioxide emissions.

iii) Carbon emissions that result [in / from / of] burning fossil fuels are likely to decrease in future.

iv) The harmful effects [of / for / on] smoking are well known.

v) Smoking can have an effect [of / for / on] not only the lungs but also the heart, brain, stomach and other organs.

vi) The increase in temperature was the cause [of / to / by] the increased rate of reaction.

vii) The increased rate of reaction was caused [of / to / by] the increase in temperature.

viii) There are several reasons [to / for / why] this change.

ix) There are several reasons [to / for / why] this change is necessary.

x) There is no reason [to / for / why] believe that reduction in fossil fuels will be harmful to the environment.

# Unit 3: **Cause & Effect**

## Exercise 5: **Language for cause and effect #3**

a) Study the following sentences and do the following:
- <u>underline</u> the part which gives the cause(s) and label it **C**;
- <u>underline</u> the part which gives the effect(s) and label it **E**;
- **highlight** the transitions which show cause/effect relationship;
- make a note of any special grammar points related to the transition, e.g. is it a sentence connector, a clause connector, what is the grammatical structure?

*Example*

                E                                                               C

**The cause of** <u>inflation</u> can be summed up in one sentence: <u>Too many dollars chasing too few goods</u>.[***]

*Language note*: <u>The cause of + sth (noun)</u>

**1.** People who are stressed often have a haggard look. A pioneering study from 2004 suggests that the reason is that stress can accelerate the cell biology of aging.[*]
*Language note*: _____

**2.** Because of the existence of stable isotopes, we must take special care when quoting the mass of an element.[**]
*Language note*: _____

**3.** The patient recently suffered a stroke in the front portion of her right hemisphere. As a result, she has great difficulty moving her left leg.[*]
*Language note*: _____

**4.** Dr. Tom Steitz is the Sterling Professor of Biochemistry and Biophysics at Yale University. As a result of his lifetime of work, he won the Nobel Prize in Chemistry in 2009.[*]
*Language note*: _____

**5.** Prader-Willi Syndrome (PWS), a rare genetic disorder, results in persistent feelings of intense hunger and reduced rates of metabolism.[*]
*Language note*: _____

**6.** Our body weight is affected by a number of factors, including gene-environment interactions, and the number of calories we consume versus the number of calories we burn in daily activity.[*]
*Language note*: _____

---

[*]    From *Psychology* by OpenStax. This OpenStax book is available for free at https://cnx.org/content/col11629/1.5.
[**]   From *University Physics* by OpenStax. Download free at https://openstax.org/details/books/university-physics-volume-3.
[***]  From *Principles of Economics* by OpenStax. Download free at https://openstax.org/details/books/principles-economics.

b) Study the following sentences and do the following:
- identify which is the cause and label it **C**;
- identify which is the effect and label it **E**;
- link the sentences, using the given transition. These are the same transitions as a). Be careful with sentence structure (you will need to rewrite some of the sentences).

Example: **The reason is**
_E_  Fossil fuels such as coal continue to be used in power plants.
_C_  They are much cheaper than other types of energy-producing fuel.
<u>Fossil fuels such as coal continue to be used in power plants. **The reason is** that they are much cheaper than other types of energy-producing fuel.</u>

### 1. Because of
___  There is a growing number of people from ethnically diverse backgrounds.
___  There is a need for therapists and psychologists to develop knowledge and skills to become culturally competent.*

### 2. As a result
___  We are more active during the night-time hours than our ancestors were.
___  Many of us sleep less than 7 hours a night and accrue a sleep debt.*

### 3. As a result of
___  Amnesia, the loss of long-term memory, occurs.
___  There is disease, physical trauma, or psychological trauma.*

### 4. Results in
___  Rheumatoid arthritis is an autoimmune disease that affects the joints.
___  There are joint pain, stiffness, and loss of function.*

### 5. To be affected by
___  Our body weight.
___  Our genes and the amount of energy we consume.*

\*  From *Psychology* by OpenStax. This OpenStax book is available for free at https://cnx.org/content/col11629/1.5.

# Unit 3: **Cause & Effect**

## Exercise 6: **Writing a cause and effect essay**

a) Choose *one* of the following topics to write a *cause and effect* essay, using either *block* or *chain* structure.

1. Global warming.
2. Air pollution.
3. Increased life expectancy.
4. Plagiarism.
5. Computer game addiction.
6. Increase in online shopping.
7. Increased demand for fast food.
8. Sleep debt (not getting enough sleep).
9. Increased urbanisation (i.e. people moving out of rural areas and into cities).
10. Refugees (people who leave their country to go to a safer foreign country).
11. Increased use of mobile phones.
12. Stress.
13. Poverty.
14. Unemployment.
15. Inflation.
16. Homelessness.
17. High crime rates in certain countries.
18. Racism.
19. Bullying (physical and/or online i.e. cyber-bullying).
20. A historical topic you know well (e.g. World War II, the American Civil War).

Use the following chart to organise your ideas.

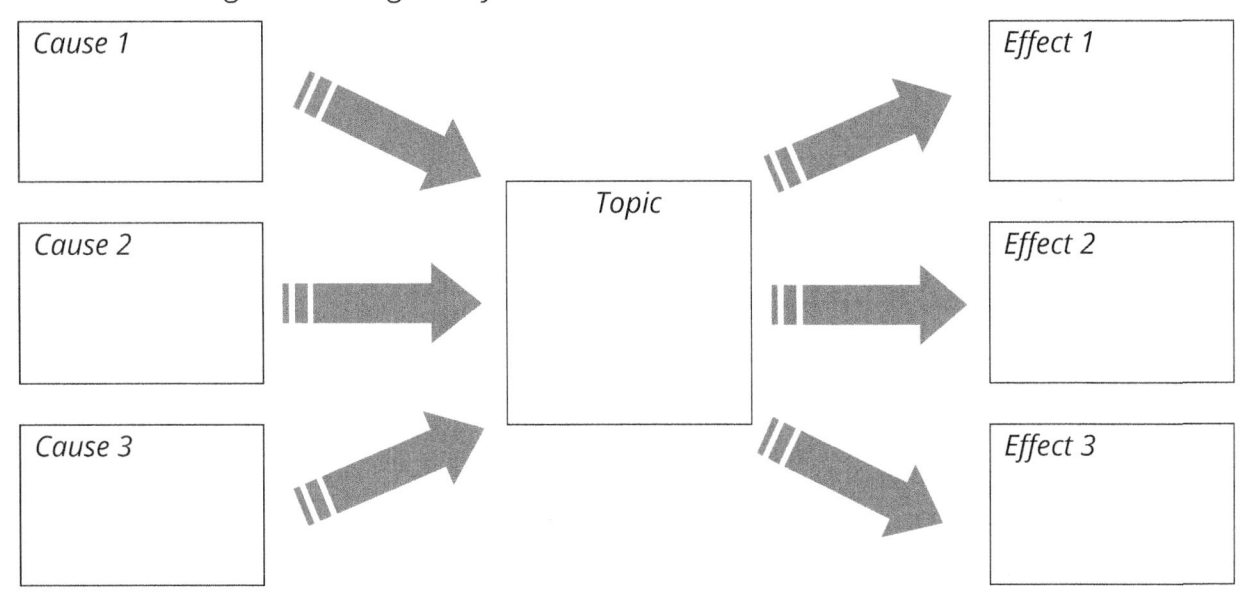

*Cause 1* → *Topic* → *Effect 1*
*Cause 2* → *Topic* → *Effect 2*
*Cause 3* → *Topic* → *Effect 3*

b) When you have finished, get a peer to check your essay, using the checklist earlier in the unit. You should also check another student's writing.

## Exercise 7: **Learning outcomes check**

a) The following are the learning outcomes for this unit. Decide how well you have mastered each one by giving it a score, as follows.

    3 = I understand/can do this well.
    2 = I understand/can do this fairly well, but I can improve with more practice.
    1 = I understand/can do this, but not well enough yet. I need to practise more.
    0 = I cannot do this yet. I need more time.

| Score | Learning Outcome |
|---|---|
| _____ | I know what a cause and effect essay is. |
| _____ | I understand different types of causes (*main, contributing, immediate, remote*). |
| _____ | I understand different types of effects (*short-term, long-term, primary, secondary*). |
| _____ | I understand ways to structure a cause and effect essay. |
| _____ | I am able to use language for showing cause and effect. |
| _____ | I can write a cause and effect essay. |
| _____ | I can peer edit a cause and effect essay, using a checklist. |

b) Use this information to review the unit and improve.

# UNIT 4 | Problem-Solution Essays

## Learning Outcomes

By the end of this unit, you should:
- understand what problem-solution and SPSE essays are;
- know what a problem-solution essay contains;
- know the two main ways to structure a problem-solution essay;
- know some common language for presenting problems and solutions.

By completing the exercises, you will also:
- study an example essay for language and content;
- practise writing solutions to problems;
- write a problem-solution essay;
- peer edit a problem-solution essay, using a checklist.

## Key Vocabulary

**Nouns**
- situation
- problem
- evaluation
- solution
- block
- chain

**Adjectives**
- problematic

**Verbs**
- solve

## Additional Vocabulary

*Academic Collocations (in the unit)*
[None]

*Academic Collocations (in the essay)*
- concerted effort (adj + n)
- increased risk (adj + n)
- physical activity (adj + n)
- rising costs (adj + n)
- significant improvement (adj + n)
- increasingly common (adv + adj)
- raise awareness (v + n)

## Contents of this section

### UNIT 4: PROBLEM-SOLUTION ESSAYS .................... 67
- Overview ..................................................................................... 68
- Structure of problem-solution essays ...................................... 69
- Language for problem-solution essays .................................... 70
- Checklist ..................................................................................... 71
- Example essay ........................................................................... 72
- Exercises ..................................................................................... 73

# Overview

Problem-solution essays consider the problem (or problems) of a particular situation, and give solutions to the problem(s). They are in some ways similar to cause and effect essays, especially in terms of structure, and will likely include the causes and effects of the problem.

Problem-solution essays are actually a sub-type of another type of essay, called the SPSE essay, which has the following four components:
- situation;
- problem;
- solution;
- evaluation.

The *situation* outlines the context of the problem. In short essays, it may be enough to include the situation in the background of the introduction. For longer essays, it will form one or more paragraphs in the main body, before the problem. The situation is likely to outline the *causes* of the problem.

The *problem* (or problems) should be clearly stated. It may be important to consider the problem from different aspects, e.g. economic vs. social vs. political, or from the point of view of different actors, e.g. students vs. teachers vs. parents. The problem is likely to consider the *effects* of the problem, since it is often the effects which make the situation problematic.

The *solutions* should relate directly to the problem (or problems). If the problem has been viewed from different perspectives (e.g. economic, social, political), the solutions should likewise be considered from these perspectives.

The *evaluation* considers how effective each of the solutions will be. For short essays, this is often included as part of the conclusion (as in the example essay in this unit). For longer essays, it will form a separate paragraph in the main body.

**In short**

Problem-solution essays (a sub-type of SPSE essays) contain the following:
- *situation* or background to the problem (often in the introduction);
- *problem(s)*;
- *solution(s)* to the problems;
- *evaluation* of the solutions (often in the conclusion).

**Ways to solve problems**

While there are many possible ways to solve problems, the following are some common *types* of solution:
- to provide funding (or resources);
- to educate;
- to create or enforce laws or rules;
- to change something (which isn't working);
- to create something new.

# Unit 4: **Problem-Solution**

# Structure of problem-solution essays

There are two main ways to structure a problem-solution essay. These are similar to the ways to structure cause and effect essays, namely using a **block** or a **chain** structure. For the *block* structure, all of the problems are listed first, and all of the solutions are listed afterwards. For the *chain* structure, each problem is followed immediately by the solution to that problem. Both types of structure have their merits. The former is generally clearer, especially for shorter essays, while the latter ensures that any solutions you present relate directly to the problems you have given.

> Block and chain structures are also used in *Cause & Effect* essays (Unit 3).

The two types of structure, *block* and *chain*, are shown in the diagram below. This is for a short essay, which includes the 'situation' in the introduction and 'evaluation' in the conclusion. A longer essay, for example one of around 1,000 words, would probably have these two sections as separate paragraphs in the main body.

> **Vocabulary in use:** *solution*
> The verb form of the word *solution* is *solve*. While the word *solute* looks like it should be the verb, it is in fact a noun used in chemistry, meaning 'a dissolved substance'.

**Block**

- Introduction (including 'situation')
- Problem 1
- Problem 2
- ...
- Transition sentence/paragraph
- Solution 1
- Solution 2
- ...
- Conclusion (including 'evaluation')

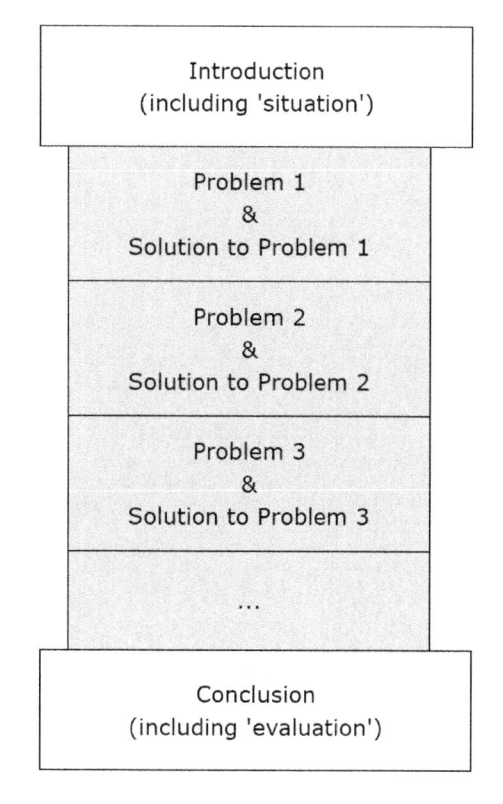

**Chain**

- Introduction (including 'situation')
- Problem 1 & Solution to Problem 1
- Problem 2 & Solution to Problem 2
- Problem 3 & Solution to Problem 3
- ...
- Conclusion (including 'evaluation')

# Language for problem-solution essays

As the *situation* will often consider the causes, while the *problem* will often include the effects, *cause* and *effect* transitions will be common in problem-solution essays. This means phrases such as 'Because of' and 'As a result of' (for *causes*) and 'This has resulted in' and 'Consequently' (for *effects*).

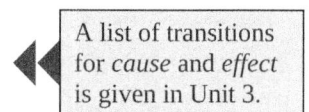

> A list of transitions for *cause* and *effect* is given in Unit 3.

When presenting solutions to problems, it is often useful to use *modal verbs*. These vary in strength and should be chosen carefully to reflect the strength of your view. Common modal verbs for offering solutions are as follows.

| Modal verb | Meaning | Strength |
|---|---|---|
| must / have to | absolute necessity, lacking any choice | *strongest* ↑ |
| need to | necessity (but having choice) | |
| should | firm suggestion | |
| can / could | suggestion | |
| might | tentative suggestion | *weakest* ↓ |

The following constructions, with a similar meaning to 'must', are also possible.

> It is essential that / It is crucial that   [X] + *do sth*

The following construction, with a similar meaning to 'need to', is also possible.

> It is necessary for [X] + *to do sth*

Examples
- In order to tackle global warming, governments **must** work together.
- In order to tackle global warming, **it is essential that** governments work together.
- In order to tackle global warming, **it is necessary for** governments to work together.
- To reduce the problem of plagiarism in undergraduate papers, universities **should** invest in plagiarism-detecting software.
- To overcome this problem, the government **could** increase taxes and use the revenue to invest in green energy.
- One way to deal with this issue **might** be for lecturers to teach paraphrasing and citation skills to their students, rather than assuming they already have these skills.

Unit 4: **Problem-Solution**

# Checklist

Below is a checklist for problem-solution essays. Use it to check your own writing, or get a peer to help you.

| Area | Item | OK? | Comments |
|---|---|---|---|
| Problem-Solution | The essay is a problem-solution essay. | | |
| | The *situation* is stated (e.g. in the Introduction), which may also show the *causes* of the problem(s). | | |
| | The *problem* is given, which may also show its *effects*. | | |
| | If appropriate, the *problem* is considered from different aspects (e.g. *economic* vs. *social*) or from the point of view of different actors (e.g. *students* vs. *teachers*). | | |
| | *Solutions* are given, which relate directly to the problem(s). | | |
| | There is *evaluation* of the solutions (e.g. in the conclusion). | | |
| | An appropriate structure is used, either *block* or *chain*. | | |
| | Problem-solution language is used accurately (e.g. *modal verbs*). | | |
| General essay skills | The essay has a clear thesis statement. | | |
| | Each paragraph has a clear topic sentence. | | |
| | Each paragraph has enough support (facts, reasons, examples, etc.). | | |
| | The conclusion includes a summary of the main points. | | |

# Example essay

Below is an example *problem-solution* essay. It is used in one of the exercises later.

*Title*: Modern lifestyles are becoming increasingly unhealthy. What are some of the problems this causes? What are some of the possible solutions to these problems?

Modern lifestyles have led us to become increasingly reliant on processed and convenience foods. At the same time, our dependence on the car, as well as modern pastimes such as watching television and surfing the internet, have led to a decrease in general levels of exercise, and therefore a decrease in fitness levels. While this kind of lifestyle is more pronounced in developed countries, it is increasingly common in developing nations, and should be considered a global phenomenon. This has led to significant health problems for individuals, as well as rising costs for governments. To tackle these problems, it is important for individuals to change their diet and levels of activity, and for governments to do more to raise awareness of the issues and promote healthy living initiatives.

One of the problems caused by unhealthy modern lifestyles is ill-health of individuals. It is well known that regular exercise can reduce the risk of heart disease and stroke, which means that those with poor fitness levels are at an increased risk of suffering from those problems. Additionally, the worsening of the average diet has been matched by an increase in the number of people who are overweight or obese. In some countries, especially industrialized ones, the number of obese people can amount to one third of the population. This is significant as overweight and obese people are more likely to suffer serious illnesses such as diabetes and heart disease, which can lead to an increase in the number of sick days, increase in unemployment, or shortened lifespan.

Unhealthy modern lifestyles also adversely affect government finance. In countries such as the UK, where there is a national health service, the cost of treatment for illnesses such as diabetes and heart disease must be borne by the government. Loss of productivity through increased sick days or unemployment also affects the economy and therefore government finances.

To tackle this problem, individuals need to make changes to their diet and their levels of physical activity. There is a reliance today on the consumption of processed foods, which have a high fat and sugar content. By preparing their own foods, and consuming more fruit and vegetables, people could ensure that their diets are healthier and more balanced, which could lead to a reduction in obesity levels. In order to improve fitness levels, people could choose to walk or cycle to work or to the shops rather than taking the car. They could also choose to walk upstairs instead of taking the lift. These simple changes could lead to a significant improvement in health and fitness levels.

Governments could also implement initiatives to improve their citizens' eating and exercise habits. This could be done through education, for example by adding classes to the curriculum about healthy diet and lifestyles. Governments could also do more to encourage their citizens to walk or cycle instead of taking the car, for instance by building more cycle lanes or increasing vehicle taxes. While some might argue that increased taxes are a unreasonable way to solve the problem, it is no different from the high taxes imposed on cigarettes to reduce cigarette consumption.

In short, obesity and poor fitness are a significant problem in modern life, leading to ill health and rising costs for governments. Individuals and governments can work together to tackle this problem and so improve diet and fitness. Of the solutions suggested, those made by individuals themselves are likely to have more impact, though it is clear that a concerted effort with the government is essential for success. With obesity levels in industrialized and industrializing countries continuing to rise, it is essential that we take action now.

# Unit 4: **Problem-Solution**

## Exercises

### Exercise 1: **Comprehension**

Answer the following questions about this unit. Either do this after reading the unit, or make notes first then use the notes to answer the questions.

1. In what way are problem-solution essays similar to cause and effect essays?

   _____

   _____

2. Problem-solution essays are a sub-type of SPSE essays. What do the letters SPSE stand for?
   - S_____
   - P_____
   - S_____
   - E_____

3. In which stage of the essay will *causes* of the problem most likely be seen? In which stage is it most likely to see *effects*? Why?

   _____

   _____

4. What happens in the 'E' stage?

   _____

5. Where might you find the first 'S' stage and the 'E' stage in a *short* essay?

   _____

   _____

6. Give examples of different ways that the problem can be viewed.

   _____

   _____

7. The following are some model verbs which can be used to present solutions. Number them in order of strength, from **1** (strongest) to **5** (weakest).

   | should | must | might | can | need to |
   |--------|------|-------|-----|---------|

# Academic Writing Genres        Sheldon Smith

## Exercise 2: **Example essay**

Study the essay on *unhealthy lifestyles* (earlier in the unit) and answer these questions.

a) What type of structure has been used? _____

b) Complete the following diagram, summarising the main ideas of the essay.

```
        Introduction

                                    PROBLEMS


                                    SOLUTIONS

        Conclusion
```

c) How has the problem been viewed in the essay (i.e. from whose viewpoint?)
_____

d) The following is a summary of the *situation* given in the introduction. Complete the summary by adding missing words from the text.

> People are eating more **i)** _____ and **ii)** _____ foods nowadays. They are also using the **iii)** _____ more and indulging in habits such as **iv)** _____ and **v)** _____, both of which mean that people are getting much less **vi)** _____ than in the past, which in turn decreases their amount of **vii)** _____. Although this is more of a problem in **viii)** _____ countries, it is also a growing problem in **ix)** _____. It is therefore a **x)** _____ situation.

d) What is the writer's *evaluation*?
_____
_____

e) The unit lists the following type of solutions. Which ones have been used in the essay?
- ☐ to provide funding (or resources)
- ☐ to change something (which isn't working)
- ☐ to educate
- ☐ to create something new
- ☐ to create or enforce laws or rules

f) Study the example essay and highlight the following:
- language for presenting solutions (including *modal verbs*);
- language for cause and effect;
- the main ideas listed in: (a) the *thesis*; (b) the *topic sentences*; (c) the *summary*.

# Unit 4: **Problem-Solution**

## Exercise 3: **Language for problem-solution**

In the following sentences, the problem has been stated. Complete each one by adding an appropriate solution. To do this, try to view the problem from a suitable aspect or from the point of view of a suitable actor. Remember to use suitable language (e.g. model verbs).
*Note: These problems relate to some of the essay topics in Exercise 4.*

**Example**
In order to tackle the problem of unhealthy lifestyles, <u>individuals need to make changes to their diet and their levels of physical activity.</u>

**i)** To deal with the problem of overuse of mobile phones by children, _____

_____

_____

**ii)** In order to address the issue of air pollution in cities, _____

_____

_____

**iii)** If countries with child labour problems are going to reverse this trend, _____

_____

_____

**iv)** To reduce the number of teenage pregnancies, _____

_____

_____

**v)** In order to tackle the problem of species extinction, _____

_____

_____

# Academic Writing Genres                                    Sheldon Smith

## Exercise 4: **Writing a problem-solution essay**

a) Choose *one* of the following topics to write a *problem-solution* essay, using either *block* or *chain* structure. It may be helpful to view the problem from different *aspects* (economic, social, political) or from the point of view of different *actors*.

1. Children are using mobile phones and computers from an earlier age and for longer hours than in the past. What problems does this cause? What are some possible solutions?
2. Civil wars and natural disasters are increasing the number of immigrants to certain nations. What problems does this cause, and what solutions are there?
3. What problems are caused by high rate of teenage pregnancy in some countries and communities? How can these problems be addressed?
4. In some countries, students need to pay for university tuition using student loans, often building up huge debts in the process. Why is this a problem? How can this be improved?
5. In some countries, child labour exists. Why is this problematic? How can it be solved?
6. In many countries, divorce rates are increasing. What are the problems and solutions?
7. Many cities in the world have high levels of air pollution. What problems does this cause? How can these problems be tackled?
8. It is increasingly difficult for working people to find a good work-life balance, with the result that many people are overworked. What problems does this cause? How can these be resolved?
9. Why is the growing extinction of animal species a problem? How can it be solved?
10. Some people are unable to afford computers or access to the internet, leading to an 'digital divide'. What are the problems this leads to, and how can these be solved?

Use the following chart to organise your ideas.

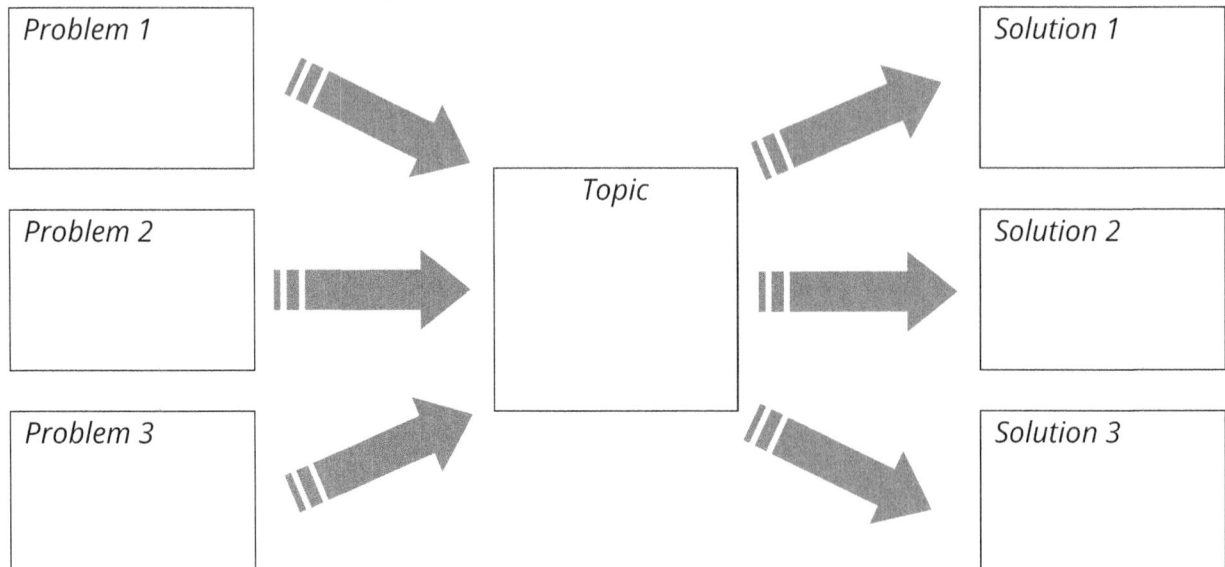

| Problem 1 |  →  |        |  →  | Solution 1 |
|-----------|-----|--------|-----|------------|
| Problem 2 |  →  | Topic  |  →  | Solution 2 |
| Problem 3 |  →  |        |  →  | Solution 3 |

b) When you have finished, get a peer to check your essay, using the checklist earlier in the unit. You should also check another student's writing.

# Unit 4: **Problem-Solution**

## Exercise 5: **Learning outcomes check**

a) The following are the learning outcomes for this unit. Decide how well you have mastered each one by giving it a score, as follows.

    3 = I understand/can do this well.
    2 = I understand/can do this fairly well, but I can improve with more practice.
    1 = I understand/can do this, but not well enough yet. I need to practise more.
    0 = I cannot do this yet. I need more time.

| Score | Learning Outcome |
|---|---|
| _____ | I understand what problem-solution and SPSE essays are. |
| _____ | I know what a problem-solution essay contains. |
| _____ | I know the two main ways to structure a problem-solution essay. |
| _____ | I know some common language for presenting problems and solution. |
| _____ | I can write solutions to problems. |
| _____ | I can write a problem-solution essay. |
| _____ | I can peer edit a problem-solution essay, using a checklist. |

b) Use this information to review the unit and improve.

# Unit 5: Classification Essays

## Learning Outcomes

By the end of this unit, you should:
- know what a classification essay is;
- understand how something can be classified (by applying a criterion);
- understand ways to structure a classification essay;
- be able to use language for classifying (to show the criterion, the result, and sub-division).

By completing the exercises, you will also:
- study an example essay for structure, language and content;
- rewrite a thesis statement to change the structure of a classification essay;
- practise using language for classification;
- complete a classification diagram;
- write a classification essay;
- peer edit a classification essay, using a checklist.

## Key Vocabulary

*Nouns*
- classification
- division
- criterion (pl. criteria)
- category
- characteristics

*Verbs*
- classify
- divide
- categorise/-ize

## Additional Vocabulary

*Academic Collocations (in the unit)*
- individual items (adj + n)
- main categories (adj + n)
- underlying principle (adj + n)
- draw conclusions (v + n)

*Academic Collocations (in the essay)*
- considerable effort (adj + n)
- fall into this category (v + n)

## Contents of this section

### Unit 5: Classification Essays ............... 79
- Overview ............... 80
- How to classify ............... 80
- Structure of classification essays ............... 81
- Language for classifying ............... 82
- Checklist ............... 84
- Example essay ............... 85
- Exercises ............... 86

# Overview

To classify means to arrange items into groups or categories. A **classification essay** (also called a **division essay**) will group or categorise people, objects, events or situations according to specific criteria or shared features or characteristics. Although it is possible for the classification to comprise a whole essay, as in this unit, sometimes this may form only part of the writing (which could be an essay, report or other genre), with the classification used to make comparisons or draw conclusions.

Classification essay questions may use verbs such as *classify* or *categorise*, or nouns such as *types, varieties, kinds* and *categories*. The following are some example questions of classification essays.

- What kinds of policies can governments use to reduce unemployment?
- Outline the four types of cellular transport.
- What are the types of solution in chemistry?
- Discuss the modes of entry an organisation can use to enter an overseas market.

> **Classify vs. divide**
> Although a *classification essay* is also called a *division essay*, the words *divide* and *classify* have different meanings. To *divide* means to separate into parts, while to *classify* means to arrange items into categories. *Dividing* starts with the whole, and there may be no underlying principle for the division. *Classifying* starts with the individual items, and there is always an underlying principle for sorting them. *Classify* and *classification* are therefore more precise terms, and are the ones used in this unit.

# How to classify

One way of classifying something is to specify a **criterion** (or **criteria**, if there is more than one) to divide the thing into different groups. For example, if you were to classify students in a university class, they could be grouped according to any of the following criteria: sex; age; nationality; ethnicity; or even favourite colour. Classifying according to sex would lead to 'male' and 'female' groups. Dividing according to age could lead to 18, 19 and so on, or ranges such as 'between 18 and 21', 'between 22 and 25', etc.

> **In short**
> Classification means dividing into categories, and can be done by identifying either:
> - a *criterion*;
> - shared characteristics.

If there is no clear criterion, or if the possible criteria do not result in logical groups for the purpose of your writing, a second way to classify is by identifying different types based on shared characteristics or features. For example, falcons and owls are two types of bird. The shared characteristics of falcons are thin, pointed wings, hooked beaks, very good eyesight, the ability to fly fast and change direction rapidly. The shared characteristics of owls, on the other hand, are a disk shaped face, forward facing eyes, ear tufts and good hearing.

# Unit 5: **Classification**

## Structure of classification essays

There are three ways to structure a classification essay, depending on the approach taken.

The first way, shown in the diagram below, is when a *single criterion* (or single way of categorising) is used, resulting in distinct categories. The purpose of this essay is to show understanding of the categories, or justify the method of classification, by giving the categories and describing their characteristics. For the single-criterion classification essay, the criterion (if there is one) should be given in the introduction, and the thesis statement should list the categories which will be described in the main body. Each body paragraph will usually describe one category in detail.

**Single criterion**

- Introduction
- **Category 1** — Description of characteristics
- **Category 2** — Description of characteristics
- **Category 3** — Description of characteristics
- …
- Conclusion

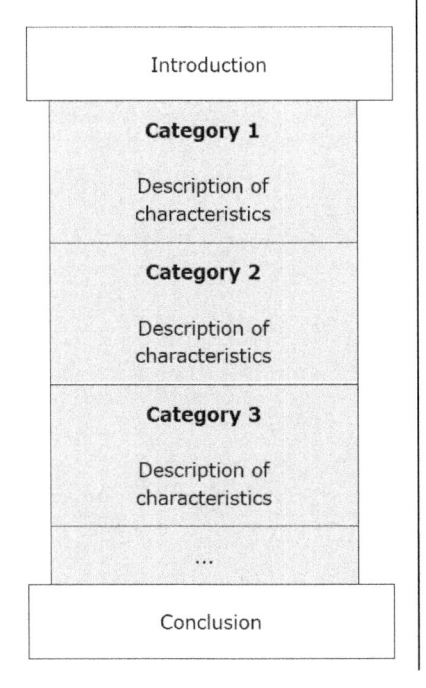

A second way, shown below, is similar to the first, except that one or more of the categories are sub-divided to create sub-categories.

**Single criterion (with sub-categories)**

- Introduction
- **Category 1** — Description of characteristics
  - Sub-category 1.1 — Examples
  - Sub-category 1.2 — Examples
  - …
- Transition sentence/paragraph
- **Category 2** — Description of characteristics
  - Sub-category 2.1 — Examples
  - Sub-category 2.2 — Examples
  - …
- Conclusion

The purpose and structure is similar to the previous one. The paragraphs describing the sub-categories may describe characteristics, but will more likely simply give examples.

**Multiple criteria**

- Introduction
- **Criterion 1** — Examples of categories
- **Criterion 2** — Examples of categories
- **Criterion 3** — Examples of categories
- …
- Conclusion

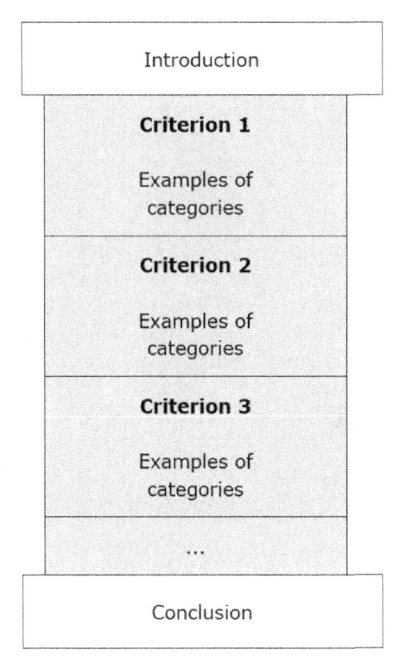

A third way, shown above, is when *multiple criteria* are used to classify the topic in different ways. The purpose of this essay is to show understanding of how the topic can be categorised, or justify the criteria for classification, by giving the criteria and showing examples of groupings using these criteria. For the multiple-criteria classification essay, the thesis statement should list the criteria which are described in the main body. Each body paragraph will usually describe the criteria and the groups it leads to. Depending on the level of detail, the examples might be broken down into separate paragraphs.

# Language for classifying

The language used for classifying depends on whether you are describing the *criterion* or the *result* of applying the criterion, or giving sub-divisions.

## Showing the criterion

The following language phrases can be used to show the *criterion*. All should be followed by a noun or noun phrase.

| [X] | can be / may be | classified / grouped | according to… / on the basis of… / depending on… / by… |

One way to classify [X] is by…

| Scientists / Researchers / Experts | classify [X] | by… |

**Language Tip: *Whether… or not***
The phrase 'whether… or not' can be used with these structures when there is no noun or noun phrase to describe the criterion. E.g.
- The students may be classified according to **whether** they are Asian **or not**.

The following examples show how these phrases can be used.
- Organisms **may be classified according to** their source of carbon.*
- Chemical disinfectants **are grouped by** the types of microbes and infectious agents they are effective against.*
- Hypersensitivity reactions **may be grouped on the basis of** their immune mechanism.
- The students **may be grouped on the basis of** age.
- The students **can be classified depending on** ethnicity.
- **One way to classify** students **is by** age.

* *From* Microbiology *by OpenStax. Download for free at https://openstax.org/details/books/microbiology.*

## Showing the result

The following language phrases can be used to show the *result*.

| [X] | can be / may be / is/are | classified / grouped | into… / as… |

| [X] | consist(s) of… / comprise(s)… |

# Unit 5: Classification

The following examples show how these can be used.
- All living organisms **are classified into** three domains of life: Archaea, Bacteria, and Eukarya.*
- Cellulose **consists of** a linear chain of glucose molecules.*
- Economics **consists of** micro-economics and macro-economics.
- Economics **comprises** micro-economics and macro-economics.

> **Vocab in use: *comprise* vs. *consist***
> The verbs *comprise* and *consist* have the same meaning. However, *consist* is followed by *of*, while *comprise* is not.

* From Microbiology by OpenStax. Download for free at https://openstax.org/details/books/microbiology.

## Showing sub-division

It may be necessary to sub-divide, that is, to divide something which has already been divided. The following shows language for this.

| | |
|---|---|
| *first division* > | classified/divided |
| *second division* > | sub-divided |
| *third division* > | further sub-divided |

For example:
- The students in the class can be classified according to sex. They can be **sub-divided** according to whether they are Asian or not. They can be **further sub-divided** according to age, into those below 25 years of age and those above 25.

According to this classification, there will be eight groups: Asian males under 25, Asian males over 25, non-Asian males under 25, etc.

## Other transition phrases

The following phrases may be useful to introduce the categories.

| The | first / second / third / final | category / type of [X] | is… |
|---|---|---|---|

| One / Another | category / type of [X] | is… |
|---|---|---|

The following examples, taken from the example essay below, show how these can be used.
- **The first type of** consumer products, unsought products, are products unplanned by the potential buyer or known products that the buyer does not actively seek.
- **The second type**, convenience products, are relatively inexpensive items that require little shopping effort.

# Checklist

Below is a checklist for classification essays. Use it to check your writing, or ask a peer.

| Aspect | Item | OK? | Comments |
|---|---|---|---|
| Classification | The essay is a classification essay. | | |
| | An appropriate structure is used, either *single-criterion* or *multiple-criteria*. | | |
| | Correct language is used for showing the criterion/criteria or the result. | | |
| For *single-criterion* structure | The introduction identifies the criterion for classification. | | |
| | The thesis statement shows the main *categories*. | | |
| | Each main body paragraph has a clear topic sentence, and covers one *category* (or *sub-category*). | | |
| | The categories in the main body match those in the thesis. | | |
| | The essay has appropriate support (including description of *categories*, with examples). | | |
| For *multiple-criteria* structure | The thesis statement shows the *criteria*. | | |
| | Each main body paragraph has a clear topic sentence, and covers one *criterion*. | | |
| | The criteria in the main body match those in the thesis. | | |
| | The essay has appropriate support (including description of *criteria*, with examples). | | |
| General essay skills | The essay has a clear thesis statement. | | |
| | Each paragraph has a clear topic sentence. | | |
| | Each paragraph has enough support (facts, reasons, examples, etc.). | | |
| | The conclusion includes a summary of the main points. | | |

# Unit 5: **Classification**

# Example essay

Below is an example *classification* essay. It is used in one of the exercises later.

*Title*: Explain, with examples, how consumer products are usually classified.

Products that are bought by the end user are called consumer products. They include electric razors, sandwiches, cars, stereos, magazines, and houses. Marketers must know how consumers view the types of consumer product their companies sell so that they can design the marketing mix to appeal to the selected target market. To help them define target markets, marketers classify consumer products by the amount of effort needed to acquire them. The four major categories under this classification are unsought products, convenience products, shopping products, and specialty products.

The first type of consumer products, unsought products, are products unplanned by the potential buyer or known products that the buyer does not actively seek. These may require no effort on the part of the consumer, for example life insurance, or considerable effort, such as burial plots.

The second type, convenience products, are relatively inexpensive items that require little shopping effort. Soft drinks, candy bars, milk, bread, and small hardware items are examples. Consumers buy them routinely without much planning.

In contrast to convenience products, the third type, shopping products, are bought only after a brand-to-brand and store-to-store comparison of price, suitability, and style. Examples are furniture, automobiles, a vacation in Europe, and some items of clothing. While convenience products are bought with little planning, shopping products may be purchased after months or even years of search and evaluation.

The final type, specialty products, are products for which consumers search long and hard and for which they refuse to accept substitutes. Expensive jewellery, designer clothing, state-of-the-art stereo equipment, limited-production automobiles, and gourmet restaurants fall into this category. Because consumers are willing to spend much time and effort to find specialty products, distribution is often limited to one or two sellers in a given region.

In conclusion, consumer products can be classified according to the effort required to obtain them, leading to four categories, namely unsought products, convenience products, shopping products, and specialty products. Although not the only way to categorise consumer products, these categories greatly assist marketers in appealing to the selected target market.

Adapted from *Chapter 11 Creating Products and Pricing Strategies to Meet Customers' Needs* (pp.434-435), from *Introduction to Business*, by OpenStax, available for free at http://cnx.org/content/col25734/1.7

# Academic Writing Genres — Sheldon Smith

# Exercises

## Exercise 1: **Comprehension**

Answer the following questions about this unit. Either do this after reading the unit, or make notes first then use the notes to answer the questions.

**1** Explain the meaning of the following terms.

- classify  _____
- criterion  _____
- sub-divide  _____

**2** Complete the diagram classifying ways to organise classification essays. Use the same missing words to complete the summary of this diagram in the box below.

**Classification Essays**
- Single-_____
  - no sub-_____
  - with sub-_____
- Multiple-_____

> Classification essays can be classified according to whether there is a _____ or not. Single-_____ essays can be sub-divided according to whether or not there are sub-_____.

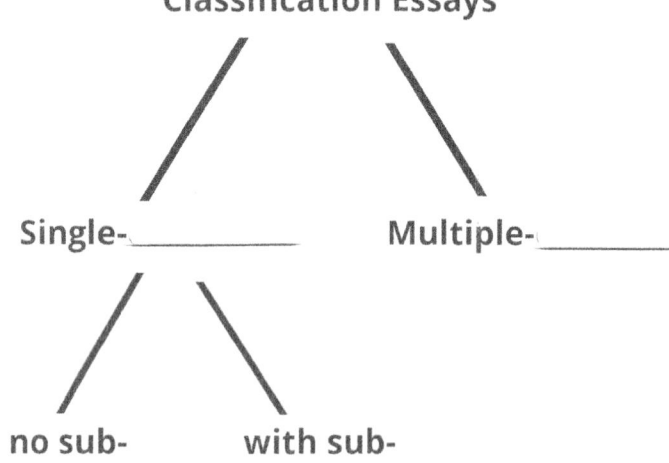

**3** Decide which type of essay (from **2** above) the following statements describe.

- the main body paragraphs describe the *criteria*  _____
- the main body paragraphs describe the *categories*  _____
- the criterion should be given in the introduction  _____
- one possible purpose is to justify the method of classification  _____
- one possible purpose is to justify the criteria for classification  _____

# Unit 5: **Classification**

## Exercise 2: **Example essay**

Study the example essay on *consumer products* (earlier in this unit) and answer the following questions.

a) What type of structure has been used? _____

b) Complete the following table showing details of the essay.

| Topic | |
|---|---|
| Definition of topic | |
| Why topic is important | |
| Criterion for classification | |

| | Name | Characteristics | Examples |
|---|---|---|---|
| Category 1 | | • <br><br>• | |
| Category 2 | | • <br><br>• | |
| Category 3 | | • <br><br>• | |
| Category 4 | | • <br><br>• | |

c) Study the example essay and highlight the following:
- language for classification;
- the criterion in: (a) the introduction; (b) the conclusion;
- transition signals to introduce the different types;
- the four types listed in: (a) the *thesis*; (b) the *topic sentences*; (c) the *summary*.

d) The following extract shows another way that consumer products can be classified.

> A second way to classify consumer products is according to durability. Consumer products that get used up, such as shampoo and potato chips, are called consumer nondurables. Those that last for a long time, such as washing machines and computers, are consumer durables.

Rewrite the introduction so that it presents a *multiple-criteria* structure. [Hint: You only need to write one sentence, namely the thesis statement.]

Original introduction

Products that are bought by the end user are called consumer products. They include electric razors, sandwiches, cars, stereos, magazines, and houses. Marketers must know how consumers view the types of consumer product their companies sell so that they can design the marketing mix to appeal to the selected target market. **To help them define target markets, marketers classify consumer products by the amount of effort needed to acquire them. The four major categories under this classification are unsought products, convenience products, shopping products, and specialty products.**

New introduction

Products that are bought by the end user are called consumer products. They include electric razors, sandwiches, cars, stereos, magazines, and houses. Marketers must know how consumers view the types of consumer product their companies sell so that they can design the marketing mix to appeal to the selected target market. _____

_____

_____

_____

# Unit 5: **Classification**

## Exercise 3: **Language for classification**

Study the following sentences. Complete each one by choosing the correct classification language to fill the gaps, based on the structure and meaning of the sentence.

1) Languages _____ according to their structural characteristics.
   a) on the basis of    b) consist of    c) can be classified

2) Languages may also _____ on the basis of their genetic relationship.
   a) classify    b) comprise    c) be grouped

3) Linguists _____ languages in two ways: according to structure and according to genetics.
   a) classify    b) comprise    c) be grouped

4) Countries can be classified _____ three kinds: low-, middle- and high-income.
   a) by    b) into    c) of

5) Animals _____ invertebrates (without a backbone) and vertebrates (having a backbone).
   a) may be grouped as    b) are classified by    c) classify into

6) Animals _____ invertebrates (without a backbone) and vertebrates (having a backbone).
   a) consist    b) comprise    c) are grouped

7) Animals can be classified according to _____ they have a backbone or not.
   a) where    b) whether    c) are

8) Computer systems _____ of hardware and software.
   a) consist    b) comprise    c) are grouped

9) Consumer products _____ durability.
   a) classify    b) may be classified by    c) are grouped into

10) _____ durability.
    a) This is classified into    b) These are categorised    c) One way to classify this is by

# Exercise 4: **Completing a classification diagram**

a) Complete the following diagram, showing classification of matter, by using the information in the text.

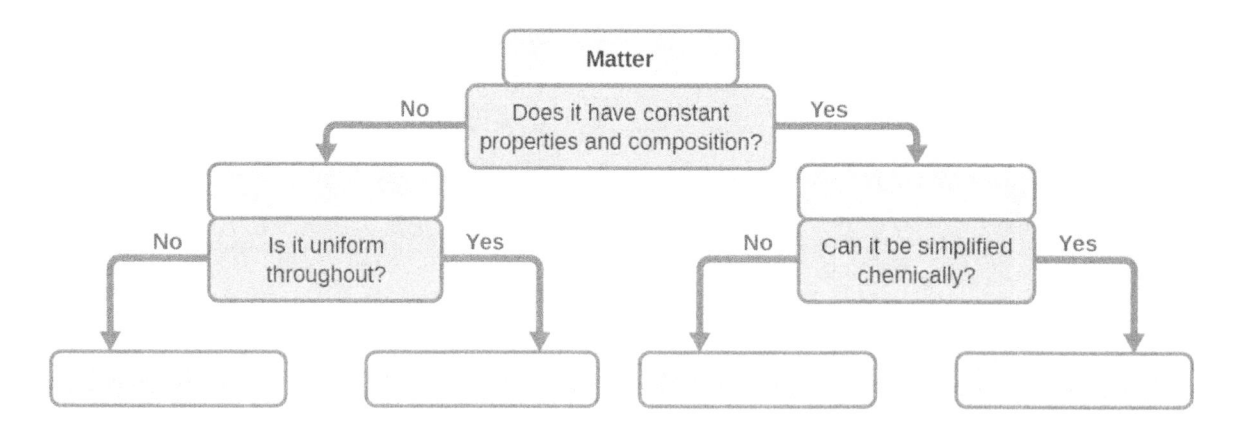

```
                          Matter
              No    Does it have constant    Yes
           ┌────── properties and composition? ──────┐
           ▼                                          ▼
       ┌───────┐                                  ┌───────┐
  No   │Is it uniform│  Yes           No    │Can it be simplified│  Yes
  ┌────│throughout?  │────┐           ┌─────│    chemically?     │─────┐
  ▼    └───────┘     ▼                ▼     └───────┘             ▼
┌────┐          ┌────┐              ┌────┐                    ┌────┐
│    │          │    │              │    │                    │    │
└────┘          └────┘              └────┘                    └────┘
```

> Matter can be classified into two broad categories: pure substances and mixtures.
>
> A pure substance has a constant composition. All specimens of a pure substance have exactly the same makeup and properties. Any sample of sucrose (table sugar) consists of 42.1% carbon, 6.5% hydrogen, and 51.4% oxygen by mass. Any sample of sucrose also has the same physical properties, such as melting point, colour, and sweetness, regardless of the source.
>
> We can divide pure substances into two classes. Pure substances that cannot be broken down into simpler substances by chemical changes are called elements. Iron, silver, gold, aluminium, sulphur, oxygen, and copper are familiar examples of the more than 100 known elements.
>
> Pure substances that can be broken down by chemical changes are called compounds. This breakdown may produce either elements or other compounds, or both. Mercury(II) oxide, an orange, crystalline solid, can be broken down by heat into the elements mercury and oxygen. When heated in the absence of air, the compound sucrose is broken down into the element carbon and the compound water.
>
> The second category of matter is mixtures. A mixture is composed of two or more types of matter that can be present in varying amounts and can be separated by physical changes, such as evaporation.
>
> Mixtures can also be broken down into two classes. A mixture which exhibits a uniform composition and appears visually the same throughout is called a homogeneous mixture. An example of a homogenous mixture is a sports drink, consisting of water, sugar, colouring, flavouring, and electrolytes mixed together uniformly. Other examples include air, maple syrup and gasoline.
>
> A mixture with a composition that varies from point to point is called a heterogeneous mixture. Italian dressing is an example of a heterogeneous mixture. It is not the same from point to point throughout the mixture—one drop may be mostly vinegar, whereas a different drop may be mostly oil or herbs. Other examples of heterogeneous mixtures are chocolate chip cookies and granite.
>
> *Adapted from* Chemistry, *pp.19-21, by OpenStax. Available free* http://cnx.org/content/col11760/1.9.

# Unit 5: Classification

b) Which structure has been used for this classification? _____

c) Use the information in the diagram and text to complete the following summary.

Matter can be divided into two general categories, namely mixtures and pure substances. A pure substance has a (1) _____ composition. Pure substances can be (2) _____ -divided into (3) _____ types, according to whether the substance can chemically simplified or not. Pure substances that (4) _____ be broken down into simpler substances are called elements, while those that (5) _____ be broken down are called (6) _____. The second general category, mixtures, can also be (7) _____ -divided into two types, depending on whether or not they are (8) _____ throughout. A mixture which exhibits a (9) _____ composition and appears visually the same throughout is called a (10) _____ mixture, while one which (11) _____ from point to point is called a heterogeneous mixture.

d) Study the passage in a) again, and the summary in b). Highlight the language which is used to classify or show categories.

# Exercise 5: **Multiple-criteria structure**

Most of the examples seen so far have been *single-criteria* structure, which is the most common. Below is a short essay using *multiple-criteria* structure. Study this essay and complete the table below.

> A joint, also called an articulation, is any place where adjacent bones come together (articulate with each other) to form a connection. Joints are classified both structurally and functionally.
>
> The structural classification of joints is based on how the joints are connected. These differences serve to divide the joints of the body into three structural classifications. A fibrous joint is where the adjacent bones are united by fibrous connective tissue. At a cartilaginous joint, the bones are joined by cartilage. At a synovial joint, the articulating surfaces of the bones are not directly connected, but instead come into contact with each other within a joint cavity that is filled with a lubricating fluid. Synovial joints allow for free movement between the bones and are the most common joints of the body.
>
> The functional classification of joints is determined by the amount of movement available between the adjacent bones. Joints are thus functionally classified as an immobile joint, a slightly moveable joint, or as a freely moveable joint. Depending on their location, fibrous joints may be functionally classified as immobile or slightly moveable. Cartilaginous joints are also functionally classified as either an immobile joint or a slightly moveable joint. All synovial joints are functionally classified as a freely moveable joint.
>
> In short, joints can be classified both structurally and functionally.
>
> *Adapted from* Chapter 9 | Joints, *p356, in* Anatomy & Physiology *by OpenStax. This OpenStax book is available for free at http://cnx.org/content/col11496/1.8*.

| Topic | |
|---|---|
| Definition of topic | |

| | Name | Defining feature or characteristics | Categories |
|---|---|---|---|
| Criteria 1 | | | • <br> • <br> • |
| Criteria 2 | | | • <br> • <br> • |

# Unit 5: Classification

## Exercise 6: **Writing a classification essay**

The following table shows information about three different types of country, viewed from an economic perspective.

a) Use this information to write a short *classification* essay.

| Topic | Classification of countries |
|---|---|
| **Why topic is important** | Allows economic comparisons to be made between different countries |
| **Criterion for classification** | Per capita GDP per year |

|  | Name | Defining characteristic | Other features | Examples |
|---|---|---|---|---|
| **Category 1** | Low-income countries | • less than $1,045 per capita GDP per year | • earn 1% of total world income<br>• represent 12% of global population<br>• 81% of population is urban | Myanmar, Ethiopia, and Somalia |
| **Category 2** | Middle-income countries | • between $1,045 and $12,745 per capita GDP per year | • earn 32% of world income<br>• represent 69% of global population<br>• 62% of population is urban | Thailand, China, and Namibia |
| **Category 3** | High-income countries | • over $12,745 per capita GDP per year | • earn 67% of world income<br>• represent 19% of the global population<br>• 28% of population is urban | United States, Germany, Canada, and the United Kingdom |

b) When you have finished, get a peer to check your essay, using the checklist earlier in the unit. You should also check another student's writing.

c) If you need more practice writing classification essays, choose one of the following topics and write an essay. Afterwards, ask a peer to check, using the checklist.
   1. Types of energy.
   2. Different groups of countries in World War II.
   3. Written assignments at university.
   4. Types of mobile applications.
   5. Types of smart device.
   6. Online learning resources.
   7. Online communication tools.
   8. Historical periods.
   9. Living organisms.
   10. University degrees.

## Exercise 7: **Learning outcomes check**

a) The following are the learning outcomes for this unit. Decide how well you have mastered each one by giving it a score, as follows.
   3 = I understand/can do this well.
   2 = I understand/can do this fairly well, but I can improve with more practice.
   1 = I understand/can do this, but not well enough yet. I need to practise more.
   0 = I cannot do this yet. I need more time.

| Score | Learning Outcome |
|---|---|
| _____ | I know what a classification essay is. |
| _____ | I understand how something can be classified (by applying a criterion). |
| _____ | I understand ways to structure a classification essay. |
| _____ | I can use language for classifying to show the *criterion*. |
| _____ | I can use language for classifying to show the *result*. |
| _____ | I can use language for classifying to show *sub-division*. |
| _____ | I can rewrite a thesis statement to change the structure of a classification essay. |
| _____ | I can complete a classification diagram. |
| _____ | I can write a classification essay. |
| _____ | I can peer edit a classification essay, using a checklist. |

b) Use this information to review the unit and improve.

# Unit 6 | Argument Essays

## Learning Outcomes

By the end of this unit, you should:
- understand what an argument essay is;
- know types of support which can be used for argument essays;
- understand how to *predict the consequence*, using appropriate language;
- understand how to use *counter-argument*, with appropriate language.

By completing the exercises, you will also:
- study an example essay for language and content;
- practise writing sentences to *predict the consequence*;
- practice writing *counter-arguments*;
- write an argument essay;
- peer edit an argument essay, using a checklist.

## Key Vocabulary

**Nouns**
- argument
- counter-argument
- consequence

**Verbs**
- argue
- persuade

## Additional Vocabulary

*Academic Collocations (in the unit)*
- academic writing (adj + n)
- artificial intelligence (adj + n)
- human activity (adj + n)
- particularly useful (adv + adj)
- generally agreed (adv + v)
- climate change (n + n)
- present arguments (v + n)

*Academic Collocations (in the essay)*
- adverse effects (adj + n)
- environmental pollution (adj + n)
- human activity (adj + n)
- modern technology (adj + n)
- nuclear weapons (adj + n)

# Academic Writing Genres — Sheldon Smith

## Contents of this section

**Unit 6: Argument Essays .................................................. 95**
- Overview ................................................................................. 96
- Types of support ................................................................... 97
  - Predicting the consequence ........................................... 97
  - Counter-argument ............................................................ 97
- Language for argument essays ........................................... 98
  - Predicting the consequence ........................................... 98
  - Counter-argument ............................................................ 99
- Checklist ................................................................................ 100
- Example essay ...................................................................... 101
- Exercises ............................................................................... 102

## Overview

Argument essays (also called *argumentative* or *argumentation* essays) are similar to discussion essays (see Unit 7) in that you will present your arguments on a topic. However, instead of presenting a balanced view, considering both sides, an argument essay will focus on one side. To argue means to present reasons for (or against) something, and your task when writing an argument essay is to present arguments to the reader in support of your position. This does not mean you will not consider the other side; indeed, doing so, via counter-argument, is an important step in strengthening your own argument.

**In short**

An argument essay looks at one side (rather than both sides), though may consider the other side through counter-arguments. Two common types of support for this essay type are:
- predicting the consequence;
- counter-argument.

Below are examples of argument essay titles.
- Give your views on same-sex schools.
- Do you agree that artificial intelligence poses a danger to mankind?
- Consider whether human activity has made the world a better place.
- Government investment in space exploration is a waste of money. To what extent do you agree or disagree with this statement?

*Note that these essay titles could also lead to discussion essays (see Unit 7), depending on the strength of your view or the extent to which you agree or disagree.*

# Unit 6: **Argument**

# Types of support

The types of support used for an argument essay are similar to other essay types, such as facts, reasons, examples and statistics. If it is a longer (researched) essay, then evidence from sources, with appropriate citations, will also be essential. There are, however, two types of support which are particularly useful for this essay type in contrast to other essay types, namely *predicting the consequence* and *counter-argument*. These are considered in more detail below.

## Predicting the consequence

Predicting the consequence helps the reader understand what will happen if something does or does not happen. For example, to convince your readers that same-sex schools are disadvantageous, you might say the following.

> If students do not go to mixed schools, they will lose many opportunities to interact with members of the opposite sex, which may hurt them in their development of important social skills.

Avoid exaggerating the consequences. For instance, saying, 'If students do not go to mixed schools, they will be shy and will not be able to talk to members of the opposite sex' exaggerates the consequences of going to single-sex schools and will make your argument less convincing.

> **Argue vs. persuade**
>
> *Argument* essays are similar to (and sometimes referred to as) *persuasion* essays, though there is a slight difference. When you argue, you present reasons for (or against) something. When you persuade, you seek to convince the reader that your position is the correct one. Persuasion is therefore stronger than argument. Both *argument* and *persuasion* rely on logical reasoning[*]. Persuasion, in addition, may make emotional appeals, or seek to assert the writer's authority on the subject[**], in order to convince the reader. The objective nature of academic writing means that *argument*, relying solely on logic, rather than *persuasion*, is more common.
>
> [*] *Logos* in Aristotle's elements of rhetoric.
> [**] *Pathos* and *ethos* respectively in Aristotle's elements of rhetoric.

## Counter-argument

A counter-argument considers the opposition's point-of-view, then presents an argument against it ('to be counter to' means 'to be against'). Showing you are aware of other arguments will strengthen your own. For example:

> Although it has been suggested that same sex schools make children more focused on study, it is generally agreed that children of the same sex are more likely to talk with each other during class.

Presenting a counter-argument can be difficult, as you need to understand who the opposition is, consider their view, and think of a good response. A counter-argument may be used within a paragraph, to strengthen your ideas. It is also possible to devote a whole paragraph to counter-argument, usually the final main body paragraph, anticipating the reader's objections to ideas in earlier paragraphs, and providing arguments to refute them.

# Language for argument essays

*Predicting the consequence* and *counter-argument* use the following language constructions.

## Predicting the consequence

This type of support is hypothetical (i.e. imaginary). It will often be introduced using 'If...' and either the first or second conditional, though other conjunctions are possible.

### First conditional

This refers to present or future time, and talks about something which is possible. The grammar of this construction is:

> *If + present tense, will + verb*

Other modal verbs, such as 'may' or 'might', can be used instead of 'will'.

Examples
- **If** governments **do not act** to tackle the problem of climate change, our earth **will suffer** catastrophic harm from which it **may** never **recover**.
- **If** students **do not go** to mixed schools, they **might lack** opportunities to interact with members of the opposite sex, which **may hurt** them in their development of important social skills.

### Second conditional

This refers to present time to talk about something which is impossible, or future time to talk about something which is improbable. This type of structure is therefore stronger than the first conditional. The grammar is:

> *If + past tense, would + verb*

Examples
- **If** laws on climate change **were repealed**, global warming **would accelerate**, which **would cause** severe harm to the earth.
- **If** government funding for schools **was decreased**, there **would be** serious effects on education, such as a shortage of teachers or lack of teaching resources.

### Other conditional conjunctions

It is also possible to use other conditional conjunctions. These include *unless* and *otherwise*, which both broadly mean 'if not'. The conjunction *unless* is only used with present tense, and is therefore used with the same meaning as first conditional (to talk about something in the future which is possible). The conjunction *otherwise* can be used with either present

# Unit 6: Argument

tense (to show something is possible) or past tense (to indicate something improbable), and is used in the 'will' or 'would' part of the clause.

The following are the previous examples, rewritten using *unless* and *otherwise*.

| Original | *If* governments **do not act** to tackle the problem of climate change, our earth **will suffer** catastrophic harm from which it **may** never **recover**. |
|---|---|
| Unless | **Unless** governments **act** to tackle the problem of climate change, our earth **will suffer** catastrophic harm from which it **may** never **recover**. |
| Otherwise | It is important for governments **to act** to tackle the problem of climate change. **Otherwise**, our earth **will suffer** catastrophic harm from which it may never **recover**. |

| Original | *If* students **do not go** to mixed schools, they **might lack** opportunities to interact with members of the opposite sex, which **may hurt** them in their development of important social skills. |
|---|---|
| Unless | **Unless** students **go** to mixed schools, they **might lack** opportunities to interact with members of the opposite sex, which **may hurt** them in their development of important social skills. |
| Otherwise | Students **need to go** to mixed schools. **Otherwise**, they **might lack** opportunities to interact with members of the opposite sex, which **may hurt** them in their development of important social skills. |

## Counter-argument

When making a counter-argument, two things need to happen. First, the counter-argument needs to be introduced. Second, this needs to be contrasted with your own argument.

The following are some useful phrases to introduce the *counter-argument*.

| Opponents<br>Many people<br>Some critics | claim<br>believe<br>argue | |
|---|---|---|
| Shaw (2008)<br>The author | claims<br>believes<br>argues<br>suggests<br>takes the view | that [*counter-argument*] |
| It has been | suggested<br>argued | |
| It might | seem<br>appear | |

# Academic Writing Genres — Sheldon Smith

To contrast your argument with the counter-argument, you will usually need to combine the phrases above with a *contrast* transition, such as 'Although...', 'While...' or 'However...'.

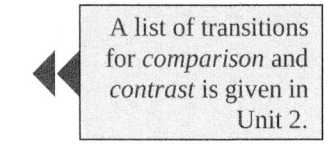

> A list of transitions for *comparison* and *contrast* is given in Unit 2.

See the following examples, which introduce *counter-arguments* for same-sex schools.

- **Opponents of** mixed schools **claim that** it is more difficult for students to concentrate when there are members of the opposite sex studying close to them. **However**, it is much easier for students to be distracted by members of the same sex.
- **Although it has been suggested that** same sex schools make children more focused on study, **it is generally agreed that** children of the same sex are more likely to talk with each other during class time.

# Checklist

Below is a checklist for argument essays. Use it to check your writing, or ask a peer.

| Area | Item | OK? | Comments |
|---|---|---|---|
| Argument | The essay is an argument essay. | | |
| | Appropriate support is used, such as *predicting the consequence* and *counter-argument*, alongside facts, reasons, examples, etc. | | |
| | Language for *predicting the consequence* is used accurately (e.g. first conditional, *unless*, *otherwise*). | | |
| | Language for *counter-argument* is used accurately (e.g. *Opponents claim that...*). | | |
| General essay skills | The essay has a clear thesis statement. | | |
| | Each paragraph has a clear topic sentence. | | |
| | The conclusion includes a summary of the main points. | | |

# Unit 6: Argument

# Example essay

Below is an example *argument* essay. It is used in one of the exercises later.

*Title*: Consider whether human activity has made the world a better place.

Mankind has made great advances in all fields since the dawn of civilisation. We have developed new technologies which allow us to enjoy luxuries that were unimaginable even a generation ago. However, the technologies that are temporarily making this world a better place to live could prove to be an ultimate disaster due to, among other things, the creation of nuclear weapons, increasing pollution, and loss of animal species.

The biggest threat to the earth caused by modern human activity comes from the creation of nuclear weapons. Although some people claim that countries need these weapons in order to defend themselves, the number and kind of weapons that some countries currently possess are far in excess of what is needed for defence. If these weapons were used, they could lead to the destruction of the entire planet.

Another harm caused by human activity to this earth is pollution. People have become reliant on modern technology, which can have adverse effects on the environment. For example, reliance on cars causes air and noise pollution. Even seemingly innocent devices, such as computers and mobile phones, use electricity, most of which is produced from coal-burning power stations, which further adds to environmental pollution. Unless we curb our direct and indirect use of fossil fuels, the harm to the environment may be catastrophic.

Animals are an important feature of this earth and the past decades have witnessed the extinction of a considerable number of animal species. This is the consequence of human encroachment on wildlife habitats, for example deforestation to expand cities. Some may argue that such loss of species is natural and has occurred throughout earth's history. However, the current rate of species loss far exceeds normal levels, and is threatening to become a mass extinction event.

In summary, there is no doubt that human activity has made the world a worse place to live as a result of the creation of nuclear weapons, pollution, and destruction of wildlife. It is important for us to see not only the short-term effects of our actions, but their long-term effects as well. Otherwise, human activity will be a step towards destruction.

**Academic Writing Genres** — Sheldon Smith

# Exercises

## Exercise 1: **Comprehension**

Answer the following questions about this unit. Either do this after reading the unit, or make notes first then use your notes to answer the questions.

1. Explain what an argument essay is. How is it different from a *discussion* essay (Unit 7)?

   _____
   _____

2. How is an *argument* essay different from a *persuasion* essay? Why is argument more common in academic writing than persuasion?

   _____
   _____

3. What two types of support are especially common/useful for an argument essay?

   - _____
   - _____

4. How are *first* and *second conditional* grammar structures formed?

   - First conditional    _____
   - Second conditional   _____

5. What type of support are *first* and *second conditional* grammar structures used for?

   _____

6. What, according to the unit, are the three steps in forming a *counter-argument*?

   - _____
   - _____
   - _____

# Unit 6: Argument

## Exercise 2: **Example essay**

Study the example essay on *human activity* (earlier in this unit) and answer these questions.

a) What is the position of the writer? Write it in the diagram below.

b) Complete the diagram by summarising the main ideas of the essay.

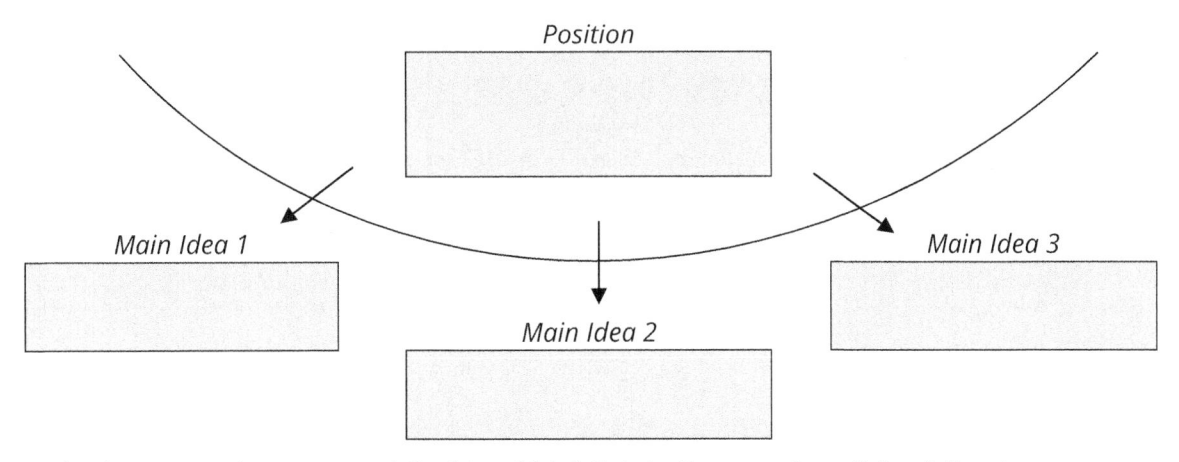

```
                    Position
                   [        ]
                  /    |    \
                 /     |     \
        Main Idea 1    |    Main Idea 3
        [        ]     |    [        ]
                       |
                  Main Idea 2
                   [        ]
```

c) Study the example essay and find (and highlight) all examples of the following:
- predicting the consequence [3 examples];
- counter-argument [2 examples].

d) Study the three examples of predicting the consequence identified in c) above and answer the following questions. Write your answers in the table below.
- What transition word is used to introduce each example?
- Which tenses are used?
- How does the choice of tense affect the meaning?

| Example | Transition | Tenses used | How choice of tense affects meaning |
|---|---|---|---|
| 1. | | | |
| 2. | | | |
| 3. | | | |

## Exercise 3: **Predicting the consequence**

In the following, only the first part of the condition has been given. Complete each one by *predicting the consequence*. Be careful to use correct grammar. Also make sure you avoid exaggerating the consequences.

**Example**
If governments do not act to tackle the problem of climate change, **our earth will suffer catastrophic harm from which it may never recover**.

**i)** If parents smoke cigarettes at home, in front of their children, _____
_____
_____

**ii)** Unless individuals change their unhealthy eating habits, _____
_____
_____

**iii)** Parents need to do more to educate their children about the dangers of social media. Otherwise, _____
_____
_____

**iv)** If countries continue to use coal and other fossil fuels as their main source of energy,
_____
_____

**v)** If schools reintroduced rules allowing teachers to hit children, _____
_____
_____

# Unit 6: Argument

## Exercise 4: Counter-argument #1

The following are paragraphs from example essays in other units. Each paragraph contains a counter-argument. For each paragraph:
- identify and underline the sentence(s) showing counter-argument;
- highlight the language used to show counter-argument.

*From example essay #2 in Unit 1*
Despite this positive short-term effect, there are also some more negative long-term effects, the most important of which is that buying on credit can lead people into a life of debt. Although some people may claim that credit gives much convenience to the consumer, it must be remembered that they pay for this convenience in the form of high interest rates. They will consequently pay much more for the products than if they had saved up and bought them, and it will thus take them much longer to pay for them. Furthermore, the ease with which credit cards can be obtained and used may lead to reckless spending. Credit card users will later be faced with monthly bills, which will use up much of their income and take them years or even a whole lifetime to pay off.

*From example essay in Unit 3*
A further effect on the family is the promotion of independence in the children. Some might argue that having both parents working might be damaging to the children because of a lack of parental attention. However, such children have to learn to look after themselves at an earlier age, and their parents often rely on them to help with the housework. This therefore teaches them important life skills.

*From example essay in Unit 4*
Governments could also implement initiatives to improve their citizens' eating and exercise habits. This could be done through education, for example by adding classes to the curriculum about healthy diet and lifestyles. Governments could also do more to encourage their citizens to walk or cycle instead of taking the car, for instance by building more cycle lanes or increasing vehicle taxes. While some might argue that increased taxes are a unreasonable way to solve the problem, it is no different from the high taxes imposed on cigarettes to reduce cigarette consumption.

# Exercise 5: **Counter-argument #2**

Write counter-arguments to the following arguments. Remember to use appropriate language. Ensure that the counter-argument relates directly to the argument given.

**Example**
Smoking cigarettes is pleasurable.
**Although opponents may claim that** smoking cigarettes is pleasurable, **this is only true in the short-term. In the long-term, the smoker may develop cancer or other life-threatening diseases, which is unpleasurable both for smokers and their loved ones.**

**i)** Individuals can do little to tackle climate change.

**ii)** Sex education at school might encourage underage children to have sex.

**iii)** Animals should not be used for medical research as they are genetically very different from human beings.

**iv)** Computer games are harmful to children.

**v)** Learning a second language is a waste of time.

# Unit 6: **Argument**

## Exercise 6: **Writing an argument essay**

a) Study the following statements. Choose *one* of them, decide which side you favour, and write an *argument* essay. Be sure to include appropriate supporting ideas (e.g. predicting the consequence, counter-argument).

1. It is essential to use animals for research in order to produce medicines and cosmetics which are safe for human use.
2. Students learn best in same sex schools.
3. Sex education is an important part of the curriculum and should be taught when students reach the age of 12.
4. Military spending is essential for national defence.
5. It is important for everyone to learn a second language.
6. Violent computer games should be banned for under-18s since they lead to violent behaviour.
7. Governments should spend a large portion of their national budget on tackling climate change.
8. Developed nations need to offer much more financial support to poorer, developing nations.
9. Eating meat is inhumane and everyone should become vegetarian.
10. All schools should have free internet access.

b) When you have finished, get a peer to check your essay, using the checklist earlier in the unit. You should also check another student's writing.

## Exercise 7: **Learning outcomes check**

a) The following are the learning outcomes for this unit. Decide how well you have mastered each one by giving it a score, as follows.

   3 = I understand/can do this well.
   2 = I understand/can do this fairly well, but I can improve with more practice.
   1 = I understand/can do this, but not well enough yet. I need to practise more.
   0 = I cannot do this yet. I need more time.

| Score | Learning Outcome |
|---|---|
| _____ | I understand what an argument essay is. |
| _____ | I know types of support which can be used for argument essays. |
| _____ | I understand how to predict the consequence, using appropriate language. |
| _____ | I understand how to use counter-argument, with appropriate language. |
| _____ | I can write an argument essay. |
| _____ | I can peer edit an argument essay, using a checklist. |

b) Use this information to review the unit and improve.

# UNIT 7 | Discussion Essays

## Learning Outcomes

By the end of this unit, you should:
- understand what a discussion essay is;
- understand the structure of a discussion essay;
- know some common language for discussion.

By completing the exercises, you will also:
- study an example essay for language and content;
- extend your vocabulary by studying forms of common discussion words;
- write a discussion essay;
- peer edit a discussion essay, using a checklist.

## Key Vocabulary

**Nouns**
- discussion
- benefit
- pro (informal)
- drawback
- con (informal)

**Adjectives**
- positive
- negative

**Verbs**
- discuss

## Additional Vocabulary

*Academic Collocations (in the unit)*
- general statements (adj + n)
- main arguments (adj + n)
- negative aspect (adj + n)
- negative side (adj + n)
- positive aspect (adj + n)
- positive feature (adj + n)
- strongest evidence (adj + n)

*Academic Collocations (in the essay)*
- financial support (adj + n)
- secondary education (adj + n)
- learning environment (n + n)

## Contents of this section

### UNIT 7: DISCUSSION ESSAYS ................................ 109

Overview ........................................................................................ 110
Structure of discussion essays ................................................... 110
Language for discussion ............................................................. 112
Checklist ....................................................................................... 112
Example essay ............................................................................. 113
Exercises ...................................................................................... 114

Academic Writing Genres — Sheldon Smith

# Overview

Some essay titles require you to examine both sides of a situation. These are known as *discussion* (or *for and against*) essays. In this sense, the academic meaning of the word *discuss* is similar to its everyday meaning, of two people talking about a topic from different sides. In a discussion essay, a balanced view is essential.

When writing a discussion essay, it is important to ensure that facts and opinions are clearly separated. Your arguments for (or against) constitute your opinions, but they will be based on and supported by facts and other types of support. In extended discussion essays, you will usually examine what other people have already said on the same subject and include this information using paraphrasing and summarising skills, as well as correct citations.

> **In short**
> A discussion essay discusses *both* sides of an issue, presenting a balanced view. You will present your opinions (arguments), based on facts (and other supporting information).

The following are examples of discussion essay topics.
- Examine the arguments for and against capital punishment.
- Schools should teach children not only academic subjects but also important life skills. Discuss.
- What are the advantages and disadvantages of technology in the classroom?
- Government investment in space exploration is a waste of money. To what extent do you agree or disagree with this statement?*

* This title could also be an argument essay (see Unit 6).

# Structure of discussion essays

Although the structure of a discussion essay may vary according to length and subject, there are several components which most discussion essays have in common. In addition to general statements and thesis statement, which all good essay introductions contain, the position of the writer will often be stated, along with relevant definitions. The main body will examine arguments for (in one or more paragraphs, usually with the most important ideas first) and arguments against (also in one or more paragraphs). The conclusion will contain a summary of the main points, and will often conclude with recommendations, based on what you think are the most important ideas in the essay. The conclusion may also contain your opinion on the topic, also based on the preceding evidence.

# Unit 7: Discussion

An overview of this structure is given in the table below.

| Stage of essay | Structural component | Purpose |
|---|---|---|
| **Introduction** | General statements | To introduce the reader to the subject of the essay. |
| | Position | To give the opinion of the writer (not always possible). |
| | Definition(s) (optional) | To explain any important technical words to the reader. |
| | Thesis | To tell the reader what parts of the topic will be included in the essay. |
| **Main body** | Arguments for | To explain to the reader the evidence for the positive side of the issue, with support. The most important ideas usually come first. This may be covered in one or more paragraphs. |
| | Arguments against | To explain to the reader the evidence for the negative side of the issue, with support. The most important ideas usually come first. This may be covered in one or more paragraphs. |
| **Conclusion** | Summary | To give the reader a brief reminder of the main ideas, while restating the issue. Sometimes also says which ideas the writer believes have the strongest evidence. |
| | Opinion & Recommendation | To give the writer's opinion, and tell the reader what the writer believes is the best action to take, considering the evidence in the essay. |

# Language for discussion

When summarising the stages in a discussion or in presenting your arguments, it can be useful to mark the *order* of the items or *degrees of importance*. The following can be used.

- First
- The most important
- Second
- The next most important
- Thirdly
- Fourth
- Finally
- Lastly

The following can be used when introducing your opinion.

- There is no doubt that...
- I believe that...
- One of the main arguments in favour of / against [X] is that...

**Pros and Cons**

It is important in writing to use synonyms rather than repeating words. The following are synonyms for **advantage**:

- benefit;
- positive aspect;
- positive feature;
- pro (informal).

Below are synonyms for **disadvantage**:

- drawback;
- negative;
- negative aspect;
- negative feature;
- con (informal).

# Checklist

Below is a checklist for discussion essays.

| Area | Item | OK? | Comments |
|---|---|---|---|
| Discussion | The essay is a discussion essay. | | |
| | There is a clear position. | | |
| | Definitions are given, if needed. | | |
| | One or more advantage paragraphs are included (including clear transition). | | |
| | One or more disadvantage paragraphs are included (including clear transition). | | |
| | The writer's opinion is given in the conclusion. | | |
| | There is a recommendation, which relates to the points in the essay. | | |
| General essay skills | The essay has a clear thesis statement. | | |
| | Each paragraph has a clear topic sentence. | | |
| | Each paragraph has enough support (facts, reasons, examples, etc.). | | |
| | The conclusion includes a summary of the main points. | | |

# Unit 7: Discussion

# Example essay

Below is an example *discussion* essay. It is used in one of the exercises later.

*Title*: *An increasing number of students are going overseas for tertiary education. To what extent does this overseas study benefit the students?*

Most people spend around fifteen years of their life in education, from primary school to university study. In the past, students only had the opportunity to study in their own country. Nowadays, however, it is increasingly easy to study overseas, especially at tertiary level. Tertiary education, also called post-secondary education, is the period of study spent at university. As the final aspect of schooling before a person begins their working life, it is arguably the most important stage of their education. While there are some undoubted benefits of this trend, such as the language environment and improved employment prospects, there is also a significant disadvantage, namely the high cost.

The first and most important advantage of overseas study is the language learning environment. Students studying overseas will not only have to cope with the local language for their study, but will also have to use it outside the classroom for their everyday life. These factors should make it relatively easy for such students to advance their language abilities.

Another important benefit is employability. Increasing globalisation means that there are more multinational companies setting up offices in all major countries. These companies will need employees who have a variety of skills, including fluency in more than one language. Students who have studied abroad should find it much easier to obtain a job in this kind of company.

There are, however, some disadvantages to overseas study which must be considered, the most notable of which is the expense. In addition to the cost of travel, which in itself is not inconsiderable, overseas students are required to pay tuition fees which are usually much higher than those of local students. Added to this is the cost of living, which is often much higher than in the students' own country. Although scholarships may be available for overseas students, there are usually very few of these, most of which will only cover a fraction of the cost. Overseas study therefore constitutes a considerable expense.

In summary, studying abroad has some clear advantages, including the language environment and increased chances of employment, in addition to the main drawback, the heavy financial burden. I believe that this experience is worthwhile for those students whose families can readily afford the expense. Students without such strong financial support should consider carefully whether the high cost outweighs the benefits to be gained.

**Academic Writing Genres**  **Sheldon Smith**

# Exercises

## Exercise 1: Comprehension

Answer the following questions about this unit. Either do this after reading the unit, or make notes first then use your notes to answer the questions.

1 What is a discussion essay?

 

 

2 How is a *discussion* essay different from an *argument* essay (see Unit 6)?

 

 

3 What elements does the *introduction* to a discussion essay usually contain?

-  
-  
-  
-  

4 What elements does the *conclusion* to a discussion essay usually contain?

-  
-  
-  

5 What is the usual order of ideas in the main body?

 

 

# Unit 7: Discussion

## Exercise 2: **Example essay**

a) Study the *Introduction* to the example essay again (below). Identify the different stages.

| | |
|---|---|
| Most people spend around fifteen years of their life in education, from primary school to university study. In the past, students only had the opportunity to study in their own country. Nowadays, however, it is increasingly easy to study overseas, especially at tertiary level. Tertiary education, also called post-secondary education, is the period of study spent at university. As the final aspect of schooling before a person begins their working life, it is arguably the most important stage of their education. While there are some undoubted benefits of this trend, such as the language environment and improved employment prospects, there is also a significant disadvantage, namely the high cost. | • General statements<br><br>• Position<br><br>• Definition<br><br>• Thesis |

b) Use the table below to record the main ideas of the essay.

| Arguments for | Arguments against |
|---|---|
|  | X |

c) Study the *Conclusion* to the model essay again (below). Identify the different stages.

| | |
|---|---|
| In summary, studying abroad has some clear advantages, including the language environment and increased chances of employment, in addition to the main drawback, the heavy financial burden. I believe that this experience is worthwhile for those students whose families can readily afford the expense. Students without such strong financial support should consider carefully whether the high cost outweighs the benefits to be gained. | • Summary<br><br>• Opinion<br><br>• Recommendation |

d) Study the essay again and identify the following:
- language to show order of importance;
- language to present the writer's opinion;
- all occurrences of the words *advantage* and *disadvantage*, or synonyms of these words.

# Academic Writing Genres          Sheldon Smith

## Exercise 3: **Vocabulary extension**

a) Complete the following table, showing different forms of some common words for advantage/disadvantage. Use a dictionary if you need to. If there is no related form, an 'X' is shown.

| Verb | Noun | Adjective | Adverb |
|---|---|---|---|
|  | benefit |  |  |
| X | advantage |  |  |
| X | disadvantage |  |  |
| X | positive |  |  |
| X | negative |  |  |

b) Use the information in the table to complete the following sentences, using the correct form of the word.

**benefit**
i) Studying overseas is _____ for students in many ways.
ii) Studying overseas can _____ students in terms of employability.
iii) Studying overseas is of _____ to students in relation to the language learning environment.

**disadvantage**
iv) Studying overseas is _____ for students in certain aspects.

**negative**
v) Studying overseas can _____ affect students financially.
vi) One _____ of studying overseas is the expense.

c) Study the sentences in b) above and make a note of the prepositions which are used with some of the words. An example has been done for you.

- beneficial __*for*__
- to be _____ benefit _____
- advantageous _____
- a positive _____

# Unit 7: Discussion

## Exercise 4: **Writing a discussion essay**

a) Choose *one* of the following topics to write a *discussion* essay.

1. Some teachers argue that students learn more effectively when they study in groups. Others believe that students learn best by studying on their own. Discuss the benefits of both, and decide which opinion you agree with.
2. In order to tackle climate change, governments need to work together. Discuss.
3. In the modern world, access to the internet is essential for students' education. Discuss.
4. Some people believe that computers and mobile phones are harmful to children's development. Others, however, believe they offer benefits. Discuss both these views.
5. Many people live far from their workplace and spend much time and money travelling to work each day. What are the advantages and disadvantages of this situation?
6. Cloning is to the benefit of mankind. Discuss.
7. In some countries, governments are encouraging industries and businesses to move out of large cities and into less populated areas. What are the pros and cons of this development?
8. Some countries restrict news content in order to protect their citizens. Others, however, allow complete freedom of the press. What are the advantages of these two approaches?
9. Examine the arguments for and against capital punishment.
10. What are the advantages and disadvantages of technology in the classroom?

b) When you have finished, get a peer to check your essay, using the checklist earlier in the unit. You should also check another student's writing.

## Exercise 5: **Learning outcomes check**

a) The following are the learning outcomes for this unit. Decide how well you have mastered each one by giving it a score, as follows.

   3 = I understand/can do this well.
   2 = I understand/can do this fairly well, but I can improve with more practice.
   1 = I understand/can do this, but not well enough yet. I need to practise more.
   0 = I cannot do this yet. I need more time.

| Score | Learning Outcome |
|---|---|
| _____ | I know what a discussion essay is. |
| _____ | I understand how to structure a discussion essay. |
| _____ | I know some common language for discussion (including *order of importance*). |
| _____ | I can use different forms of common discussion words (*advantage*, *benefit*, etc.) |
| _____ | I can write a discussion essay. |
| _____ | I can peer edit a discussion essay, using a checklist. |

b) Use this information to review the unit and improve.

# Unit 8 | Definition Essays

## Learning Outcomes

By the end of this unit, you should:
- understand what a definition essay is;
- understand how to structure a definition essay (using etymology, exemplification, etc.);
- know some common language for defining.

By completing the exercises, you will also:
- study an example essay for language, content and structure;
- write formal definitions, using appropriate structure and language;
- write a definition essay;
- peer edit an essay, using a checklist.

## Key Vocabulary

*Nouns*
- definition
- etymology
- negation
- enumeration
- analogy

*Verbs*
- define

## Additional Vocabulary

*Academic Collocations (in the unit)*
- academic writing (adj + n)
- appropriate language (adj + n)
- appropriate ways (adj + n)
- economic activity (adj + n)
- general category (adj + n)
- low incomes (adj + n)
- precise definitions (adj + n)
- secondary education (adj + n)
- wide range (adj + n)

*Academic Collocations (in the essay)*
- appropriate action (adj + n)
- internal structures (adj + n)

## Contents of this section

### Unit 8: Definition Essays ........................................ 119

- Overview ........................................................................... 120
- Structure of definition essays ........................................... 120
- Language for definition essays ......................................... 121
- Checklist ........................................................................... 122
- Example essay .................................................................. 123
- Exercises ........................................................................... 124

# Overview

It is often necessary in academic writing to define some of the terms which are used, usually in the introduction. Definitions of this sort will generally be only a sentence long, and will give the formal, dictionary definition of a word, stating the general category it belongs to and then providing enough details to distinguish it from others in the same category. It is also possible to write extended definitions, which may be one paragraph long, with the formal definition serving as the topic sentence. It is also possible to extend the definition to a whole essay, as considered in this section.

# Structure of definition essays

There are many ways to organise a definition essay. Some of these use structures covered in other units (e.g. *comparison*, Unit 2; *classification*, Unit 5). Each of the following might form a single paragraph in the main body, though not all of these would be used, as the essay would be too long. If the extended definition is only one paragraph long, these could be used as supporting ideas in the paragraph.

- **Etymology**. The *etymology*, i.e. the origin of the word, can add to the definition. A paragraph covering this might show not only the origin, but also how the meaning or usage has changed over time. This is a common way to begin the main body.
- **Exemplification**. Giving *examples* is a common way to extend the definition of a word. [See Unit 10 for more on exemplification.]
- **Comparison**. If the word being defined is very complex or unusual, it can help the definition by giving an *analogy*, in other words *comparing* it to something which is simpler or more familiar to the reader. [See Unit 2 for more on comparison.]
- **Contrast**. It is possible to extend the definition of a word by *contrasting* it with other words in the same category which are close in meaning to the word being defined. [See Unit 2 for more on contrast.]
- **Classification**. If the word you are defining can be divided into different types, *classification* can be used to extend the definition. [See Unit 5 for classification.]
- **Process**. If the word being defined is a process, or is used to carry out a process, then the definition can be extended by explaining the *process*. [See Unit 9 for more on describing a process.]
- **Negation**. It is sometimes helpful to extend the definition of the word by using *negation*, in other words explaining what it is *not*, in order to explain what it is.
- **Description**. If the word being defined is something physical, then a *description* of its characteristics, possibly including a diagram, might be appropriate. [See Unit 11.]
- **Enumeration**. If the word being defined has many characteristics, then it might be helpful to *enumerate* or list each of these characteristics in detail.

# Unit 8: Definition

# Language for definition essays

The most important language for a definition essay relates to giving a formal definition of the word or phrase which the essay is about. The most common way to write a formal definition is to use a relative clause. See the following examples.

- Academic English **is the branch of English which** is used for study, research, teaching and universities.
- Tertiary education **may be defined as the period of study which** is spent at university.
- A university **is a place where** students go to study after finishing secondary education.
- A teacher **is a person who** educates or instructs others, especially in a school.
- Astronomy **is defined as the study of the objects which** lie beyond our planet Earth and the processes by which these objects interact with one another.[*]

**Tip: writing definitions**
Writing definitions can seem straightforward, but be careful to make sure:
- the category is not too broad or too narrow;
- the word you are defining is not repeated in a different form in the characteristics (A teacher is a person who teaches).

[*] Adapted from Astronomy by OpenStax. Download for free at https://openstax.org/details/books/astronomy.

In each case, the following structure is used.

> Word to be defined + **verb** + **category** + **wh-word** + characteristics

In the examples above, the verbs (or verb phrases) are 'is', 'is defined as' and 'may be defined as'. The categories are 'the branch of English', 'the period of study', 'a place', 'a person' and 'the study of objects'. Wh-words are 'which', 'where' and 'who'.

In addition to relative clauses, the following phrases are useful.

- is concerned with…
- deals with…
- relates to…
- involves…

**Using the right wh-word**
Remember that:
- **which** is used for objects and animals (can be replaced by **that**);
- **where** is used for places;
- **who** is used for people;
- **when** is used for time.

These phrases are generally *not* used to give precise definitions, since the class is usually missing; instead, they are used to list some or all of the characteristics.

The following are some examples of these phrases in use.
- Economics **is concerned with** the well-being of all people, including those with jobs and those without jobs, as well as those with high incomes and those with low incomes.[**]
- Organizational psychology **is concerned with** the effects of interactions among people in the workplace on the employees themselves and on organizational productivity.[***]
- The special theory of relativity **deals with** changes when objects move very fast.[*]
- Social psychology **deals with** all kinds of interactions between people, spanning a wide range of how we connect: from moments of confrontation to moments of working together and helping others.[***]
- Cognitive empathy, also known as theory-of-mind, **relates to** the ability to take the perspective of others and feel concern for others.[***]
- Radar astronomy **involves** transmitting as well as receiving.[*]
- Monetary policy **involves** managing interest rates and credit conditions, which influences the level of economic activity, as described in more detail below.[**]

[*] From Astronomy by OpenStax. Download for free at https://openstax.org/details/books/astronomy.
[**] From Principles of Economics by OpenStax. Download for free at https://openstax.org/details/books/principles-economics.
[***] From Psychology by OpenStax. Download for free at https://openstax.org/details/books/psychology.

# Checklist

Below is a checklist for definition essays. Use it to check your writing, or ask a peer to help.

| Area | Item | OK? | Comments |
|---|---|---|---|
| Definition | The essay is a definition essay. | | |
| | Appropriate ways to organise ideas have been used (*etymology, exemplification, comparison, contrast, classification, process, negation, description, enumeration*). | | |
| | Appropriate language has been used for the formal definition. | | |
| General essay skills | The essay has a clear thesis statement. | | |
| | Each paragraph has a clear topic sentence. | | |
| | Each paragraph has enough support. | | |
| | The conclusion includes a summary of the main points. | | |

# Unit 8: Definition

# Example essay

Below is an example *definition* essay. It is used in one of the exercises later.

Anatomy is a required component of many medical courses. An understanding of anatomy is not only fundamental to any career in the health professions, but can also be beneficial to health. Familiarity with the human body can help people make healthful choices and prompt them to take appropriate action when signs of illness arise. Human anatomy is the branch of science which studies the body's structures. Some of these structures are very small and can only be observed and analyzed with the assistance of a microscope, for example muscle tissue and nerve cells. Other larger structures can readily be seen, manipulated, measured, and weighed, such as the heart and brain. This essay considers the origins of anatomy, different specialisms of anatomy, different approaches to anatomy, and how it is different from physiology.

Anatomy has evolved considerably over the centuries. The word "anatomy" comes from a Greek root that means "to cut apart". Human anatomy was first studied by observing the exterior of the body and observing the wounds of soldiers and other injuries. Later, physicians were allowed to dissect bodies of the dead to augment their knowledge. When a body is dissected, its structures are cut apart in order to observe their physical attributes and their relationships to one another. Dissection is still used in medical schools, anatomy courses, and in pathology labs. In order to observe structures in living people, however, a number of imaging techniques have been developed. These techniques allow clinicians to visualize structures inside the living body such as a cancerous tumour or a fractured bone.

Like most scientific disciplines, anatomy has areas of specialization. *Gross anatomy* is the study of the larger structures of the body, those visible without the aid of magnification. Macro- means "large", thus, gross anatomy is also referred to as *macroscopic anatomy*. In contrast, micro- means "small" and *microscopic anatomy* is the study of structures that can be observed only with the use of a microscope or other magnification devices. Microscopic anatomy includes cytology, the study of cells, and histology, the study of tissues. As the technology of microscopes has advanced, anatomists have been able to observe smaller and smaller structures of the body, from slices of large structures like the heart, to the three-dimensional structures of large molecules in the body.

Anatomy can also be classified according to the approach to the study of the body's structures. Regional anatomy is the study of the interrelationships of all of the structures in a specific body region, such as the abdomen. Studying regional anatomy helps us appreciate the interrelationships of body structures, such as how muscles, nerves, blood vessels, and other structures work together to serve a particular body region. In contrast, systemic anatomy is the study of the structures that make up a discrete body system—that is, a group of structures that work together to perform a unique body function. For example, a systemic anatomical study of the muscular system would consider all of the skeletal muscles of the body.

Anatomy is usually studied alongside physiology, though it has an important difference. Whereas anatomy is about structure, physiology is about function. Human physiology is the scientific study of the chemistry and physics of the structures of the body and ways in which they work together to support the functions of life.

In short, human anatomy, which originated in the external study of wounds, has advanced to include not only macroscopic study of organs but microscopic study of the body's internal structures. It can be classified into regional and systemic anatomy, and differs from physiology in that it studies structure rather than function. Knowledge of anatomy is helpful in understanding news about nutrition, medications, medical devices and procedures. At some point, everyone will have a problem with some aspect of his or her body and knowledge of anatomy can help them be a better parent, spouse, partner, friend, colleague, or caregiver.

Adapted from *Anatomy and Physiology* by OpenStax. Download for free at https://openstax.org/details/books/anatomy-and-physiology.

# Exercises

## Exercise 1: **Comprehension**

Answer the following questions about this unit. Either do this after reading the unit, or make notes first then use your notes to answer the questions.

**1** The following are possible components of a definition essay. Explain what they mean.

- Etymology _____
- Negation _____
- Enumeration _____

**2** Give another *three* possible components of a definition essay.
[Note: A total of nine are given in the unit, so there are another six possible components.]

- _____
- _____
- _____

**3** What is the usual way to write a formal definition? [Hint: it uses a *wh-* word.]

_____
_____

**4** Which *wh-* words are used with the following?

- People _____
- Places _____
- Time _____
- Objects _____

**5** How are definitions given using phrases like 'is concerned with' and 'deals with' different from formal definitions (using the structure in Q3 above)?

_____
_____

# Unit 8: Definition

## Exercise 2: **Example essay**

Study the example definition essay earlier in the unit and answer the following questions.

a) What is being defined? _____

b) Find the formal definition (given in the introduction), then identify following.

- category          _____
- characteristics   _____

c) The essay introduction uses *exemplification* following the formal definition. What are the examples of?
_____

d) The essay uses *etymology* in the first main body paragraph. What is the *etymology* of the word?
_____

e) The essay uses *classification* in two of the main body paragraphs. In what ways can anatomy be classified?

1) _____
2) _____

f) The essay uses *contrast* in the final main body paragraph. What things are being contrasted? What is the difference between them?
_____
_____
_____

# Exercise 3: **Writing formal definitions**

a) Complete the following *formal* definitions by adding a category and wh-word. An example has been given.

|      | Word being defined | Verb | Category | Wh-word | Characteristics |
|------|--------------------|------|----------|---------|-----------------|
| E.g. | A teacher          | is   | **a person** | **who** | educates or instructs others, especially in a school. |
| 1.   | A pollutant        | is   |          |         | contaminates the water or air or soil. |
| 2.   | Lungs              | are  |          |         | remove carbon dioxide and provide oxygen to the blood. |
| 3.   | A dentist          | is   |          |         | deals with the anatomy, development and diseases of teeth. |
| 4.   | A battlefield      | is   |          |         | battles or other forms of conflict are or have been fought. |
| 5.   | An equinox         | is   |          |         | the sun crosses the earth's equator and the day and night are of equal length (usually March 21 and September 23). |
| 6.   | Steel              | is   |          |         | is formed by mixing iron with small amounts of carbon. |
| 7.   | A celebrity        | is   |          |         | is widely known. |
| 8.   | Plagiarism         | is   |          |         | has been copied from someone else and is presented as being your own original work. |
| 9.   | A bee              | is   |          |         | has a hairy body, usually living in a honey-producing hive. |
| 10.  | A terminus         | is   |          |         | something begins or ends (e.g. a bus route). |

b) Now write formal definitions of the following words. If you are unsure of the meaning, use a dictionary to check – but do *not* just copy from the dictionary.

- A CEO (chief executive officer): _____

_____

- Biology: _____

_____

- Feminism: _____

_____

# Unit 8: Definition

## Exercise 4: **Writing a definition essay**

a) Choose one of the following topics to write a definition essay. Be sure to include a *formal* definition of the word (in the introduction), using appropriate language. Structure your response in an appropriate way, e.g. by using *etymology, exemplification, comparison, contrast, classification, process, negation, description* or *enumeration*.

- A subject you are familiar with (e.g. mathematics, economics, business studies, literature).
- An important term in your field of study (e.g. *homeostasis* in biology, *scarcity* in economics, *cognition* in psychology).
- Cyberbullying.
- Language.
- Intelligence.

b) When you have finished, get a peer to check your essay, using the checklist earlier in the unit. You should also check another student's writing.

## Exercise 5: **Learning outcomes check**

a) The following are the learning outcomes for this unit. Decide how well you have mastered each one by giving it a score, as follows.

- 3 = I understand/can do this well.
- 2 = I understand/can do this fairly well, but I can improve with more practice.
- 1 = I understand/can do this, but not well enough yet. I need to practise more.
- 0 = I cannot do this yet. I need more time.

| Score | Learning Outcome |
|---|---|
| _____ | I understand what a definition essay is. |
| _____ | I understand how to structure a definition essay (using etymology, exemplification, etc.). |
| _____ | I know some common language for defining. |
| _____ | I can write *formal* definitions, using appropriate structure and language. |
| _____ | I can write a definition essay. |
| _____ | I can peer edit a definition essay, using a checklist. |

b) Use this information to review the unit and improve.

# Unit 9 | Process Essays

## Learning Outcomes

By the end of this unit, you should:
- understand what a process essay is;
- understand how to structure a process essay;
- know some common language for describing a process;
- understand different types of process description (informational, habitual, particular, directional).

By completing the exercises, you will also:
- study an example process essay for structure and content;
- complete a diagram, using a process description;
- use a flowchart to write a process description;
- write a process essay;
- peer edit an essay, using a checklist.

## Key Vocabulary

*Nouns*
- process

*Adjectives*
- informational
- habitual
- particular
- directional

## Additional Vocabulary

*Academic Collocations (in the unit)*
- academic writing (adj + n)
- negative feedback (adj + n)
- immediately following (adv + adj)
- describe a process (v + n)
- give information (v + n)

*Academic Collocations (in the essay)*
- human activity (adj + n)
- key role (adj + n)
- recent study (adj + n)
- climate change (n + n)

## Contents of this section

### Unit 9: Process Essays .................................... 129

    Overview ............................................................. 130
    Types of process description ............................. 130
    Structure of process essays ............................... 130
    Language for describing a process .................... 131
    Checklist ............................................................. 132
    Example essay .................................................... 133
    Exercises ............................................................. 134

# Overview

A process description presents a series of stages to explain how something is or was done or how something happens. It is a common part of other genres such as laboratory reports (see Unit 13), where it will normally form a section or paragraph, though it is possible to construct a whole essay describing a process.

# Types of process description

There are two types of process description which can be used. The first and most common type used in academic writing is **informational process**. The purpose is to inform the reader so that they can understand the process. They are not expected to reproduce it. This type can be sub-divided into **habitual process**, which describes how something usually or always happens (e.g. how the biological process of cellular respiration occurs), and **particular process**, which describes how a particular thing happened (e.g. how an experiment was conducted).

The second type is a **directional process** description. This type gives the reader directions they can follow (e.g. how to bake a cake). The purpose is for the reader to be able to reproduce the process, if they wish.

| In short |
|---|
| A process essay explains how something is or was done. There are two types, and two sub-types:<br>1. *informational process* (to give information);<br>　a) *habitual* (always happens);<br>　b) *particular* (a particular thing, in the past);<br>2. *directional process* (so the reader can repeat it). |

# Structure of process essays

The introduction and conclusion to a process essay are much like any other essay. The process description itself will appear in the main body. A separate paragraph should be used for each stage in the process, which means that, before writing, you should be clear what the different stages are. These stages are usually presented in *chronological order*, in other words in the time order in which they occur. Each stage may have only one step, or may consist of several steps. You need to ensure that the purpose of each stage is clear to the reader. You may need to add definitions or explanations for any unfamiliar terms or materials. It is common to include a diagram to aid understanding. For a *directional process*, you should note optional steps, and warn the reader of possible problems they might encounter. For an *informational (particular)* process which describes a process you carried

| In short |
|---|
| For this essay type:<br>• use a separate paragraph for each stage;<br>• present stages in chronological order;<br>• use a diagram, if possible;<br>• note optional steps (for *directional* process);<br>• note precautions for accuracy (for *informational* process such as lab experiment). |

# Unit 9: Process

out, such as a laboratory experiment, it is common to describe precautions you took to ensure the process was carried out accurately.

# Language for describing a process

The language used for process description depends on the type.

### Informational process (habitual)
To describe how something happens (e.g. a biological process), you will usually use present simple tense. See the following example, describing the biological process of homeostasis. Present simple verbs related to the process are in bold.

- When a change **occurs** in an animal's environment, an adjustment must be made. The receptor **senses** the change in the environment, then **sends** a signal to the control centre (in most cases, the brain) which in turn **generates** a response that **is** signalled to an effector. The effector is a muscle (that **contracts** or **relaxes**) or a gland that **secretes**. Homeostasis **is** maintained by negative feedback loops.

*From* Biology 2e *by OpenStax. Download for free at https://openstax.org/details/books/biology-2e.*

### Informational process (particular)
To describe how something happened (e.g. an experiment, a survey), you will either use personal pronouns, usually 'I' or 'we', or past passive. While past passive is considered more academic by some, personal pronouns are possible, especially for the social sciences.

- First, the reactants were placed in the beaker. [*past passive*]
- We first asked the respondents a series of questions about their professions. [*using 'we'*]

### Directional process
For *directional process*, it is common to use 'you' or imperative. This type of writing is less academic than for the other process type, and is therefore much less common in university writing. The following are examples.

- First, place the reactants in the beaker. [*imperative*]
- You should first place the reactants in the beaker. [*using 'you'*]

It is also helpful to use transition words and phrases to ensure that each stage, and each step within each stage, links together logically. Be careful, however, not to overuse these.

| *Sequence transitions* | | *Time signals* |
|---|---|---|
| • First | • After | • After a few hours |
| • To begin with | • Afterwards | • At the same time |
| • Second | • After that | • During |
| • Next | • Immediately following this | • Meanwhile |
| • The next step | • In turn | • In the meantime |
| • Then | • Finally | • Later |
| • Before | • Lastly | • Eventually |

# Academic Writing Genres — Sheldon Smith

Below is the previous example for homeostasis, with the process transitions in bold.
- When a change occurs in an animal's environment, an adjustment must be made. The receptor senses the change in the environment, **then** sends a signal to the control centre (in most cases, the brain) which **in turn** generates a response that is signalled to an effector. The effector is a muscle (that contracts or relaxes) or a gland that secretes. Homeostasis is maintained by negative feedback loops.

# Checklist

Below is a checklist for process essays. Use it to check your writing, or ask a peer to help.

| Aspect | Item | OK? | Comments |
|---|---|---|---|
| Process | The essay is a *process* essay (either *informational* or *directional*). | | |
| | Each paragraph covers one stage of the process. | | |
| | All stages have been included. | | |
| | Stages are presented in *chronological* order. | | |
| | A diagram has been included, if possible. | | |
| | Transition signals are used, sparingly (e.g. *First, Next, In turn*). | | |
| For *informational* process | Sufficient detail has been included to understand the process. | | |
| | If appropriate, precautions for accuracy are given (for *particular* process). | | |
| | Correct tense has been used (present tense for *habitual* process, past tense for *particular* process). | | |
| For *directional* process | Sufficient detail has been included to reproduce the process. | | |
| | If appropriate, optional steps or potential problems are shown. | | |
| | Correct tense or sentence structure has been used (imperative or 'you'). | | |
| General essay skills | The essay has a clear thesis statement. | | |
| | Each paragraph has a clear topic sentence. | | |
| | The conclusion includes a summary of the main points. | | |

# Unit 9: Process

# Example essay

Below is an example *process* description. It is used in one of the exercises later.

*Title: Outline the processes involved in the Nitrogen Cycle.*

Getting nitrogen into the living world is difficult. Plants and phytoplankton are not equipped to incorporate nitrogen from the atmosphere (which exists as tightly bonded, triple covalent $N_2$) even though this molecule comprises approximately 78 percent of the atmosphere. Nitrogen enters the living world via free-living and symbiotic bacteria, which incorporate nitrogen into their macromolecules through nitrogen fixation (conversion of $N_2$). There are several bacteria involved in this process, such as cyanobacteria in aquatic ecosystems, rhizobium bacteria, which live symbiotically in the root nodules of legumes (such as peas, beans, and peanuts), and free-living bacteria, such as Azotobacter. This essay considers the nitrogen cycle in terrestrial systems, the nitrogen cycle in marine food webs, and examines how human activity releases nitrogen.

The process of nitrogen fixation occurs in three steps in terrestrial food webs. As shown in Figure 46.17, the nitrogen that enters living systems by nitrogen fixation is successively converted from organic nitrogen back into nitrogen gas by bacteria. First, the ammonification process converts nitrogenous waste from living animals or from the remains of dead animals into ammonium ($NH_4^+$) by certain bacteria and fungi. Second, through nitrification, the ammonium is converted to nitrites ($NO_2^-$) by nitrifying bacteria, such as Nitrosomonas, which are in turn converted to nitrates ($NO_3^-$) by similar organisms. Third, the process of denitrification occurs, whereby bacteria, such as Pseudomonas and Clostridium, convert the nitrates into nitrogen gas, allowing it to re-enter the atmosphere.

A similar process occurs in the marine nitrogen cycle, where the ammonification, nitrification, and denitrification processes are performed by marine bacteria. Some of this nitrogen falls to the ocean floor as sediments, which can then be moved to land in geologic time by uplift of the Earth's surface and thereby incorporated into terrestrial rock. Although the movement of nitrogen from rock directly into living systems has been traditionally seen as insignificant compared with nitrogen fixed from the atmosphere, a recent study showed that this process may indeed be significant and should be included in any study of the global nitrogen cycle.

Human activity can release nitrogen into the environment by two primary means. The first is the combustion of fossil fuels, which releases different nitrogen oxides. Atmospheric nitrogen is associated with several effects on Earth's ecosystems including the production of acid rain (as nitric acid, $HNO_3$) and greenhouse gas (as nitrous oxide, $N_2O$) potentially causing climate change. The second way human activity releases nitrogen is by the use of artificial fertilizers in agriculture, which are then washed into lakes, streams, and rivers by surface runoff. A major effect from fertilizer runoff is saltwater and freshwater eutrophication, a process whereby nutrient runoff causes the excess growth of microorganisms, depleting dissolved oxygen levels and killing ecosystem fauna.

In short, there are many bacteria which are involved in fixing nitrogen, which involves three steps in both terrestrial and marine systems, namely ammonification, nitrification and denitrification. Human activity also contributes to the amount of nitrogen in the environment.

*Text adapted from* Biology 2e *by OpenStax. Download for free at https://openstax.org/details/books/biology-2e*

# Academic Writing Genres

**Sheldon Smith**

# Exercises

## Exercise 1: **Comprehension**

Answer the following questions about this unit. Either do this after reading the unit, or make notes first then use your notes to answer the questions.

**1** Explain what is meant by a process description.

_____
_____

**2** The following are the two main types of process description. Explain how they are different.

- Informational _____
- Directional _____

**3** *Informational* process description can be sub-divided into the following two types. Explain the difference between them.

- Habitual _____
- Particular _____

**4** Complete the following summary about the structure of a process essay.

For the main body of a process essay, a **i)**_____ paragraph should be used for each **ii)**_____ in the process. These should be presented in **iii)**_____ order. It is important to ensure that the **iv)**_____ of each is clear to the reader. It may be necessary to include **v)**_____ or explanations for any unfamiliar terms or materials. It is common to include a **vi)**_____ to aid understanding. For a **vii)**_____ process, **viii)**_____ steps should be noted, and the reader should be warned of possible **ix)**_____ they might encounter. For an *informational (particular)* process, it is common to describe **x)**_____ which were taken to ensure the process was carried out accurately.

**5** Complete the following table giving information about language for different process types.

| Type | Language |
|---|---|
| Informational (habitual) | Usually uses **i)**_____ tense. |
| Information (particular) | Usually uses **ii)**_____ pronouns or **iii)**_____ tense. |
| Directional | Uses **iv)**_____ or **v)**_____. |

Unit 9: **Process**

## Exercise 2: **Example essay**

Study the example process essay earlier in the unit and answer the following questions.

a) What process is being described? _____

b) What type of process is it? Choose one of the following three.

   i. informational (habitual)
   ii. informational (particular)
   iii. directional

c) Highlight all examples of process transitions used in the text.

d) Complete the following diagram by using information from the example essay.

**The Nitrogen Cycle**

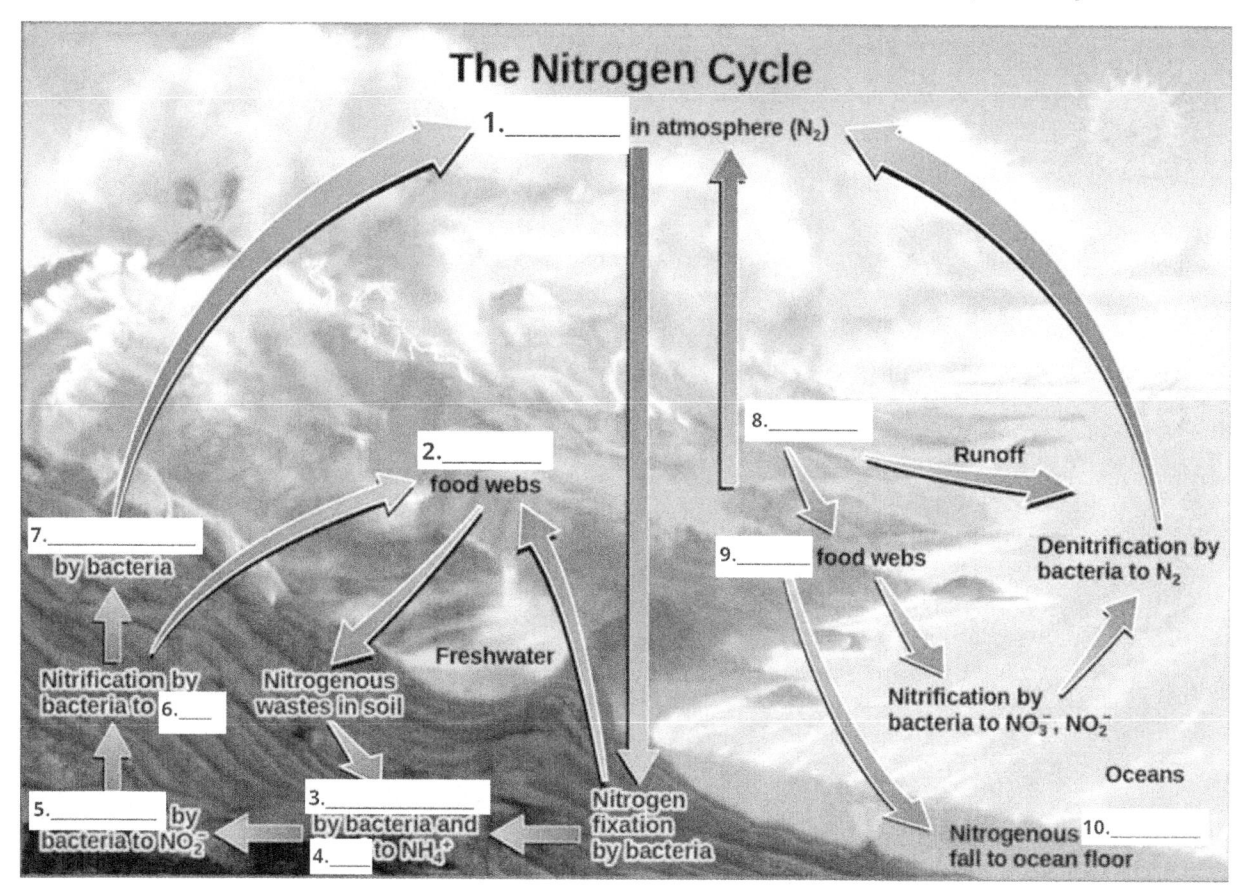

1. _____ in atmosphere ($N_2$)
2. _____ food webs
3. _____ by bacteria and
4. _____ to $NH_4^+$
5. _____ by bacteria to $NO_2^-$
6. _____
7. _____ by bacteria
   Nitrification by bacteria to 6.
8. _____
9. _____ food webs
10. _____
   Nitrogenous wastes in soil
   Freshwater
   Nitrogen fixation by bacteria
   Runoff
   Denitrification by bacteria to $N_2$
   Nitrification by bacteria to $NO_3^-$, $NO_2^-$
   Oceans
   Nitrogenous 10._____ fall to ocean floor

**Figure 46.17**. The Nitrogen Cycle. (credit: modification of work by John M. Evans and Howard Perlman, USGS). Taken from Biology 2e *by OpenStax. Download for free at* https://openstax.org/details/books/biology-2e.

## Exercise 3: **Using a flowchart**

Study the following flowchart. Use it to write a process description *paragraph*. Be sure to use appropriate transitions and verb tense.

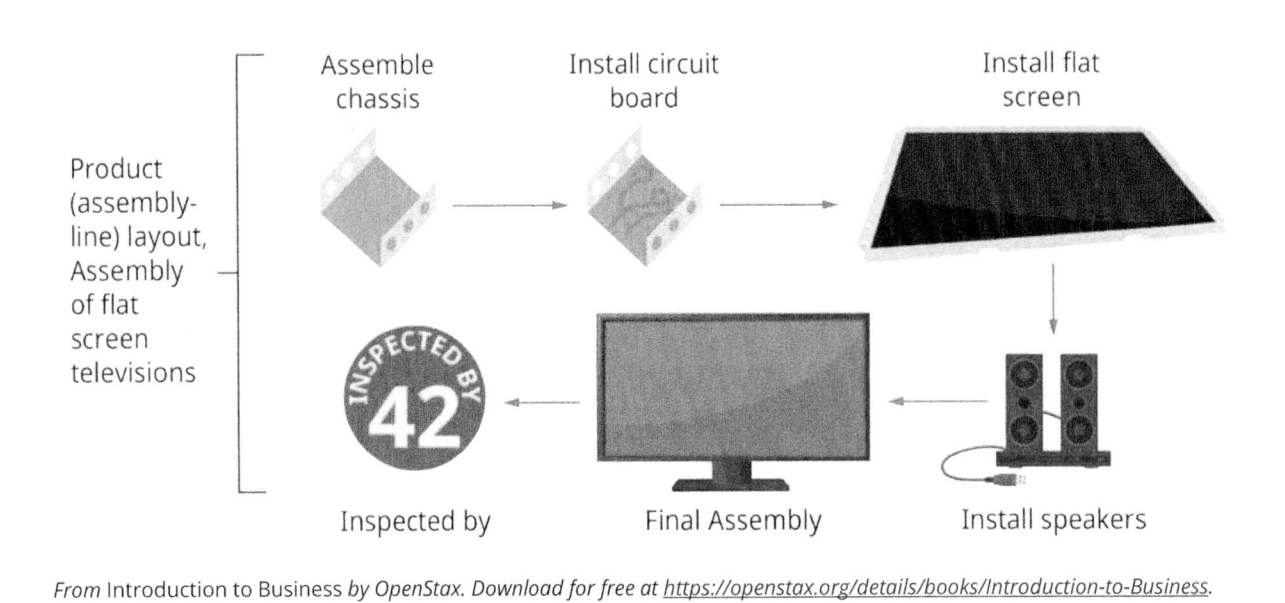

Product (assembly-line) layout, Assembly of flat screen televisions:
- Assemble chassis
- Install circuit board
- Install flat screen
- Install speakers
- Final Assembly
- Inspected by

*From* Introduction to Business *by OpenStax. Download for free at* https://openstax.org/details/books/Introduction-to-Business.

# Unit 9: **Process**

## Exercise 4: **Writing an essay**

a) Choose one of the following topics to write a process essay.

- Essay writing is often described as a process. Write about the process of writing an essay, from understanding the title to proofreading the final draft. [Note: For more about the writing process, see https://www.eapfoundation.com/writing/process/.]
- How to find source material for a researched essay.
- How to improve your writing when you have received feedback (from a peer or from your teacher).
- How to prepare for an exam.
- How to start a business.
- How bad habits develop.
- How to prepare for an interview.

b) When you have finished, get a peer to check your essay, using the checklist earlier in the unit. You should also check another student's writing.

## Exercise 5: **Learning outcomes check**

a) The following are the learning outcomes for this unit. Decide how well you have mastered each one by giving it a score, as follows.

    3 = I understand/can do this well.
    2 = I understand/can do this fairly well, but I can improve with more practice.
    1 = I understand/can do this, but not well enough yet. I need to practise more.
    0 = I cannot do this yet. I need more time.

| Score | Learning Outcome |
|---|---|
| _____ | I understand what a process essay is. |
| _____ | I understand how to structure a process essay. |
| _____ | I know some common language for describing a process. |
| _____ | I understand different types of process description (informational, habitual, particular, directional). |
| _____ | I can complete a diagram, using a process description. |
| _____ | I can use a flowchart to write a process description. |
| _____ | I can write a process essay. |
| _____ | I can peer edit a process essay, using a checklist. |

b) Use this information to review the unit and improve.

# Unit 10: Exemplification Essays

## Learning Outcomes

By the end of this unit, you should:
- understand what an exemplification essay is;
- understand how to structure an exemplification essay;
- know some common language for giving examples.

By completing the exercises, you will also:
- study an example essay for language, content and structure;
- practise using exemplification transitions;
- write an exemplification essay;
- peer edit an essay, using a checklist.

## Key Vocabulary

**Nouns**
- exemplification
- chronology

**Adverb**
- chronologically

## Additional Vocabulary

*Academic Collocations (in the unit)*
- appropriate way (adj + n)
- use this format (v + n)

*Academic Collocations (in the essay)*
- social responsibility (adj + n)
- socially responsible (adv + adj)

## Contents of this section

### Unit 10: Exemplification Essays ........................ 139

- Overview ........................................................... 140
- Structure of exemplification essays ................ 140
- Language for exemplification .......................... 141
- Checklist ........................................................... 142
- Example essay .................................................. 143
- Exercises ........................................................... 144

# Overview

Exemplification means 'showing by giving examples'. Although exemplification is most often used at the paragraph level, it is also possible to write a whole essay using this format.

# Structure of exemplification essays

The structure of an exemplification essay is like any other essay, with an introduction, main body, and conclusion. Exemplification essays can be divided into three main types.

- **Extended example**. This type uses a single, extended example for the whole essay. Different aspects of the example are explored in each paragraph.
- **Multiple examples**. This type focuses on one separate example in each paragraph.
- **Themed examples**. This type has multiple examples in each paragraph, which are linked together according to some theme.

When deciding on the order of the aspects (for the first type) or the order of the examples within the essay or paragraph (for the other two types), it may be useful to do so as follows.

- **Chronologically**. List the aspects or examples in time sequence, starting from the one which occurred first and finishing with the one which occurred last.
- **Order of importance**. List the aspects or examples in order of importance, either from the most to the least important, or the least to the most important.
- **Order of complexity**. List the aspects/examples from the simplest to most complex. Note that this is *not* reversible: going from most to least complex can be confusing.

The following diagram summarises these different ways to organise exemplification essays.

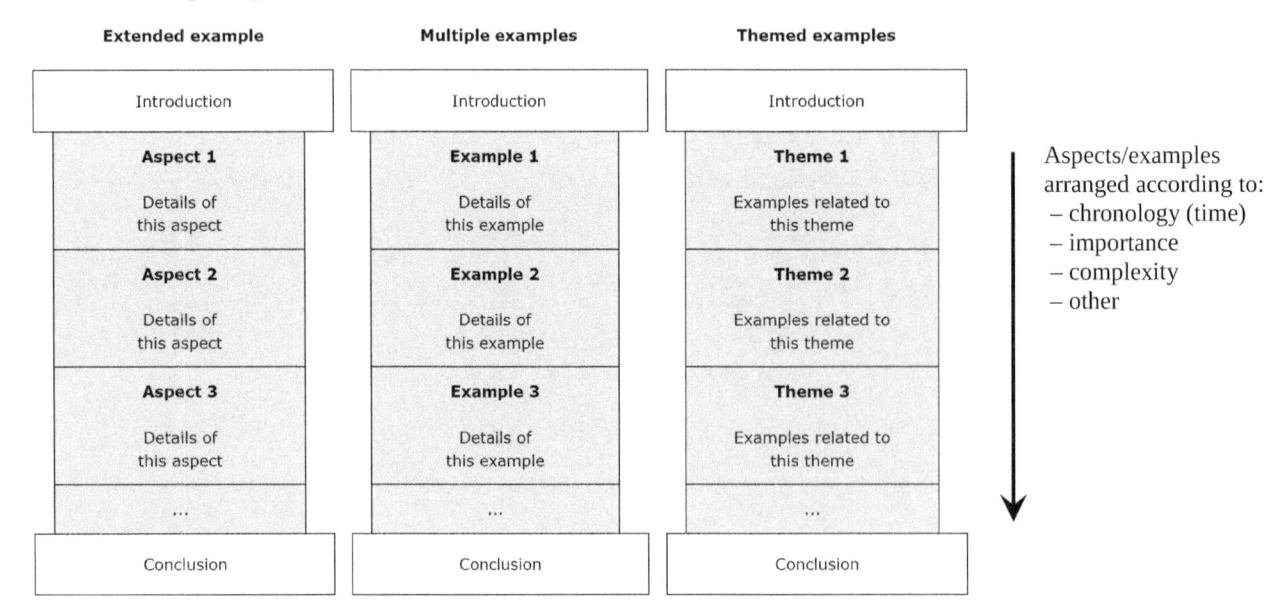

| Extended example | Multiple examples | Themed examples |
|---|---|---|
| Introduction | Introduction | Introduction |
| **Aspect 1** — Details of this aspect | **Example 1** — Details of this example | **Theme 1** — Examples related to this theme |
| **Aspect 2** — Details of this aspect | **Example 2** — Details of this example | **Theme 2** — Examples related to this theme |
| **Aspect 3** — Details of this aspect | **Example 3** — Details of this example | **Theme 3** — Examples related to this theme |
| ... | ... | ... |
| Conclusion | Conclusion | Conclusion |

Aspects/examples arranged according to:
– chronology (time)
– importance
– complexity
– other

# Unit 10: **Exemplification**

# Language for exemplification

The following are some common transition signals which can be used for giving examples, organised by type.

| Sentence connectors | Clause connectors | Other |
| --- | --- | --- |
| - For example<br>- For instance<br>- In this case | - like* | - such as<br>- (to be) an example of<br>- one example of this (is)<br>- take the case of<br>- to demonstrate<br>- to illustrate |

*Note: *like* is informal when used as an exemplification transition.

The following are some examples of these transition signals in use. All examples are taken from *Biology 2e* by OpenStax (available for free at http://cnx.org/content/col24361/1.8).

- Energy exists in different forms. **For example**, electrical energy, light energy, and heat energy are all different energy types.
- Consider statins **for example** – which is a class of drugs that reduces cholesterol levels.
- Chemical differences in the cell-surface receptors among hosts mean that a virus that infects a specific species (**for example**, humans) often cannot infect another (**for example**, chickens).
- When more than two genes are being considered, the Punnett-square method becomes unwieldy. **For instance**, examining a cross involving four genes would require a 16 × 16 grid containing 256 boxes.
- Moving water, **such as** in a waterfall or a rapidly flowing river, has kinetic energy.
- Myopia (near-sightedness) occurs when an eyeball is elongated and the image focus falls in front of the retina. **In this case**, images in the distance are blurry but images nearby are clear.
- When fertilization occurs between two true-breeding parents that differ in only one characteristic, the process is called a monohybrid cross, and the resulting offspring are monohybrids. **To demonstrate** a monohybrid cross, consider the case of true-breeding pea plants with yellow versus green pea seeds.
- If the solution's volume on both sides of the membrane is the same, but the solute's concentrations are different, then there are different amounts of water, the solvent, on either side of the membrane. **To illustrate** this, imagine two full water glasses. One has a single teaspoon of sugar in it, whereas the second one contains one quarter of a cup of sugar. If…
- The elbow **is an example of** a hinge joint.
- **An example of** a pivot joint **is** the joint of the first and second vertebrae of the neck that allows the head to move back and forth.
- One way in which the mutant allele can interfere is by enhancing the function of the wild-type gene product or changing its distribution in the body. **One example of this is** the Antennapedia mutation in Drosophila.

# Checklist

Below is a checklist for exemplification essays. Use it to check your writing, or ask a peer.

| Area | Item | OK? | Comments |
|---|---|---|---|
| Process | The essay is an *exemplification* essay. | | |
| | The essay uses an appropriate method of organisation (*extended example, multiple examples,* or *themed examples*). | | |
| | The examples are ordered in an appropriate way (*chronologically,* by order of *importance,* by order of *complexity,* or another logical way). | | |
| | The essay uses appropriate transitions (e.g. *for example, for instance, such as, to illustrate*). | | |
| General essay skills | The essay has a clear thesis statement. | | |
| | Each paragraph has a clear topic sentence. | | |
| | Each paragraph has enough support. | | |
| | The conclusion includes a summary of the main points. | | |

# Unit 10: **Exemplification**

# Example essay

Below is an example *exemplification* essay. It is used in one of the exercises later.

*Title*: Explain, with examples, what corporate social responsibility (CSR) is.

Corporate social responsibility (CSR) is the concern of businesses for the welfare of society as a whole. Acting in an ethical manner involves obligations beyond those required by law or union contract. Many companies continue to work hard to make the world a better place to live, with recent data suggesting that Fortune 500 companies spend more than $15 billion annually on CSR activities. Three examples of companies which engage in CSR are Starbucks, Salesforce and Deloitte.

Starbucks has many initiatives which help it to act in a socially responsible way. For example, it has a goal of 100 percent pay equity for gender and race, which it has achieved in the U.S (Starbucks, 2017). It also donates food to food banks every night. Additionally, it endeavours to ensure its coffee is ethically sourced, with a goal of reaching 100 percent, and currently achieving 99 percent ethically sourced coffee (Starbucks, 2017). A final initiative is donating coffee trees to farmers to replace trees lost to age and disease.

Salesforce is another example of a company with an ethical outlook. Salesforce encourages its employees to volunteer in community activities and pays them for doing so. Employees who participate in seven days of volunteerism in one year are given a $1,000 grant by the company to donate to any non-profit organisation the employee chooses (Salesforce, 2018).

A final example of a company which engages in CSR is Deloitte. Employees who work for Deloitte can get paid for up to 48 hours of volunteer work each year. In 2016, more than 27,000 Deloitte professionals contributed more than 353,000 volunteer hours to their communities around the world (Williams and Marshall, 2019).

In short, many companies are engaging in socially responsible ways, with Starbucks, Salesforce and Deloitte being three examples. If more companies can embrace CSR rather than solely pursuing profits, the world will be a better place for all.

References
Salesforce (2018) *Employee Volunteering & Giving*. Available from: https://www.salesforce.org/volunteers/ (Accessed 15 February 2019).

Starbucks (2017) *Global Social Impact: 2017 Performance Report*. Available from: https://globalassets.starbucks.com/assets/8c1f8c07efde407e9d48bfaf518c0b45.pdf (Accessed 15 February 2019).

Williams, D. and Marshall, D. (2019) *Celebrating Volunteerism at Deloitte and in Our Communities*. Available from: https://www2.deloitte.com/us/en/pages/about-deloitte/articles/celebrating-volunteerism.html (Accessed 15 February 2019).

*Adapted from* Introduction to Business *by OpenStax. Download free at https://openstax.org/details/books/Introduction-to-Business.*

**Academic Writing Genres**              **Sheldon Smith**

# Exercises

## Exercise 1: **Comprehension**

Answer the following questions about this unit. Either do this after reading the unit, or make notes first then use your notes to answer the questions.

**1** Explain what is meant by exemplification.

_____

_____

**2** The following are ways to structure the main body of an exemplification essay.

    **a)** How many examples are used (single example or multiple examples)?
    **b)** What do the paragraphs in the main body contain?

- Extended example   a) _____
  
                                         b) _____

- Multiple examples   a) _____
  
                                         b) _____

- Themed examples   a) _____
  
                                         b) _____

**3** The unit gives three ways to order the content of the main body. What are the ways? Complete the following gaps (the first letter of each missing word has been given).

- C_____ order
- Order of i_____
- Order of c_____

**4** Which of the three ways given in **Q3** above cannot be reversed? Why?

_____

_____

# Unit 10: **Exemplification**

## Exercise 2: **Example essay**

Study the example exemplification essay earlier in the unit and answer these questions.

a) What type of structure has been used? _____

b) Complete the following diagram, summarising the main ideas of the essay.

```
┌─────────────────────────────┐
│        Introduction         │
└─────────────────────────────┘
     │
     ├──────────────────────┐
     ├──────────────────────┤   EXAMPLES
     ├──────────────────────┤
     │
┌─────────────────────────────┐
│         Conclusion          │
└─────────────────────────────┘
```

c) The following is a possible paragraph from an essay organised in a different way, namely using **themed examples**. Complete the paragraph by using information from the text.
[*Note: The first answer, to question i), is the **theme** of this paragraph.*]

> Another way which is used by many companies to make them socially responsible is encouraging or rewarding employees who take part in **i)** _____ activities. For instance, Salesforce encourages its employees to take part in activities in the **ii)** _____. Employees who participate for **iii)** _____ days in a year receive **iv)** _____ which they can give to any **v)** _____ they choose. Another example is **vi)** _____. Employees who work for this company can receive pay for as much as **vii)** _____ paid volunteer work a year. In 2016, over **viii)** _____ individuals working for that company took advantage, together working for a total of **ix)** _____ hours for their communities **x)** _____.

d) What other *themes* are suggested by the text?
[Hint: Look at the other example paragraph, which is not used in c) above.]

- _____
- _____
- _____
- _____

e) Highlight all examples of exemplification transitions used in:
- the example essay;
- the paragraph in c) above.

# Academic Writing Genres — Sheldon Smith

## Exercise 3: **Exemplification transitions**

Complete each sentence by choosing the correct exemplification phrase to fill the gap.

**1)** The scientific names of sugars can be recognized by the suffix *-ose* at the end of the name (_____, fruit sugar is called *fructose* and milk sugar is called *lactose*).
a) for instance    b) is an example of    c) such as

**2)** Iron typically exhibits a charge of either 2+ or 3+, and the two corresponding compound formulas are $FeCl_2$ and $FeCl_3$. The simplest name, *iron chloride*, will, _____, be ambiguous, as it does not distinguish between these two compounds.
a) in this case    b) to demonstrate    c) such as

**3)** Group 15 elements _____ nitrogen have five valence electrons in the atomic Lewis symbol: one lone pair and three unpaired electrons.
a) for example    b) is an example of    c) such as

**4)** The formula $H_2O$, which can describe water at either the macroscopic or microscopic levels, _____ the symbolic domain.
a) for example    b) is an example of    c) such as

**5)** As stated in the text, convincing examples that _____ the law of conservation of matter outside of the laboratory are few and far between.
a) is an illustration of    b) illustration    c) demonstrate

**6)** Figure 6.27 _____ the traditional way to remember the filling order for orbitals.
a) such as    b) illustration    c) illustrates

**7)** Extensive properties depend on the amount of matter, _____, the mass of gold. Intensive properties do not, _____, the density of gold.
a) for example    b) is an example of    c) such as

**8)** Heat _____ an extensive property, and temperature _____ an intensive property.
a) for example    b) is an example of    c) such as

**9)** Traditionally, the discoverer (or discoverers) of a new element names the element. _____, element 106 is now known as *seaborgium* (Sg) in honour of Glenn Seaborg.
a) For example    b) An example of    c) Such as

**10)** It is essential to remember that energy must be added to break chemical bonds, whereas forming chemical bonds releases energy. _____ $H_2$, the covalent bond is very strong, which means a large amount of energy must be added to break it.
a) For example    b) In the case of    c) Example is

All examples adapted from *Chemistry* by OpenStax. Download for free at https://openstax.org/details/books/chemistry.

# Unit 10: **Exemplification**

## Exercise 4: **Writing an exemplification essay**

a) Write an exemplification essay on one of the following topics.

- Describe, with examples, the types of writing that students may be required to produce at university.
- Explain, with examples, how technology can be beneficial for education.
- Give examples of types of energy.
- In what ways can technology be harmful to social relationships? Give examples.
- How has society changed over the past twenty years? Give examples.
- Which modern historical figure has had the biggest impact on your country? Justify your answer with examples.
- Choose a field of study (e.g. economics, biology, psychology) and gives examples of how this field is important to the modern world.
- Choose a field of study (or a career) and give examples of some of the skills required to be successful in that field (or career).

b) When you have finished, get a peer to check your essay, using the checklist earlier in the unit. You should also check another student's writing.

## Exercise 5: **Learning outcomes check**

a) The following are the learning outcomes for this unit. Decide how well you have mastered each one by giving it a score, as follows.

   3 = I understand/can do this well.
   2 = I understand/can do this fairly well, but I can improve with more practice.
   1 = I understand/can do this, but not well enough yet. I need to practise more.
   0 = I cannot do this yet. I need more time.

| Score | Learning Outcome |
|---|---|
| _____ | I understand what an exemplification essay is. |
| _____ | I understand how to structure an exemplification essay. |
| _____ | I know some common language for giving examples. |
| _____ | I can use exemplification transitions accurately. |
| _____ | I can write an exemplification essay. |
| _____ | I can edit an exemplification essay, using a checklist. |

b) Use this information to review the unit and improve.

# Unit 11 | Description Essays

## Learning Outcomes

By the end of this unit, you should:
- understand what a description essay is;
- understand different aspects which can be described (size, function, etc.).

By completing the exercises, you will also:
- study descriptive paragraphs for language and content;
- complete a diagram, using information from a descriptive paragraph;
- identify language used for description;
- write a description paragraph/essay;
- peer edit a paragraph/essay, using a checklist.

## Key Vocabulary

**Nouns**
- description

**Adjective**
- descriptive

## Additional Vocabulary

**Academic Collocations (in the unit)**
- academic writing (adj + n)
- appropriate language (adj + n)

**Academic Collocations (in the essay)**
- digital information (adj + n)
- external environment (adj + n)
- main function (adj + n)

## Contents of this section

### Unit 11: Description Essays ................................. 149

Overview ............................................................................. 150
What to describe ................................................................ 150
Structure of description essays ......................................... 151
Language for description ................................................... 151
Checklist .............................................................................. 152
Example paragraphs ........................................................... 153
Exercises ............................................................................. 154

# Overview

Description is used to tell the reader about the characteristics of a physical object or something abstract such as an organisation. Description is a common part of academic writing and may form part of essays, reports or other genres. For example, a laboratory report (see Unit 13) might describe the apparatus used in the experiment, while a process essay (see Unit 9) outlining the process of respiration might describe the lungs and other organs involved in respiration. Description can also be used for a whole essay, as considered in this unit.

# What to describe

Description in academic writing should be objective, in other words focusing on the object itself, rather than your personal feelings about it. If it is a physical object, you may want to describe observable or measurable aspects such as weight, size, colour, shape, and position. You can also consider other aspects such as function, structure and properties

If it is an organisation, there are other things you can describe. Some are similar to the above. For example, size might be important, but it will not be measured in a physical sense; it will be measured by the number of employees, the number of customers or clients (if it is a business), the annual turnover (i.e. the budget for one year), and so on. Instead of position, its location may be important (e.g. where the headquarters are, whether it has any regional offices). Function, as with a physics object, is important. Structure is also important, though in this case it will refer to the structure of the organisation (e.g. what departments it has, how the leadership is organised). It is also possible to describe the origin of the organisation (e.g. who founded it, when was it founded, where and why).

---

**Make it visual**

Your goal in descriptive writing is to enable the reader to form a mental picture of what you are describing. This is much easier if there *is* a picture, such as:
- a diagram;
- a photograph;
- a drawing.

If using a visual, be sure to include it as close as possible to the description, and refer to it using appropriate language, e.g.:
- *As shown in Figure 1…*

---

**In short**

For things, you can describe:
- weight;
- size;
- colour;
- shape;
- position;
- function;
- structure;
- properties.

For organisations, you can describe:
- size;
- location;
- function;
- structure;
- origin.

# Unit 11: Description

## Structure of description essays

A description essay will contain an introduction, main body and conclusion, like any other essay. There is no prescribed structure for the main body of a description essay. It is likely that the *function*, if it is given, will appear first, as this gives purpose to the whole description. It is also likely that basic, physical aspects such as weight, size and so on will appear before more complex aspects such as structure and properties.

## Language for description

Description often uses either the *present simple* tense (e.g. to describe physical objects which still exist) or *past simple* (e.g. for apparatus used in an experiment, which is past). Description may make use of various words and phrases to describe the previously mentioned aspects. Some of these are straightforward, and are not included here (e.g. *square* or *circular* for shape, *long* or *high* for size, *weigh* for weight). Some useful transition words or phrases for description are given below.

**Position**
- above
- below
- at the bottom
- at the top
- next to
- over
- under
- behind
- in front of
- in the middle
- on the left of
- on the right of
- diagonally below
- between
- opposite

**Function (thing)**

The { function / purpose / role } of [X] is to…

**Structure**

[X] { consists of / contains / is divided into / is connected to }

**Function (organisation)**

[X] / The organisation / The company { builds / designs / manufactures / produces / provides }

**Location**

[X] / The organisation / The company { is { located / headquartered } / has { offices / branches / stores } } in

**Origin**

[X] was founded { in (+ year) / by (+ person) }

# Academic Writing Genres — Sheldon Smith

# Checklist

Below is a checklist for description essays. Use it to check your writing, or ask a peer to help.

| Area | Item | OK? | Comments |
|---|---|---|---|
| Description | The essay is a *description* essay. | | |
| | If possible, the essay uses a diagram or other visual to aid understanding. | | |
| | Appropriate aspects have been described (e.g. *size, function, structure*). | | |
| | Appropriate tense has been used (e.g. *present simple* for things which still exist, or *past simple* e.g. for experiment apparatus). | | |
| | Appropriate language has been used (e.g. position transitions). | | |
| | The description is clear and detailed enough to enable the reader to visualise the thing being described. | | |
| General essay skills | The essay has a clear thesis statement. | | |
| | Each paragraph has a clear topic sentence. | | |
| | The conclusion includes a summary of the main points. | | |

# Unit 11: **Description**

# Example paragraphs

Below are two example *descriptions*. Both of these are single paragraphs, rather than whole essays, since this type of organisation is more frequently encountered at the paragraph level rather than the essay level. These examples are used in one of the exercises later.

**1**

From the nasal cavity, air passes through the pharynx (throat) and the larynx (voice box), as it makes its way to the trachea (Figure 39.7). The main function of the trachea is to funnel the inhaled air to the lungs and the exhaled air back out of the body. The human trachea is a cylinder about 10 to 12 cm long and 2 cm in diameter that sits in front of the oesophagus and extends from the larynx into the chest cavity where it divides into the two primary bronchi at the mid-thorax (Figure 39.8). It is made of incomplete rings of hyaline cartilage and smooth muscle. The trachea is lined with mucus-producing goblet cells and ciliated epithelia. The cilia propel foreign particles trapped in the mucus toward the pharynx. The cartilage provides strength and support to the trachea to keep the passage open. The smooth muscle can contract, decreasing the trachea's diameter, which causes expired air to rush upwards from the lungs at a great force. The forced exhalation helps expel mucus when we cough. Smooth muscle can contract or relax, depending on stimuli from the external environment or the body's nervous system.

*From* Biology 2e *by OpenStax. Download for free at https://openstax.org/details/books/biology-2e.*

**2**

The leader in cybercrimes technology is Guidance Software, founded in 1997 to develop solutions that search, identify, recover, and deliver digital information in a forensically sound and cost-effective manner. Headquartered in Pasadena, California, the company employs 391 people at offices and training facilities in Chicago, Illinois; Washington, DC; San Francisco, California; Houston, Texas; New York City; and Brazil, England, and Singapore. The company's more than 20,000 high-profile clients include leading police agencies, government investigation and law enforcement agencies, and Fortune 1000 corporations in the financial service, insurance, high-tech and consulting, health care, and utility industries.

*From* Introduction to Business *by OpenStax. Download for free at https://openstax.org/details/books/Introduction-to-Business.*

# Academic Writing Genres — Sheldon Smith

## Exercises

### Exercise 1: Comprehension

Answer the following questions about this unit. Either do this after reading the unit, or make notes first then use your notes to answer the questions.

1 The following is a list of aspects, given in the unit, which might form part of the description of a *physical object*. The first two letters of each is given. Complete the words.

- we_____
- si_____
- co_____
- sh_____
- po_____
- fu_____
- st_____
- pr_____

2 Which of the aspects, given in question 1 above, might appear *first*? Why?
_____
_____

3 Which of the aspects, given in question 1 above, might appear *last*? Why?
_____
_____

4 What aspects from 1 above might appear in a description of an *organisation*? Which other aspects might be used?

- _____
- _____
- _____
- _____
- _____

5 What tenses are often used in descriptions?
_____
_____

# Unit 11: Description

## Exercise 2: **Example paragraphs**

Study example paragraphs **1** and **2** earlier in the unit and answer the following questions.

### Example Paragraph 1

a) What is being described? _____

b) Identify as many of the following aspects in the description as possible.

- Weight
- Size
- Colour
- Shape
- Position
- Function
- Structure
- Properties

c) Highlight useful words/phrases in the text related to the above aspects.

d) Use the description to label the missing words in these diagrams.

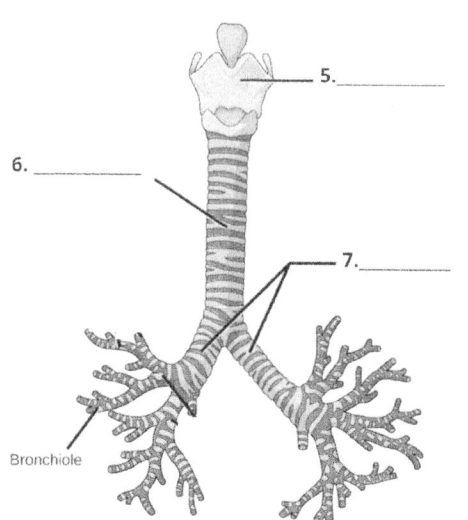

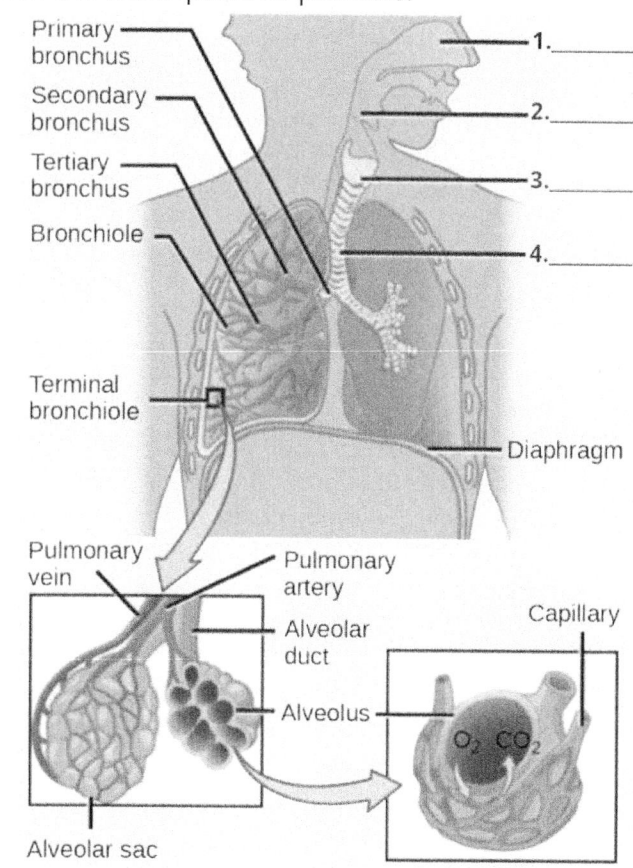

Figure 39.8 (credit: modification of work by Gray's Anatomy)   Figure 39.7 (credit: modification of work by NCI)

### Example Paragraph 2

e) What is being described? _____

f) Identify as many of the following aspects in the description as possible.

- Size
- Location
- Function
- Structure
- Origin

g) Highlight useful words/phrases in the text related to the above aspects.

# Exercise 3: **Language for description**

Study the following phrases and:
   a) identify the aspects that they are associated with.
   b) **highlight** the words/phrases used for description;
An example has been done for you.

### Physical object

| Sentence | Aspect |
|---|---|
| The human small intestine is over 6m **long**. | *size* |
| The human small intestine is divided into three parts: the duodenum, the jejunum, and the ileum. | |
| The inner the ear consists of the cochlea and the vestibular system. | |
| The iris, which is the coloured part of the eye, is a circular muscular ring. | |
| The iris lies between the lens and cornea. | |
| The role of the iris is to regulate the amount of light entering the eye. | |
| Some dinosaurs were nearly 40 meters (130 feet) in length. | |
| Some dinosaurs weighed at least 80,000 kg (88 tons). | |
| The algae contain phycoerythrins, accessory photopigments that are red in colour and obscure the green tint of chlorophyll in some species. | |

*Sentences adapted from* Biology 2e *by OpenStax. Download for free at https://openstax.org/details/books/biology-2e.*

### Organisation

| Sentence | Aspect |
|---|---|
| NASDAQ was founded in 1971. | |
| It has about 3,600 companies. | |
| NASDAQ is a sophisticated telecommunications network that links dealers throughout the United States. | |
| NASDAQ lists more companies than the NYSE, but the NYSE still leads in total market capitalization, making it the second largest in the world. | |
| Like the NYSE, it is located in New York City. | |
| An average of 1.6 billion shares were exchanged daily in 2016 through NASDAQ. | |
| It provides up-to-date bid and ask prices on about 3,700 of the most active OTC securities. | |
| The NASDAQ Stock Market has three different market tiers: Capital Market (small cap); Global Market (mid cap); and Global Select Market. | |

*Sentences adapted from* Introduction to Business Studies *by OpenStax. Download for free at https://openstax.org/details/books/Introduction-to-Business.*

# Unit 11: **Description**

## Exercise 4: **Writing an essay**

a) Write a paragraph or essay on one of the following topics.

- Write a description of a physical object which is important or commonly used in your field of study. Try to describe as many aspects as you can (e.g. size, shape, function).
- Describe an organisation which you know about or which is important in your field of study (e.g. WTO, IMF, WWF, UN, EU, OPEC, UNESCO). Try to describe as many aspects as you can (e.g. size, function, origin), researching online if necessary.

*Note: Because this essay type is more commonly encountered at paragraph rather than essay level, the above can be written as a paragraph rather than a whole essay, though a whole essay is also possible.*

b) When you have finished, get a peer to check your essay, using the checklist earlier in the unit. You should also check another student's writing.

## Exercise 5: **Learning outcomes check**

a) The following are the learning outcomes for this unit. Decide how well you have mastered each one by giving it a score, as follows.

    3 = I understand/can do this well.
    2 = I understand/can do this fairly well, but I can improve with more practice.
    1 = I understand/can do this, but not well enough yet. I need to practise more.
    0 = I cannot do this yet. I need more time.

| Score | Learning Outcome |
| --- | --- |
| _____ | I understand what a description essay is. |
| _____ | I know some common language for describing. |
| _____ | I understand different aspects which can be described (size, function, etc.). |
| _____ | I can complete a diagram, using information from a description. |
| _____ | I can identify language used for description. |
| _____ | I can write a description essay/paragraph. |
| _____ | I can peer edit a description essay/paragraph, using a checklist. |

b) Use this information to review the unit and improve.

# Part II:
Reports

# Unit 12 | About the Report Genre

## Learning Outcomes

By the end of this unit, you should:
- understand what a report is;
- be aware of different types of report;
- understand the differences between a report and an essay;
- understand the different sections of a report and the functions of each;
- be aware of language phrases for different report sections.

By completing the exercises, you will also:
- study an example report for content, structure and language.

## Key Vocabulary

**Nouns**
- primary research
- preliminaries
- abstract
- end matter
- appendix (pl. appendices)

## Additional Vocabulary

*Academic Collocations (in unit)*
- additional information (adj + n)
- appropriate language (adj + n)
- detailed information (adj + n)
- further research (adj + n)
- key areas (adj + n)
- main features (adj + n)
- main findings (adj + n)
- primary research (adj + n)
- relevant information (adj + n)
- significant effect (adj + n)
- specific information (adj + n)
- broadly similar (adv + adj)
- clearly defined (adv + past)
- commonly found (adv + past)
- commonly used (adv + past)
- gathering data (v + n)
- give information (v + n)
- present an argument (v + n)
- support an argument (v + n)

*Academic Collocations (in report)*
- certain aspects (adj + n)
- further studies (adj + n)
- high percentage (adj + n)
- increasing proportion (adj + n)
- qualitative studies (adj + n)
- substantial differences (adj + n)
- partly responsible (adv + adj)
- statistically significant (adv + adj)
- strongly agree/disagree (adv + v)
- give/provide evidence (v + n)

## Contents of this section

### Unit 12: About the Report Genre .................... 161

- Overview .................................................................. 162
- What is a report? ....................................................... 162
- How is a report different from an essay? ........................ 163
- Structure of reports .................................................... 164
- Language for reports .................................................. 168
- Checklist .................................................................. 169
- Example report ......................................................... 170
- Exercises ................................................................. 174

# Academic Writing Genres — Sheldon Smith

## Overview

After essays, the second most common form of writing which you are likely to undertake at university is the report. This unit describes what a report is, how to structure a report, and language phrases which may be used in different report sections.

## What is a report?

A report is a very structured form of writing which presents and analyses information clearly and briefly for a particular audience. They are common not only at university, but also in industry and government. There are many types of report, though the type you write at university depends on your course. Each report will have a different format and writing conventions, though the structure and language are broadly similar for all reports. The following are some of the types of report you may be required to write at university.

- **Laboratory report**. This report explains and analyses the results of an experiment. *See Unit 13.*
- **Business report**. This report analyses a situation and uses business theory to provide solutions or recommendations. *See Unit 14.*
- **Research report**. This gives the results of research which has been conducted, for example through surveys (via questionnaires or interviews). *See Unit 15.*
- **Case study report**. This examines a real-world situation (the 'case') and analyses it using appropriate theory (the 'study'). *See Unit 15.*
- **Progress report**. This informs a supervisor or customer about progress on a project over a certain period of time. *See Unit 15.*
- **Project report**. This reports on project work which has been conducted. *See Unit 15.*
- **Design report**. This report describes and evaluates a design used to solve a particular problem. *See Unit 15.*
- **Field report**. This combines theory and practice by describing an observed person, place or event and analysing the observation. *See Unit 15.*
- **Technical report**. This report describes technical research, written by engineers for the government, managers, clients or other engineers. *See Unit 15.*

---

**In short**

A report:
- has many different types;
- is very structured, with contents page, headings, sub-headings etc.;
- usually contains primary research;
- is different from an essay.

**Report names**

Reports go by many different names. For example:
- **laboratory reports** are also called *lab reports*, *experimental reports*, or *science reports*;
- **technical reports** are also called *scientific reports*;
- **business reports** include many types such as *market research reports*, *marketing reports*, and *financial reports*.

# Unit 12: About reports

# How is a report different from an essay?

Although many of the writing skills required for essays also apply to reports, such as use of topic sentences, cohesion, comparing information, reports are quite unlike essays in several regards. Unlike an essay, which uses the writer's own ideas or information from other sources, the information in a report is usually the result of primary research. Rather than continuous paragraphs, a report will contain headings and sub-headings, as well as graphs, charts and tables (sometimes you may be asked to write an essay with headings, but this is not a report, since all the other features, aside from headings, are the same as an essay). Reports often use the information to present recommendations for future action.

> **Primary research**
> Primary research involves gathering data yourself, for example from an experiment, investigation, questionnaire or survey.

The table below outlines the main features of reports, in comparison to essays.

| Category | Aspect | Report | Essay |
|---|---|---|---|
| General | Purpose | Provides specific information to the reader. | Presents an argument. |
| | Readability | Allows information to be found quickly in specific sections. | Requires careful reading to follow the argument. |
| | Writing skills | Demonstrates research skills and ability to analyse information. | Demonstrates ability to support an argument (thesis) via knowledge and understanding of the topic |
| | Length | Will always be a long assignment. | May be relatively short (e.g. for an exam) or a long assignment. |
| Structure | Sections | Has clearly defined sections, each with a different function. | Uses well-ordered paragraphs, *not* sections. |
| | Headings | Uses headings and sub-headings for the different sections (often numbered). | Does *not* usually use headings, sub-headings or numbering. |
| | Bullet points | May contain bullet points. | Usually uses continuous paragraphs. |
| | Contents page | Will often include a Contents page to show report sections. | Will *not* usually include a Contents page. |
| Content | Graphics | Usually uses graphics such as tables, graphs, charts. | Does *not* usually include graphics. |
| | Research | Usually includes *primary* research (e.g. from experiment, survey) in addition to *secondary* research. | Generally only includes *secondary* research (e.g. citations from books or journals). |
| | Recommendations | Often has recommendations. | Only *certain* essay types (e.g. discussion) have recommendations. |
| | Appendices | May include appendices with additional information. | Unlikely to include appendices. |

# Academic Writing Genres — Sheldon Smith

## Structure of reports

Although the exact nature of your report will vary according to the discipline you are studying, the general structure is broadly similar for all disciplines. Below is the structure of a typical report. Each part is discussed in more detail later.

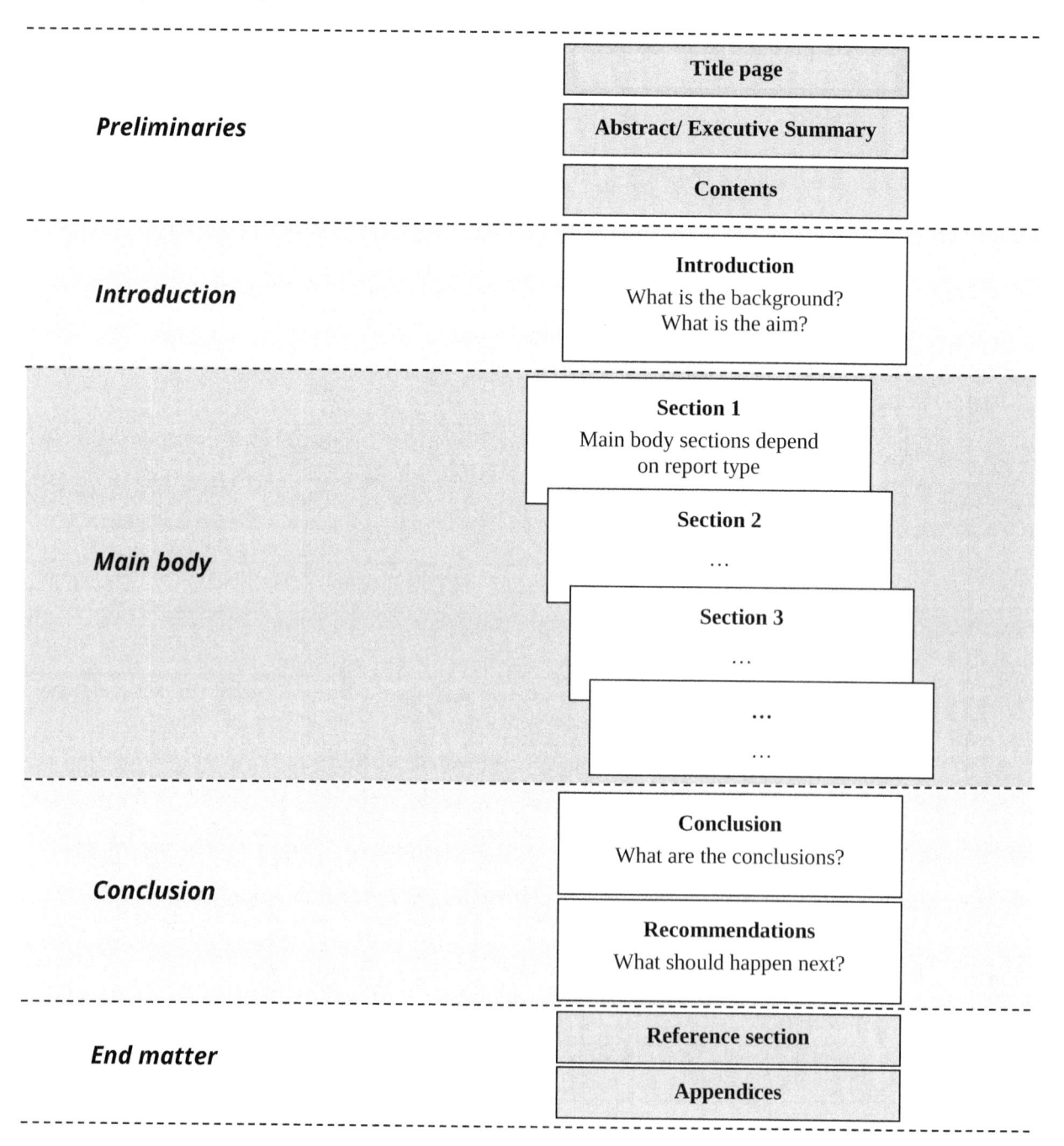

**Preliminaries**
- Title page
- Abstract/ Executive Summary
- Contents

**Introduction**
- Introduction
  What is the background?
  What is the aim?

**Main body**
- Section 1 — Main body sections depend on report type
- Section 2 …
- Section 3 …
- …
- …

**Conclusion**
- Conclusion
  What are the conclusions?
- Recommendations
  What should happen next?

**End matter**
- Reference section
- Appendices

# Unit 12: **About reports**

## *Preliminaries*

The *preliminaries* (or *front matter*) are parts that go at the beginning of the report, before the main content. There are several parts which are placed here.

Your report will probably have a **Title page**. Information which could be given on this page includes the following.
- The title of the report.
- The name(s) of the author(s).
- Your student number(s).
- Name of the lecturer the report is for.
- Date of submission.
- Number of words.

> **In short**
> A report usually contains the following sections.
> - Title page
> - Abstract
> - Contents page
> - Introduction (background, aim, theory)
> - Main body (sections depend on report type)
> - Conclusion
> - Recommendations
> - Reference section
> - Appendices

Many longer reports will contain an **Abstract** (or **Executive Summary**). This is a summary of the whole report, and should contain details of the key areas (e.g. for a laboratory report, this would mean the background, method, main findings and conclusions). An abstract is not usually needed for short reports.

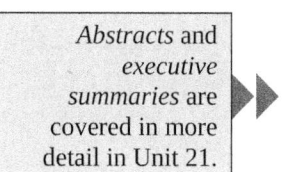

> *Abstracts* and *executive summaries* are covered in more detail in Unit 21.

Many reports will contain a **Contents** page. This should list all the headings and sub-headings in the report, together with the page numbers. Most word processing software can build a table of contents automatically.

## *Introduction*

The first main section of your report will be the **Introduction**. This will contain several elements, which can be combined in the Introduction section, or given as subsections with their own sub-headings. One important element is *background* information on the topic. Many reports, for example laboratory reports (see Unit 13), will contain essential *theory*, such as equations which will be used later. The *aim* (or aims) should also be stated. This is especially important as it explains why you are writing the report. You may need to give *definitions* of key terms and classify information. It is likely that the Introduction will contain material from other sources, in which case appropriate citations will be needed. You may also give the *scope* of the report in the introduction, i.e. what aspects will be covered in the report and what will be excluded.

## Main body

There are many possible sections which can go in the main body of the report. These depend on the report type and the approach. A laboratory report will usually contain sections giving the *Method*, the *Results* and a *Discussion* of what the results mean. This structure is commonly used for other report types. A business report may contain a *Literature Review* before the *Method* section. See later units for more details.

## Conclusion

The conclusion of the report usually consists of two sections, which may be combined. The first of these, **Conclusion**, presents conclusions which result from the information and analysis in the main body of the report. The conclusions, which should be clear and concise, should relate directly to the aims of the report, and state whether these have been fulfilled. At this stage in the report, there should be no new information.

Many reports conclude with a **Recommendations** section, giving recommendations for future action. These should be specific. As with the conclusions, the recommendations should derive from the main body of the report.

## End matter

*End matter* (or *back matter*) goes at the end of the report, after the main content. It comprises two parts. The first is a **Reference section** (called a *Works Cited List* for MLA style referencing). This lists all sources cited in the text.

The second is **Appendices**. These are used to provide any detailed information which your readers may need for reference, but which do not contain key information and which you therefore do not want to include in the body of the report. Examples are a questionnaire used in a survey or a letter of consent for interview participants. Appendices must be relevant, and should be numbered so they can be referred to in the main body, i.e. Appendix 1, Appendix 2, etc. (*appendices* is the plural form of *appendix*).

---

**IMRAD/AIMRAD**

The most common way to structure a report is often referred to as IMRAD, which is short for Introduction, Method, Results And Discussion. This structure is used not only for laboratory reports (Unit 13) and scientific articles, but is the default structure for many report types, as well as other genres (e.g. theses, Unit 20). As such reports often begin with an Abstract, the structure may also be referred to as AIMRAD.

**Conclusions vs. recommendations**

The main difference between conclusions and recommendations is time. Conclusions relate to the *past*, i.e. what was found through the research or investigation in the report. Recommendations relate to the *future*, i.e. what actions can be taken later.

# Unit 12: **About reports**

The following chart summarises the stages of a report, the structural components, and the purpose of each component.

| Stage of report | Structural component | Purpose |
|---|---|---|
| **Preliminaries** | Title page | Gives information such as the title of the report, name(s) of the author(s), date of submission, word count. |
| | Abstract | Gives a summary of the whole report. For some report types, may be called *Summary* or *Executive Summary*. |
| | Contents page | Lists all the headings and sub-headings in the report, together with the page numbers. |
| **Introduction** | Introduction | Gives background information needed to understand the report. May also contain theory and scope of the report. Should state aim(s). |
| **Main body** | *Depends on the report type.* | Gives the main content of the report. The sections depend on the report (common sections are Method, Results and Discussion). |
| **Conclusion** | Conclusion | Summarises the main conclusions of the report. |
| | Recommend-ations | Gives recommendations for future action, based on the conclusions. |
| **End matter** | Reference section | Lists any sources cited in the text, with full details. |
| | Appendices | Provides any detailed information which readers may need for reference, but which do not contain key information (e.g. questionnaire used in a survey, letter of consent). Should be numbered, Appendix 1, Appendix 2, etc. |

# Language for reports

There are many language phrases which are useful for different stages of the report. Some are below. Others depend on the content of the main body, and are covered in later units.

## Introduction

The *Background* section of your introduction is likely to require in-text citations. Check the referencing system required by your course.

The tense you use for the *Aims* will depend on whether the subject of the sentence is the report (which still exists) or something such as an experiment or survey (which has finished). If you are referring to the report, you should use *present* tense. If you are referring to an experiment or survey, which has finished, you should use *past* tense. E.g.

| The | aim / purpose | (of this report) is firstly to / (of this experiment) was to | research [sth] measure [sth] discover [wh-] investigate [sth or wh-] find out [sth or wh-] |
|---|---|---|---|

The experiment aimed to

Examples of some of these phrases in use are given below.
- **The aim of this report is to investigate** whether class size affects student achievement.
- **The aim of this experiment was to measure** the value of gravity using a simple pendulum.

## Conclusion

The *Recommendations* can use the following modal verb constructions:

| [X] should It is recommended that [X] One recommendation is that [X] | [verb] |
|---|---|

For example:
- Further research **should be** carried out to find out if these opinions are true in other markets.
- Based on the conclusions above, **it is recommended that** the company **consider** paying more attention to above-the-line promotion in order to attract new customers.
- **A final recommendation is that** the company **streamline** its overseas operations.

## End matter

Although there is no language for *Appendices*, the following may be used in the main body.

A complete copy of [X] is shown in Appendix 1.
For more details, refer to Appendix 1, which shows...
See Appendix 1 for more information.

Unit 12: **About reports**

# Checklist

Below is a general checklist for reports (checklists for specific report types are given in later units). You can use this to check your own writing, or ask a peer to help.

| Stage | Section | Item | OK? | Comments |
|---|---|---|---|---|
| Preliminaries | Title page | The report has a clear and informative title. | | |
| | | Other relevant information is included on the title page (e.g. student name, student ID, name of lecturer, word count). | | |
| | Abstract | An abstract (or executive summary) has been included, if necessary. | | |
| | Contents page | There is a Contents page, listing all sections, subsections and page numbers | | |
| Introduction | Background | Relevant background information has been included, including theory, if necessary. | | |
| | Aims | The aim is clearly stated, with appropriate language (e.g. *The aim of the experiment was to...*). | | |
| Main body | [Sections depend on report type] | The main body has sections and subsections relevant to the type of report. | | |
| Conclusion | Conclusions | There are clear conclusions. | | |
| | Recommend-ations | Recommendations are given. | | |
| | | Appropriate language is used (e.g. *It is recommended that...*). | | |
| End matter | Reference section | There is a reference section, with full details of all sources. | | |
| | Appendices | Appendices are clearly numbered. | | |

# Example report

Below is an example report. It is used in one of the exercises later. For simplicity, the report does not include title page or contents. The report is adapted from the following source: https://bmcmededuc.biomedcentral.com/articles/10.1186/1472-6920-7-38.
© Cave *et al*; licensee BioMed Central Ltd. 2007.

## Newly qualified doctors' views about whether their medical school had trained them well: questionnaire surveys

### Abstract

**Background**: A survey of newly qualified doctors in the UK in 2000/2001 found that 42% of them felt unprepared for their first year of employment in clinical posts. We report on how preparedness has changed since then, and on the impact of course changes upon preparedness.

**Methods**: Postal questionnaires were sent to all doctors who qualified from UK medical schools, in their first year of clinical work, in 2003 (n = 4257) and 2005 (n = 4784); and findings were compared with those in 2000/2001 (n = 5330). The response rates were 67% in 2000/2001, 65% in 2003, and 43% in 2005. The outcome measure was the percentage of doctors agreeing with the statement *'My experience at medical school has prepared me well for the jobs I have undertaken so far'*.

**Results**: In the 2000/2001 survey 36.3% strongly agreed or agreed with the statement, as did 50.3% in the 2003 survey and 58.5% in 2005. Between 1998 and 2006 all UK medical schools updated their courses. Within each cohort a significantly higher percentage of the respondents from schools with updated courses felt well prepared.

**Conclusion**: UK medical schools are now training doctors who feel better prepared for work than in the past. Some of the improvement may be attributable to curricular change.

### Background

A survey of newly qualified doctors from all medical schools in the UK, who undertook their first year of clinical work in 2000/2001, found that 42% of them felt unprepared by their medical school for their first clinical posts [1]. The survey also found significant and substantial differences between medical schools in how well prepared their graduates felt.

There is no consensus on how to train students to be good doctors or on how to select medical students who will make good doctors [2,3]. There is a clear consensus however, emphasised by the General Medical Council (GMC) in its document on undergraduate training entitled *Tomorrow's Doctors*, that medical schools should improve their preparation of students for their first year of working life. Following the publication of the first edition of *Tomorrow's Doctors* in 1993 [4], all UK medical schools initiated major curricular changes to bring their courses into line with the recommendations. The extent of changes necessary varied between medical schools, but all schools underwent major curricular revisions and changes to student assessment practices, with some introducing for example problem based learning. The GMC visited all medical schools to advise on the changes and to monitor progress.

Lack of preparedness has been linked to stress in junior doctors [5], and it is therefore important to investigate what might help junior doctors feel better prepared.

Our main aim in this study is to report on the views of newly qualified doctors in 2003 and 2005, compared with those in 2000/2001, about their preparation for their first year of clinical work. A secondary aim is to begin to investigate whether the increased attention to preparedness for practice, manifested through curricular changes at UK medical schools, has resulted in improvements in the way newly qualified doctors feel.

## Methods
### Participants and questionnaires
Questionnaires asking about preparedness were sent to newly qualified doctors in the UK in 2000, 2001, 2003 and 2005. The questionnaires were sent to doctors approximately 9 months after their graduation. We have grouped the 2000 and 2001 cohorts, which included all newly qualified doctors in 2000 and a random 25% sample of those in 2001, together. The 2003 and 2005 cohorts included all graduates from those two years. All questionnaires included the statement '*My experience at medical school has prepared me well for the jobs I have undertaken so far*', presented in the same format in each survey. Respondents were invited to state their level of agreement with the statement on a five-point scale from 'strongly agree' to 'strongly disagree'.

### Administration of the questionnaires
In 2000, 2001 and 2003, questionnaires were posted directly to doctors' registered addresses, obtained from the GMC register. Up to four reminders were sent to non-responders. In 2005 the GMC was unable to provide doctors' addresses so the survey was administered through postgraduate deaneries.

## Results
Questionnaires were sent to 5330 doctors in 2000/2001, 4257 doctors in 2003, and 4784 doctors in 2005. The response rates were 67%, 65%, and 43% respectively. The results from the 2003 and 2005 surveys were compared to those from the 2000/2001 survey. The proportion of doctors who agreed, partly agreed, or disagreed with the statement '*My experience at medical school prepared me well for the jobs I have undertaken so far*' is shown in Table 1.

**Table 1: Percentage responses to the statement that 'My experience at medical school prepared me well for the jobs I have undertaken so far'**

| Year of survey | % who agree or strongly agree | % who neither agree or disagree | % who disagree or strongly disagree |
| --- | --- | --- | --- |
| 2000/2001 | 36.2 (n = 1111) | 22.5 (n = 689) | 41.3 (n = 1262) |
| 2003 | 50.3 (n = 1382) | 18.9 (n = 519) | 30.8 (n = 844) |
| 2005 | 58.5 (n = 1195) | 26.1 (n = 533) | 15.3 (n = 308) |

Between 1998 and 2006, all UK medical schools implemented updated or 'new' courses (where implementation is defined as meaning that the majority of graduating doctors had undergone the new course) [4]. Figure 1 shows the percentage of respondents from schools using the old course and the new course who felt well prepared in the year under study.

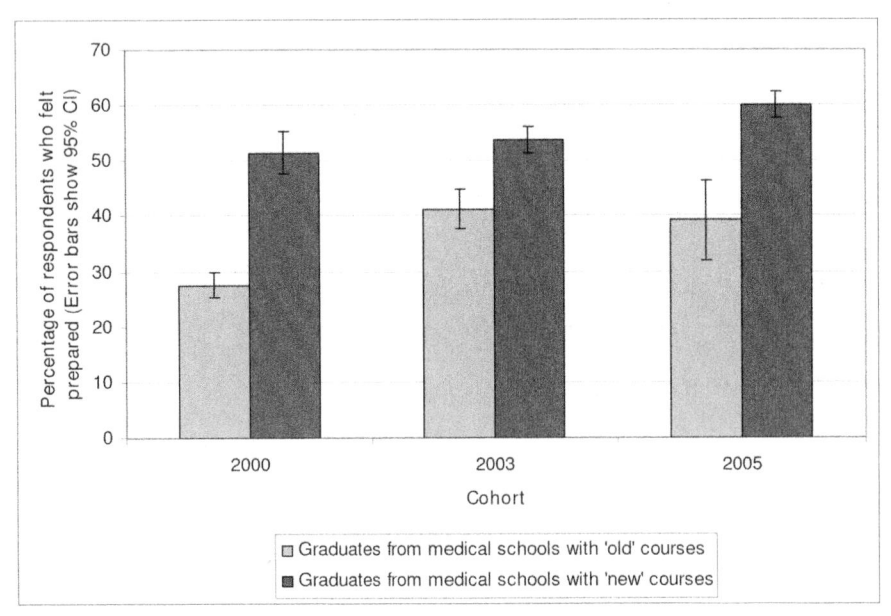

**Figure 1: Comparison of schools with new and old courses.**

## Discussion

The fact that such a high percentage of the newly qualified doctors in 2000/2001 did not feel well prepared for their first year of medical work was a concern. The results from the more recent qualifiers are reassuring for two reasons. First, they show that preparedness has improved significantly. In each successive cohort, an increasing proportion of doctors agreed with the statement *'My experience at medical school prepared me well for the jobs I have undertaken so far'*. In the 2000/2001 cohort, 36.3% strongly agreed or agreed, in the 2003 cohort, the corresponding percentage was 50.3% and in the 2005 cohort, it was 58.5% (see Table 1). Second, the results suggest that changes in medical school courses may be partly responsible for the improvements. Figure 1 shows that, within each cohort, a statistically significantly higher percentage of the respondents from schools with new courses felt well prepared. There is evidence from qualitative studies of junior doctors that certain aspects of modernised courses, for example periods of shadowing, are related to improvements in preparedness [6].

The major limitation to this study is the use of a subjective outcome measure. While subjective measures such as preparedness have strong face validity, there is no good evidence that those who feel more prepared are in fact more prepared.

The results of this study are encouraging, but they give cause for some continuing professional concern because, despite the improvements, in 2005 the percentage who agreed or strongly agreed that they had been well prepared was still only 59%. Whether the results should cause public concern is less clear. As stated above, there is no good evidence that those who feel unprepared are in fact unprepared; and doctors' first year of medical work provides a supervised transition from medical student to fully registered medical practitioner.

## Conclusion
In conclusion, this paper provides evidence that doctors feel more prepared for their first year of medical work. It also gives evidence that medical schools have given increasing recognition to the importance of preparing doctors for their first year of practice, and that they have implemented course changes to improve preparedness.

## Recommendations
Further studies are required to explore the relationship between subjective and objective measures of preparedness, as well as to follow up the long-term impact of the course changes. It is essential to study junior doctors' views about their training and competencies, especially during the present period of rapid evolution in the UK of both undergraduate and postgraduate medical education and training.

## References
1. Goldacre MJ, Lambert T, Evans J, Turner G: **Pre-registration house officers' views on whether their experience at medical school prepared them well for their jobs: national questionnaire survey**. *BMJ* 2003, **326**:1011-2.

2. Hurwitz B, Vass A: **What's a good doctor, and how can you make one?** *BMJ* 2002, **325**:667-668.

3. Parry J, Mathers J, Stevens A, Parsons A, Lilford R, Spurgeon P, Thomas H: **Admissions processes for five year medical courses at English schools: review.** *BMJ* 2006, **332**:1005-9.

4. General Medical Council: *Tomorrow's doctors. Recommendations on undergraduate medical education*. London 2003.

5. Paice E, Rutter H, Wetherell M, Winder B, McManus IC: **Stressful incidents, stress and coping strategies in the pre-registration house officer year**. *Med Educ* 2002, **36**:56-65.

6. Watmough S, Garden A, Taylor D: **Pre-registration house officers' views on studying under a reformed medical curriculum in the UK**. *Med Educ* 2006, **40(9)**:893-899.

7. National Health Service Management Executive: **Junior Doctors –The New Deal.** London: Department of Health; 1991.

8. Hayes K, Feather A, Hall A, Sedgwick P, Wannan G, Wessier-Smith A, Green T, McCrorie P: **Anxiety in medical students: is preparation for full-time clinical attachments more dependent upon differences in maturity or on educational programmes for undergraduate and graduate entry students?** *Med Educ* 2004, **38(11)**:1154-1163.

# Academic Writing Genres — Sheldon Smith

## Exercises

### Exercise 1: Comprehension

Answer the following questions about this unit. Either do this after reading the unit, or make notes first then use the notes to answer the questions.

1  What is a report?

___

2  Match the following report types with their description.

| Report type | Description |
| --- | --- |
| i. Laboratory report | a. This examines a real-world situation and analyses it using appropriate theory. |
| ii. Business report | b. This type of report explains and analyses the results of an experiment. |
| iii. Research report | c. This combines theory and practice by describing an observed person, place or event and analysing the observation. |
| iv. Project report | d. This analyses a situation and uses theory to provide solutions or recommendations. |
| v. Case study report | e. This report is written by engineers and describes technical research. |
| vi. Progress report | f. This reports the results of research which has been conducted, for example through surveys (using questionnaires or interviews). |
| vii. Field report | g. This informs a supervisor or customer about progress that has been made on a project over a certain period of time. |
| viii. Technical report | h. This report describes and evaluates a design used to solve a particular problem. |
| ix. Design report | i. This reports on work which has been done or is planned. |

3  What information will usually go in the Introduction to a report?

___

4  What is an Appendix? What kind of information will go here? What is the plural of this word?

___

# Unit 12: About reports

**5** Study the following sentences. Decide if each one is a feature of a **report**, an **essay**, or **both**. An example has been done.

| | | | | |
|---|---|---|---|---|
| E.g. | Has different types such as *laboratory, business, case study* and *field*. | report | essay | both |
| i. | Allows information to be found quickly in specific sections. | report | essay | both |
| ii. | Demonstrates ability to support an argument (thesis) through knowledge and understanding of the topic. | report | essay | both |
| iii. | Requires good writing skills, such as the ability to construct paragraphs with clear topic sentences. | report | essay | both |
| iv. | Has clearly defined sections, each with a different function. | report | essay | both |
| v. | Uses headings and sub-headings. | report | essay | both |
| vi. | Requires accurate use of vocabulary and grammar. | report | essay | both |
| vii. | Will often include a Contents page. | report | essay | both |
| viii. | Does not usually include graphics such as tables, graphs, charts. | report | essay | both |
| ix. | Generally only includes secondary research (e.g. citations from books or journals). | report | essay | both |
| x. | May include appendices with additional information. | report | essay | both |

**6** The following are typical components or sections of a report. Number them (from 1-9) according to the order in which they usually occur.

Recommendations  Main body  Title page  Reference section
Appendices  Conclusion  Abstract  Contents page
Introduction

**7** The following are extracts from reports. Decide which of the sections in **Q6** (above) they are likely to go in, based on the language used or the content.

| Extract | | Section |
|---|---|---|
| i. | It is recommended that the company implement measures to reduce the high turnover of staff. | |
| ii. | The aim of this report is to investigate whether class size has an effect on learning outcomes. | |
| iii. | As can be seen from the graph, the average GDP increased significantly during the five year period. | |
| iv. | Spielman (2017) defines the fundamental attribution error as the tendency to assume that the behaviour of a person is the result of their personality, failing to recognise the effect of the situation on their behaviour. | |
| v. | Spielman, R.M. (2017) *Psychology*. Houston: OpenStax. | |
| vi. | This report has shown that having diabetes increases the risk of heart disease. | |

**Academic Writing Genres**                                                                   **Sheldon Smith**

## Exercise 2: **Example report**

Study the example report and answer the following questions.

a) What type of report is this? How do you know?

_____

b) The report contains answers to the following questions.
- First, decide which section(s) you think will contain the answer. Do this for *all* of the questions *before* looking for the answer. [Hint: Choose from *Title, Abstract, Background, Method, Results, Discussion, Conclusions, Recommendations, References.*]
- Then, look through the report to find the answer to each question. Try to do this as *quickly as possible*. [Hint: Use the headings to help.]
- At the same time, check to see whether the answer was in the section you expected.

| Question | Section(s) | Answer |
|---|---|---|
| 1. What is the topic of the report? | | |
| 2. How was data gathered? | | |
| 3. What percentage of newly trained doctors felt well prepared in: 2000/2001, 2003 and 2005? | | |
| 4. What may have been responsible for changes in preparedness? | | |
| 5. Do the writers feel that doctors are more prepared now than in the past? | | |
| 6. What further studies are recommended by the writers? | | |
| 7. What is the source of this statement: 'Lack of preparedness has been linked to stress in junior doctors [5]'? | | |
| 8. What are the limitations of the study? | | |
| 9. What are the aims of the study? | | |
| 10. How long after graduation were questionnaires sent to doctors? | | |

Unit 12: **About reports**

c) Study the report again and find examples of *language phrases* for all of the following:
- stating aims;
- referring to tables or graphs;
- two uses of the pronoun 'we', and one use of the pronoun 'our';
- stating limitations;
- giving conclusions.

d) What is the difference between the two phrases which refer to **Figure 1**?

_____

_____

_____

## Exercise 3: **Learning outcomes check**

a) The following are the learning outcomes for this unit. Decide how well you have mastered each one by giving it a score, as follows.

    3 = I understand/can do this well.
    2 = I understand/can do this fairly well, but I can improve with more practice.
    1 = I understand/can do this, but not well enough yet. I need to practise more.
    0 = I do not understand/cannot do this yet. I need more time.

| Score | Learning Outcome |
|---|---|
| _____ | I understand what a report is. |
| _____ | I am aware of different types of report. |
| _____ | I understand the differences between a report and an essay. |
| _____ | I understand the different sections of a report and the functions of each. |
| _____ | I am aware of language phrases for different report sections. |

b) Use this information to review the unit and improve.

# Unit 13 | Laboratory Reports

## Learning Outcomes

By the end of this unit, you should:
- understand what a laboratory report is;
- understand the different sections of a typical laboratory report;
- understand the function of each section;
- be aware of language phrases to use in different sections of a laboratory report.

By completing the exercises, you will also:
- study a laboratory report for content, structure and language.

## Key Vocabulary

**Nouns**
- method
- results
- discussion

## Additional Vocabulary

*Academic Collocations (in the unit)*
- academic writing (adj + n)
- appropriate language (adj + n)
- human behaviour (adj + n)
- main findings (adj + n)
- natural world (adj + n)
- possible sources (adj + n)
- raw data (adj + n)
- relevant information (adj + n)
- secondary sources (adj + n)
- immediately following (adv + adj)
- slightly different (adv + adj)
- primarily concerned (adj + past)
- draw conclusions (v + n)
- gather information (v + n)
- give information (v + n)
- interpret data (v + n)
- present data (v + n)
- use the method (v + n)

*Academic Collocations (in the report)*
- empirical study (adj + n)
- possible sources (adj + n)

## Contents of this section

### Unit 13: Laboratory Reports ............................ 179

    Overview ............................................................................................................... 180
    What is a laboratory report? ................................................................................ 180
    Structure of laboratory reports ............................................................................ 181
    Language for laboratory reports ......................................................................... 185
    Checklist ................................................................................................................ 188
    Example report .................................................................................................... 190
    Exercises ............................................................................................................... 194

## Overview

Both in the laboratory and in the field, scientists perform experiments, interpret data, and seek to share their findings with other scientists. These can be natural scientists, such as biologists, chemists and physicists investigating the natural world, or social scientists such as psychologists investigating human behaviour. The medium for sharing their findings is the *laboratory report*. This section explains what a laboratory report is, how it is structured, and language phrases used in this report type.

## What is a laboratory report?

A laboratory report, also called a *scientific report* or an *experimental report*, explains the results of an experiment, usually to other specialists in the same field. Laboratory reports are published in scientific journals – and used as assessment tools on university or pre-university courses. A laboratory report is arguably the most important form of communication in the sciences.

There are many functions a laboratory report needs to achieve. It should outline the background of the experiment and the reason for conducting it. The report should also explain the procedure, in such a way that the reader is not only able to follow the process but replicate it, should they wish. The report needs to detail not only the results but also their significance, including whether they agree with the underlying theory and any errors that may have arisen. Improvements in the procedure or equipment may also be given.

# Unit 13: **Lab Reports**

## Structure of laboratory reports

A laboratory report follows the general structure of a report as given in Unit 12, with the most common sections of the main body being *Method*, *Results* and *Discussion*. The following summarises the structure of a typical laboratory report. Each section is described in more detail on the next page.

**Preliminaries**
- Title page
- Abstract/Summary
- Contents

**Introduction**
- Introduction
  What is the background?
  Is there any important theory?
  What is the aim?

**Main body**
- Method
  What apparatus was used?
  How was data gathered?
- Results
  What were the results?
- Discussion
  What do the results mean?
  How accurate are they?

**Conclusion**
- Conclusion
  What are the conclusions?
  Are there any recommendations?

**End matter**
- Reference section
- Appendices

# Academic Writing Genres     Sheldon Smith

The *Preliminaries* are the same as for a general report (see Unit 12). There should be a **Title page**, which includes a brief, clear and informative title (around 5 to 15 words). For a laboratory report, an **Abstract** is used, rather than *Executive Summary*. The *Abstract* should give a summary of the whole report, stating what was done, why, what the results were and what the conclusions were. For most reports, the *Abstract* will be around 100-200 words, though for long reports, it may be up to a page, while for short reports, this part may be omitted. A **Contents page** is usually included for long reports, omitted for short ones.

The **Introduction** will contain general *background* information. This part should be very brief. A laboratory report will usually consider important *theory*, which is either tested in the experiment or which the experiment relies on. This might form a separate subsection (called *Theory* or *Theoretical Background*). It may contain equations, which should be numbered for easy reference later in the report. The theory section should define any specialist terms. There should also be a clear *aim* (or aims), which briefly states what you were trying to find out by conducting the experiment.

> **In short**
> A laboratory report usually contains the following.
> - **Title page** (title 5-15 words)
> - **Abstract** (100-200 words)
> - **Contents page**
> - **Introduction**:
>   - Background
>   - Theory
>   - Aims – *why* experiment was conducted
> - **Method** – *how*, *where* and *when* data was gathered
> - **Results** – *what* the data is
> - **Discussion** – *why* the results matter, *how* they compare to expected values, sources of error
> - **Conclusion**
> - **Reference section**
> - **Appendices**

The first section of the *main body* is typically the **Method** section, also called *Procedure*, *Experimental* or *Methods and Materials*. This section outlines how you gathered information, where from and how much. A report of an experiment may answer these questions here.
- What apparatus was used?
- How did you conduct the experiment?
- How many times did you repeat the procedure?
- What precautions did you take to increase accuracy?

It is usual to include a labelled diagram of any apparatus in the *Method* section.

The **Results** section, also called *Findings* or *Data*, explains what you found out, in other words the data that has been collected from the experiment. The data will often be presented in tables. Be sure to include correct units in the table. This section is primarily concerned with description; there should be no calculations.

# Unit 13: Lab Reports

The **Discussion** section, also called *Analysis*, is where you develop your ideas. It draws together the background information or theory from the *Introduction* with the data from the *Results* section, explaining why the results occurred and what they mean. This section will look at the relationship between the results and theory and identify trends. The *Discussion* will often include figures (graphs or other visual material), as this will help the reader to understand the main points. It is always preferable to present results in graphs if at all possible, as it is easier to understand information this way. If data is presented in a graph, the same data should *not* be repeated in a table (though this tabulated data can be given in an appendix). Any calculations made from the results will appear in this section. This section should fulfil the aims in the *Introduction*.

> **Presenting tables/figures**
>
> When presenting information in tables and figures, remember to:
> - include a legend (heading), explaining what each one shows;
> - number tables and figures separately, e.g. Table 1, Figure 1, Figure 2, Table 2;
> - put headings for tables at the *top* of the table, and headings for figures *underneath*;
> - be sure to include correct units in tables and figures;
> - make sure axes of graphs are clearly labelled.

The *Discussion* section may consider how the results compare to the expected values. It should also consider any possible sources of error, and how these could have been overcome. These could arise from problems with the theoretical assumptions, measurement errors, or problems with the apparatus. Suggested improvements, in the apparatus or method, should also be given.

As with any report, there will be a **Conclusion** section. This section should restate the main findings in the report, and state whether the aim was achieved. It should not contain any new information that was not in the *Discussion*. The *Conclusion* will usually also summarise possible suggestions (i.e. recommendations) for improvement, which, unlike for the general report shown in Unit 12, are usually part of the *Conclusion*, rather than forming a separate section.

As with any report, there should be suitable *End matter*. This is likely to be a **Reference section** for any sources cited. A laboratory report may contain **Appendices**, for example lab diary or raw data.

# Academic Writing Genres — Sheldon Smith

The following chart summarises the stages of a laboratory report, the structural components, and the purpose of each component.

| Stage of report | Structural component | Purpose |
| --- | --- | --- |
| **Preliminaries** | Title page | Gives information such as the title of the report, name(s) of the author(s), date of submission, word count. |
| | Abstract | Gives a summary of the whole report (what was done, why, what the results and conclusions were). |
| | Contents page | Lists all the headings and sub-headings in the report, together with the page numbers. |
| **Introduction** | Introduction | Gives background information. Presents important theory, possibly including equations, and defines any specialist terms. States aim(s). |
| **Main body** | Method | Lists apparatus used in the experiment (with diagram) and describes how the experiment was conducted. |
| | Results | Gives the data from the experiment, usually in the form of tables. |
| | Discussion | Analyses the data from the experiment, often using graphs and calculations. May consider how results compare to the expected values. Considers possible sources of error, and suggests improvements in the apparatus or method. |
| **Conclusion** | Conclusion | Summarises the main findings of the report and suggestions for improvement. |
| **End matter** | Reference section | Lists any sources cited in the text, with full details. |
| | Appendices | Provides any detailed information not needed for the main body (e.g. lab diary, raw data). |

# Unit 13: **Lab Reports**

# Language for laboratory reports

The general language for reports, given in Unit 12, also applies to laboratory reports. There are, however, additional phrases for different sections, as outlined below.

## *Preliminaries*

The *Title* of your report will depend very much on the subject matter, and will be very individual. Nonetheless, there are some useful verbs and phrases which can be used in laboratory report titles. These include the following.

- Investigating [X]
- Calculating [X]
- Measuring [X]
- Demonstrating [X]
- Analysing [X]
- Determining [X]
- An Investigation into [X]
- A Demonstration of [X]
- An Analysis of [X]

In the above, [X] represents a noun phrase, for example: *Measuring the value of gravity using a simple pendulum.*

## *Introduction (Theory)*

If you want to refer to theories or principles, you can use the following structures.

> **According to** Newton's First Law, ...
> Newton's First law **states that**...

The following structures can be used for presenting equations.

> The equation for [Z] is...
> The equation of [Z] can be written as...
> The following equation of [Z] can be obtained: ...
> [Z] can be expressed as...

The following phrases can be used for stating what something stands for or represents.

[X] ...where [X] { is / stands for / represents / denotes / symbolises } ...

... is { represented / denoted } by [X].

For example:
- **The equation for** velocity with constant acceleration **is** $v = u + at$, **where** $t$ **is** the time, $v$ **is** the velocity at time $t$, $u$ **is** the velocity a time 0, and $a$ **represents** acceleration.
- Boyle's law **can be expressed as** $P_i V_i = P_f V_f$, **where** $P_i$ **is** the initial pressure, $V_i$ **is** the initial volume, $P_f$ **is** the final pressure, and $V_f$ **is** the final volume.

## Method

Science reports will usually include apparatus for conducting the experiment. The following phrases can be used for describing the apparatus.

| The apparatus | consisted of... |
|---|---|
| | comprised... |
| | was set up as shown in the diagram below. |

Because academic writing does not usually use 'I' or 'we', this section will often contain passive structures when describing how you gathered information, usually the *past passive* (because the experiment is finished). Because the method of conducting an experiment or survey is a *process*, it can be useful to use process transitions, as follows.

*Process description is covered in Unit 9.*

*Sequence transitions*
- First
- To begin with
- Second
- Next
- The next step
- Then
- Before
- After
- Afterwards
- After that
- Immediately following this
- In turn
- Finally
- Lastly

*Time signals*
- After a few minutes
- During
- At the same time
- Meanwhile
- In the meantime
- Later
- Eventually

For example:
- **After** measuring the length of the string, the bob **was moved** several degrees.

## Results

If you use tables, charts, etc., the following language can be used to refer to these. Note that this language is description, i.e. it does not analyse or draw conclusions.

| Figure 1 | gives | ... |
|---|---|---|
| Table 1 | shows | information about ... |
| | indicates | |

# Unit 13: **Lab Reports**

## Discussion

The following language can be used for referring to graphs, charts and tables in the *Discussion* section. Unlike similar phrases used for the *Findings* section, which merely describe, this language discusses, i.e. it says what the information means.

| As can be seen from<br>According to<br>As is shown in | the chart<br>the figure<br>the table<br>the graph | , ... |
|---|---|---|
| It can be seen from | Table 1<br>Figure 2 | that... |

The following phrases can be used when comparing the values or results to those expected.

| This value<br>The calculated answer | agrees with<br>is close to<br>differs slightly from<br>is slightly different from | the accepted value of [X], which is...<br>the true value of [X].<br>the expected value of [X]. |
|---|---|---|
| The results | agree with<br>are close to<br>differ slightly from<br>are slightly different from | |

The following phrases can be used when discussing how errors may have affected the results.

| Errors | may have arisen | in the measurement of [X], thereby affecting the results. |
|---|---|---|
| A further error | | from neglect of [X], which might have affected results. |

## Conclusion

The following conditional structures can be used to indicate how the process could have been improved.

If [X] had been [done] (instead of Y) the results might have been more accurate.

The results might have been more accurate if [X] had been [done] (instead of Y).

# Checklist

Below is a checklist for laboratory reports. Use it to check your writing, or ask a peer to help.

| Stage | Area | Item | OK? | Comments |
|---|---|---|---|---|
| Preliminaries | Title page | The report has a clear and informative title (5-15 words). | | |
| | | Other relevant information is included on the title page (e.g. student name, student ID, name of lecturer, word count). | | |
| | Abstract | There is an abstract summarising the report, around 100-200 words (may be omitted for short reports). | | |
| | Contents page | A contents page is included (may be omitted for short reports). | | |
| Introduction | Introduction | Relevant background is included. | | |
| | | Relevant theory is included, if necessary (e.g. equations, definitions of key terms). | | |
| | | The aim is clearly stated, with appropriate language (e.g. *The aim of the experiment was to...*). | | |
| Main body | Method | There is a description of apparatus, with diagram. | | |
| | | The procedure is clearly explained, using past passive tense. | | |
| | | There is a description of precautions for accuracy. | | |
| | Findings | Results are in tables or lists (with correct units). | | |
| | | Appropriate language is used for referring to tables etc. (e.g. *Table 1 shows...*). | | |

# Unit 13: **Lab Reports**

| | | | | |
|---|---|---|---|---|
| **Main body** | **Discussion** | Data is processed and displayed appropriately (e.g. graphs). | | |
| | | The discussion links the results to the information in the *Introduction/theory* section. | | |
| | | There is an explanation of whether observations agree with those expected, using appropriate language. | | |
| | | Possible sources of error are given, with appropriate language. | | |
| | | Suggestions for possible improvement are given, using appropriate language. | | |
| **Conclusion** | **Conclusion** | The conclusions are clearly stated. | | |
| | | There is a statement of success or otherwise, referring to the aim in the introduction. | | |
| **End matter** | **Reference section** | There is a reference section with full details of all sources. | | |
| | **Appendices** | Appendices, if used, are clearly numbered. | | |
| | **General** | All tables and figures have suitable headings, which are placed *above* the tables and *beneath* the figures. | | |
| | | Suitable font and font size have been used. | | |
| | | The report is within the specified word limit. | | |
| | | Secondary sources (usually in the *background* and *theory*) are paraphrased and have suitable in-text citations. | | |

# Academic Writing Genres                                    Sheldon Smith

# Example report

Below is an example physics laboratory report. It is used in one of the exercises later. For simplicity, the report does not include title page or contents.

Determination of $g$, the acceleration due to gravity,<br>from pendulum oscillations in Guangzhou, China.

**Abstract**
Using a simple pendulum, the acceleration due to gravity in Guangzhou, China was calculated and found to be 9.71 ms$^{-2}$. The value was obtained by measuring the period of a pendulum for different lengths and plotting the lengths against the square of the period, with the gradient of the line of best fit used to calculate the value of $g$ from the equation $g = 4\pi^2$ x gradient. This experimental value for gravity is in close agreement with the accepted value for this location. An improved value could be obtained by using a photogate timer, or by increasing the number of trials and using the average value of T at each length.

## 1. Introduction
### 1.1 Background
In the early 17th century, Galileo conducted experiments on pendulums and discovered that two pendulums of equal length kept time together, regardless of the arc of their swing (Van Helden, 1995). This discovery led, half a century later, to the pendulum clock, invented by Christiaan Huygens (Van Helden, 1995), which was the most accurate timekeeper until the invention of the quartz clock in the early 20th century.

### 1.2 Theory
A simple pendulum consists of a light string, fixed at one end, with a mass $m$ suspended from the other end. The mass swings back and forth with a period $T$, where period is defined as the time required for one complete oscillation, in other words, for the mass to swing back and forth once (Nedungadi, Raman and McGregor, 2013). According to Ling, Sanny and Moebs (2017), the period is independent of mass and the maximum displacement, and depends only on the length of the pendulum, assuming gravity is constant. The period of a pendulum is almost independent of amplitude, especially if the amplitude is less than 15° (Ling, Sanny and Moebs, 2017).

Nedungadi, Raman and McGregor (2013) state that the period $T$ of a pendulum is given by the following equation:

(1) $T = 2\pi\sqrt{(l/g)}$

where $l$ is the length of the pendulum and $g$ is acceleration due to gravity.

This equation can be rewritten as:

(2) $T^2 = 4\pi^2(l/g)$

If the period of the pendulum is measured for different values of $l$ and the results used to plot a graph of $l$ against $T^2$, the gradient will be $g/4\pi^2$. In other words, $g$ can be calculated from the following equation:

(3) $g = 4\pi^2$ x gradient

The value of $g$ in Guangzhou, China is 9.79 ms$^{-2}$ (Wolfram Alpha LLC, 2019; SensorsONE, 2019).

# Unit 13: Lab Reports

### 1.3 Aim
The aim of the experiment was to measure acceleration due to gravity in Guangzhou, China by using a simple pendulum.

### 2. Method
The apparatus, shown in Figure 1, comprised a string, a metal bob of mass 500g, a support stand with a clamp, and a stopwatch. The metal bob was attached to one end of the string, while the other end of the string was attached to the stand. An initial length of 0.6m was used. The pendulum was set to an angle of 10° and allowed to swing freely. The time for ten oscillations was measured, using a stopwatch. A relatively large number of oscillations was chosen in order to reduce the error in measuring the time. The process was conducted a total of eight times, with the string lengthened each time in increments of 0.2m, up to a final length of 2m.

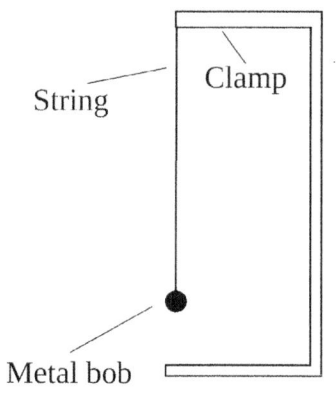

Figure 1. Experimental set-up.

### 3. Results.
The results of the eight measurements are shown in Table 1. Column 1 shows the length of the pendulum, measured in metres, while column 2 shows the time for ten oscillations, measured in seconds.

Table 1. Length and time data from the experiment.

| $l$ (m) | T for 10 oscillations (s) |
|---|---|
| 0.6 | 15.5 |
| 0.8 | 18.0 |
| 1.0 | 20.0 |
| 1.2 | 22.0 |
| 1.4 | 24.8 |
| 1.6 | 25.4 |
| 1.8 | 26.9 |
| 2.0 | 28.5 |

### 4. Discussion
The time for one oscillation at each length, and the square value, were calculated from the data (Table 2).

Table 2. Calculations of T for one oscillation and $T^2$.

| $l$ (m) | T for 10 oscillations (s) | T for one oscillation (s) | $T^2$ (s$^2$) |
|---|---|---|---|
| 0.6 | 15.5 | 1.55 | 2.40 |
| 0.8 | 18.0 | 1.80 | 3.24 |
| 1.0 | 20.0 | 2.00 | 4.00 |
| 1.2 | 22.0 | 2.20 | 4.84 |
| 1.4 | 24.8 | 2.48 | 5.66 |
| 1.6 | 25.4 | 2.54 | 6.45 |
| 1.8 | 26.9 | 2.69 | 7.24 |
| 2.0 | 28.5 | 2.85 | 8.12 |

Excel was used to plot this data on a graph of pendulum length against period squared (Figure 2). The data has been fit to a straight line, with the equation y=0.02463x + 0.0083. Multiplying the gradient by $4\pi^2$ to calculate $g$ gives a value of 9.71 ms$^{-2}$, which is close to the accepted value of 9.79 ms$^{-2}$.

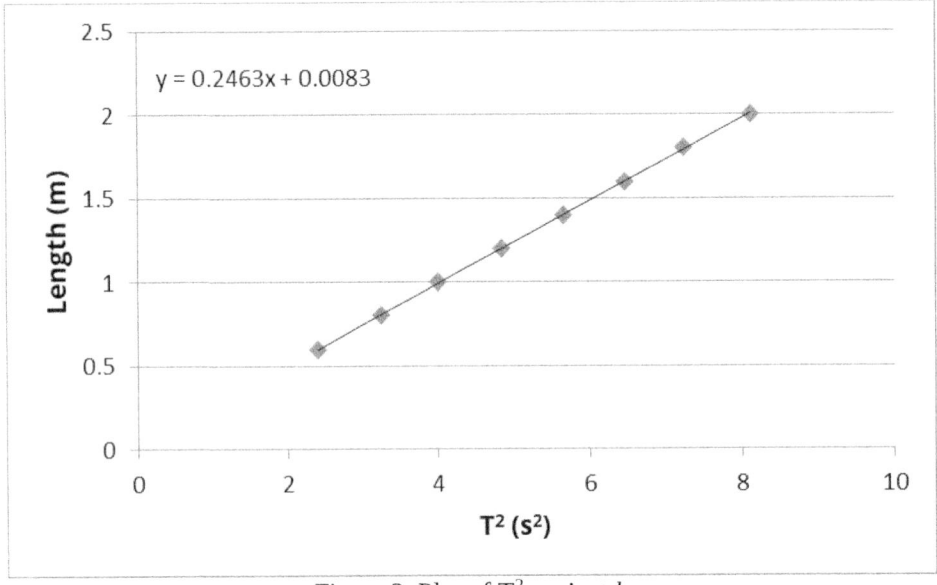

Figure 2. Plot of $T^2$ against $l$.

There are various possible sources of error. One of these is the reaction time of the experimenter. As ten oscillations were used, a 0.1s error would lead to a 0.01s error for T, which for a time of around 2s would mean a fractional error of 0.02s. Another possible error is in measuring the length of the string. A 1mm error would mean a fractional 0.001m for length 1m. The timing error is therefore more significant than the length error.

The experiment could be improved with more precise timing of the period. This could be achieved by using a photogate timer. Additionally, the experiment could be repeated for the same lengths and the average value of T could be used.

## 5. Conclusion
Using a simple pendulum, a value of $g$ = 9.71 ms$^{-2}$ has been obtained as the value of gravity in Guangzhou,

which is close to the accepted value for this location, which is 9.79 ms$^{-2}$. An improved value could be obtained by using a photogate timer, or by increasing the number of trials and using the average value of T at each length.

**References**

Ling, S., Sanny, J. and Moebs, W. (2017), *University Physics: Volume 1*. Houston: OpenStax.

Nedungadi P., Raman R. & McGregor M. (2013). 'Enhanced STEM learning with Online Labs: Empirical study comparing physical labs, tablets and desktops', in *Frontiers in Education Conference, 2013 IEEE* (pp. 1585-1590).

SensorsONE (2019), *Local Gravity Calculator*. Available at: https://www.sensorsone.com/local-gravity-calculator/ (Accessd 28 February 2019).

Van Helden, A. (1995), *Pendulum Clock*. Available from http://galileo.rice.edu/sci/instruments/pendulum.html (Accessed 28 February 2019).

Wolfram Alpha LLC (2019). Available at: https://www.wolframalpha.com/input/?i=acceleration+due+to+gravity+guangzhou+china (Accessed 28 February 2019).

# Exercises

## Exercise 1: **Comprehension**

Answer the following questions about this unit. Either do this after reading the unit, or make notes first then use the notes to answer the questions.

1  What is a laboratory report?

   _____

   _____

2  The following shows the usual components or sections of a laboratory report. The first letter of each is given. Complete the word(s). An example has been done.
   [Note: some answers are *two* words.]
   - Title page
   - A_____
   - C_____
   - I_____
     - B_____
     - T_____
     - A_____
   - M_____
   - R_____
   - D_____
   - C_____
   - R_____
   - A_____

3  What may be contained in the 'T' section (see Q2 above) of a laboratory report? Where would you find this section? What other name might it have?

   _____

   _____

4  Why are calculations part of the 'D' section, rather than the section before?

   _____

   _____

5  Apart from analysis (and calculations), what else may be contained in the 'D' section?

   _____

   _____

# Unit 13: Lab Reports

**6** The following are extracts from laboratory reports. Decide which section they are likely to go in, based on the language and content.

| | Extract | Section |
|---|---|---|
| i. | The test apparatus consisted of a 50 cm long and 6 cm wide metal bar with two cube-shaped opaque PVC boxes with a side length of 5.5 cm attached to it at a distance of 22 cm from each other.** | |
| ii. | These results are in line with the hypothesis that fruit odour in *C. macrocarpa* and *L. cymosa* is an evolved signal to seed-dispersing primates and/or other contemporary or extinct frugivores.** | |
| iii. | The aim of this preliminary study was to compare the effectiveness of the extraction of bioactive components from poplar propolis (phenolics, flavones/flavonols and flavanones/dihydroflavonols) using the maceration method, MAE and UE.* | |
| iv. | MAE of bioactive phenolics and flavonoids from poplar type propolis was found to be a very fast extraction method, compared to maceration and even UE.* | |
| v. | Different extraction methods of biologically active components from propolis: a preliminary study* | |
| vi. | The use of propolis as a remedy has a long history [1]. In addition, preparations, as well as food and beverage additives containing propolis extracts can be found on the market in numerous countries [2].* | |
| vii. | The sample was placed in an Erlenmayer flask with the corresponding amount of solvent and was treated with ultrasound at 25°C for a given duration.* | |
| viii. | The results demonstrate that the use of ultrasound and of microwave extractions greatly reduce the extraction time.* | |
| ix. | MAE (microwave assisted extraction) is the process of using microwave energy to heat solvents in contact with a sample in order to partition some chemical components from the matrix into the solvent.* | |
| x. | Three extraction methods were employed in order to obtain the biologically active components of poplar type (European) propolis. The results are summarized in Table 1.* | |

\* Adapted from *Different extraction methods of biologically active components from propolis: a preliminary study*, by Boryana Trusheva, Dorina Trunkova and Vassya Bankova. Available from https://bmcchem.biomedcentral.com/articles/10.1186/1752-153X-1-13.

\*\* Adapted from *Chemical recognition of fruit ripeness in spider monkeys (Ateles geoffroyi)*, by Nevo, Omer *et al*. Available from https://www.nature.com/articles/srep14895

# Exercise 2: **Example report**

Study the example report on *determination of g* (earlier in this unit) and answer the following questions.

a) The report contains answers to the following questions.
- First, decide which section(s) you think will contain the answer. Do this for *all* of the questions *before* looking at the report.
- Then, look through the report to find the answer to each question. Try to do this as *quickly as possible*. [Hint: Use the headings to help.]
- At the same time, check to see whether the answer was in the section you expected.

| Question | Section(s) | Answer |
|---|---|---|
| 1. What was the value of $g$ obtained in the experiment? | | |
| 2. When did Galileo conduct experiments studying the pendulum? | | |
| 3. What apparatus was used in the experiment? | | |
| 4. What two sources of error are given? | | |
| 5. What do $T$, $l$ and $g$ represent in the follow equation? $T = 2\pi\sqrt{(l/g)}$ | | |
| 6. Why was the time for ten oscillations measured, rather than the time for a single oscillation? | | |
| 7. What was the time for 10 oscillations when the length was 1.2m? | | |
| 8. How could the experiment be improved? | | |
| 9. What was the aim of the experiment? | | |
| 10. What is the equation for the line of best fit (of the graph)? | | |

Unit 13: **Lab Reports**

b) Study the report again and find examples of *language phrases* for all of the following:
- stating aims;
- referring to tables or graphs;
- listing the apparatus;
- giving improvements.

c) The following table has extracts from the report. It also shows the section the extracts are in, the function of the extracts, and the tense(s) used. Complete the table by:
- identifying the correct tense (or tenses, if more than one);
- completing the gaps in the examples, using the correct form of the verb in brackets.

When you have finished, check your answers by finding the sentences in the report.

| Section | Function | Tense(s) | Extract |
|---|---|---|---|
| Introduction (Background) | To describe past events | | In the early 17th century, Galileo **(i)**_____ (conduct) experiments on pendulums and **(ii)**_____ (discover) that two pendulums of equal length **(iii)**_____ (keep) time together, regardless of the arc of their swing. |
| Introduction (Theory) | To give theory | | A simple pendulum **(iv)**_____ (consist) of a light string, fixed at one end, with a mass $m$ suspended from the other end. The mass **(v)**_____ (swing) back and forth with a period $T$. |
| Introduction (Aim) | To state the aim | | The aim of the experiment **(vi)**_____ (be) to measure acceleration due to gravity. |
| Method | To show the equipment | | The apparatus, shown in Figure 1, **(vii)**_____ (comprise) a string, a metal bob of mass 500g, a support stand with a clamp, and a stopwatch. |
| Method | To give the method | | The metal bob **(viii)**_____ (attached) one end of the string, while the other **(ix)**_____ (attached) to the stand. An initial length of 0.6m **(x)**_____ (use). |
| Results | To describe graphs | | The results of the eight measurements **(xi)**_____ (show) in Table 1. Column 1 **(xii)**_____ (show) the length of the pendulum, measured in metres |
| Discussion | Showing results of calculations | | Multiplying the gradient by $4\pi^2$ to calculate $g$ **(xiii)**_____ (give) a value of 9.71 ms$^{-2}$, which **(xiv)**_____ (be) close to the accepted value of 9.79 ms$^{-2}$. |
| Discussion | Showing sources of error | | There **(xv)**_____ (be) various possible sources of error. |
| Conclusion | To state conclusion | | Using a simple pendulum, a value of $g = 9.71$ ms$^{-2}$ **(xvi)**_____ (obtain) as the value of gravity in Guangzhou, which is close to the accepted value. |

# Exercise 3: **Learning outcomes check**

a) The following are the learning outcomes for this unit. Decide how well you have mastered each one by giving it a score, as follows.

    3 = I understand/can do this well.
    2 = I understand/can do this fairly well, but I can improve with more practice.
    1 = I understand/can do this, but not well enough yet. I need to practise more.
    0 = I do not understand/cannot do this yet. I need more time.

| Score | Learning Outcome |
|---|---|
| _____ | I understand what a laboratory report is. |
| _____ | I understand the different sections of a typical laboratory report . |
| _____ | I understand the function of each section. |
| _____ | I am aware of language phrases to use in different sections of a laboratory report. |

b) Use this information to review the unit and improve.

# Unit 14 | Business Reports

## Learning Outcomes

By the end of this unit, you should:
- understand what a business report is;
- understand the different sections of a business report;
- understand the function of each section.

By completing the exercises, you will also:
- study a business report for content, structure and language.

## Key Vocabulary

*Nouns*
- letter of transmittal
- literature review

## Additional Vocabulary

*Academic Collocations (in unit)*
- additional information (adj + n)
- existing research (adj + n)
- main findings (adj + n)
- relevant information (adj + n)
- secondary sources (adj + n)
- seem unlikely (v + adj)
- achieve an objective (v + n)
- gather information (v + n)
- identify problems (v + n)
- make recommendations (v + n)

*Academic Collocations (in report)*
- higher value (adj + n)
- publicly available (adv + adj)
- significantly higher (adv + adj)
- slightly higher (adv +adj)

# Contents of this section

## Unit 14: Business Reports .................................. 199
- Overview .................................................................. 200
- What is a business report? ........................................ 200
- Structure of business reports ................................... 201
- Checklist ................................................................. 205
- Example report ....................................................... 207
- Exercises ................................................................. 213

## Overview

Business reports are essential in the world of business, and are therefore often used as assessments in disciplines such as accounting, finance, management and marketing. This section considers what a business report is and how to structure this type of report.

## What is a business report?

In industry, a business report is written in order to help an organisation achieve an objective, for example to increase sales of a particular product or to improve its financial situation. At university, business reports simulate this real-world experience by asking you to analyse a situation (real or simulated) and apply business theory in order to come up with solutions or recommendations. In finance, for example, you might be asked to analyse a company's financial data and write a report on the findings; in marketing, you might be required to write a report on the marketing mix of a company and make recommendations; in management, you might be required to write a report on the management structure of an organisation and suggest ways it could be improved. Key skills in business report writing are therefore the ability to apply business theory to real world situations, to identify problems, to suggest solutions, to interpret information and to make recommendations.

**Consider the audience**

For any kind of writing, it is important to consider the audience. This is especially so for a business report, since there are many possible people the report might be intended for (e.g. finance personnel, marketing staff, the CEO). At university, the audience might be simulated, e.g. 'Write a report for the CEO…'. Understanding who the audience is, what they know, why they need the report and what they will do with the information, will help you decide how to write the report and what to include (and exclude).

# Unit 14: **Business Reports**

## Structure of business reports

The exact structure of a business report may vary according to discipline, but is likely to follow the general pattern outlined below. Each area is discussed in more detail later.

**Preliminaries**
- Title page
- Letter of Transmittal
- Executive Summary
- Contents

**Introduction**
- Introduction
  Background, purpose, scope.
  Outline of report, key terms.

**Main body**
- Literature Review
  What do other writers say?
- Methodology
  How did you collect data?
- Findings
  What is the data?
- Discussion
  What does the data mean?

**Conclusion**
- Conclusion
  What are the conclusions?
- Recommendations
  What should happen next?

**End matter**
- Reference section
- Appendices

# Academic Writing Genres     Sheldon Smith

The *Preliminaries* for a business report are mostly similar to a general report (Unit 12). There should be a **Title page**, with a brief, clear and informative title, as well as other details such as author's name, name of person the report is written for, and date of submission. One unique element of a business report is the **Letter of Transmittal**. This is a brief cover letter to the person who requested the report, with information such as scope of the report and the problems which the report addresses. It is *not* usually used for reports at university. A business report will usually need an **Executive Summary**. The purpose of the *Executive Summary* is to save a busy executive time by giving them the main points so they do not need to read the whole report. As such, it should summarise key information such as the purpose, scope, main findings, conclusions and recommendations. It should be short, around 10-15% of the length of the report, often on a separate (single) page, probably between one and three paragraphs in length. Finally, long reports should include a **Contents page** (this may be omitted for short reports).

> **In short**
> A business report usually contains the following.
> - **Title page**
> - **Letter of Transmittal**
> - **Executive Summary** (10-15% of report)
> - **Contents page**
> - **Introduction** – background, key terms, purpose, scope, outline
> - **Literature Review** – what other writers say
> - **Methodology** – *how*, *where* and *when* data was gathered
> - **Findings** – *what* the data is
> - **Discussion** – *why* the data is important, i.e. what it means
> - **Conclusion**
> - **Recommendations**
> - **Reference section**
> - **Appendices**

The **Introduction** should provide all the information necessary for the reader to understand the body of the report. It will usually begin with *background* information, which may, for example, give the events which led to problem which the report addresses and outline the context, such as company size, management structure, or main activities the company is engaged in. It may also be necessary to define *key terms* required in the body of the report. The Introduction should also give the *purpose* of the report, the *scope* (what aspects will be covered, what will be excluded), and an *outline* of the report structure.

The *main body* can have many possible sections, depending on the nature of the report. The structure of a business report is not as prescribed as a laboratory report (Unit 13), which means there will be much more variation of sections and (especially) subsections.

The main body of a Business report may begin with a **Literature Review**. This gives a critical summary of the existing research in the field to identify gaps and create a starting point for your own research. Not all reports require this section. If you are including it in your report, make sure it is needed.

> *Literature reviews are covered in more detail in Unit 22.*

# Unit 14: Business Reports

Another common section is **Methodology**. This will outline how you gathered information, when and where. This section, if included, is likely to be very brief.

A **Findings** section is where you present the data you gathered through the research tools given in the *Methodology*. This section is factual, i.e. it does not contain opinion. It may be sub-divided, depending on the nature of the findings.

The **Discussion** section is where you analyse the facts presented earlier. This is where you will present your opinions. These should be 'expert' opinions, inasmuch as they are grounded in theory (which should be suitably cited). This section is likely to have many subsections, depending on the scope and purpose of the report. *Marketing* reports, for example, may contain subsections related to standard marketing tools such as *PESTEL* (Political, Economic, Social, Technological, Environmental, Legal), *PEST*, *SWOT* (Strengths, Weaknesses, Opportunities, Threats), *STP* (Segmentation, Targeting, Positioning) and *Target Market Analysis*. In *Management accounting* reports there may be subsections such as *financial analysis* or *NPV (Net Present Value) analysis*.

| Effective headings |
| --- |
| When using headings, try to: <br> • make them clearly describe the section content; <br> • ensure all content relates to the heading; <br> • use sentence format (capital for the first letter only, not all words); <br> • use parallel form for headings at the same level (e.g. all noun phrases, or all beginning with a verb); <br> • use font size to show hierarchy of headings (main headings larger, sub-headings smaller). |

It is possible to combine the *Discussion* section with the *Findings* section, to create a section called *Findings and discussion*, or just *Findings*, though it is important to remember that the facts (findings) should be separated from your opinions (discussion). This section may include figures (graphs or other visual material), or refer the reader to the appendices. It is more common in business reports than laboratory reports for additional material to be put in the appendices rather than in the main body.

The **Conclusion** section should summarise the key points in the *Discussion*. No new points should be included. A business report is likely to finish with **Recommendations**. This will suggest possible actions and who should carry them out. The recommendations may be numbered. If some of the recommendations seem unlikely to be adopted, giving alternatives may be helpful. This section may be combined with the *Conclusion* section.

As with any report, there should be suitable *End matter*. This means a **Reference section** for any sources cited, and **Appendices** of additional information, such as visuals or data collection tools such as questionnaires or interview questions.

The following chart summarises the stages of a business report, the structural components, and the purpose of each component.

| Stage of report | Structural component | Purpose |
| --- | --- | --- |
| **Preliminaries** | Title page | Gives information such as the title of report, name(s) of the author(s), date of submission, word count. |
| | Letter of transmittal | Gives scope of the report and problems which the report addresses (written as a cover letter). |
| | Executive summary | Summarises key information (purpose, scope, main findings, conclusions and recommendations). |
| | Contents page | Lists all the headings and sub-headings in the report, together with the page numbers. |
| **Introduction** | Introduction | Gives background information. Defines key terms. States purpose, scope and outline of report. |
| **Main body** | Literature review | Gives a critical summary of existing research. |
| | Methodology | Outlines how/when/where information was gathered. |
| | Findings | Presents the data. |
| | Discussion | Analyses the data to give 'expert' opinions, grounded in theory. May include graphs and other figures. |
| **Conclusion** | Conclusion | Summarises the main points of the report. |
| | Recommendations | Suggests possible actions and who will carry them out. |
| **End matter** | Reference section | Lists any sources cited in the text, with full details. |
| | Appendices | Provides any detailed information not needed for the main body (e.g. questionnaires, interview questions). |

Unit 14: **Business Reports**

# Checklist

Below is a checklist for business reports. You can use this to check your own writing, or ask a peer to help.

| Stage | Section | Item | OK? | Comments |
|---|---|---|---|---|
| **Preliminaries** | **Title page** | The report has a clear and informative title. | | |
| | | Other relevant information is included on the title page (e.g. student name, student ID, name of lecturer, word count). | | |
| | **Letter of Transmittal** | There is a Letter of Transmittal, if necessary. | | |
| | **Executive Summary** | An Executive Summary has been included (if necessary), which is between 10-15%, one to three paragraphs in length, on a separate sheet. | | |
| | **Contents page** | A contents page is included, if appropriate (may be omitted for short reports). | | |
| **Introduction** | **Background** | The Introduction contains necessary background information (e.g. origin of the problem, company size, management structure, main activities of the company). | | |
| | **Definitions** | There are definitions of key terms required in the body. | | |
| | **Purpose and Scope** | The Introduction gives the purpose of the report and the scope (what aspects will be covered, what will be excluded). | | |
| | **Outline** | There is an outline of the report structure | | |

| | | | | |
|---|---|---|---|---|
| **Main body** | **Literature Review** | If necessary, there is a critical review of existing research. | | |
| | **Methodology** | There is an outline of how information was gathered, when and where. | | |
| | **Findings** | The findings (factual data) are presented. *May be combined with Discussion.* | | |
| | **Discussion** | The findings are analysed and 'expert' opinions are given, referring to theory. | | |
| | | There are suitable subsections, e.g. Strengths, Weaknesses, Opportunities, Threats (SWOT). | | |
| **Conclusion** | **Conclusions** | There is a summary of the main points. | | |
| | **Recommend-ations** | There are recommendations for future action, including who should carry them out. *May be combined with Conclusions.* | | |
| **End matter** | **Reference section** | There is a reference section with full details of all sources cited. | | |
| | **Appendices** | Appendices are clearly presented. | | |
| | **General** | Tables and figures have suitable headings, placed *above* the tables and *beneath* the figures. | | |
| | | Suitable font and font size have been used (including larger size for headings). | | |
| | | The report is within the specified word limit. | | |
| | | Secondary sources (in the *Literature Review* or *Discussion*) are paraphrased and have suitable in-text citations. | | |
| | | Headings clearly describe the section content, use sentence format (capital for the first letter only), and have parallel form (e.g. all noun phrases). | | |

Unit 14: **Business Reports**

# Example report

Below is an example business report. It is used in one of the exercises later. For simplicity, the report does not include title page, contents or appendices. Some of the main body content has also been removed to make it more concise.

This report is adapted from: https://www.scirp.org/journal/PaperInformation.aspx?PaperID=69287#t2. Data and some of the structure and content have been retained from the original, but graphs have been replotted, and most of the content has been altered.

**Ratio Analysis of Tesco Plc between 2010 and 2014 in Comparison to Sainsbury and Morrisons**

## Executive summary

This report analyzes the financial performance of Tesco Plc between 2010 and 2014 and compares it with the performance of Morrisons and Sainsbury during the same period. The publicly available financial statements of these three companies were used as the data source. From the data analysis, it is clear that from 2010 to 2014, the performance of the company was unsatisfactory when compared to other companies in the same industry. It is recommended that Tesco proceed with caution with its international expansion, first ensuring it has a strong position in relation to its competitors in its core UK market base.

## 1. Introduction

### 1.1 Ratio analysis

Ratio analysis is a method of assessing the condition and performance of a company by using the company's financial statements (Gitman *et al.*, 2018). This can be done by comparing the performance in a particular year to previous years, by comparing it to industry averages, or, as in this report, to comparing it to other companies in the same industry over the same time period.

### 1.2 Tesco Plc

Tesco Plc is a leading global retailer, with over 3,400 stores and 300,000 employees in the UK (Tesco, 2018a). It was founded in 1919 in Hackney, London, and is now headquartered in Welwyn Garden City, Hertfordshire, UK (Tesco, 2018b). As shown in Figure 1, Tesco is the leading supermarket in the UK, with a 27.7% market share (Kantar WorldPanel, 2018). Its closest competitors are Sainsbury (15.7%), Asda (15.5%) and Morrisons (10.5%). This report will compare Tesco to Sainsbury and Morrisons, since full financial data is not available for Asda.

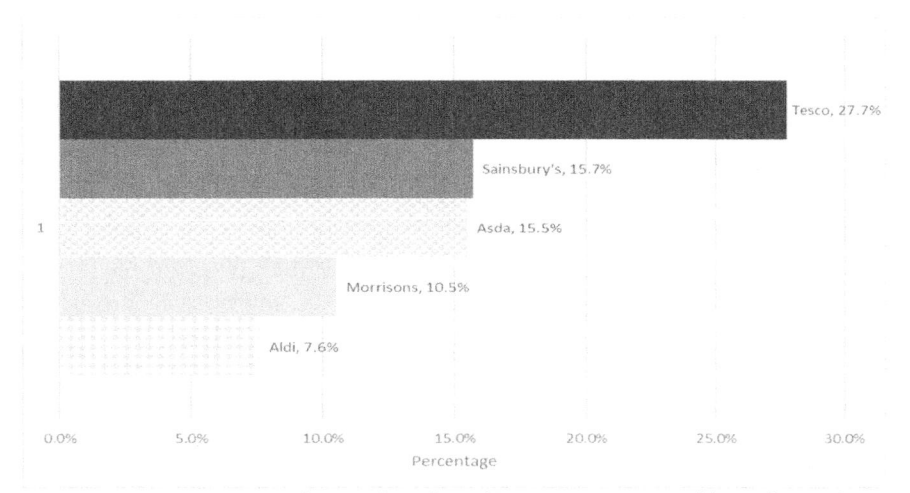

Figure 1. UK supermarket market share (Source: Kantar WorldPanel, 2018)

Globally Tesco has over 6,800 stores and 440,000 employees (Tesco, 2018c). Total sales of the Tesco group in

2016/17 financial year amount to £51 billion, with profits of £1.8 billion (Tesco, 2018d). Berlingske Media (2018) states that Tesco focuses mainly on food products, with strong brand recognition in the UK which it has used to expand into the banking sector. It has used its growth to expand internationally, especially into Asia, including the Chinese market, as well as the western US market (Berlingske Media, 2018).

### 1.3 Aim
The aim of this report is to assess the performance of Tesco Plc between 2010 and 2014 by comparing it to two of its closest rivals.

## 2. Methodology
The data for this report was taken from publicly available financial statements of Tesco, Sainsbury and Morrisons for the years 2010 to 2014.

## 3. Findings and discussion
This report considers a range of ratios to analyse Tesco's performance over the period covered. The ratios used are profitability ratios, efficiency ratios, liquidity ratios, financial ratios, and shareholders ratios.

### 3.1. Profitability ratios
According to Gitman *et al.* (2018), profitability ratios measure how efficiently a company is being managed and how well it is using its resources to generate profit. For the majority of these ratios, having a higher value in relation to a competitor, or to a previous period for the same company, is an indication that the company is performing well. Two important profitability ratios are *Return on capital employed (ROCE)* and *net profit margin*.

#### 3.1.1 Return on capital employed
*Return on capital employed (ROCE)* measures the relationship between profit and capital employed (Fernandes, 2014). It is significant since it highlights the success of the business from the shareholder's perspective and demonstrates how efficient the handling of the company's investment is. The higher the ratio, the better the business is doing. ROCE is given by the following equation.

$$ROCE = \frac{\text{Operating Profit (before interest and tax)}}{\text{Ordinary Share Capital + Reserve + Long-term borrowing}}$$

Table 1 shows the ROCE for Tesco from 2010 to 2014. Tesco's ROCE was generally stable from year to year, though there was a decline in 2013.

| Year | 2010 | 2011 | 2012 | 2013 | 2014 |
|---|---|---|---|---|---|
| Operating Profit | 3,457 | 3,811 | 4,182 | 2,188 | 2,631 |
| Ordinary share + Reserve | 14,596 | 16,535 | 17,775 | 16,643 | 14,715 |
| Long term borrowing | 11,580 | 9,541 | 9,777 | 9,946 | 9,188 |
| ROCE | 13.21% | 14.61% | 15.17% | 8.22% | 11.00% |

Table 1. Return on capital employed of Tesco Plc from 2010 to 2014
(Source: Tesco Plc financial reports in 2010, 2011, 2012, 2013 and 2014).

Figure 2 shows the ROCE of Tesco in comparison to its rivals (full data given in Appendix 1). It is generally higher than both Sainsbury and Morrisons, though Sainsbury has overtaken it in the final two years, while Morrisons has seen a sharp decline.

Unit 14: **Business Reports**

ROCE

| | 2010 | 2011 | 2012 | 2013 | 2014 |
|---|---|---|---|---|---|
| Tesco | 13.21% | 14.61% | 15.17% | 8.22% | 11.00% |
| Sainsbury | 9.70% | 10.96% | 10.60% | 10.62% | 12.22% |
| Morrisons | 13.73% | 12.80% | 12.88% | 11.58% | 1.20% |

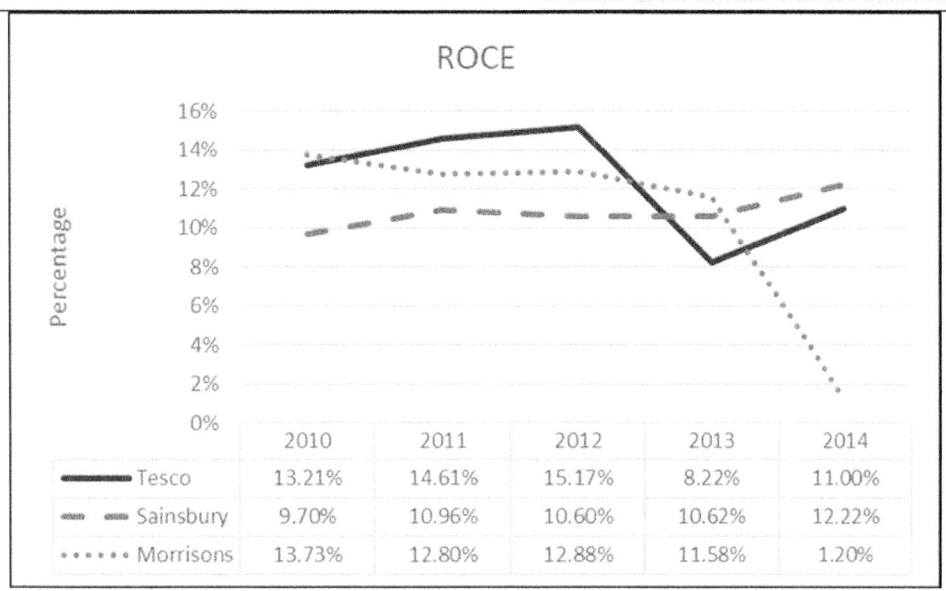

Figure 2. ROCE for Tesco Plc, Sainsbury and Morrissons.

### 3.1.2 Net profit margin

The *net profit margin,* also called *return on sales,* gives a percentage of the amount of money remaining once all expenses, including tax, have been deducted (Gitman *et al.,* 2018). Higher values are better than lower ones. The equation for this ratio is given below.

$$\text{Net Profit Margin} = \frac{\text{Net Profit}}{\text{Revenue}}$$

Net profit margin for Tesco over this period is shown in Table 2. The figures ranged from 5.94% to 3.02%, with a sharp downward trend over the final two years.

| Year | Net Profit Margin |
|---|---|
| 2010 | 5.58% |
| 2011 | 5.80% |
| 2012 | 5.94% |
| 2013 | 3.02% |
| 2014 | 3.55% |

Table 2. Tesco Plc's net profit margin from 2010 to 2014
(Sources: Tesco Plc's financial reports in 2010, 2011, 2012, 2013 & 2014).

Figure 3 compares Tesco's performance with that of Morrisons and Sainsbury (for full data, see Appendix 1). Tesco performed well during this period in comparison to its rivals, with a significantly higher net profit margin than Sainsbury and slightly higher than Morrisons between 2010 and 2012, and significantly higher than Morrisons in 2014, though slightly lower than Sainsbury in this year. Only in 2013 was its performance unsatisfactory, and then only in relation to Morrisons.

## Net Profit Margin

| | 2010 | 2011 | 2012 | 2013 | 2014 |
|---|---|---|---|---|---|
| Tesco | 5.58% | 5.80% | 5.94% | 3.02% | 3.55% |
| Sainsbury | 3.67% | 3.91% | 3.58% | 3.31% | 3.75% |
| Morrisons | 5.57% | 5.30% | 5.36% | 4.85% | 0.99% |

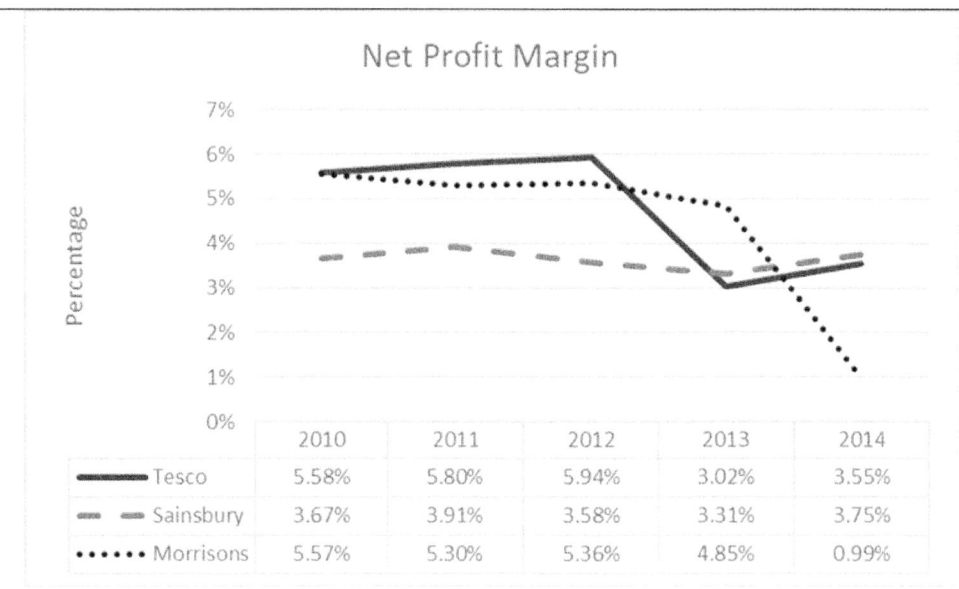

Figure 3. Net profit ratio.

## 3.2 Efficiency ratios

These ratios analyze how well an organization makes use of its resources to generate revenue. A key efficiency ratio is the *asset turnover ratio*.

### 3.2.1 Asset turnover ratio

According to Bodie, Kane and Marcus (2004), *asset turnover ratio* measures how well a company uses its assets to generate profit. The formula is as follows.

$$\text{Asset Turnover Ratio} = \frac{\text{Revenue}}{\text{Average total assets}}$$

As shown in Table 3, Tesco's asset turnover ratio increased over the period, from 2.17 in 2010 to 2.66 in 2014.

| Year | Revenue | Average total assets | Asset turnover ratio |
|---|---|---|---|
| 2010 | 56,910 | 26,176 | 2.17 |
| 2011 | 60,931 | 26,076 | 2.33 |
| 2012 | 64,539 | 27,552 | 2.34 |
| 2013 | 64,826 | 26,589 | 2.44 |
| 2014 | 63,557 | 23,903 | 2.66 |

Table 3. Assets turnover of Tesco Plc from 2010 to 2014.

Figure 4, however, indicates that Sainsbury performed better than Tesco with regard to its asset turnover ratio in the period under review. Sainsbury's asset turnover ratio is higher than that of Tesco in each year. Indeed, its lowest figure, of 2.70 in 2012, is higher than Tesco's highest figure, of 2.66 in 2014. While initially below Morrisons at the start of this period, Tesco has pulled above this competitor during the final three years.

## Asset Turnover Ratio

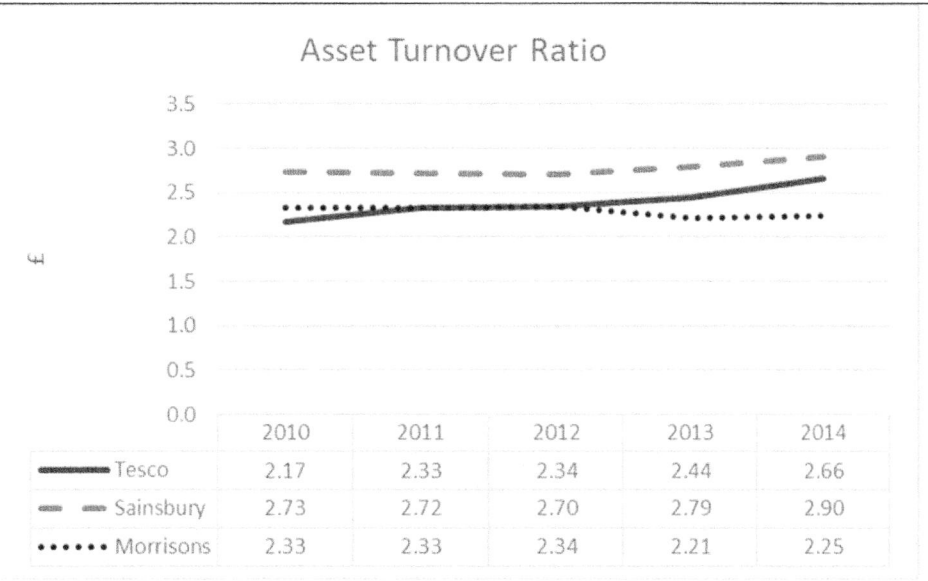

| | 2010 | 2011 | 2012 | 2013 | 2014 |
|---|---|---|---|---|---|
| Tesco | 2.17 | 2.33 | 2.34 | 2.44 | 2.66 |
| Sainsbury | 2.73 | 2.72 | 2.70 | 2.79 | 2.90 |
| Morrisons | 2.33 | 2.33 | 2.34 | 2.21 | 2.25 |

Figure 4. Asset turnover of Tesco Plc compared with Sainsbury and Morrisons.

### 3.3 Liquidity ratios

Liquidity ratios are used to measure a company's ability to meet short-term debts (Gitman *et al.*, 2018). A company with good liquidity can obtain funds more easily in comparison to competitors with lower liquidity. Companies compare liquidity with competitors on an annual basis in order to make decisions (Lundholm, and Sloan, 2012). The three main measures of liquidity are the *current ratio,* the *acid-test (quick) ratio,* and *net working capital.*

-----
*[Note: For brevity, the rest of the main body has not been included. The headings are retained, as is the Conclusion and Recommendations section and the References.]*
-----

#### 3.3.1 Current ratio
...

#### 3.3.2 Acid-test (quick) ratio
...

#### 3.3.3 Net working capital
...

### 3.4 Financial ratios
...

#### 3.4.1 Gearing ratio
...

#### 3.4.2 Interest coverage ratio
...

### 3.5 Shareholders ratios
...

### 3.5.1 Price/earnings ratio
...

### 3.5.2 Dividend cover
...

https://html.scirp.org/file/ 4-2670078_12.htm

## 4. Conclusion and recommendations
In summary, the ratio analysis of Tesco Plc shows that overall, the company performance between 2010 and 2014 was unsatisfactory when compared to other companies in the same industry, namely Sainsbury and Morrisons. While some ratios, such as the profitability ratios ROCE and net profit margin, show a positive performance for Tesco, most ratios demonstrate the opposite trend. It is recommended that Tesco proceed with caution with its international expansion, first ensuring it has a strong position in relation to its competitors in its core UK market base.

## References
Berlingske Media (2018) *Company profile*. Available from: https://www.euroinvestor.com/exchanges/xetra/tesco-plc-ls-05/10090477 (Accessed 20 December 2018).

Bodie, Z., Kane, A. and Marcus, A.J. (2004) *Essentials of Investments*, 5th ed. New York: McGraw-Hill.

Fernandes, N. (2014) *Finance for Executives: A Practical Guide for Managers*. New York: NPV Publishing.

Gitman, L.J., McDaniel, C., Shah, A., Reece, M., Koffel, L., Talsma, B. and Hyatt, J.C. (2018) *Introduction to Business*. Houston: OpenStax.

Kantar WorldPanel (2018) *Grocery Market Share (12 weeks ending)*. Available from: https://www.kantarworldpanel.com/en/grocery-market-share/great-britain (Accessed 20 December 2018).

Lundholm, R. and Sloan, R. (2012) *Equity Valuation and Analysis*. New York.: McGraw Hill/Irwin.

Tesco (2018a) *Tesco UK*. Available from: https://www.tescoplc.com/about-us/our-businesses/tesco-uk/tesco-in-the-uk/ (Accessed 1 December 2018).

Tesco (2018b) *History*. Available from: https://www.tescoplc.com/about-us/history/ (Accessed 1 December 2018).

Tesco (2018c) *Our Business*. Available from: https://www.tescoplc.com/about-us/our-businesses/ (Accessed 1 December 2018).

Tesco (2018d) *Key Facts*. Available from: https://www.tescoplc.com/about-us/key-facts/ (Accessed 1 December 2018).

Unit 14: **Business Reports**

# Exercises

## Exercise 1: **Comprehension**

Answer the following questions about this unit. Either do this after reading the unit, or make notes first then use the notes to answer the questions.

1 What is a business report?

_____

_____

2 What are some of the key skills involved in writing a business report?

_____

_____

3 The following shows common components or sections of a business report. The first letter of each is given. Complete the word(s). Some examples have been done.
 [Note: some answers are *more than one* word.]

- T_____
- Letter of transmittal
- Executive summary
- C_____
- I_____
- L_____
- M_____
- F_____
- D_____
- C_____
- R_____
- A_____

4 What is a *Letter of transmittal*?

_____

_____

5 What is an *Executive summary*? How long should it be? How is it usually formatted?

_____

_____

_____

**6** What elements may be contained in the *Introduction* section of a business report?

- _____
- _____
- _____
- _____
- _____

**7** What is the difference between the *Findings* and the *Discussion* section?

_____
_____
_____

**8** Give examples of some business tools which could be used to structure the *Discussion* section of the text.

_____
_____
_____
_____

**9** Which sections of a business report are sometimes combined?

_____
_____
_____

**10** Why is the audience especially important for a business report?

_____
_____
_____

# Unit 14: Business Reports

## Exercise 2: **Example report**

Study the example report on *ratio analysis of Tesco Plc* (earlier in this unit) and answer the following questions.

a) The following shows a *Table of contents* for the report. Some headings are missing. Complete the missing headings by referring to the report.

1. Introduction .................................................................1
    1.1 Ratio analysis........................................................1
    1.2 **(i)** _____ ...............................1
    1.3 Aim .......................................................................1
2. Methodology ...............................................................2
3. Findings and discussion..............................................2
    3.1 **(ii)** _____ ratios ....................2
        3.1.1 Return on capital employed.....................2
        3.1.2 **(iii)** _____ ..................3
    3.2 **(iv)** _____ ratios...................4
        3.2.1 Asset turnover ratio ................................4
    3.3 **(v)** _____ ratios......................5
        3.3.1 **(vi)** _____ ratio ..............5
        3.3.2 **(vii)** _____ ratio.............5
        3.3.3 Net working capital ................................5
    3.4 Financial ratios .................................................5
        3.4.1 **(viii)** _____ ratio............5
        3.4.2 Interest coverage ratio ............................5
    3.5 Shareholders ratios ..........................................6
        3.5.1 **(ix)** _____ ratio .............6
        3.5.2 Dividend cover .......................................6
4. Conclusion and recommendations............................6
**(x)** _____ ................................................6
Appendices ......................................................................6

b) Complete the following summary of the report, by using the *Executive summary*.

> The report gives an analysis of the **(i)** _____ performance of **(ii)** _____ between 2010 and **(iii)** _____ by comparing it to the performance of **(iv)** _____ and **(v)** _____. The performance of the company was **(vi)** _____ when compared to those other companies. The recommendation is for Tesco to move carefully as it expands into **(vii)** _____ markets, by first making sure it has a relatively strong position in the **(viii)** _____ market.

c) The report contains answers to the following questions.
- First, decide which section(s) or subsection(s) you think will contain the answer. Do this for *all* of the questions *before* looking at the report for the answer. Use the *Table of contents* above to help.
- Then, look through the report to find the answer to each question. Try to do this as *quickly as possible*. [Hint: Use the headings to help.]
- At the same time, check to see whether the answer was in the section you expected.

| Question | Section(s) | Answer |
|---|---|---|
| 1. In which year was Tesco's net profit margin at its lowest? What was the value in that year? | | |
| 2. What action for the future does the author recommend? | | |
| 3. What is the source of the financial data? | | |
| 4. Which two companies was Tesco compared with in the report? | | |
| 5. What is the equation for *asset turnover ratio*? | | |
| 6. In section 3.2.1, the author cites Bodie, Kane and Marcus (2004). What is the name of the book the author has read for this citation? | | |
| 7. How many people work for Tesco Plc in the UK, and how many people work for the company worldwide? | | |
| 8. What is the overall performance of Tesco Plc from 2010-2014? | | |
| 9. What is ratio analysis? | | |
| 10. Which company had the highest ROCE in 2014? | | |

d) Study the report again and find examples of *language phrases* for all of the following:
- stating the aim;
- referring to tables or graphs;
- giving recommendations.

# Unit 14: **Business Reports**

## Exercise 3: **Learning outcomes check**

a) The following are the learning outcomes for this unit. Decide how well you have mastered each one by giving it a score, as follows.

    3 = I understand/can do this well.
    2 = I understand/can do this fairly well, but I can improve with more practice.
    1 = I understand/can do this, but not well enough yet. I need to practise more.
    0 = I do not understand/cannot do this yet. I need more time.

| Score | Learning Outcome |
|---|---|
| _____ | I understand what a business report is. |
| _____ | I understand the different sections of a business report. |
| _____ | I understand and the function of each section. |

b) Use this information to review the unit and improve.

# Unit 15 | Other Report Types

## Learning Outcomes

By the end of this unit, you should:
- understand what the following report types are: research report, case study report, progress report, project report, design report, field report, and technical report;
- understand the content of the above report types;
- know how to structure each of the above report types.

## Key Vocabulary

**Nouns**
- case study

**Adjectives**
- illustrative
- exploratory
- explanatory
- cumulative
- critical

## Additional Vocabulary

*Academic Collocations*
- common themes (adj + n)
- considerable variation (adj + n)
- external sources (adj + n)
- future research (adj + n)
- initial research (adj + n)
- key issues (adj + n)
- main findings (adj + n)
- possible sources (adj + n)
- previous research (adj + n)
- relevant literature (adj + n)
- typical example (adj + n)
- collect data (v + n)
- collect information (v + n)
- describe methods (v + n)
- give information (v + n)
- make recommendations (v + n)
- test theory (v + n)

## Contents of this section

### Unit 15: Other Report Types .......................... 219
  Overview ................................................................. 220
  Research reports ..................................................... 220
  Case study reports .................................................. 221
  Progress reports ..................................................... 222
  Project reports ....................................................... 223
  Design reports ....................................................... 224
  Field reports .......................................................... 225
  Technical reports ................................................... 226
  Exercises ............................................................... 227

# Academic Writing Genres                                          Sheldon Smith

## Overview

There are many other reports which can be written at university. Some of the most common, considered in this section, are *research reports, case study reports, progress reports, project reports, design reports, field reports,* and *technical reports*. Each report type is explained briefly, and a suggested structure is given.

## Research reports

A research report gives the results of research which has been conducted, for example through surveys using questionnaires or interviews. Research reports are similar to laboratory reports (Unit 13) in many ways. Both involve a method used to collect data, which will be analysed and presented in the form of tables, graphs or charts. The main difference is that rather than testing theory or a hypothesis, research reports seek to find answers to research questions. The following is a possible structure.

[*Note: An example research report is given in Unit 12.*]

| Section | Contents |
| --- | --- |
| **Title page** | Includes details such as title of report, number of words, name of author. |
| **Executive summary/Abstract** | Summarises the report contents (including what the research problem is, why it is important, methods of collecting data, findings and what the findings mean). |
| **Contents** | Lists the sections in the report, with page numbers. |
| **Introduction** | Outlines the context, background and purpose of the research. Defines necessary terms, and gives the scope (limits) of the research. |
| **Literature review** | Gives a critical discussion of previous research on the topic, which provides further context as well as justification for the research. Not all research reports include this. |
| **Methodology** | Explains how research was conducted. For example, for the results of a survey, the reader will need to know how, when and where the survey was conducted, how the target group was selected, how many people were surveyed, how they were surveyed (interview or questionnaire), and why this approach was chosen. |
| **Results** | Gives the results of the research, often using tables or graphs. This section should contain facts (no interpretation). May be combined with *Discussion*. |
| **Discussion** | Interprets and evaluates the results, with reference to literature. May give potential errors and ways to improve the research design. |
| **Conclusion** | Restates the research problem and summarises the main findings and their significance. May also state problems with the research. |
| **Recommendations** | Gives recommendations for future research. May be combined with *Conclusion*. |
| **References** | Lists any external sources referred to in the report. |
| **Appendices** | Gives information not crucial to the main body of the report, e.g. questionnaire, interview questions, consent form. |

# Unit 15: Other Reports

# Case study reports

A case study report, also called case study, case write-up or case report, analyses a single, typical example (the 'case') using specialist concepts (the 'study'). The case could be an organization, an event, a location, a person or a group of people. The case study is common in the field of business (where the case may be, for example, a particular company), though it is used in other disciplines, including education (where the case could be a school) and medicine (where the case may be a hospital, a ward, or a single patient).

There are several types of case study which can form the basis of a case study report. **Illustrative case studies** describe a case, explain what is happening and why, and bring it to the attention of the reader. **Exploratory cases studies**, also called *pilot case studies*, are initial research conducted before future, large-scale research. **Explanatory case studies** explain why and how something happened. **Cumulative case studies**, also called *collective case studies*, collect information from several past studies. **Critical instance case studies** explain a unique case and its particular characteristics, without attempting to generalise.

As with most reports, there are many ways to structure a case study report. The following provides a possible structure for a case study report, following the typical IMRAD structure.

| Section | Content |
| --- | --- |
| Title page | Includes details such as title, number of words, name of author. |
| Executive summary | Summarises the report contents. |
| Contents | Lists the sections in the report, with page numbers. |
| Introduction | Outlines the situation and identifies key issues or factors involved. Gives a detailed description of the case. |
| Literature review | Describes and evaluates previous research or theories which relate to the case. |
| Method | Outlines the methods used to get information, and why you chose them. |
| Results | Outlines the results. |
| Discussion | Analyses the results. Gives the causes (e.g. for *explanatory* case study) or possible solutions, related to the research considered earlier and your own experience. |
| Conclusion | Summarises the main findings of the report. If the case has a central problem, this section will give the strategy you propose to tackle the problem. |
| Recommendations | Gives recommendations for future work, or an action plan. May be combined with *Conclusion*. |
| Reflection | Reflects on the experience of writing the case study report. This section sometimes forms part of undergraduate reports, though is not part of formal reports. |
| References | Lists any external sources referred to in the report. |
| Appendices | Gives information not crucial to the main body of the report. |

# Progress reports

A progress report informs a supervisor or commercial organisation about progress that has been made on an activity over a certain period of time. The report may be needed to show that the work you are doing is on track according to your original proposal, that your results are meaningful, and (in the case of externally funded research) that the investment in the research is worthwhile. Progress reports may be required on a regular basis, or only at certain times during the activity.

If the report is requested by an organization or company, the commercial benefits are likely to be more important than the academic implications, which means that these should be emphasized. In such cases, the report is likely to be read by non-experts, and should be written accordingly, for example by including a glossary of terms.

There will usually be guidelines to follow in terms of structure, and there can be considerable variation. If the report is intended primarily for technical (research) personnel, a typical IMRAD structure may be appropriate. The following shows the possible contents of a progress report, following an IMRAD structure.

| Section | Contents |
| --- | --- |
| **Title page** | Includes details such as title of project, report number, date, name of author. |
| **Abstract** | Summarises the report contents. Could alternatively be an Executive Summary if the report is for a company rather than an academic body. |
| **Contents** | Lists the sections in the report, with page numbers. |
| **Glossary** | Explains terms and abbreviations so that non-experts will understand them. |
| **Introduction** | Outlines the period of work covered by the report and what was planned. |
| **Method** | Outlines the techniques used. These may have changed, in which case you should explain how and why. Even if they are the same, you should still describe them, though it is not necessary to go into much detail. Should refer back to any previous reports. |
| **Results** | Outlines what has been completed. |
| **Discussion** | Gives information on how your work has developed, how you have deviated from the original plan, the work planned for the future and an updated plan, with a clear description of the stages and timeline (possibly including future report dates). |
| **Conclusion** | Summarises the report. Gives an overall appraisal of the progress to date. |
| **Recommendations** | Gives appropriate recommendations, for example how the work can be further developed. |
| **References** | Lists any external sources referred to in the report. |
| **Appendices** | Gives information not crucial to the main body of the report. |

# Unit 15: **Other Reports**

# Project reports

A project report is used to report on a project which has been conducted. Before undertaking the project, be sure to discuss with your lecturer or supervisor to make sure it is appropriate.

The structure of the project report may be given by your lecturer or supervisor, and may be standard for your course. If not, the following is a possible structure for a project report, following the IMRAD structure of a typical report (though many other ways to structure this type of report are possible).

| Section | Contents |
| --- | --- |
| **Title page** | Includes details such as title of project, number of words, name of author. |
| **Abstract** | Summarises the report contents. |
| **Contents** | Lists the sections in the report, with page numbers. |
| **Introduction** | Outlines the project, including scope and aims. Gives any necessary background which the reader needs to know to understand the report. |
| **Method** | Outlines the project design and how information was gathered. For some disciplines, such as computer science, this section may be replaced with other sections, usually *Project Specification* (describes what the system does), *Design* (describes how it does it) and *Implementation* (describes specification and design in more detail, e.g. including computer code). |
| **Results** | Outlines the results of the project. |
| **Discussion** | Analyses the results and, if appropriate, evaluates the project design. |
| **Conclusion** | Summarises the report by stating what the main results were and whether the aims were met. |
| **Recommendations** | Gives recommendations, for example how the project design could be improved or how the work can be further developed. |
| **References** | Lists any external sources referred to in the report. |
| **Appendices** | Gives information not crucial to the main body of the report. |

# Design reports

A design report describes and evaluates a design which has been used to solve a particular problem. It is usually written for a supervisor or colleague whose knowledge is equal to or greater than yours. Design reports are common in Engineering.

There will usually be guidelines to follow in terms of structure. The following shows the possible contents of a design report.

| Section | Contents |
| --- | --- |
| **Title page** | Includes details such as title of report, number of words, name of author. |
| **Executive Summary** | Summarises the report contents. Should include elements of each of the main body areas (design problem, design description, design evaluation). |
| **Contents** | Lists the sections in the report, with page numbers. |
| **Design problem** | Describes the problem and gives the objectives of the design project. Provides the background to the design (why the problem is important, how it is currently solved). Gives criteria for evaluating the success of the design (e.g. cost, weight, comfort, durability), with the source of the criteria (e.g. from customer needs). Criteria should be measurable, and may be presented in a table. |
| **Design description** | Describes the design. Gives information on what the design does and how it works, with diagrams. Should contain subsections to break down the design description (which is likely to be very technical), for example looking at mechanical, electrical and software aspects. Should explain how the design is used. This section is likely to be the largest in the report. |
| **Design evaluation** | Evaluates the success of the design by comparing performance (via computer modelling or physical model) to design criteria. Physical models that were constructed should be described here. Summarises strengths and weaknesses of the design. Gives recommendations for future work. |
| **References** | Lists any external sources referred to in the report. |
| **Appendices** | Gives information not crucial to the main body of the report, e.g. drawings, rejected designs, cost of materials. |

# Unit 15: Other Reports

# Field reports

A field report combines theory and practice by describing an observed person, place or event in the natural environment (the 'field') and analysing the observation in order to identify common themes. The field report represents your interpretation of the meaning of the data that is gathered during the field study. This is a common assignment in disciplines such as social work, anthropology, education, law, and health care, where bridging theory and practice is important.

When conducting a field study, the person, place or event needs to be systematically observed and the details accurately recorded. This is done through activities such as note-taking, photography, video recording, audio recording, or drawing.

A field report can be structured in many ways, including the IMRAD structure. The following shows the possible contents of a field report, following an IMRAD structure.

| Section | Contents |
| --- | --- |
| **Title page** | Includes details such as title of report, number of words, name of author. |
| **Abstract** | Summarises the report contents. |
| **Contents** | Lists the sections in the report, with page numbers. |
| **Introduction** | Describes the background and purpose of the field study. Defines necessary terms. States the focus of the study. Reviews relevant literature on the topic. |
| **Method** | Describes methods used to collect data. Gives information on where the data was gathered, when, who or what was observed, why they were chosen for observation, and how the observation was conducted. |
| **Results** | Gives information on the data obtained in the field study. May be presented in the form of tables, graphs, photographs, diagrams, maps, sketches, or the results of interviews. |
| **Discussion** | Analyses and interprets the data from the field study, in relation to the theory (literature) described in the introduction. The theory will help you decide which observations are worth evaluating. Interpretation should be based on observation, rather than speculation. |
| **Conclusion and recommendations** | Summarises the main findings of the report. If the field study was intended to solve a problem, there should also be recommendations. |
| **References** | Lists any external sources referred to in the report. |
| **Appendices** | Gives information not crucial to the main body of the report, e.g. pictures, maps, drawings, transcripts of interviews. |

# Technical reports

Technical reports are written by engineers for the government, managers, clients or other engineers to describe technical research. The purpose of a technical report might be to convince stakeholders to pursue a particular course of action, to inform them of the outcomes or benefits of a project, to persuade them to choose one design rather than another, or simply to instruct others who will work from the design plans.

There are many ways to structure this type of report. The following shows one possible way, giving sections and contents.

| Section | Contents |
| --- | --- |
| **Title page** | Includes details such as title of report, number of words, name of author. |
| **Abstract** | Summarises the report contents. |
| **Contents** | Lists the sections in the report, with page numbers. |
| **Introduction** | Gives the purpose and scope of the report. Defines necessary terms. |
| **Background** | Gives background theory relevant to the report. May be replaced by Literature Review (critical discussion of previous research on the topic), if appropriate. |
| **Project description** | Gives details of the research project design. |
| **Findings and discussion** | Presents the results and analyses what the results mean. Likely to use tables and graphs. Considers possible sources of error. |
| **Conclusion and recommendations** | Summarises the main findings of the report. Makes recommendations. |
| **References** | Lists any external sources referred to in the report. |
| **Appendices** | Gives information not crucial to the main body of the report. |

# Unit 15: Other Reports

# Exercises

*Note: Since many of the reports covered in this section are very specialized, no example report is given, and there are no specific exercises. There is, however, an example research report in Unit 12, because this is a more common report type and is organized in a fairly standard way, making it a good general report to study.*

## Exercise 1: **Learning outcomes check**

a) The following are the learning outcomes for this unit. Decide how well you have mastered each one by giving it a score, as follows.

    3 = I understand/can do this well.
    2 = I understand/can do this fairly well, but I can improve with more practice.
    1 = I understand/can do this, but not well enough yet. I need to practise more.
    0 = I cannot do this yet. I need more time.

| Score | Learning Outcome |
|---|---|
| | I understand what the following report types* are: |
| _____ |    research report; |
| _____ |    case study report; |
| _____ |    progress report; |
| _____ |    project report; |
| _____ |    design report; |
| _____ |    field report; |
| _____ |    technical report. |
| _____ | I understand the content of the above report types (if required by my course*). |
| _____ | I know how to structure each of the above report types (if required*). |

*Your course of study may not require all of these report types. Study only the ones which are necessary.

b) Use this information to review the unit and improve.

# Part III:
# Other Genres

# Unit 16 | Posters

## Learning Outcomes

By the end of this unit, you should:
- know how to plan a poster;
- understand key elements of poster design;
- understand the type of content that is suitable for a poster.

By completing the exercises, you will also:
- compare and contrast two example posters;
- decide which poster you prefer, based on design and content;
- plan, design and create a poster;
- peer edit a poster, using a checklist.

## Key Vocabulary

**Nouns**
- main message
- illustrations
- design
- layout
- white space
- font
- sketch

**Verbs**
- laminate

## Additional Vocabulary

*Academic Collocations (unit)*
- further consideration (adj + n)
- key aspect (adj + n)
- little information (adj + n)
- personal contact (adj + n)
- relevant information (adj + n)
- carefully selected (adv + past)

*Academic Collocations (examples)*
- crucial importance (adj + n)
- technological development (adj + n)
- alternative strategies (adj + n)

## Contents of this section

### Unit 16: Posters ................................................. 231

- Overview ........................................................................ 232
- Planning a poster ........................................................... 233
- Poster design ................................................................. 234
- Poster content ............................................................... 236
- Checklist ........................................................................ 238
- Example poster #1 ......................................................... 240
- Example poster #2 ......................................................... 241
- Exercises ........................................................................ 242

# Overview

Posters are a common way to present work, for example at conferences. In some respects, a poster resembles a presentation visual aid, in that information must be presented clearly, succinctly and with visual impact. Posters differ from presentation visual aids, however, in that they must be self-contained, they usually take more time to prepare, and they cost more to produce.

Two examples of conference posters are shown below (Figure 16.1a, in portrait orientation, and Figure 16.2b, same dimensions but landscape orientation).

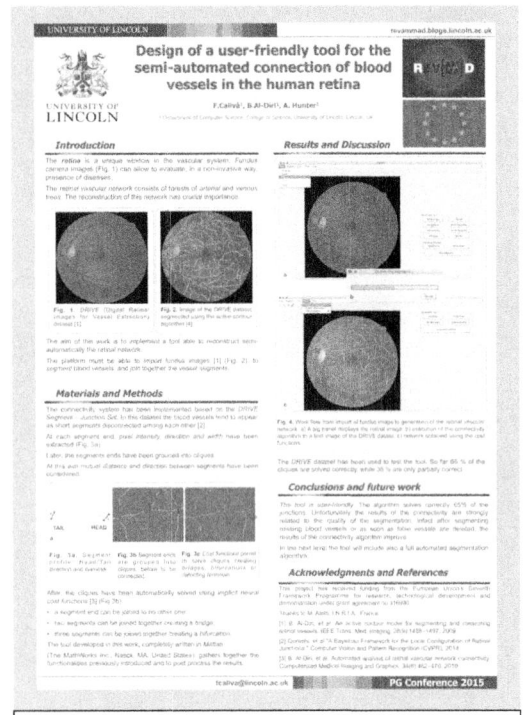

Figure 16.1a: An example conference poster (portrait orientation)

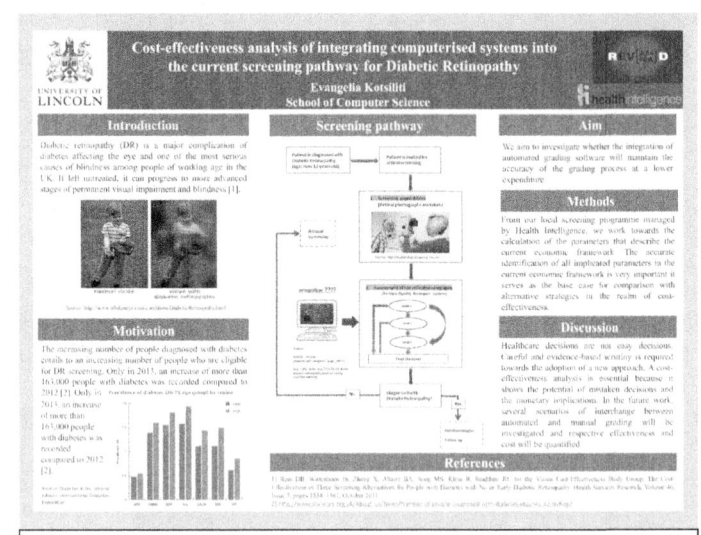

Figure 16.1b: An example conference poster (landscape orientation).

Source (16.1a): http://eprints.lincoln.ac.uk/16931/4/__ddat01_staffhome_bjones_RDS_Desktop_2015%20posters_CalivaFrancescoPGconf2.pdf

Source (16.1b): http://eprints.lincoln.ac.uk/16931/9/__ddat01_staffhome_bjones_RDS_Desktop_2015%20posters_PGR%20conference_poster%20Evi%20Kotsiliti.pdf

There are several benefits of presenting information via a poster. First, they offer choice, as participants can decide which to read, and how carefully, in contrast to having to sit through presentation after presentation. A poster is also beneficial to the presenter, as it can give them more personal contact with those who are interested in the information than is possible when giving a formal presentation. At the same time, unlike a presentation with a captive audience, the participants at a conference are free to view or ignore the poster as

# Unit 16: Posters

they please, and it can be depressing to spend a long time preparing a poster only to see many people walk past without even giving it a glace.

To maximise the chances that viewers will look at the poster, and to increase reader engagement, you need to make sure that it looks professional, and has the right balance between text and visuals. The rest of this unit gives guidelines to help.

Note that if you are planning to present a poster at a conference you will probably have to submit an abstract first so the organisers can decide who to invite to present their work.

> **In short**
> Posters, which are self-contained visual aids, are common at conferences. They allow:
> - participants to choose;
> - you to make more personal contact with the audience.

> *Abstracts* are covered in more detail in Unit 21.

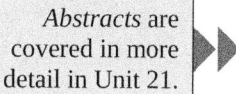

## Planning a poster

Before you start designing your poster and thinking about content, you need to plan what you will include. The first step is to consider what your **main message** is. What *one* thing do you want people to remember after they have viewed your poster?

Once you have decided on your main message, you will be able to decide **which points to include** to support the message. A poster will contain far less information than a report or research paper, and you will therefore need to be very *selective*.

A next step will be to consider which **illustrations** to use in the poster. These are arguably the most important part, as viewers are likely to focus much more on the illustrations than they do on the text, which they might just skim through. The illustrations you choose need to support your main message and add to the flow of information.

> **Tip: Be creative**
> Do not just cut up your conference paper and attach it to a large piece of card. It will contain far too much text and will not be appealing. Major yawn! Don't expect anyone to read it except friends and those who take pity on you.

When planning your poster, make sure you know the **size** your final poster will (or should) be. A typical size is 1.2m wide by 0.75m high (see Figure 16.2), though this will vary from conference to conference. The exact dimensions will determine the amount of information you can include and the overall design.

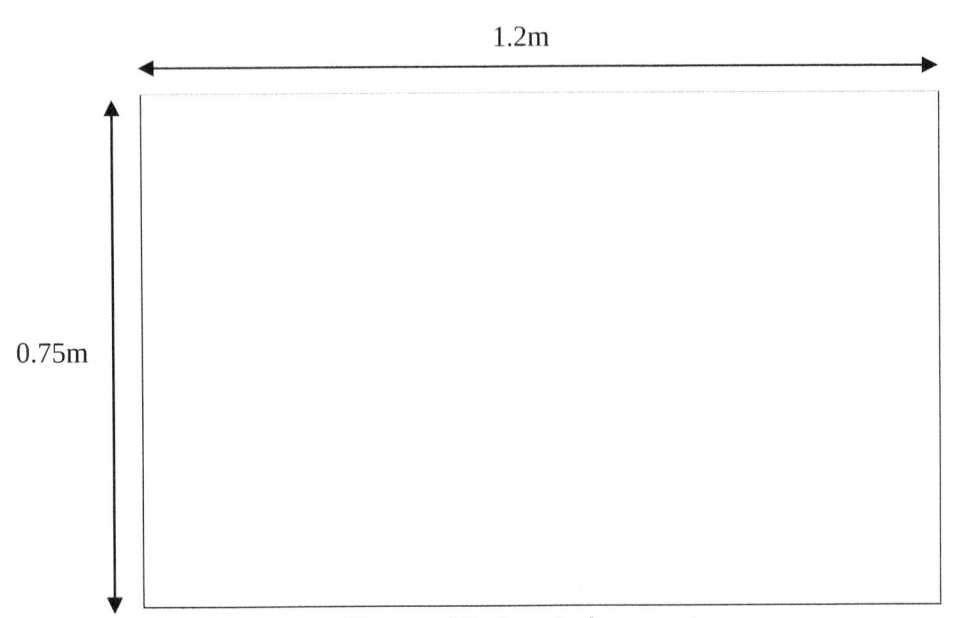

Figure 16.2: A typical poster size.

# Poster design

There are many ways to design your poster. Your aim is to produce something which attracts viewers to come closer and read it; in other words, something which is *visually appealing*. This can be achieved by paying attention to the following aspects: colour; illustrations; positioning of information; white space; font size; and font.

One key aspect to visual appeal is **colour**. Colour can be especially useful in connecting similar parts of the poster. In general it is better to use only two to three colours, each of which should have a clear purpose.

Another aspect of visual appeal is **illustrations**. As noted above, viewers will concentrate most on the illustrations and may only skim the text, so as far as possible try to make them self-explanatory, with clear titles and captions. As the illustrations are likely to be the main attraction, you might want to plan your poster around them. When creating illustrations, try to use bigger lines than you would use in a report or research paper. This will add to their visual appeal. The illustrations will probably need to

> **Tip: Make a sketch**
> To help with poster design, especially positioning of information, it is useful to make a **sketch** of the poster. A smaller piece of paper (e.g. A4 or A3) can be used. In particular, the sketch will show where the different sections will be placed and where the figures will go. It can also be used to plan the colours and borders.

## Unit 16: **Posters**

be different from (generally simpler than) those in your paper. It is best to avoid using tables, as these generally do not work well in posters.

Another important consideration is **layout**. The viewer is likely to read from top to bottom and left to right, and the sections should be positioned this way. This allows readers to move from one column to the next, which is helpful if there are two or more people viewing the poster at the same time. It is generally best to put the title at the top, in the centre. Below this there will usually be two or three columns, depending on the amount of information. Possible layouts are shown in Figure 16.3.

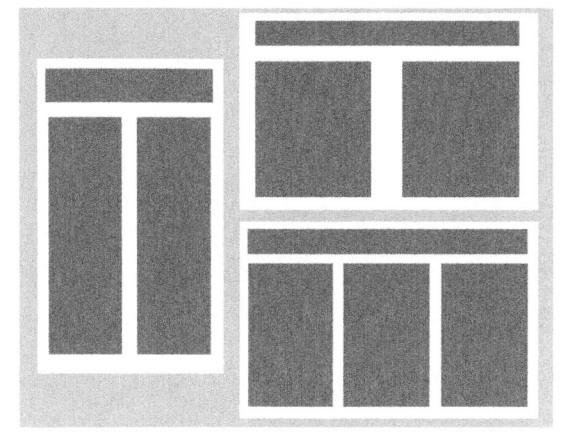

Figure 16.3: Three different ways to position information.

Another important aspect of a poster is **white space**. White space refers to the parts of the poster where there are no images or text. It is important to leave a lot of white space so that the information on the poster is not too dense, and white space should be thought of not as blank space but as part of the poster design. It is especially important to leave space between the sections so they are distinct and clearly separate from one another. Think also about the border to the whole poster. Bullet points will also help to break up the page and add to the amount of white space.

A further consideration in poster design is **font size**. The title, the first text on the poster which is likely to be read, should be the largest font size out of all text on the poster. Headings should also be in large font, though smaller than the title (see Figure 16.4). As the font size will differentiate them as headings, it is not necessary to underline them or use capitals. The main text should be large enough to be read from one to two metres away, a comfortable standing distance without crowding the poster. In practice, this means a text size of at least 18 point, up to a possible maximum of 30 point. There is a trade-off between impact (larger font size) and amount of information (smaller font size). You will need to decide on the correct balance. Sometimes, the level of light where the poster is displayed may be poor, which is another reason why a larger font size is needed.

| In short |
| --- |
| When designing a poster, consider:<br>• colour;<br>• illustrations;<br>• layout;<br>• white space;<br>• font size;<br>• font. |

> **Title (largest)**
> Headings (large)
> Text (can be read from 1-2m)

Figure 16.4: Relative font size for different poster elements

The **font** itself is also important. Try to use at most two different fonts (e.g. one for titles, one for text). A single font for the whole poster may be enough. Most writers agree that a *sans serif font* is best for posters. This type of font is simple and easy to read. The font you are reading now is a *sans serif* font, called Open Sans. Other examples are Arial and Helvetica. [If you want to see a *serif* font for contrast, try Times New Roman, the most common *serif* font. The *In Short* and *Tip* boxes in this book use a *serif* font.]

> **Tip: Laminate**
> Laminating the different parts of the poster, or the whole poster, will help to protect it (useful for transporting) as well as make it look more professional.

## Poster content

The poster should include all the **relevant information** required to achieve your main message. If you are starting from a paper you have already written (the most likely approach), you will need to summarise the sections to ensure you have included the main points. Many presenters include far too much information without enough editing. Few people will have enough time to read such posters and the main message will be lost on almost everyone who sees it.

To compensate for the lack of detail in the poster, you can **prepare a handout** with additional points, or even give out a copy of your whole paper to those who are interested. Make sure that your name and contact information are contained on any supplementary material you hand out.

# Unit 16: **Posters**

If you are creating a poster from scratch, you are more likely to include too little information than too much, and your goal will therefore be to ensure that each point is sufficiently detailed.

The **headings** of the poster should show the flow of information. These do not have to be the same as the paper the poster is based on (if there is one), though many posters will simply follow the IMRAD structure (Introduction, Method, Results and Discussion), and this can be a useful fall-back if you are unsure of other ways to structure the poster.

As viewers are likely to skim through the text fairly quickly (noted above), **short paragraphs and sentences** are preferable to the long paragraphs and complex language which is often present in a written paper. Breaking the text up by using bullet points is also helpful in keeping things simple (as well as increasing the amount of white space, as noted earlier).

> **Tip: Check**
> When you have finished your poster, try to:
> - view it from a distance to gauge its impact and decide if the font size is appropriate;
> - view it in dimly lit conditions to make sure it can still be read;
> - get someone else to view the poster to make sure they understand the main message.

Wherever possible, **use an illustration instead of text**. This is especially useful for equipment or procedures; use a schematic diagram instead. A picture is worth a thousand words!

# Checklist

Below is a checklist for posters. Use it to assess your poster, or ask a peer to help.

| Area | Aspect | Item | OK? | Comments |
|---|---|---|---|---|
| **Planning** | Main message | The main message of the poster is clear (i.e. the *one* thing you want people to remember after they have viewed your poster). | | |
| | Selection of information | The main points have been carefully selected and support the main message. | | |
| | | The illustrations have been carefully selected and support the main message and flow of information. | | |
| | Size | The size of the poster matches the requirements. | | |
| **Design** | Colour | Colour has been used well e.g. to connect similar parts. | | |
| | | Each colour has a clear purpose. | | |
| | | No more than three colours have been used. | | |
| | Illustrations | Illustrations are self-explanatory (clear titles and captions). | | |
| | | Illustrations use bigger lines than in the report/paper. | | |
| | | Illustrations are clear and simple. | | |

## Unit 16: **Posters**

| | | | | |
|---|---|---|---|---|
| **Design (cont'd)** | Layout | Flow of information is logical (e.g. top to bottom, left to right). | | |
| | | Title is placed at the top centre. | | |
| | | A maximum of three columns has been used. | | |
| | White space | There is a good amount of white space, e.g. border, between sections. | | |
| | Font size | The title has the largest font size. | | |
| | | Headings have larger font than the text. | | |
| | | The text can be read from 1-2m away (18-30 point). | | |
| | Font | A maximum of 2 fonts has been used. | | |
| | | The fonts are *san serif* (e.g. Arial, Helvetica). | | |
| **Content** | Information | All relevant information is included. | | |
| | | There is not too much (or too little) information. | | |
| | | A handout (or copy of the paper) has been prepared, if necessary. | | |
| | Headings | Headings are logical and aid to flow of information. | | |
| | Conciseness | Paragraphs and sentences are short. | | |
| | | Text is broken up e.g. by use of bullet points. | | |
| | | Illustrations are used in place of text wherever possible (e.g. schematic for procedure). | | |

Academic Writing Genres Sheldon Smith

# Example poster #1

Below is an example conference poster. It is used in one of the exercises later. This is a larger version of the poster used earlier in the unit (Figure 16.1a).

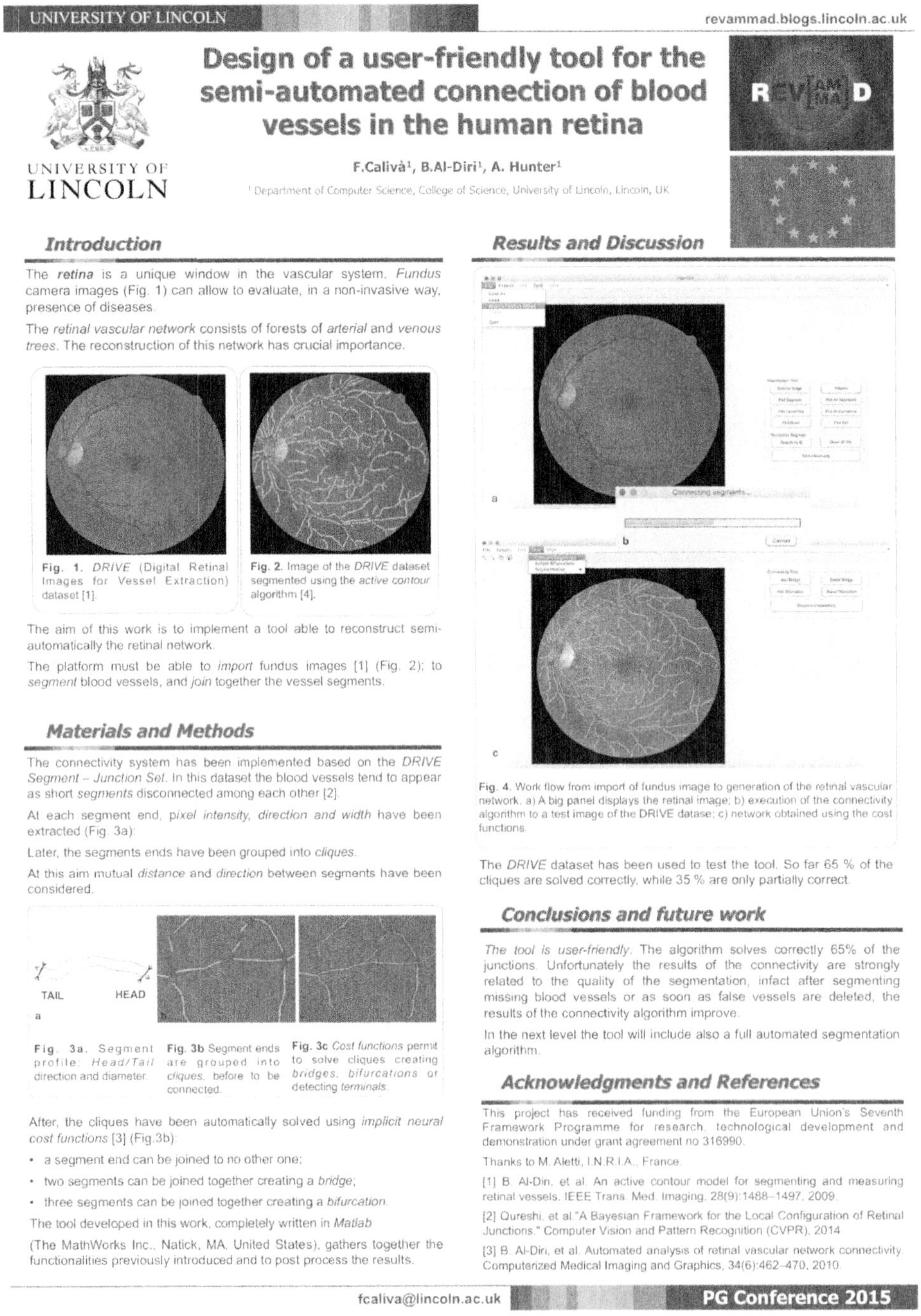

Source: http://eprints.lincoln.ac.uk/16931/4/__ddat01_staffhome_bjones_RDS_Desktop_2015%20posters_CalivaFrancescoPGconf2.pdf

## Unit 16: Posters

# Example poster #2

Below is another example conference poster. It is also used in one of the exercises later. This is a larger version of the poster used earlier in the unit (Figure 16.1b).

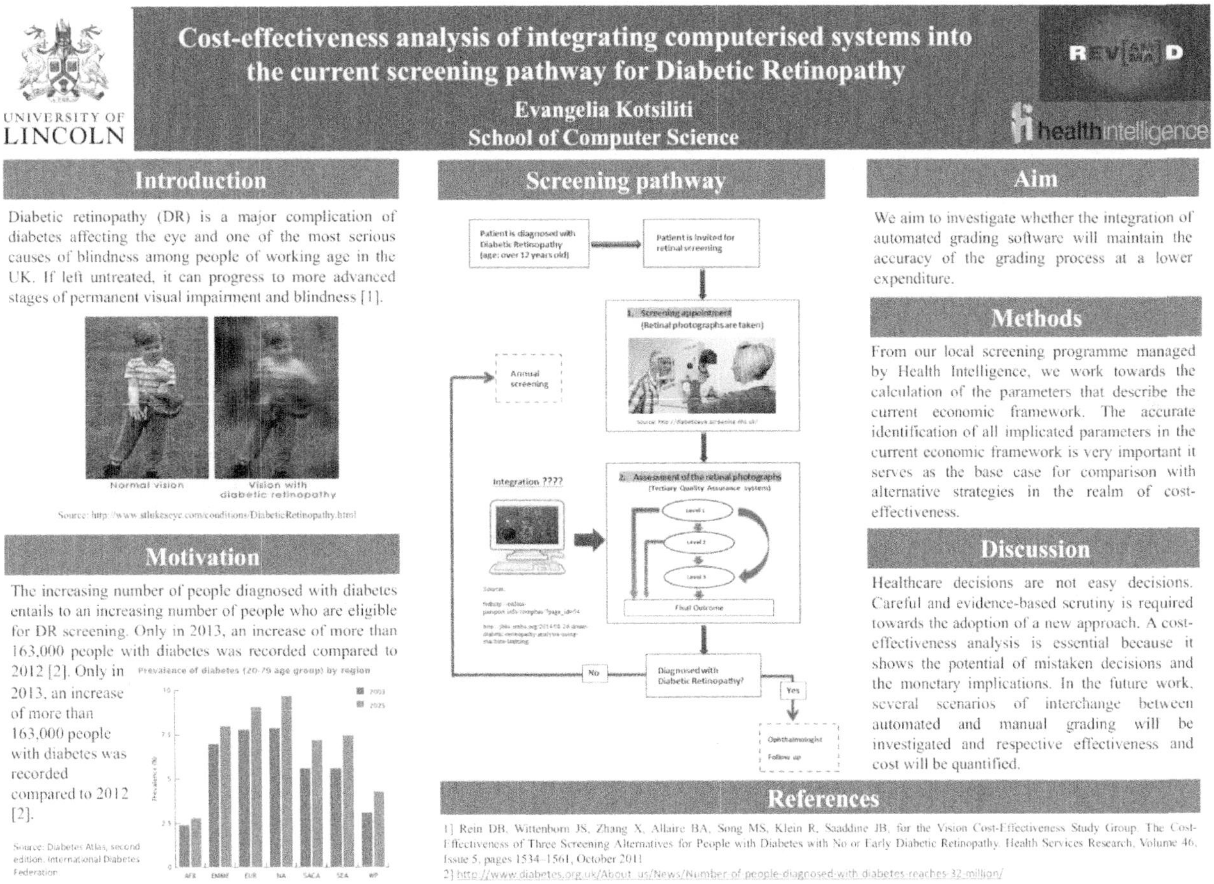

Source: http://eprints.lincoln.ac.uk/16931/9/__ddat01_staffhome_bjones_RDS_Desktop_2015%20posters_PGR%20conference_poster%20Evi%20Kotsiliti.pdf

# Exercises

## Exercise 1: **Comprehension**

Answer the following questions about this unit. Either do this after reading the unit, or make notes first then use the notes to answer the questions.

**1** How is a poster similar to and how is it different from a presentation visual aid?
_____
_____

**2** What are the benefits of a poster for:
- the viewer    _____
- the presenter _____

**3** Complete the following flowchart, showing the process of **planning a poster**.

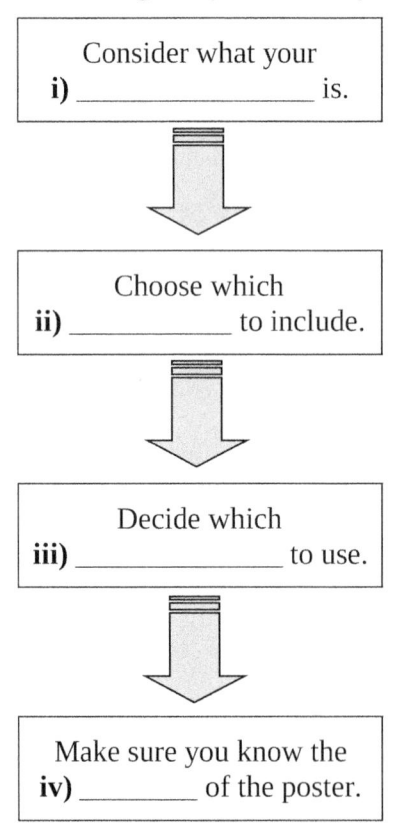

```
┌─────────────────────────────┐
│   Consider what your        │
│ i) _____ is.        │
└─────────────────────────────┘
              ↓
┌─────────────────────────────┐
│   Choose which              │
│ ii) _____ to include.   │
└─────────────────────────────┘
              ↓
┌─────────────────────────────┐
│   Decide which              │
│ iii) _____ to use.      │
└─────────────────────────────┘
              ↓
┌─────────────────────────────┐
│   Make sure you know the    │
│ iv) _____ of the poster.  │
└─────────────────────────────┘
```

## Unit 16: **Posters**

**4** The following is a list of aspects, given in the unit, which you should consider when you **design the poster**. The first letter of each is given. Complete the words.

- C_____
- I_____
- L_____
- W_____ s_____
- F_____ s_____
- F_____

**5** What information is given in the unit about the size of the following aspects of text?
- Title          _____
- Headings       _____
- Main text      _____

**6** Which type of font is recommended for text on a poster: *serif* or *sans serif*? Why? Give some common examples of the recommended font.
_____
_____

**7** Give **two** reasons why bullet points are helpful for a poster.
_____
_____

**8** What is the function of the poster's headings? Is it essential to use the same headings as the paper that the poster is based on (e.g. IMRAD)?
_____
_____

**9** What can you do to compensate for the lack of detail in your poster?
_____
_____

**10** How much information should be included in the poster? What problems are you likely to encounter with the amount of information if you are starting from a paper already written?
_____
_____

# Academic Writing Genres — Sheldon Smith

## Exercise 2: **Example posers**

a) Compare and contrast the two example posters earlier in the unit. How are they similar? How do they differ? Record your answers in the Venn diagram below.

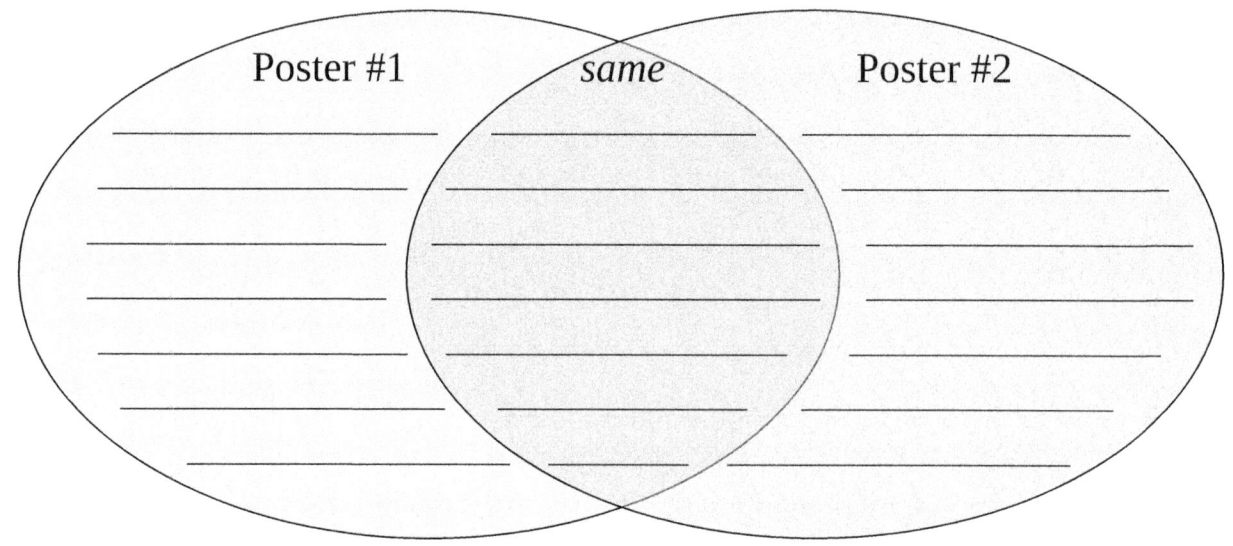

[Venn diagram with three regions: Poster #1, same, Poster #2]

b) The following is a modified form of the checklist from earlier in the unit. It considers all design and content aspects except colour (as the paperback version of this book is black-and-white). Compare the two posters and decide **which one you prefer for each aspect**.

| Area | Aspect | Look for: | Preferred poster |
|------|--------|-----------|------------------|
| **Design** | Illustrations | Clear illustrations, clear titles and captions. | ① ② |
| | Layout | Logical flow of information, positioning of title, number of columns. | ① ② |
| | White space | Amount of white space. | ① ② |
| | Font size | Title has largest size, headings are larger than text, text is large enough. | ① ② |
| | Font | San serif, easy to read. | ① ② |
| **Content** | Information | Not too much or too little information. | ① ② |
| | Headings | Logical headings which aid to the flow of information. | ① ② |
| | Conciseness | Short paragraphs and sentences, bullet points to break up the text. | ① ② |

c) When you have finished, use the information to decide which one you prefer overall.

Unit 16: **Posters**

## Exercise 3: **Designing a poster**

a) Create a poster, using one of the following options.
- Use a paper you have written (ideally one with headings such as a report).
- Use one of the reports in Part II of this book (additional reports are available online).
- Design a short survey, with up to 10 questions, using a mix of question types (open-ended, multiple choice, rating, ranking). Survey your classmates, using the questions. Present the results of the survey in poster format. The questions should all relate to a single topic, e.g. *Use of free time, Eating habits, Attitudes towards the environment.*

Follow these steps to create the poster.
1. Plan the poster. Think carefully about your *main message*, which *points to include* and what *illustrations* you will use. Make sure you know the size of the poster.
2. Design the poster. Think carefully about colour, illustrations, layout, white space, font size and font (if it is typewritten). **Use the space below to sketch out your design before you move to the next step.**
3. Create the poster. Make sure you include all relevant information, have useful headings, keep information brief and use bullet points if possible.

*Poster sketch (turn book around if using portrait layout).*

b) When you have finished, get a peer to check your poster, using the checklist earlier in the unit. You should also check another student's poster.

# Academic Writing Genres — Sheldon Smith

## Exercise 4: **Learning outcomes check**

a) The following are the learning outcomes for this unit. Decide how well you have mastered each one by giving it a score, as follows.

    3 = I understand/can do this well.
    2 = I understand/can do this fairly well, but I can improve with more practice.
    1 = I understand/can do this, but not well enough yet. I need to practise more.
    0 = I cannot do this yet. I need more time.

| Score | Learning Outcome |
|---|---|
| _____ | I know how to plan a poster. |
| _____ | I understand key elements of poster design. |
| _____ | I understand the type of content that is suitable for a poster. |
| _____ | I can compare and contrast two posters. |
| _____ | I can decide which poster I prefer, based on design and content. |
| _____ | I can plan, design and create a poster. |
| _____ | I can peer edit a poster, using a checklist. |

b) Use this information to review the unit and improve.

# Unit 17 | Reflective Writing

## Learning Outcomes

By the end of this unit, you should:
- understand what reflective writing is;
- understand the learning cycle and its connection to reflection;
- know about two models of reflective writing (Gibbs and Johns);
- be aware of some questions to ask when reflecting on an experience;
- know some language to use for reflective writing.

By completing the exercises, you will also:
- study an example reflection for structure.

## Key Vocabulary

**Nouns**
- reflection

**Adjectives**
- aesthetic
- ethical
- empirical
- reflexive

## Additional Vocabulary

*Academic Collocations (in the unit)*
- academic writing (adj + n)
- ethical questions (adj + n)
- experiential learning (adj + n)
- main issue (adj + n)
- previous experiences (adj + n)
- similar situations (adj + n)
- frequently used (adv + past)
- widely known (adv + past)
- add information (v + n)
- draw conclusions (v + n)

*Academic Collocations (in reflection)*
- add information (v + n)

## Contents of this section

### Unit 17: Reflective Writing ...................................247

Overview ....................................................................................248
The learning cycle ......................................................................248
Models of reflection ...................................................................248
Language for reflecting ..............................................................251
Checklist ....................................................................................252
Example reflection .....................................................................254
Exercises ....................................................................................255

# Overview

Many courses ask students to reflect on a practical experience in order to make sense of it and continue to develop. Reflective writing is especially common in practical courses such as education and health, though it is applicable to all disciplines. The writing will usually be in the form of a reflective essay, a learning log or a learning portfolio.

# The learning cycle

The idea of learning through reflection is underpinned by the learning cycle. According to the learning cycle, learning does not come about simply through doing, but rather as a result of reflecting on the experience, concluding, planning what to do next, then doing it, reflecting again, and so on, in a continual loop. The most widely known version of the learning cycle is Kolb's experiential learning cycle, shown in Figure 17.1.

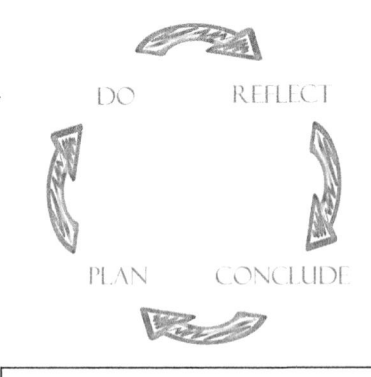

Figure 17.1: Kolb's Experiential Learning Cycle

# Models of reflection

While the Kolb learning cycle provides a good context for understanding how learning works and the importance of reflection, it is not the most practical when it comes to *writing* about the experience. Your course of study may have a particular model or form that you are required to follow when reflecting. If it does not, the following two models, namely the Gibbs reflective cycle and the Johns' structured model of reflection, are ones which are frequently used to help learners reflect.

## *The Gibbs reflective cycle*

The Gibbs reflective cycle (Figure 17.2) is based on the Kolb cycle. In the Gibbs reflective cycle, you should go through a series of stages which will get you to reflect on your experiences. This begins with fairly concrete questions that ask you to **describe** what happened, and how you **feel**. You should then **evaluate** the positives, which you want to repeat next time, as well as the negatives, which you want to avoid or overcome. The questions become more abstract when you start to **analyse** and try to understand why you had the problems you did. This is where feedback, from peers or a teacher, can be especially useful, since it is not always easy to identify your own problems. Although the Kolb cycle shows reflect/conclude/plan as three separate parts of the cycle, many tutors, when they ask you to reflect, will expect you to do all three, i.e. not just reflect but draw conclusions and plan how to move forward. The Gibbs reflective cycle includes these final

# Unit 17: **Reflective writing**

two stages, and if you follow this cycle you will need to **conclude** what you have learnt from the experience, and to **plan** for future experiences.

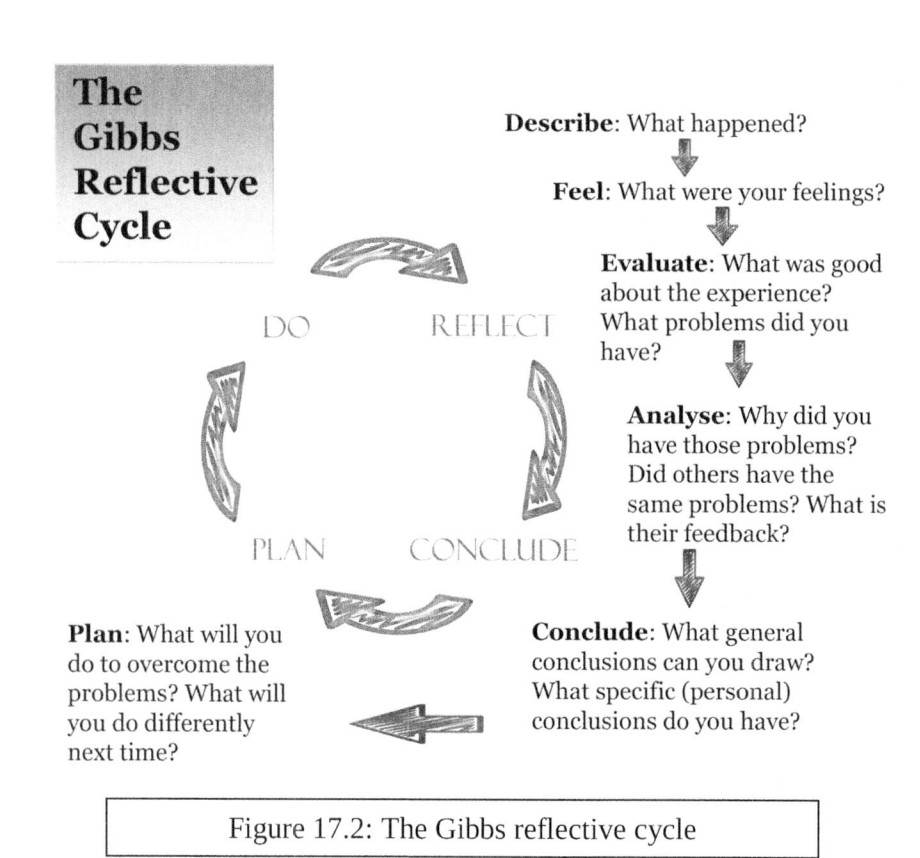

**The Gibbs Reflective Cycle**

**Describe**: What happened?

**Feel**: What were your feelings?

**Evaluate**: What was good about the experience? What problems did you have?

**Analyse**: Why did you have those problems? Did others have the same problems? What is their feedback?

**Conclude**: What general conclusions can you draw? What specific (personal) conclusions do you have?

**Plan**: What will you do to overcome the problems? What will you do differently next time?

DO — REFLECT — CONCLUDE — PLAN

| In short |
|---|
| To reflect using the Gibbs reflective cycle, you should:<br>• describe what happened;<br>• explain how you feel;<br>• evaluate positives and negatives;<br>• analyse the reasons;<br>• conclude what you learnt from the experience;<br>• plan how to improve. |

Figure 17.2: The Gibbs reflective cycle

## *Johns' model of structured reflection*

Johns' model of structured reflection was developed by Professor Christopher Johns for nursing professionals, though it is applicable to other fields. It is intended to be used with a colleague or mentor, in order to increase the rate of learning. The model requires initial description of the experience, after which you ask yourself questions based on five different ways of knowing, namely: aesthetic, personal, ethical, empirical and reflexive. The order does not have to be followed, and not all questions need to be asked (and, if appropriate, some questions can be repeated).

| In short |
|---|
| The Johns' model considers:<br>• description;<br>• aesthetic questions;<br>• personal questions;<br>• ethical questions;<br>• empirical questions;<br>• reflexive questions. |

The questions to ask are shown on the next page (Figure 17.3).

| Area | Question(s) | Notes |
|---|---|---|
| **Descriptive** | Write a description of the experience. | |
| **Aesthetic** | - What was I trying to achieve?<br>- Why did I respond as I did?<br>- What were the consequences of that (for the patient*/others/myself)?<br>- How was this person (or these persons) feeling?<br>- How did I know this?<br>*\* Can be changed depending on context, e.g. 'students' for teaching.* | *These questions relate to concrete actions (in the here and now).* |
| **Personal** | - How did I feel in this situation?<br>- What internal factors were influencing me? | *These questions relate to your reactions and motivation.* |
| **Ethical** | - How did my actions match with my beliefs?<br>- What factors made me act in incongruent ways? | *These questions relate to how your actions match the way you want to act.* |
| **Empirical** | - What knowledge did or should have informed me? | *This question relates to how you use your knowledge.* |
| **Reflexive** | - How does this connect with previous experiences?<br>- Could I handle this better in similar situations?<br>- What would the consequences of alternative actions be (for the patient*/others/myself)?<br>- How do I now feel about this experience?<br>- Can I support myself and others better as a consequence?<br>- Has this changed my ways of knowing? | *These questions require final reflection on the experience.* |

Figure 17.3: Johns' Model of Structured Reflection
(Source: Johns, C.C. (1995) ' Framing learning through reflection',
*Journal of Advanced Nursing*, **22**, 226-234)

# Unit 17: **Reflective writing**

## Language for reflecting

Reflective writing is unlike most other forms of writing required at university. Since the reflection is based on your own experience, it is common to use the first person ('I'). The writing is likely to use more informal language and be less structured than other forms of academic writing. It may also be more subjective in nature. At the same time, there are still many academic elements. For example, as with other forms of academic writing, you may need to refer to academic literature, e.g. to explain why and how something happened.

When writing about what happened or how you felt, you should use *past simple* tense (*I felt that...*). When referring to theory, you should use *present simple* (e.g. *Johns (1993) suggests...*).

The following are some possible phrases to use for different components of a reflection. These are just some suggestions; many more expressions are possible.

*Identifying the main issue*

| The most | meaningful / significant / relevant | aspect / experience / issue | was... |

*Describing thoughts, feelings, reactions etc. (and showing sequence)*

| At first / Initially / ... / Subsequently / Later | I | felt/did not feel... / thought/did not think... / knew/did not know... / noticed/did not notice... / realised/did not realise... |

*Giving reasons*

| This | might be / could be / is probably | due to... / because of... / related to... |

*Giving conclusions*

| Having | read... / discussed... / analysed... | I now | believe... / know... / realise... |

From this experience, I have learned...

| I feel I have | developed / improved | my understanding of... / my knowledge of... / my ability to... |

*Giving plans*
I now need to...
I next plan to...

# Checklist

Below is a checklist for reflection **using the Gibbs reflective cycle** (one for the Johns' model is on the next page). Use it to assess your reflection, or ask a peer to help.

| Area | Aspect | Item | OK? | Comments |
|---|---|---|---|---|
| **Gibbs reflective cycle** | Description | There is a description of the experience. | | |
| | Feelings | The reflection explains how you felt. | | |
| | Evaluation | Positives of the experience are given. | | |
| | | Negatives of the experience are given. | | |
| | Analysis | Reasons for problems or negatives are given. | | |
| | | Feedback from others is included, if obtained. | | |
| | Conclusion | Conclusions (general and specific) are given. | | |
| | | The conclusions show what you have learnt from the experience. | | |
| | Plan | There is a plan for future action. | | |
| **Language** | Formality | The language is informal (using 'I'). | | |
| | Tense | Suitable tense is used (past tense for the experience and feelings, present tense for theory). | | |
| | Language phrases | Suitable phrases are used for different parts of the reflection (e.g. *At first, I felt...*). | | |
| **Other** | Sources | Reference to theory is made if/where appropriate. | | |

# Unit 17: **Reflective writing**

Below is a checklist for reflection **using the Johns' model of structured reflection**. Use it to assess your reflection (if you have followed this model), or ask a peer to help.

| Area | Aspect | Item | OK? | Comments |
|---|---|---|---|---|
| Johns' model of structured reflection | Descriptive | There is a description of the experience. | | |
| | Aesthetic | There are details of concrete actions (what you were trying to achieve, your response, the consequences of your actions, how others felt). | | |
| | Personal | The reflection explains how *you* felt, and why you felt this way. | | |
| | Ethical | There is an explanation of how your actions matched with your beliefs. | | |
| | Empirical | Knowledge that did (or should have) influenced you is considered. | | |
| | Reflexive | The experience is linked to previous experiences. | | |
| | | Alternative actions (and their consequences) are considered. | | |
| | | Final feelings of the experience are expressed. | | |
| | | Personal improvements are considered (e.g. ability to handle similar situations, ways of knowing). | | |
| Language | Formality | The language is informal (using 'I'). | | |
| | Tense | Suitable tense is used (past for the experience and feelings, present for theory). | | |
| | Language phrases | Suitable phrases are used for different parts of the reflection (e.g. *At first, I felt...*). | | |
| Other | Sources | Reference to theory is made if/where appropriate. | | |

# Example reflection

Below is an example reflection. It is used in one of the exercises later.
[Note: It is written as a single paragraph because of the exercise it is used for later.]

> My students are getting ready to submit a reflective assignment. I have seen some of their drafts and can see that they have a general understanding of how to reflect, but tend to be too descriptive, without thinking deeply enough. This is not surprising since they have not, in their prior studies, had to engage in reflective practice. Boud, Keogh and Walker (2013) observe that reflection is easily neglected since it is both unique to the learner and impossible to observe directly. They cite Duley (1981, p.611) in pointing out that reflection is 'The skill of experiential learning in which people tend to be the most deficient'. I decided to add information to a learning website I use to help my students with their studies. Although I had several handouts from which I could get information, I felt they were rather too simple. I therefore searched for more information about the learning cycle and reflection in text books and online. I was initially quite confused at the different models, none of which quite matched the one I was used to, namely the Kolb model, despite the fact that this is the one most frequently used by lecturers (Hilsdon, 2005). I was a little worried that I had been teaching students in the wrong way. However, I found the different models and ideas stimulating, and liked the fact that the information challenged what I already knew and made me think more deeply. After reading more about the topic I felt I already had a good understanding of what reflection means, but I had problems deciding how to present the information in a useful way on the learning website. This is partly because of the many different models, which I felt would confuse my students. It is also because the website information needs to be fairly brief, but at the same time needs to be accurate and useful. In a lesson, I can help students by adding explanations and working individually with them, but on the website, I cannot do this. I discussed the information with colleagues, which helped to clarify my ideas. I also asked them to look at an initial version of the page on the website and give me some feedback, which also helped to improve the content. I came to the conclusion that it would be best to use a single model. According to Hilsdon (2005), the reflective models of Gibbs (1988) and Johns (1993, 1998) are commonly used since they 'offer structured approaches to reflection', in the form of headings in a cycle for the former and a series of questions for the latter. Although Hilsdon cautions that reflection 'needs to involve more than simply thinking about and describing our own actions according to models such as that of Gibbs or Johns', and needs to involve a 'recognition of how our identity and subject position may be structured in the discourse forms we use', he is talking about native speakers on graduate courses. In the case the undergraduate ESL learners I teach, who are just beginning their reflective journey, these structured models provide the best next step. I decided that the Gibbs reflective cycle would be most suitable for my students, since it is based on the Kolb cycle I had previously been using, but it has more structure, with a clearer set of stages and questions to help students reflect. As mentioned above, my students' reflections tend to be too descriptive. One advantage of using the Gibbs reflective cycle is that it shows students they have made a useful beginning (by describing), but that this is only a first step towards reflection, and they need to go further by explaining how they feel, by evaluating, analysing, concluding and planning. Once the information is on the website and I have used it to guide students in their reflection, I will examine how well students use this information to reflect, and consider how it can be improved to help other students in the future.
>
> **References**
> Boud, D., Keogh, R., and Walker, D. (Eds.) (2013) *Reflection: Turning experience into learning.* New York: Routledge.
> Hilsdon, J. (2005) 'Rethinking reflection: A study involving students of nursing', *Journal of Practice Teaching*, 6(1) 2005, pp.57-70.

# Unit 17: Reflective writing

# Exercises

## Exercise 1: Comprehension

Answer the following questions about this unit. Either do this after reading the unit, or make notes first then use your notes to answer the questions.

**1** What is the purpose of reflection?
_____

**2** Give examples of reflective assignments you might encounter at university.
- _____
- _____
- _____

**3** Complete the four stages of Kolb's learning cycle as shown in the diagram.

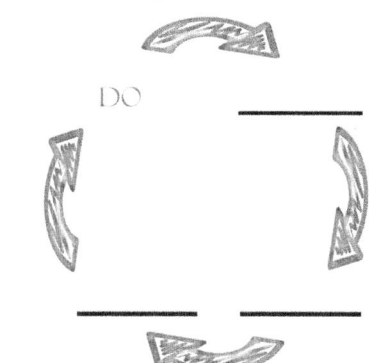

**The Kolb Learning Cycle**

**4** The following shows the different areas of Johns' model of structured reflection. Match each area with the correct description (right). An example has been done.

| Area | Description (what it relates to) |
|---|---|
| Descriptive | *Relates to the final reflection on the experience.* |
| Aesthetic | *Relates to your reactions and motivation.* |
| Personal | *Relates to how your actions match the way you want to act.* |
| Ethical | *Relates to description of the experience.* |
| Empirical | *Relates to concrete actions (in the here and now).* |
| Reflexive | *Relates to how you use your knowledge.* |

**Academic Writing Genres**                                                     **Sheldon Smith**

5  Which of the areas above do the following questions relate to?
   [Hint: There is one for each area, except *descriptive*, which does not use questions.]

- How did my actions match with my beliefs?     _____
- How did I feel in this situation?     _____
- Why did I respond as I did?     _____
- Could I handle this better in similar situations?     _____
- What knowledge did or should have informed me?     _____

6  Complete the following flowchart, showing the stages of the Gibbs reflective cycle.

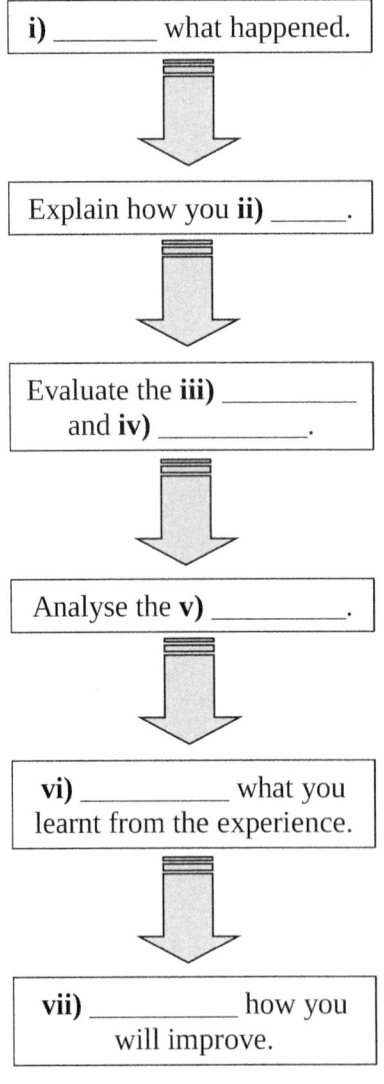

> **i)** _____ what happened.
>
> ⬇
>
> Explain how you **ii)** _____.
>
> ⬇
>
> Evaluate the **iii)** _____ and **iv)** _____.
>
> ⬇
>
> Analyse the **v)** _____.
>
> ⬇
>
> **vi)** _____ what you learnt from the experience.
>
> ⬇
>
> **vii)** _____ how you will improve.

# Unit 17: **Reflective writing**

**7** How is reflective writing different from regular academic writing? How is it similar. Write your answers in the table below

|  | Reflective writing | Regular academic writing |
|---|---|---|
| Differences | • _____ <br> • _____ <br> • _____ <br> • _____ | • _____ <br> • _____ <br> • _____ <br> • _____ |
| Similarities | | |

## Exercise 2: **Example reflection**

Study the example reflection earlier in the unit. The reflection follows the Gibbs reflective cycle. Read the reflection and identify each of the stages:
- description;
- feeling;
- evaluation;
- analysis;
- conclusion;
- plan.

## Exercise 3: **Learning outcomes check**

a) The following are the learning outcomes for this unit. Decide how well you have mastered each one by giving it a score, as follows.

    3 = I understand/can do this well.
    2 = I understand/can do this fairly well, but I can improve with more practice.
    1 = I understand/can do this, but not well enough yet. I need to practise more.
    0 = I cannot do this yet. I need more time.

| Score | Learning Outcome |
|---|---|
| _____ | I understand what reflective writing is. |
| _____ | I understand the learning cycle and its connection to reflection. |
| _____ | I know about two models of reflective writing (Gibbs and Johns). |
| _____ | I am aware of some questions to ask when reflecting on an experience. |
| _____ | I know some language to use for reflective writing. |

b) Use this information to review the unit and improve.

# Unit 18 | Book Reviews

## Learning Outcomes

By the end of this unit, you should:
- understand what a book review is;
- know the difference between a book review and a book report;
- understand how to prepare to write a book review;
- know the structure of a book review;
- understand the content of a typical book review;
- be aware of some language for different parts of a book review.

By completing the exercises, you will also:
- study an example book review for structure, content and language.

## Key Vocabulary

*Adjectives*
- bibliographic
- critical

## Additional Vocabulary

*Academic Collocations (in the unit)*
- academic journals (adj + n)
- critical evaluation (adj + n)
- final chapter (adj + n)
- key areas (adj + n)
- main arguments (adj + n)
- opening chapter (adj + n)
- previous work (adj + n)
- similar approach (adj + n)
- critically evaluate (adv + v)
- give information (v + n)

*Academic Collocations (in the review)*
- comprehensive review (adj + n)
- main focus (adj + n)
- major components (adj + n)
- negative effects (adj + n)
- specific forms (adj + n)

## Contents of this section

## Unit 18: Book Reviews .................................................. 259

Overview ................................................................................................ 260
Preparing to write a book review ........................................................ 260
Structure of book reviews .................................................................... 260
Language for book reviews .................................................................. 262
Checklist ................................................................................................ 263
Example book review ........................................................................... 264
Exercises ................................................................................................ 266

## Overview

A book review describes and critically evaluates a (usually recent) book. Like any kind of review, for example a review of a film or television programme, it will offer a description of the main points, consider the strengths and weaknesses, and give an overall evaluation, in order to allow the reader to decide whether or not it will be of interest to them and therefore a good investment of their time and money. Book reviews are sometimes used as assignments on undergraduate courses, and are a common component of academic journals. They are typically short pieces of work, around 500-750 words in length; they may sometimes be shorter or longer, but will rarely exceed 1000 words. A book review should not be confused with a book report, which is a relatively short and purely descriptive assignment, common in high school (rather than university) courses.

## Preparing to write a book review

In order to write an effective book review, you first need to read the book. If possible (if you have time), read it carefully, making notes as you go along. It is helpful to identify quotations which you might use later when you write your review. As you read the book, try to identify the author's purpose, the intended audience, the author's main arguments and themes, and how evidence is used.

## Structure of book reviews

A book review will usually begin with **bibliographic information**. This means details such as the name of the book, the name(s) of the author(s), and the publisher. Other details may be helpful, e.g.: date and place of publication; format; edition; number of pages; price; ISBN.

The text of the review should begin with an **introduction**. As the review will be fairly brief, it is common to begin with an anecdote or quotation which captures the main idea of the book. The introduction will identify the author and title, specify the type of book, and state the book's subject matter. Further background detail to place the book in context may be given, for example previous work by the author in the same field, prior work by other writers in the same field, or information about the book series (if the book is part of a series). The thesis of the book, i.e. its specific contribution, may also be given, along with your own thesis, i.e. your initial appraisal of the work and key observations.

The main body of the review will provide *description* and *critical evaluation* of the text. These may be dealt with separately, with description first and evaluation next, or in combination.

# Unit 18: **Book reviews**

Although the evaluation is the more important part, the description may still take up half or two thirds of the content of the main body, in order to lay the foundation for the evaluation.

The **description** of the text will summarise the book. Evidence from the book, such as quotations, may be used to support the points. This part might give information on the following areas, which can later be used as criteria for evaluating the book:
- content of the book (possibly by chapter-by-chapter);
- the author's purpose;
- the intended audience;
- the author's arguments and themes;
- sources used in the book;
- how the book is organised or laid out.

The **critical evaluation** will present your reaction to the book. You might compare it to other (similar) books in the field, and consider its relative strengths and weaknesses. In this part you may respond to the areas above by considering key questions, as follows, to further highlight the strengths and weaknesses of the book.
- *Content of the book.* Is everything included? Is there too much information? Is anything essential left out?
- *The author's purpose.* Has the author succeeded in their purpose?
- *The intended audience*. Is the book appropriate for the intended audience? Why (not)? Who else might benefit from reading it?
- *The author's arguments and themes.* How valid or effective are the arguments and themes? Do you agree with the author's opinions? Why (not)?
- *Sources used in the book.* How strong are the sources? Are there enough?
- *How the book is organised or laid out.* Is it organised in a logical or useful way? Are there any problems? Is the layout clear and easy to use?

Finally, there should be a **conclusion** to the book review. This will sum up your thoughts on the book. This means summarising the book's strengths and weaknesses, indicating whether this is a useful book, whether it will make a lasting contribution to its field, whether you recommend it, and who will benefit from reading it.

Note that the above is the structure for a book review for a non-fiction work, which is the most common kind of review for university study. For a work of fiction, a similar approach can be used, though in place of the points for *argument* and *sources*, you would consider *setting, plot, characters, use of language* and *voice* when describing the book, and consider how effective each of these elements are when evaluating it.

# Language for book reviews

It is important is to make sure that your views are distinct from the author's. This can be done by using the author's name, or referring to 'The author' or 'The book'.

The following phrases might be useful for summarising the contents of the book.

- The book is divided into the following parts.
- This text is divided into four main chapters focusing on…
- Section one of the book
- The opening chapter
- The second section
- Chapter three
- The next chapter
- The final chapter

| details |
| reviews |
| focuses on |
| defines |
| explores |

The following phrases can be used to highlight weaknesses.

The book would benefit from…
A nice addition to the book would be…
The weakest area of the book is…

The | only / main / greatest | weakness / drawback | of the book is…

The following phrases can be used to indicate a suitable audience for the book.

- The book should appeal to those who…
- This book is applicable to…
- It would be an excellent resource for…
- The book is particularly interesting for…
- The book will be of interest to…
- This book is highly recommended to…
- … are likely to find the book useful.
- … would find it valuable.

The following adjectives can be used to give a positive review (negatives of these can be used for a negative review).

- informative
- interesting
- well-organised
- concise
- up-to-date
- thorough
- substantial
- comprehensive
- clear
- readable

# Unit 18: Book reviews

# Checklist

Below is a checklist for book reviews. Use it to check your writing.

| Area | Item | OK? | Comments |
|---|---|---|---|
| **Biographical details** | Essential details are given, e.g. name of book, author, publisher, date/place of publication, format, edition, number of pages, price, ISBN. | | |
| **Introduction** | There is an interesting beginning (e.g. anecdote or quotation). | | |
| | The introduction identifies the author, title, and type of book. | | |
| | The introduction states what the book is about. | | |
| | Background is given, e.g. previous work by the author or others in the same field, information about the book series (if part of a series). | | |
| | The thesis of the book is given, i.e. its specific contribution. | | |
| | Your thesis is given, i.e. your initial appraisal of the work and key observations. | | |
| **Description** | There is a description of key areas, e.g. summary of content, author's purpose, intended audience, arguments, sources, organisation and layout. | | |
| | Quotations are used as evidence. | | |
| **Evaluation** | There is critical evaluation of key areas, e.g. content (is everything included?), purpose (is it achieved?), audience (is it suitable?), arguments (are they valid?), evidence (is it strong?), organisation and layout (it is logical and clear?). | | |
| | Strengths and weaknesses are given. | | |
| **Conclusion** | There is a summary of the book's strengths and weaknesses. | | |
| | There is an indication of whether the book is useful or makes a lasting contribution. | | |
| | The conclusion states whether you recommend the book, and what audience it suits. | | |

Academic Writing Genres                                                    Sheldon Smith

# Example book review

Below is an example *book review*. It is taken from the following source: https://link.springer.com/content/pdf/10.1186%2F1747-1028-2-27.pdf.

Book review
**Review of "The Cell Cycle: Principles of Control" by David O. Morgan**
Mignon A Keaton

**Book details**
Morgan, D.O.: The Cell Cycle: Principles of Control (Primers in Biology) London: New Science Press Ltd; 2007:297. ISBN: 978-0-9539181-2-6

"The Cell Cycle: Principles of Control" by David Morgan is the second publication in the Primers In Biology series from New Science Press Ltd. This text aims to provide "a clear and concise guidebook" to our knowledge of the complex network of signalling pathways, regulatory circuits, and biochemical machines employed during cell reproduction. The result is a well-written book that is ideal for both students and seasoned scientists who are new-comers to the cell cycle field. Upper-level undergraduates and new graduate students will find it easy to follow, thanks to numerous colour figures whose schematics are used throughout the book. Each of the twelve chapters is divided into modular two-page sections that address specific topics (histone synthesis in S phase, for example). This webpage-like format is ideal for students who are used to retrieving information online, but readers looking for a thorough discussion of a topic may be frustrated by the limitations that a two-page partition imposes. Although molecular details are often included, this text is not a comprehensive review of the field. Instead, each chapter provides background for further reading and includes references for reviews and primary literature in each section.

A welcome aspect of the book is Morgan's attempt to integrate information gained from the study of different model organisms. In order to do so, Chapter 2 is dedicated to the organization of (both budding and fission) yeast, *Drosophila*, *Xenopus*, and mammalian cell cycles. This is especially helpful for understanding the data figures in the book as well as those in the primary literature. While most sections compare regulatory mechanisms in multiple systems (usually comparing budding yeast with mammalian cells), some sections only discuss the system in which the most complete information is known. Tables correlating protein homologues across multiple species are present throughout the text.

Morgan introduces the "cell-cycle control system" as the regulatory network that acts as a biological timer to ensure the execution of cell cycle events in a timely and consistent way. Cyclin-dependent kinases (CDKs) are the major components of this system, and an understanding of CDK regulation is an important foundation for studying the cell cycle. Thus, CDK regulation by phosphorylation and cyclin degradation is introduced before any stage of the cell cycle is covered in detail. A main focus of Chapter 3 is the inherent bistability of the system that allows for switch-like transitions between G1/S and G2/M and

# Unit 18: Book reviews

the establishment of a self-perpetuating oscillator. Sections 3–7, 3–8, and 3–11 are the best explanations of these mechanisms that I've read to date.

After establishing the principles of CDK regulation, how the cell-cycle control system executes DNA replication, nuclear division, and cytokinesis is described in Chapters 4–8. This allows Morgan to address seamlessly both the underlying mechanisms and the regulation of those mechanisms at each step in the cell cycle. Ultimately, this approach gives the reader a more fluid view of the cell cycle and a firmer understanding of how regulatory circuits in one phase can mediate regulation of the following phases.

Although this book is entitled "The Cell Cycle: Principles of Control," the mechanics of cell cycle events are equally addressed. The mitotic spindle is discussed in detail in Chapter 6. A thorough introduction to microtubule structure and behaviour is given. The roles of microtubule motors and kinetochores in establishing a spindle with bi-oriented chromosomes is discussed. Morgan presents the enigmatic processes of kinetochore attachment, microtubule flux, and chromosome congress ion by discussing proposed models in the context of published data. Similarly, the mechanics of the actin-myosin contractile ring during cytokinesis is detailed in Chapter 8 and the structural connections between homologous chromosomes during meiosis are emphasized in Chapter 9. Researchers whose work focuses on other aspects of the cell cycle may particularly appreciate the attention given to these events.

A review of the cell cycle would not be complete without a discussion of the effects that extracellular signalling path-ways have on cell proliferation. Morgan goes a step further by also discussing the regulation of cell size and the influence of cell metabolism on the cell-cycle control system. In addition, the negative effects of hyperproliferation and telomere shortening are included.

One of the attractive aspects of this book is Morgan's excellent description of the principles of tumorigenesis in Chapter 12. The development of improved detection methods and treatments for cancer is one of the main goals of understanding cell cycle regulation. Researchers will appreciate the sections covering the different mechanisms of acquiring mutations and genomic instability, the nomenclature describing the tissue specificity of tumours, and the genes most commonly mutated in specific forms of cancer. This chapter is a very good primer for reading cancer-related studies, which can often be very clinical in nature.

Overall, this book offers an excellent portrait of the fascinating complexity of cell division. The principles behind the detailed mechanisms of ensuring timely and control-led progression through the cell cycle are well communicated. Morgan often cross-references related sections, allowing the reader to skip around chapters as needed. Published data is presented in a clear and useful way. For these reasons, I believe this book would be an ideal text for an advanced undergraduate or graduate-level class. As a young researcher in the cell cycle field, I also believe this book has the potential to inspire students to join other researchers in the endeavour to further our understanding of cell reproduction.

**Academic Writing Genres**  **Sheldon Smith**

# Exercises

## Exercise 1: **Comprehension**

Answer the following questions about this unit. Either do this after reading the unit, or make notes first then use your notes to answer the questions.

1 What features does a book review share with other kinds of review (e.g. film review, review of TV programmes)?

- _____
- _____
- _____
- _____

2 How long is a typical book review?
_____
_____

3 How is a book *review* different from a book *report*?
_____
_____

4 Explain, with examples, what *bibliographic details* are. Where you would normally find them?
_____
_____
_____
_____

5 Explain the following terms.
- The thesis of the *book*. _____
- The thesis of the *review*. _____

## Unit 18: **Book reviews**

**6** Which is more important, *description* or *evaluation*? Which part is usually longer? Why?

_____
_____
_____

**7** Complete the missing words in the table below (first column), showing areas which might be considered when describing/evaluating the book. To help you, some key questions for each area are included (these are slightly modified from earlier in the unit).

| Area | Key questions |
| --- | --- |
| **(i)** _____ of the book | Is everything included? Is there too much information? Is anything essential left out? |
| The author's **(ii)** _____ | Has the author succeeded? |
| The intended **(iii)** _____ | Is the book appropriate for them? Why (not)? Who else might benefit from reading it? |
| The author's **(iv)** _____ and **(v)** _____ | How valid or effective are they? Do you agree with the author's opinions? Why (not)? |
| **(vi)** _____ used in the book | How strong are they? Are there enough? |
| How the book is **(vii)** _____ | Is it logical or useful? Are there any problems? Is the book clear and easy to use? |

**8** What may be achieved in the introduction to a book review?

- _____
- _____
- _____
- _____
- _____

**9** Give examples of the kind of background that may be given in the introduction.

- _____
- _____
- _____

**10** The following are some positive adjectives which could be used to describe a book. However, the letters are mixed up. Unscramble them to form the adjective. To help you, the first letter has been given, and there is an example.

- relac ⇨ c<u>lear</u>
- prechenomvies ⇨ c_____
- noccies ⇨ c_____
- verimfation ⇨ i_____
- nittinegers ⇨ i_____
- bealared ⇨ r_____
- lusstibanta ⇨ s_____
- hugothor ⇨ t_____
- poutated ⇨ u_____-_____-_____
- gellowdranies ⇨ w_____-_____

## Exercise 2: **Example book review**

Study the example book review earlier in the unit and answer the following questions.

a) The *Introduction* to the example book review is copied below. Identify the different elements (shown to the right).

| | |
|---|---|
| "The Cell Cycle: Principles of Control" by David Morgan is the second publication in the Primers In Biology series from New Science Press Ltd. This text aims to provide "a clear and concise guidebook" to our knowledge of the complex network of signalling pathways, regulatory circuits, and biochemical machines employed during cell reproduction. The result is a well-written book that is ideal for both students and seasoned scientists who are new-comers to the cell cycle field. Upper-level undergraduates and new graduate students will find it easy to follow, thanks to numerous colour figures whose schematics are used throughout the book. Each of the twelve chapters is divided into modular two-page sections that address specific topics (histone synthesis in S phase, for example).This webpage-like format is ideal for students who are used to retrieving information online, but readers looking for a thorough discussion of a topic may be frustrated by the limitations that a two-page partition imposes. Although molecular details are often included, this text is not a comprehensive review of the field. Instead, each chapter provides background for further reading and includes references for reviews and primary literature in each section. | • The author and title.<br><br>• Information about the book series.<br><br>• An anecdote or quotation at the beginning.<br><br>• What the book is about.<br><br>• The thesis of the book, i.e. its specific contribution.<br><br>• The writer's thesis, i.e. their appraisal of the work and key observations. |

## Unit 18: Book reviews

b) How is the book review organised: description then evaluation, or the two combined?

_____

c) How many chapters are contained in the book? _____

d) Who does the writer suggest would be a suitable audience for the book?

_____
_____

e) How does the writer organise the description of the content of the book (e.g. by theme, by chapter, other)? _____

f) How is the book organised (i.e. what is the layout of the book)?

_____
_____

g) Give an example of a weakness of the book. [Hint: It is given in the Introduction]

_____
_____

h) Which area does the following paragraph of the review consider? What does it tell you about the book?

> A review of the cell cycle would not be complete without a discussion of the effects that extracellular signalling path-ways have on cell proliferation. Morgan goes a step further by also discussing the regulation of cell size and the influence of cell metabolism on the cell-cycle control system. In addition, the negative effects of hyperproliferation and telomere shortening are included.

_____
_____
_____

# Academic Writing Genres                                    Sheldon Smith

i) Is the review positive or negative? How do you know? Find examples of adjectives or phrases to support your opinion.

- _____
- _____
- _____
- _____
- _____
- _____

- _____
- _____
- _____
- _____
- _____
- _____

## Exercise 3: Learning outcomes check

a) The following are the learning outcomes for this unit. Decide how well you have mastered each one by giving it a score, as follows.

    3 = I understand/can do this well.
    2 = I understand/can do this fairly well, but I can improve with more practice.
    1 = I understand/can do this, but not well enough yet. I need to practise more.
    0 = I cannot do this yet. I need more time.

| Score | Learning Outcome |
| --- | --- |
| _____ | I understand what a book review is. |
| _____ | I know the difference between a book review and a book report. |
| _____ | I understand how to prepare to write a book review. |
| _____ | I know the structure of a book review. |
| _____ | I understand the content of a typical book review. |
| _____ | I am aware of some language for different parts of a book review. |

b) Use this information to review the unit and improve.

# Unit 19: Research Proposals

## Learning Outcomes

By the end of this unit, you should:
- understand what a research proposal is;
- know the two kinds of research proposal;
- understand the different sections of a research proposal;
- understand the function and content of each section.

## Key Vocabulary

*Nouns*
- approval
- funding
- timeline

## Additional Vocabulary

*Academic Collocations*
- detailed information (adj + n)
- key areas (adj + n)
- previous research (adj + n)
- frequently used (adv + past)
- pilot study (n + n)
- research methodology (n + n)
- give information (v + n)
- require resources (v + n)

## Contents of this section

Unit 19: Research Proposals .................................. 271
    Overview ........................................................................ 272
    Structure of research proposals ................................... 272
    Checklist ........................................................................ 275
    Exercises ....................................................................... 277

# Overview

Research proposals are written before research is conducted in order to gain approval or funding for the research. There are two types of research proposal, as follows.
- **Approval proposal**. This type of proposal is written before undertaking a final project, dissertation or thesis, and is submitted to your supervisor for approval.
- **Funding proposal**. This type of proposal is submitted to an external organisation in order to seek funding for your research.

For an *approval proposal*, your supervisor needs to see that your research is worthwhile and has been carefully planned before you begin. This means presenting information such as the purpose of the research, its importance, previous research in the same area, how your research will be conducted, a timeframe, and the resources that will be needed.

For a *funding approval*, the organisation needs to see that your research represents a worthwhile investment of available funds. As such, this type of proposal is not a mere presentation of information, but rather a form of persuasive writing. You will need to demonstrate the validity of your research design, the significance of the research, how it is relevant to the organisation, your competence as a researcher, the fitness of the research facilities, and the appropriateness of your research budget.

# Structure of research proposals

Many research proposals are submitted using an application form, meaning that a formally structured document is not required. If there is no form, the following is a possible structure for a research proposal. This structure is for an *approval proposal*, as this is the one likely to be encountered for university study.

The proposal should begin with a **Title page**. This will provide a preliminary (or proposed) title for your research. Other details such as your name, university name, and supervisor's name may also appear here.

Following this, there should be a **Summary** of the research proposal. This will give the key areas in the proposal, i.e. the aim, objectives, research questions, method, and timeline.

There should be an **Introduction** to the proposal. This will give *background information* and a description of the research area. It may also give the motivation for the research and explain its importance. The overall *aim* of the research will be given, in other words what your research will achieve. This will be accompanied by more specific *research objectives*,

# Unit 19: **Research proposals**

which outline the issues to be addressed in order to achieve the aim. These will be followed by the *research questions* which enable the objectives to be achieved (usually Why, How or What questions).

There should be a preliminary **Literature review**. This section provides a critical summary of previous research in the area, identifying possible gaps and how your research will fill them. This section may help to justify your research and show why it is important. Although at this stage your review of literature may not be complete, your supervisor will still need to see the general framework that your research exists within, and examples of previous research in the area, in order to be confident you are approaching the research in the correct way.

Next there will be a **Methodology** section. This section will give information on how your research will be conducted. This includes the kind of data which will be obtained (e.g. quantitative or qualitative), the source of data, the research methodology and why this approach has been chosen. Ethical and safety issues may also be identified. Required resources may also be listed, e.g. facilities, laboratory equipment and technical help.

> **Future tense**
> As the research has not yet been conducted, the method will use future tense rather than the usual past passive.

The proposal should include a **Timeline**. This section will show how you plan to finish the research within the allotted time. It should include when important aspects of the research will start and finish, for instance the literature review, stages of experiments, and chapters of the final written work (likely to be a thesis or dissertation). The timeline can be formatted as a table or a list; a GANTT chart, listing tasks (vertical axis) and time (horizontal axis), is also frequently used.

There should be a **References** section, which gives full details of any sources cited in the research proposal.

Finally, there will be **Appendices**, which give additional information not needed in the main body. This could include interview questions, questionnaires, and pilot study data.

Other sections are also possible. For example, there may be sections on *Expected results*, *Expected chapter outline*, *Supervision* or *Dissemination of results*.

# Academic Writing Genres       Sheldon Smith

The following chart summarises the sections of a research proposal.

| Section | Purpose |
|---|---|
| Title page | Gives a proposed title for the research, as well as information such as the name of the author, university name, and supervisor's name. |
| Summary | Gives a summary of the research proposal. |
| Introduction | Describes the research area and provides necessary background information. Gives aim of the research, research objectives, and research questions. |
| Literature review | Provides a (preliminary) summary of previous literature in the area. Identifies possible gaps and how the research will fill them. |
| Methodology | Gives information on how the research will be conducted. May also identify ethical and safety issues and list required resources. |
| Timeline | Gives expected start/end dates of important aspects of the research. |
| Reference section | Lists any sources cited in the proposal, with full details. |
| Appendices | Provides any detailed information which readers may need for reference (e.g. interview questions, questionnaires, pilot study data). |

# Unit 19: Research proposals

# Checklist

Below is a checklist for research proposals. Use it to assess your proposal, or ask a peer.

| Section | Item | Details | OK? | Comments |
|---|---|---|---|---|
| **Title page** | Title | There is a proposed title for the research. | | |
| | Details | The title page includes details such as name of author, university name, supervisor's name. | | |
| **Summary** | / | There is a summary of key areas of the proposal (aim, research questions, method, timeline). | | |
| **Introduction** | Background | The research area is described. | | |
| | Aim | The overall aim of the research is given. | | |
| | Research objectives | There are clear and specific research objectives. | | |
| | Research questions | The research questions are stated. | | |
| **Literature review** | Critical summary | There is a critical summary of previous research in the area. | | |
| | Research gaps | Gaps are identified, as well as how your research will fill them. | | |

| | | | | |
|---|---|---|---|---|
| **Methodology** | Data type/ source | There is information on the type and source of data which will be obtained. | | |
| | Methodology | There are details of the research methodology and why this approach has been chosen. | | |
| | Ethics/safety | Ethical and safety issues are identified, if necessary. | | |
| | Resources | Required resources are listed. | | |
| **Timeline** | Start/end dates | A timeline is given, showing start/end dates of key aspects. | | |
| | Format | The timeline is suitably formatted, e.g. table, list, GANTT chart. | | |
| **Reference section** | / | Full details are given for all sources cited in the research proposal. | | |
| **Appendices** | / | Appendices give additional details not needed in main text. | | |
| **Other sections** | / | Other sections included, if appropriate (e.g. *Expected results*, *Expected chapter outline, Supervision, Dissemination of results*). | | |

# Unit 19: **Research proposals**

## Exercises

### Exercise 1: **Comprehension**

Answer the following questions about this unit. Either do this after reading the unit, or make notes first then use your notes to answer the questions.

1. What is a research proposal?

   _____

   _____

2. What are the two types of research proposal? What is the difference between them?

   _____

   _____

   _____

   _____

3. Which type of proposal is more common for university study?

   _____

4. True or false: A research proposal is a formally structured document. Justify your answer.

   _____

   _____

5. What elements might the *Introduction* contain?

   - _____
   - _____
   - _____
   - _____
   - _____
   - _____
   - _____

# Academic Writing Genres  Sheldon Smith

**6** How is the *Literature review* in a research proposal similar to the one in the final document? How is it different?

_____
_____

**7** What tense is usually used to describe the method? Why is this tense used? How and why is this different from the tense used in the final document?

_____
_____
_____

**8** What elements might the *Methodology* contain?

- _____
- _____
- _____
- _____
- _____
- _____
- _____

**9** The proposal should include a *timeline*. Give *brief* answers to the following questions about the timeline.

- Why is it important?  _____
- What should it contain?  _____
- How can it be formatted?  _____

**10** What other sections could a research proposal contain?

- _____
- _____
- _____
- _____

# Unit 19: **Research proposals**

## Exercise 2: **Learning outcomes check**

a) The following are the learning outcomes for this unit. Decide how well you have mastered each one by giving it a score, as follows.

    3 = I understand/can do this well.
    2 = I understand/can do this fairly well, but I can improve with more practice.
    1 = I understand/can do this, but not well enough yet. I need to practise more.
    0 = I cannot do this yet. I need more time.

| Score | Learning Outcome |
|---|---|
| _____ | I understand what a research proposal is. |
| _____ | I know the two kinds of research proposal. |
| _____ | I understand the different sections of a research proposal. |
| _____ | I understand the function and content of each section. |

b) Use this information to review the unit and improve.

# Unit 20: Theses/Dissertations

## Learning Outcomes

By the end of this unit, you should:
- know what a thesis/dissertation is;
- understand the difference between a thesis and a dissertation;
- understand how to prepare to write thesis/dissertation;
- know some key requirements to be aware of before writing a thesis/dissertation;
- know how to structure a thesis/dissertation;
- understand the contents of each chapter of a thesis/dissertation.

## Key Vocabulary

**Nouns**
- thesis
- dissertation

## Additional Vocabulary

*Academic Collocations*
- detailed information (adj + n)
- earlier research (adj + n)
- existing research (adj + n)
- final stage (adj + n)
- major differences (adj + n)
- qualitative data (adj + n)
- quantitative data (adj + n)
- relevant information (adj + n)
- significant amount (adj + n)
- commonly found (adv + past)
- pilot studies (n + n)
- gather information (v + n)
- gather data (v + n)
- give information (v + n)

## Contents of this section

Unit 20: Theses/Dissertations .......................... 281
    Overview ................................................................. 282
    Thesis vs. Dissertation ........................................... 282
    Preparing to write a thesis/dissertation ............. 282
    Structure of a thesis/dissertation ....................... 283
    Checklist .................................................................. 287
    Exercises ................................................................. 289

# Overview

If you are studying for a Master's or a PhD, you will need to write a thesis or dissertation as the final stage. This section explains the difference between these two terms, gives ideas for how to prepare to write one, and gives information on their structure.

# Thesis vs. Dissertation

The meaning of the terms *thesis* and *dissertation* vary according to the country of study. In the UK, a *thesis* (also called a *doctoral thesis*) is written at the end of a PhD, and a *dissertation* (also called a *Master's dissertation*) is written at the end of a Master's degree. This contrasts with the USA, where a *thesis* is written at the end of a Master's degree, and a *dissertation* is written at the end of a PhD. In Australia, both of these pieces of writing are called *thesis*, though there is a distinction between a *Master's minor thesis*, which demonstrates knowledge, and a *Master's major thesis*, which contributes to knowledge.

The dissertation and thesis have a similar structure. The main difference between them as pieces of writing is the length, with a Master's thesis/dissertation being shorter, around 15,000-20,000 words, and a PhD thesis/dissertation up to 80,000 words.

# Preparing to write a thesis/dissertation

Writing a thesis/dissertation can seem a daunting task. To help, most Master's and PhD programmes will require you to complete a **research proposal** first, which will allow you to begin planning and establish a timeline. You will also normally need to write a **literature review** as an assignment, which, again, will help you prepare. Other similar tasks may be required to help build towards this end goal, for example pilot studies or learning journals.

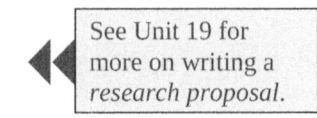

> See Unit 19 for more on writing a *research proposal*.

As part of your preparation, you should check the requirements. The mark scheme, if provided, should help with this. In particular, be sure to check the following.
- **Word limits**. What is the word limit for the whole document? Does this include or exclude Abstract, References and Appendices? Is there a minimum number of words? Are there any word limits for individual parts (e.g. Abstract)?
- **Required chapters/content**. Are there any chapters which must be included? Is there a specific order for chapters? Is there a guide to what each one should contain?
- **Content of appendices**. What should go in the Appendices versus the main body?

# Unit 20: Theses/Dissertations

## Structure of a thesis/dissertation

There are many ways to structure a thesis/dissertation, which, like reports, can vary according to discipline. A traditional thesis/dissertation will be broadly organised using the IMRAD structure. Below are the sections (typically called 'chapters' for writing of this length) which are commonly found. Each is discussed in more detail later.

**Preliminaries**
- Title page
- Abstract
- Acknowledgements
- Contents

**Introduction**
- Introduction
  What is the background?
  What is the aim?

**Main body**
- Literature review
  What other research has been done?
  What gaps exist?
- Method
  How/when/where was data gathered?
- Results
  What were the results?
- Discussion
  What do the results mean?

**Conclusion**
- Conclusion
  What are the conclusions?
- Recommendations
  What should happen in future?

**End matter**
- Reference section
- Appendices

## Preliminaries

There are several parts which go at the beginning, before the main content. There should first be a **Title page**. This will include the title, which should be short, specific and clear. Details such as name of author, name of university, name of supervisor, and word count, may also appear here. The format of the title page may be specified, so check first.

Next, there should be an **Abstract**. This is a stand-alone piece of writing which summarises the document. It should contain details of the aim, objectives, background, methods, results, conclusions, and recommendations. There is often a strict word limit for the Abstract, which can be difficult to meet. Although this appears first, it is usually best to write it last, when the whole document is finished and you are sure of the content.

> *Abstracts* are covered in more detail in Unit 21.

Unlike a report, a thesis/dissertation requires **Acknowledgements**. This is used to thank your supervisor(s) and the other people who have helped in your research and in the writing of your thesis/dissertation. It may also give a declaration that the work is your own and is free of plagiarism.

Finally, the preliminaries should conclude with a **Contents** page. This should list all the *headings and sub-headings* in the document, together with the page numbers. There will usually also be a separate *List of illustrations*, giving the numbers, titles and page numbers of all the figures, a *List of tables* for the tables, and *List of abbreviations* used in the text.

## Introduction

This chapter should give sufficient background to enable the reader to understand the main body of the thesis/dissertation. This means providing the context of the research, why the subject is important, and the aim and objectives of the research. There should also be information on how the thesis/dissertation is organized.

## Literature review

The main body is likely to begin with a **Literature Review**, though for some disciplines this section might be omitted. This gives a critical summary of the existing research in the field, indicating authors who have worked or are working in the area and their main contributions. The main purpose is to identify gaps in knowledge and justify your own research. The review will lead in to the research problem or questions you are addressing.

> *Literature reviews* are covered in more detail in Unit 22.

# Unit 20: **Theses/Dissertations**

## Methodology

This chapter will outline the method and materials of your research, in other words how, when and where you gathered information. This chapter is likely to also justify the research process. In addition, you are likely to explain why other methods, which you did not use, were rejected.

> **Method vs. methodology**
> The term *method* is used to describe what you did. The term *methodology* has a broader meaning, including not only the method but the philosophy behind it.

## Results

This chapter presents the results of the research. There is likely to be a significant amount of data, which will need to be organised and presented in a logical way. Graphs and pie charts are common ways of presenting quantitative data. Qualitative data, such as results of interviews, can be summarised and presented in tables, along with quoted excerpts. Research questions might be used to create subsections to further organise the data. Problems with gathering data should also be considered in this section.

## Discussion

This chapter draws together prior elements by analyzing the results, grounded in theory (e.g. from the literature review), and showing their implications. Major differences or similarities between your findings and those of earlier research should be shown. Limitations of the research should also be given.

## Conclusion

The conclusion consists of two chapters. The first, **Conclusion**, summarises information, and states the extent to which the aim and objectives of the research have been met.

There may also be a **Recommendations** chapter. This will give recommendations for future action, which should derive from the main body. If appropriate, ways to further develop your work will be given in this chapter.

## End matter

The thesis/dissertation will conclude with two sections. The first is a **Reference section**, listing all sources cited in the text. The extensive writing process means it is easy to omit one or more references, or include one or more which are not cited, so be sure to check.

The second is the **Appendices**, which provide any detailed information which your readers may need for reference, but which you do not want to include in the body.

# Academic Writing Genres — Sheldon Smith

The following chart summarises the structure of a thesis/dissertation.

| Stage | Section/Chapter | Purpose |
|---|---|---|
| Preliminaries | Title page | Gives the title, plus details such as name of author, name of university, name of supervisor, word count. |
| | Abstract | Gives a summary of the document (aim, objectives, background, methods, results, conclusions, recommendations). Should be a stand-alone piece of writing. |
| | Acknowledgements | Thanks your supervisor(s) and the other people who have helped in your research. |
| | Contents | Gives all the headings and sub-headings, with page numbers. Also gives List of illustrations, List of tables, and List of abbreviations. |
| Introduction | Introduction | Provides context of the research. Says why the subject is important. States the aim and objectives of the research. Shows how the document is organized. |
| Main body | Literature review | Gives a critical summary of existing research in the field. Indicates authors who have worked or are working in the area and their main contributions. Identifies gaps in knowledge. Justifies the research. |
| | Methodology | Outlines the method and materials of the research. Explains why other methods were rejected. |
| | Results | Presents results of the research via graphs, pie charts, tables etc. |
| | Discussion | Analyses the results and shows their implications. Shows differences or similarities between findings and earlier research. Gives limitations of the research. |
| Conclusion | Conclusion | Summarises information in the document. States the extent to which the aim and objectives were met. |
| | Recommendations | Gives recommendations for future action and ways to further develop the work. |
| End matter | Reference section | Lists all sources cited in the text. |
| | Appendices | Provides any detailed information which readers may need for reference which is not in the main body. |

# Unit 20: **Theses/Dissertations**

# Checklist

Below is a checklist for a thesis/dissertation. Use it to check your writing, or ask a peer.

| Stage | Section | Item | OK? | Comments |
|---|---|---|---|---|
| Preliminaries | Title page | The thesis/dissertation has a clear and informative title. | | |
| | | Other relevant information is included (e.g. name of author, word count). | | |
| | Abstract | There is an Abstract which summarises the whole document. | | |
| | Acknowledgements | There is an Acknowledgements page. | | |
| | Contents page | A contents page is included, listing all the headings and sub-headings | | |
| | | There is a separate *List of illustrations*, *List of tables* and *List of abbreviations*. | | |
| Introduction | Background | The Introduction contains necessary background, including context of the research and why subject is important. | | |
| | Aim and objectives | The research aim/objectives are given. | | |
| | Outline | There is an outline of how the thesis/dissertation is organised. | | |
| Main body | Literature Review | There is a critical summary of existing research. | | |
| | | The review cites authors who have worked/are working in the area and their main contributions. | | |
| | | Gaps in knowledge are identified. | | |
| | Methodology | There is an outline of how information was gathered, when and where. | | |
| | | The research process is justified. | | |
| | | Other (rejected) methods are explained. | | |
| | Findings | Data is presented in a logical way (graphs, pie charts, tables). | | |
| | | Problems with gathering data are considered. | | |

| | | | | |
|---|---|---|---|---|
| **Main body (cont'd)** | **Discussion** | The results are analysed, grounded in theory (e.g. from the literature review). | | |
| | | Major differences/similarities between findings and earlier research is shown. | | |
| | | Limitations of the research are given. | | |
| **Conclusion** | **Conclusion** | There is a summary of the main points, and a statement of the extent to which the aim and objectives have been met. | | |
| | **Recommend-ations** | There are recommendations for future action, and/or ways to further develop the research. | | |
| **End matter** | **Reference section** | There is a reference section with full details of sources cited. | | |
| | | Reference section entries are correctly formatted. | | |
| | | All sources cited in the text are in the reference section. | | |
| | | All sources in the reference section are cited in the text. | | |
| | **Appendices** | Appendices are clearly presented and numbered. | | |
| | | Appendices contain appropriate material (not essential for main body). | | |
| **Other requirements** | **Word limits** | The document is within the word limit. | | |
| | | Each section is within the word limit, if this is specified. | | |
| | **Chapters** | All required chapters are included. | | |
| | | Chapters are in the required order, if the order is specified. | | |
| | **Other** | The document fulfils other requirements, e.g. those indicated by the mark scheme. | | |

# Unit 20: Theses/Dissertations

## Exercises

### Exercise 1: Comprehension

Answer the following questions about this unit. Either do this after reading the unit, or make notes first then use your notes to answer the questions.

1 What is the difference between a *thesis* and a *dissertation*?

   _____
   _____
   _____

2 How long (number of words) is a typical thesis/dissertation?

   _____
   _____

3 Give examples of assignments that might be part of a Master's or PhD programme that might help you prepare to write a thesis/dissertation.

   - _____
   - _____
   - _____
   - _____

4 Give examples of requirements you should consider before writing your thesis/dissertation.

   - _____
   - _____
   - _____

# Academic Writing Genres                              Sheldon Smith

5  The following are the components of a typical thesis/dissertation. However, they are in the *wrong order*. Number them (from 1-13) according to the order they usually go in. An example has been done.
   - Abstract                    _____
   - Acknowledgements            _____
   - Appendices                  _____
   - Conclusion                  _____
   - Contents page               _____
   - Discussion                  _____
   - Findings                    _____
   - Introduction                _____
   - Literature Review           _____
   - Methodology                 _____
   - Recommendations             _____
   - Reference section           _____
   - Title page                  ___1___

6  What elements of a thesis/dissertation are *not* usually found in reports?
   _____
   _____

7  Why might it be best to write the Abstract *last*?
   _____
   _____

8  What is the purpose of the Introduction? What should it contain?
   _____
   _____
   _____

9  How might the following types of data be represented in the *Results* chapter?
   - Quantitative data    _____
   - Qualitative data     _____

10  What problems might you encounter when preparing the *Reference section* for a thesis/dissertation? How can you overcome these problems?
   _____
   _____

# Unit 20: **Theses/Dissertations**

## Exercise 2: **Learning outcomes check**

a) The following are the learning outcomes for this unit. Decide how well you have mastered each one by giving it a score, as follows.

    3 = I understand/can do this well.
    2 = I understand/can do this fairly well, but I can improve with more practice.
    1 = I understand/can do this, but not well enough yet. I need to practise more.
    0 = I cannot do this yet. I need more time.

| Score | Learning Outcome |
|---|---|
| _____ | I know what a thesis/dissertation is. |
| _____ | I understand the difference between a thesis and a dissertation. |
| _____ | I understand how to prepare to write a thesis/dissertation. |
| _____ | I know some key requirements to be aware of before writing a thesis/dissertation. |
| _____ | I know how to structure a thesis/dissertation. |
| _____ | I understand the contents of each chapter of a thesis/dissertation. |

b) Use this information to review the unit and improve.

# PART IV:
## GENRE ELEMENTS

# Unit 21 | Abstracts

## Learning Outcomes

By the end of this unit, you should:
- know what an abstract is;
- understand the difference between an *abstract* and an *executive summary*;
- understand the difference between an *informative* abstract and a *descriptive* abstract;
- know which type of abstract is most commonly used;
- understand how to structure an abstract;
- understand the typical content of an abstract (and what *not* to include);
- know language to use for writing abstracts.

By completing the exercises, you will also:
- study example abstracts for language and type.

## Key Vocabulary

**Nouns**
- abstract
- executive summary

**Adjectives**
- informative
- descriptive

## Additional Vocabulary

**Academic Collocations (in unit)**
- appropriate language (adj + n)
- further research (adj + n)
- main findings (adj + n)
- numerical data (adj + n)
- original research (adj + n)
- specific information (adj + n)
- technical expertise (adj + n)
- increasingly common (adv + adj)

**Collocations (in example abstracts)**
- current research (adj + n)
- further studies (adj + n)
- qualitative research (adj + n)
- related issues (adj + n)
- research findings (n + n)
- address the issue (v + n)
- assess the impact (v + n)
- consider issues (v + n)

## Contents of this section

### Unit 21: Abstracts .......................................... 295

Overview .......................................................................................... 296
Abstract vs. Executive Summary ..................................................... 296
Types of abstract ............................................................................. 297
Word length .................................................................................... 297
Structure and content of abstracts ................................................. 297
Language for abstracts ................................................................... 298
Checklist ......................................................................................... 299
Example abstracts .......................................................................... 300
Exercises ......................................................................................... 301

## Overview

An abstract is a shortened version of an academic paper, such as a report, a conference paper or a journal article, appearing before the paper itself. It is intended for someone who has not read the article, and its purpose is to provide concise information to the reader so that they can decide whether to read the article in detail. It is therefore the most frequently read part of any paper, apart from the title. Abstracts for journal papers are often reprinted in special abstracting journals or electronic indexing services.

## Abstract vs. Executive Summary

Some types of documents require an *abstract*, while others use an *executive summary* instead. They are similar in that both present a summary of the whole document. They have several differences, however. One is the audience. An *abstract* is intended for an expert audience. In contrast, an *executive summary* presents an overview of the document to a non-expert audience, such as management personnel. A second difference is purpose. While an *abstract* is intended to allow the reader to decide whether to read the whole document, the purpose of an *executive summary* is to provide enough information so the reader does not have to read the whole document. As such, an *executive summary* is usually more detailed and longer than an *abstract*. An *executive summary* is common in government, management or consulting, and is a component of report types such as business reports (Unit 14).

> **In short**
> The differences:
> - **abstract**: for expert audience, helps them decide whether to read the whole document;
> - **executive summary**: for non-expert audience, more detailed, allows them to avoid reading the whole document.

# Unit 21: **Abstracts**

## Types of abstract

There are two kinds of abstract which can be written.
- **Informative abstract**. This type of abstract summarises the information in the main sections of the paper. It is *the most common type* of abstract, and is suitable for papers or reports about original research.
- **Descriptive abstract**. This type of abstract describes the structure of the document. This type is far less common, although it might be appropriate for review articles or research the results of which you do not want to reveal to the reader until they have read the whole paper.

## Word length

An abstract should be as brief as possible, providing only the important information which the reader needs to know rather than presenting a complete summary. For a conference or journal paper, the word limit will usually be stated. If there is no limit, a general rule is between 5% and 10% of the original. For a short document (up to 2000 words), this might mean 100 to 200 words. For a PhD thesis, the abstract might be as long as 800 words. *Descriptive* abstracts are shorter than *informative* abstracts, typically fewer than 100 words. An *executive summary*, in comparison, is typically 10-20% the length of the original.

## Structure and content of abstracts

An abstract is generally written as a single paragraph, though it is increasingly common for journals to request abstracts using headings. The contents of the abstract will depend on how the paper is structured. For a typical IMRAD structure (Introduction, Method, Results and Discussion), an abstract will normally include the following elements:
- **background** (the background to the research);
- **aim** (the aim of the research);
- **method** (how the research was conducted);
- **results** (what the main findings were);
- **conclusions** (what the findings mean).

The abstract may also contain **recommendations** (e.g. for further research) and **limitations** (what the limitations of the research were). The following would ***not*** normally be included in an abstract: information not contained in the paper itself; tables and diagrams; citations.

The abstract will usually follow the order given above, which matches the order in a typical research paper. However, it can be useful to put the most important ideas first, so that readers will know the main point of the paper even if they only read the first sentence of the abstract. The description of the methods is likely to be very brief (unless the paper is presenting a new method), while the results are likely to take up the greatest number of words. The description should be as quantitative as possible, in other words using numerical data.

Although the abstract appears before the article, it is often written last. This is mainly because the abstract can only be written when the findings have been analysed, conclusions have been drawn and recommendations made.

## Language for abstracts

It is advisable to use short, simple sentences and active statements in order to convey the information as effectively as possible. Non-standard abbreviations should be avoided for clarity; most journals will be able to provide a list of standard abbreviations. It is common in abstracts to refer to the researchers using the third person plural pronoun 'we' or possessive pronoun 'our', as in the following examples.

> In this review, we discuss…
> Our | findings | suggest that…
>     | results  | show that…
> We show that…
> We also found…
> We provide recommendations…

There are some differences in language depending on the type of abstract. If you are writing an *informative abstract*, it is likely that *past* tense will be used most often to describe what you did or found out in your research. The language will be fairly precise and specific.

On the other hand, if you are writing a *descriptive abstract*, the *present* tense is more common as you describe what your paper does. The language may include more generalised vocabulary and phrases, such as the following.

> The paper  | describes |
> This paper | explores  | [X].
>            | considers |
> [X] is analysed.

# Unit 21: **Abstracts**

# Checklist

Below is a checklist for abstracts. Use it to check your writing, or ask a peer to help.

| Area | Item | OK? | Comments |
|---|---|---|---|
| **General** | Appropriate type of abstract is used (*informative* or *descriptive*). | | |
| | The abstract gives the reader a clear idea of what the research is about. | | |
| **Structure** | The abstract is written as a single paragraph (using headings if required). | | |
| **Content** | All relevant parts have been included, e.g. background, aim, method, results, conclusions. | | |
| | The information on the method is very brief (unless a new method is presented). | | |
| | The results take up the largest amount. | | |
| | The results are stated in a quantitative way (i.e. using numerical data). | | |
| | All important information is included. | | |
| | All information in the abstract is contained in the paper. | | |
| **Language** | Appropriate language is used (e.g. precise and specific for *informative* abstract, general for *descriptive* abstract). | | |
| | Appropriate tense is used (usually *past* tense for *informative* abstract, *present* tense for *descriptive* abstract). | | |
| | Non-standard abbreviations are avoided. | | |
| **Other** | The abstract is within the word limit (if this is specified). | | |
| | Tables and diagrams are *not* used. | | |
| | Citations are *not* used. | | |

# Example abstracts

Below are two example *abstracts*. They are used in the exercises later in the unit.

**1**

In this paper the author considers issues of quality in phenomenographic research. Research rigor, which is traditionally evaluated by validity and reliability criteria, ensures that research findings reflect the object of study. Quality in research subsumes rigor and extends considerably beyond satisfying the criteria for rigor. A piece of research has to convince readers of its quality when evaluated against criteria that have been developed through contributions and agreements within the research community. This paper tackles the quality issue in phenomenographic research in three steps. First, criteria for quality in qualitative research are discussed. Second and drawing on the literature, related issues when the criteria are applied to phenomenographic studies and the ways of addressing the issues are examined. Finally, the phenomenographic process is analyzed and suggestions are made for enhancing quality at each stage of the process. New phenomenographic researchers especially will find this paper as a useful guide.

Abstract taken from Sin, S. (2010) 'Considerations of Quality in Phenomenographic Research', *International Journal of Qualitative Methods*, pp. 305–319. doi: 10.1177/160940691000900401.

**2**

There are concerns that the marketing of e-cigarettes may increase the appeal of tobacco smoking in children. We examined this concern by assessing the impact on appeal of tobacco smoking after exposure to advertisements for e-cigarettes with and without candy-like flavours, such as bubble gum and milk chocolate. We assigned 598 English school children (aged 11–16 years) to 1 of 3 different conditions corresponding to the adverts to which they were exposed: adverts for flavoured e-cigarettes, adverts for non-flavoured e-cigarettes or a control condition in which no adverts were shown. The primary endpoint was appeal of tobacco smoking. Secondary endpoints were: appeal of using e-cigarettes, susceptibility to tobacco smoking, perceived harm of tobacco, appeal of e-cigarette adverts and interest in buying and trying e-cigarettes. Tobacco smokers and e-cigarette users were excluded from analyses (final sample=471). Exposure to either set of adverts did not increase the appeal of tobacco smoking, the appeal of using e-cigarettes, or susceptibility to tobacco smoking. Also, it did not reduce the perceived harm of tobacco smoking, which was high. Flavoured e-cigarette adverts were, however, more appealing than adverts for non-flavoured e-cigarettes and elicited greater interest in buying and trying e-cigarettes. Exposure to adverts for e-cigarettes does not seem to increase the appeal of tobacco smoking in children. Flavoured, compared with non-flavoured, e-cigarette adverts did, however, elicit greater appeal and interest in buying and trying e-cigarettes. Further studies extending the current research are needed to elucidate the impact of flavoured and non-flavoured e-cigarette adverts.

Abstract adapted from *Vasiljevic M, Petrescu DC, Marteau TM (2016) 'Impact of advertisements promoting candy-like flavoured e-cigarettes on appeal of tobacco smoking among children: an experimental study',* Tobacco Control, 2016;25:e107-e112.

# Unit 21: Abstracts

## Exercises

### Exercise 1: Comprehension

Answer the following questions about this unit. Either do this after reading the unit, or make notes first then use your notes to answer the questions.

1 What is an abstract? What is the purpose of an abstract?

_____
_____
_____

2 How are an *abstract* and an *executive summary* similar? How are they different?

_____
_____
_____
_____

3 What are the two types of abstract? Which one is most commonly used?

- _____
- _____

4 How long is a typical abstract? How long is an executive summary?

_____
_____

5 Complete the following summary of language for abstracts, using words from the box.

| general | tense | non-standard | past |
|---------|-------|--------------|------|
| present | simple | precise | active |

In order to convey information effectively, abstracts usually use a)_____ sentences and b)_____ statements. c)_____ abbreviations should be avoided. The verb d)_____ often differs according to the type of abstract, for example e)_____ for *descriptive* abstracts and f)_____ for *informative* ones. *Descriptive* abstracts usually use g)_____ words and phrases, while *informative* abstracts tend to use more h)_____ language.

# Academic Writing Genres        Sheldon Smith

## Exercise 2: **Example abstracts**

Study the two example abstracts (earlier in the unit) and answer the following questions.

a) Which abstract is *informative* and which is *descriptive*? How do you know?

_____

_____

_____

b) What tense is most common in each abstract? In each one, find examples of:
- present tense
- past tense

c) Study the second extract again (copied below). Identify and label the following elements:
- Background
- Methods
- Results
- Conclusions

> There are concerns that the marketing of e-cigarettes may increase the appeal of tobacco smoking in children. We examined this concern by assessing the impact on appeal of tobacco smoking after exposure to advertisements for e-cigarettes with and without candy-like flavours, such as bubble gum and milk chocolate. We assigned 598 English school children (aged 11–16 years) to 1 of 3 different conditions corresponding to the adverts to which they were exposed: adverts for flavoured e-cigarettes, adverts for non-flavoured e-cigarettes or a control condition in which no adverts were shown. The primary endpoint was appeal of tobacco smoking. Secondary endpoints were: appeal of using e-cigarettes, susceptibility to tobacco smoking, perceived harm of tobacco, appeal of e-cigarette adverts and interest in buying and trying e-cigarettes. Tobacco smokers and e-cigarette users were excluded from analyses (final sample=471). Exposure to either set of adverts did not increase the appeal of tobacco smoking, the appeal of using e-cigarettes, or susceptibility to tobacco smoking. Also, it did not reduce the perceived harm of tobacco smoking, which was high. Flavoured e-cigarette adverts were, however, more appealing than adverts for non-flavoured e-cigarettes and elicited greater interest in buying and trying e-cigarettes. Exposure to adverts for e-cigarettes does not seem to increase the appeal of tobacco smoking in children. Flavoured, compared with non-flavoured, e-cigarette adverts did, however, elicit greater appeal and interest in buying and trying e-cigarettes. Further studies extending the current research are needed to elucidate the impact of flavoured and non-flavoured e-cigarette adverts.
>
> Abstract adapted from *Vasiljevic M, Petrescu DC, Marteau TM (2016) 'Impact of advertisements promoting candy-like flavoured e-cigarettes on appeal of tobacco smoking among children: an experimental study'*, Tobacco Control, 2016;25:e107-e112.

# Unit 21: **Abstracts**

## Exercise 3: **Learning outcomes check**

a) The following are the learning outcomes for this unit. Decide how well you have mastered each one by giving it a score, as follows.

   3 = I understand/can do this well.
   2 = I understand/can do this fairly well, but I can improve with more practice.
   1 = I understand/can do this, but not well enough yet. I need to practise more.
   0 = I cannot do this yet. I need more time.

| Score | Learning Outcome |
|-------|------------------|
| _____ | I know what an abstract is. |
| _____ | I understand the difference between an *abstract* and *executive summary*. |
| _____ | I understand the difference between an *informative* and a *descriptive* abstract. |
| _____ | I know which type of abstract is most commonly used. |
| _____ | I understand how to structure an abstract. |
| _____ | I understand the typical content of an abstract (and what *not* to include). |
| _____ | I know language to use for writing abstracts. |

b) Use this information to review the unit and improve.

# Unit 22 | Literature Reviews

## Learning Outcomes

By the end of this unit, you should:
- know what a literature review is;
- understand how to structure a literature review;
- be aware of some writing guidelines for literature reviews.

By completing the exercises, you will also:
- study an example literature review for structure and content.

## Key Vocabulary

**Nouns**
- chronology

**Adjectives**
- critical

**Verbs**
- synthesise/-ize

## Additional Vocabulary

*Academic Collocations (in the unit)*
- academic writing (adj + n)
- existing research (adj + n)
- future study (adj + n)
- historical development (adj + n)
- key concepts (adj + n)
- original meaning (adj + n)
- previous studies (adj + n)
- quantitative approaches (adj + n)
- give an overview (v + n)
- provide context (v + n)
- provide support (v + n)

*Academic Collocations (in the review)*
- high levels (adj + n)
- increased productivity (adj + n)
- insufficient evidence (adj + n)
- numerous studies (adj + n)
- potential impact (adj + n)
- previous research (adj + n)
- previous studies (adj + n)
- recent study (adj + n)
- increasingly common (adv + adj)
- research evidence (n + n)
- survey data (n + n)
- provide evidence (v + n)

## Contents of this section

### Unit 22: Literature Reviews..................................305
Overview ........................................................................................................ 306
What is a literature review?......................................................................... 306
Structure of literature reviews..................................................................... 307
Checklist ........................................................................................................ 309
Example literature review............................................................................ 310
Exercises........................................................................................................ 312

## Overview

Literature reviews often form part of larger pieces of writing, such as reports, journal articles, theses or dissertations, though they may also be stand-alone pieces of writing. This section considers what a literature review is, how to structure one, and provides some guidelines for writing a literature review.

## What is a literature review?

A literature review gives a critical summary of the existing research in the field in order to identify gaps and create a starting point for your own research. A literature review is often conducted and written before you embark on research for a thesis or dissertation, and might help you to decide on the direction of your research.

| In short |
|---|
| A literature review:<br>• provides a critical summary of existing research;<br>• identifies gaps in knowledge;<br>• justifies your own research;<br>• describes and evaluates information. |

While in places the review may be descriptive, for the most part it should evaluate and analyse. This will be done by:
- summarising information;
- finding links or similarities between different areas;
- finding contradictions or differences;
- highlighting weaknesses or inconsistencies with the research;
- identifying a gap in the research.

# Unit 22: **Literature reviews**

# Structure of literature reviews

The structure of a literature review in part depends on the length. Literature reviews in reports or journal articles may be only one or two paragraphs long, and will therefore be less structured. Literature reviews written as stand-alone assignments or as part of a Master's thesis/dissertation will be much longer (around 2000-3000 words), while those for a PhD thesis/dissertation will be longer still (8,000-10,000 words), and these types of literature review will be much more structured pieces of writing, with an introduction, main body and conclusion.

## *Introduction*

An introduction to a literature review, if there is one, needs to accomplish several tasks. These include:
- outlining the topic or issue, in order to provide context for the review;
- explaining key concepts or terms;
- outlining how the main body will be organised;
- giving the scope (i.e. why certain literature is included and other literature excluded).

## *Main body*

The main body will describe, evaluate and analyse the literature findings. This will usually be done by grouping the findings according to a specific principle. Common principles for organisation are as follows.
- **Chronology**. Literature is organised according to when it was published.
- **Theme**. Literature is linked according to a theme.
- **Conclusions**. Literature can be linked according to the conclusions of the writers.
- **Methodology**. Literature may be linked according to the methodology used in previous studies, for example qualitative versus quantitative.

It is often possible to combine these methods of organisation, for example, literature linked by a theme may still be considered chronologically within that theme.

---

**Identifying a gap**

When identifying a gap, be sure that it is a *real* gap, and not simply the result of an inadequate search of the literature. Types of gap you might uncover are:
- *knowledge gap* – the most common;
- *relationship gap* – when it is not known how two things are connected;
- *theory gap* – when theory has not been thoroughly tested;
- *method gap* – when a method has not been used in a particular way;
- *analysis gap* – when something has not been analysed in a particular way, e.g. qualitative vs. quantitative.

---

**In short**

A literature review has:
- an introduction, outlining topic, stating key terms, giving organisation and scope;
- a main body, which can be organised in many ways (chronologically etc.);
- a conclusion, summarising findings.

# Academic Writing Genres — Sheldon Smith

The main body may also review the methods or materials relevant to your own study. This will provide support for your own choice of method.

It is likely that the main body with use sub-headings to further organise the information.

## *Conclusion*

The conclusion to the review, if there is one, will:
- summarise the most significant findings of your review;
- identify gaps in knowledge.

---

**Writing guidelines**

When writing your review, you should:
- use evidence – back up points by referring to specific writers/studies;
- be relevant – only include information related to the review focus;
- be selective – only include the most important points;
- be brief – summarise main points, rather than paraphrase or use quotations;
- show importance – the more important a study is, the more space it should take up;
- compare and contrast – highlight any similarities or differences in the findings;
- synthesise – link sources together if they say the same thing;
- be cautious – do not make claims the evidence does not show.

# Unit 22: **Literature reviews**

# Checklist

Below is a checklist for literature reviews. Use it to check your writing, or ask a peer to help.

| Stage | Section | Item | OK? | Comments |
|---|---|---|---|---|
| Introduction | Context | The introduction gives an outline of the topic or issue. | | |
| Introduction | Definitions | Key concepts or terms are explained, if necessary. | | |
| Introduction | Organisation | The organisation of the main body is given. | | |
| Introduction | Scope | The scope is given (what literature is included/excluded). | | |
| Main body | Organising principle | Literature is grouped appropriately (by *chronology*, *theme*, *conclusions*, or *methodology*). | | |
| Main body | Sub-headings | Main body uses sub-headings, if necessary (long reviews only). | | |
| Main body | Methods | Methods/materials relevant to the study have been reviewed. | | |
| Conclusion | Summary | There is a summary of the most significant findings. | | |
| Conclusion | Gaps | Gaps in knowledge are identified. | | |
| Other | Evaluation | The review evaluates findings (rather than just describing). | | |
| Other | Evidence | Specific writers or studies are referred to, to support points. | | |
| Other | Relevance | All information is related to the focus of the review. | | |
| Other | Selection | Only the most important information is included. | | |
| Other | Brevity | Main ideas of writers/studies are summarised (rather than paraphrased or quoted). | | |
| Other | Importance | More important findings take up more space. | | |
| Other | Comparison/contrast | Similarities/differences between findings are highlighted. | | |
| Other | Synthesis | Sources are linked together if they say the same thing. | | |
| Other | Caution | The findings are not overstated. | | |

# Example literature review

The following is the introduction to a journal article. It contains a literature review. It is taken from the following source: https://bmjopen.bmj.com/content/5/9/e008331.

## 1. Introduction

### 1.1 Background

Job satisfaction and burnout in the nursing workforce are global concerns,[1, 2] both due to their potential impact on quality and safety of patient care[3] and because low job satisfaction is a contributing factor associated with nurses leaving their job and the profession.[4] Numerous studies previously reported different rates of nurses' job satisfaction, burnout and intention to leave.[5, 6]

Shift patterns have been identified as an important factor in determining well-being and satisfaction among nurses.[7, 8] Providing in-patient nursing care inevitably involves shift work. Shifts of 12 h or longer have become increasingly common for nurses in hospitals in some countries in Europe.[9] This change is mainly driven by managers' perceptions of improved efficiency from reducing the number of nurse shifts a day, therefore resulting in fewer handovers between shifts, less interruptions to clinical care provision and increased productivity due to a reduction in the overlap between two shifts.[10] From the nurse perspective, longer shifts offer a potential to benefit from a compressed working week, with fewer work days and more days off-work, lower commuting costs and increased flexibility.[11, 12] However, previous studies on shift length in Europe did not provide evidence of nurses working a compressed work week, so it is not clear if working 12 h shifts is associated with fewer days at work.[9] These scheduling practices have not been systematically evaluated and the movement to longer shifts for nurses has not been based on research evidence of improved outcomes for nurses and an absence of harm to patients.[9, 13, 14]

### 1.2 Literature review

In the limited research literature on the outcomes of nurse work hours, results have been mixed.[14-17] Estabrooks[18] *et al.* found insufficient evidence of effects of shift length on nurse job satisfaction and burnout, while a more recent systematic review reported evidence of adverse nurse outcomes associated with shifts of 12 or more hours, including burnout, job dissatisfaction, intention to leave and fatigue from a number of studies, mostly from the US.[19] A recent study among European nurses investigated the association between shift length and nurses' psychological well-being. The findings show that nurses preferred 12 h shifts because more time off helped them balance work and personal commitments, although the nature of these was not examined (e.g., having a second job, having caring responsibilities at home and other potential confounders on the impact of 12 h shifts on nurse outcomes). Paradoxically, the study also found that nurses who worked 12 h shifts were more likely to experience high levels of burnout than nurses working shorter shifts.[20] Similarly, Stimpfel[16] reported that American nurses working extended shifts, particularly longer than 13 h, were more satisfied with their work schedules but were more likely to experience burnout and job dissatisfaction than nurses who worked shifts of 8 or 9 h. However, the US study did not disentangle scheduled shift length from extended shifts due to overtime worked, a common limitation in previous research on nurses' shift lengths.

Differences between work hour regulations between countries may limit the generalisability of US research. The US has regulations governing nurses' work hours that differ from the European Working Time Directive, in terms of limiting weekly hours, including overtime, and providing extra protection for between-shift rest hours and night work.[21]

### 1.3 Aims

The present study aims to examine the extent to which European hospital nurses' extended shifts (12 h or more) are associated with burnout, job dissatisfaction, satisfaction with work schedule flexibility and intention to leave the job.

*[The rest of the article is not included]*

# Unit 22: **Literature reviews**

**References**

1. McHugh MD, Kutney-Lee A, Cimiotti JP, *et al*. Nurses' widespread job dissatisfaction, burnout, and frustration with health benefits signal problems for patient care. *Health Aff (Millwood)* 2011;**30**:202–10. doi:10.1377/hlthaff.2010.0100
2. Rafferty AM, Clarke SP, Coles J, *et al*. Outcomes of variation in hospital nurse staffing in English hospitals: cross-sectional analysis of survey data and discharge records. *Int J Nurs Stud* 2007;**44**:175–82. doi:10.1016/j.ijnurstu.2006.08.003
3. Van Bogaert P, Kowalski C, Weeks SM, *et al*. The relationship between nurse practice environment, nurse work characteristics, burnout and job outcome and quality of nursing care: a cross-sectional survey. *Int J Nurs Stud* 2013;*50*:1667–77. doi:10.1016/j.ijnurstu.2013.05.010
4. Ramoo V, Abdullah KL, Piaw CY. The relationship between job satisfaction and intention to leave current employment among registered nurses in a teaching hospital. *J Clin Nurs* 2013;**22**:3141–52. doi:10.1111/jocn.12260
5. Aiken LH, Sloane DM, Bruyneel L, *et al*. Nurses' reports of working conditions and hospital quality of care in 12 countries in Europe. *Int J Nurs Stud* 2013;**50**:143–53. doi:10.1016/j.ijnurstu.2012.11.009
6. Aiken LH, Sermeus W, Van den Heede K, *et al*. Patient safety, satisfaction, and quality of hospital care: cross sectional surveys of nurses and patients in 12 countries in Europe and the United States. *BMJ* 2012;**344**:e1717. doi:10.1136/bmj.e1717
7. Andrews DR, Dziegielewski SF. The nurse manager: job satisfaction, the nursing shortage and retention. *J Nurs Manag* 2005;**13**:286–95. doi:10.1111/j.1365-2934.2005.00567.x
8. Simon M, Müller BH, Hasselhorn HM. Leaving the organization or the profession—a multilevel analysis of nurses' intentions. *J Adv Nurs* 2010;**66**:616–26. doi:10.1111/j.1365-2648.2009.05204.x
9. Griffiths P, Dall'Ora C, Simon M, *et al*. Nurses' shift length and overtime working in 12 European countries: the association with perceived quality of care and patient safety. *Med Care* 2014;**52**:975–81. doi:10.1097/MLR.0000000000000233
10. NHS Evidence. *Moving to 12-hour shift patterns: to increase continuity and reduce costs*. Basingstoke and North Hampshire NHS Foundation Trust, 2010.
11. Stone PW, Du Y, Cowell R, *et al*. Comparison of nurse, system and quality patient care outcomes in 8-hour and 12-hour shifts. *Med Care* 2006;**44**:1099–106. doi:10.1097/01.mlr.0000237180.72275.82
12. Dwyer T, Jamieson L, Moxham L, *et al*. Evaluation of the 12-hour Shift Trial in a Regional Intensive Care Unit. *J Nurs Manag* 2007;**15**:711–20. doi:10.1111/j.1365-2934.2006.00737.x
13. Geiger-Brown J, Trinkoff AM. Is it time to pull the plug on 12-hour shifts?: Part 1. The evidence. *J Nurs Adm* 2010;**40**:100–2. doi:10.1097/NNA.0b013e3181d0414e
14. Garrett C. The effect of nurse staffing patterns on medical errors and nurse burnout. *AORN J* 2008;**87**:1191–204. doi:10.1016/j.aorn.2008.01.022
15. Macken L, Hyrkas K. Retention, fatigue, burnout and job satisfaction: new aspects and challenges. *J Nurs Manag* 2014;**22**:541–2. doi:10.1111/jonm.12254
16. Stimpfel AW, Sloane DM, Aiken LH. The longer the shifts for hospital nurses, the higher the levels of burnout and patient dissatisfaction. *Health Aff (Millwood)* 2012;**31**:2501–9. doi:10.1377/hlthaff.2011.1377
17. Peters VP, de Rijk AE, Boumans NP. Nurses' satisfaction with shiftwork and associations with work, home and health characteristics: a survey in the Netherlands. *J Adv Nurs* 2009;**65**:2689–700. doi:10.1111/j.1365-2648.2009.05123.x
18. Estabrooks CA, Cummings GG, Olivo SA, *et al*. Effects of shift length on quality of patient care and health provider outcomes: systematic review. *Qual Saf Health Care* 2009;**18**:181–8. doi:10.1136/qshc.2007.024232
19. Bae SH, Fabry D. Assessing the relationships between nurse work hours/overtime and nurse and patient outcomes: systematic literature review. *Nurs Outlook* 2014;**62**:138–56. doi:10.1016/j.outlook.2013.10.009
20. Estryn-Behar M, Van der Heijden BI. Effects of extended work shifts on employee fatigue, health, satisfaction, work/family balance, and patient safety. *Work* 2012;**41**(Suppl 1):4283–90.
21. European Parliament & Council of the EU. Directive 2003/88/EC of the European Parliament and of the Council of 4 November 2003 concerning certain aspects of the organisation of working time: L 299, 2003–11–18, p.9, 2003.

**Academic Writing Genres**      **Sheldon Smith**

# Exercises

## Exercise 1: **Comprehension**

Answer the following questions about this unit. Either do this after reading the unit, or make notes first then use your notes to answer the questions.

1 What is a literature review? What is its purpose?

_____

_____

2 True or false: A literature review is a stand-alone piece of writing. Explain your answer.

_____

_____

3 What do you need to do in the introduction to a literature review?

- _____
- _____
- _____
- _____

4 What do you need to do in the conclusion to a literature review?

- _____
- _____
- _____
- _____

# Unit 22: Literature reviews

**5** The ideas in the main body are usually linked according to a common principle. What are the organising principles given in the text?

- _____
- _____
- _____
- _____

**6** When reviewing a particular study, how can you demonstrate its importance?

_____
_____

**7** Complete the following summary of writing guidelines for literature reviews, using words from the box.

| writers | synthesise | brief | selective |
| cautious | relevant | evidence | quotations |

When writing the review, you should use a)_____ from specific b)_____ or studies to support your points. You should be c)_____ and include only the most important points. It is important for the literature to be d)_____ to the focus of your review. It is also important to be e)_____, which means summarising information rather than using f)_____. If more than one writer says the same thing, you should g)_____ the information, in other words, link the sources together. Finally it is important to be h)_____ in how you report findings, and not overstate the claims made in the findings.

# Exercise 2: **Example literature review**

Study the example literature review (earlier in the unit) and answer the following questions.

a) Complete the following summary of the *background* of the article, which provides the context for the literature review.

Job satisfaction and burnout in the **i)** _____ industry are of **ii)** _____ importance for two reasons: first, because of their effect on quality and **iii)** _____ of patient care; and second, because low **iv)** _____ can lead to nurses leaving their job. Shifts of **v)** _____ or longer have become increasingly common in Europe, mainly because of managers' ideas of improved **vi)** _____. Longer shifts may be beneficial to nurses because they lead to fewer **vii)** _____ and more **viii)** _____. This in turn means lower **ix)** _____ and greater **x)** _____. However, **xi)** _____ in Europe have not shown evidence of nurses working fewer days in a week. The trend for longer shifts for nurses has not been based on **xii)** _____ of improved benefits for nurses and a lack of **xiii)** _____ to patients.

b) The following four sources are all listed in the literature review (only the first two have names used in the review): **16. Stimpfel, 18. Estabrooks *et al.*, 19,** and **20**. Which of the sources are associated with the following findings?

| Findings | Source(s) |
|---|---|
| a) Nurses working extended shifts were more satisfied with their *work schedules* or *work-life balance*. | |
| b) Nurses working longer shifts were more likely to experience *burnout*. | |
| c) Nurses working longer shifts were more likely to experience *job dissatisfaction*. | |
| d) Nurses working longer shifts were more likely to *leave their job*. | |
| e) There was not enough evidence that shift length affected nurse job satisfaction and burnout. | |

# Unit 22: Literature reviews

c) The following table is modified from the checklist earlier in the unit, with questions added and space for answers. Study the example literature review to answer the questions.

| Section | Item | Questions | Answers |
|---|---|---|---|
| **Context** | The introduction gives an outline of the topic or issue. | *1. What is the topic or issue covered in the literature review?* | |
| **Scope** | The scope is given (what literature is included/excluded). | *2. What is the scope of the research paper?* | |
| | | *3. How is the scope of the literature review different from the research paper?* | |
| | | *4. What problem does the writer identify with using this broader scope for the literature review?* | |
| | | *5. How might this problem help to justify the writer's own research?* | |
| **Organising principle** | Literature is grouped appropriately (by *chronology, theme, conclusions,* or *methodology*). | *6. How is the literature review organised?* | |
| **Sub-headings** | Main body uses sub-headings, if necessary (long reviews only). | *7. Are sub-headings used? Why (not)?* | |
| **Evidence** | Specific writers or studies are referred to, to support points. | *8. How many writers or studies are referred to in the review?* | |
| **Brevity** | Main ideas of writers/studies are summarised (rather than paraphrased or quoted). | *9. How many quotations are used in the review?* | |
| **Importance** | More important findings take up more space. | *10. Which two sources are most important, i.e. which ones take up most space?* | |
| **Comparison/ contrast** | Similarities/ differences between findings are highlighted. | *11. Identify at least one transition signal to show comparison and at least one to show contrast.* | |
| **Synthesis** | Sources are linked together if they say the same thing. | *12. Give examples of sources which are linked in (i) the background and (ii) the review.* | |

# Exercise 3: **Learning outcomes check**

a) The following are the learning outcomes for this unit. Decide how well you have mastered each one by giving it a score, as follows.

    3 = I understand/can do this well.
    2 = I understand/can do this fairly well, but I can improve with more practice.
    1 = I understand/can do this, but not well enough yet. I need to practise more.
    0 = I cannot do this yet. I need more time.

| Score | Learning Outcome |
| --- | --- |
| _____ | I know what a literature review is. |
| _____ | I understand how to structure a literature review. |
| _____ | I am aware of some writing guidelines for literature reviews. |

b) Use this information to review the unit and improve.

# Appendices

# Appendix 1 | Accessing online resources

## About online resources

There are additional online resources for each unit. These resources include worksheets, copies of checklists, teaching tips, lesson plans and mp3 recordings (for books in the speaking and listening series). These resources are available free of charge. All you need is an access code (see below).

## How to access online resources

Follow these steps to access the resources.
1) Go to https://www.evidentpress.com/resources/.
2) To access the resources, you will first need to register. If you have already done this, skip to step 3). If not, click on **Register** and follow the onscreen instructions, which will require you to enter a username, your first name, last name, email address and password.
3) Use your login details to log in to the site. This will take you to your **Resources** page. This screen will tell you which books you already have access to, if any.
4) Click on the button **Add Resources**. Enter the access code to gain access to the resources. The code for *EAP Foundation: Academic Writing Genres* is shown below.

### ACCESS CODE: 3Kj7fR2

You will only need to enter this code once. In future when you log in, the resources for this book will automatically be available.

If you follow the above steps, you should be able to access all the resources for the book. If you have any difficulty entering the code, registering or logging in, please contact Evident Press by using the form on the Evident Press contact page, or directly at contact@evidentpress.com.

Once registered, you will automatically receive notification of any updates to the resources.

# Appendix 2 | Answers to exercises

## Contents of this section

### Appendix 2: Answers to exercises .................... 319
- Unit 1: About the Essay Genre ..............................................................320
- Unit 2: Compare & Contrast Essays ......................................................327
- Unit 3: Cause & Effect Essays ................................................................333
- Unit 4: Problem-Solution Essays ..........................................................340
- Unit 5: Classification Essays ..................................................................344
- Unit 6: Argument Essays .......................................................................351
- Unit 7: Discussion Essays ......................................................................357
- Unit 8: Definition Essays .......................................................................361
- Unit 9: Process Essays ...........................................................................364
- Unit 10: Exemplification Essays ............................................................368
- Unit 11: Description Essays ...................................................................372
- Unit 12: About the Report Genre .........................................................377
- Unit 13: Laboratory Reports .................................................................381
- Unit 14: Business Reports .....................................................................385
- Unit 15: Other Report Types .................................................................389
- Unit 16: Posters .....................................................................................390
- Unit 17: Reflective Writing ....................................................................393
- Unit 18: Book Reviews ..........................................................................396
- Unit 19: Research Proposals .................................................................400
- Unit 20: Theses/Dissertations ...............................................................402
- Unit 21: Abstracts ..................................................................................404
- Unit 22: Literature Reviews ..................................................................407

Academic Writing Genres                                      Sheldon Smith

# Unit 1: About the Essay Genre

## Unit 1, Exercise 1: **Comprehension**

**1** What are the three parts of a typical *essay*?
- Introduction
- Main body
- Conclusion

**2** What is the main purpose of the introduction?

The introduction should: (1) introduce the topic of the essay; (2) give a general background of the topic; (3) indicate the overall plan of the essay.

**3** In the diagram at the start of the unit, the introduction has a 'funnel' shape (right). Why?

Because the introduction becomes more specific as it progresses.

**4** List some features of the *thesis statement*.
- It states the specific topic of the essay.
- It often lists the main (controlling) ideas of the essay.
- It may indicate the method of organisation of the essay.
- It is usually at the end of the introduction.
- It is usually one sentence.

**5** What are the three components of a typical *paragraph*?
- Topic sentence
- Supporting sentences
- Concluding sentence

**6** Why might the final component of a paragraph be missing?

The concluding sentence is most useful for long paragraphs, as it helps the reader to remember of the main ideas. It will often be missing from shorter paragraphs.

# Appendix 2: Answers

**7** What is the *controlling idea*? Where would you find it?

The controlling idea limits the paragraph to one or two areas that can be discussed fully in one paragraph.

It is found in the *topic sentence.*

**8** Why is the topic sentence important to:
- the writer   has a clear idea what information to include (and exclude)
- the reader   has a clear idea what the paragraph will discuss, which aids understanding

**9** Is the following statement true or **false**: *The topic sentence is the most specific in the paragraph.* Justify your answer.
It is **false**. The topic sentence is the most **general** sentence in the paragraph.

**10** Give examples of types of support that a paragraph might contain.
- reasons
- examples
- facts
- statistics
- citations

**11** What are the two components of a typical conclusion?
- A summary of the main points.
- The writer's final comment on the subject.

# Academic Writing Genres

**Sheldon Smith**

## Unit 1, Exercise 2: **Example essay**

a) Highlight the following aspects of the essay:
- background;
- thesis statement;
- topic sentences;
- summary;
- final comment.

| | |
|---|---|
| background | Society is becoming increasingly materialistic. There is an ever-increasing array of new products which advertising makes us desire. To help consumers meet this desire, it is becoming easier to buy goods on credit. **While there are some obvious, positive short-term benefits of this, most notably an improved quality of life, there are also many long-term, mainly negative effects, such as the possibility of life-long debt.** |
| thesis | |
| Topic sentence #1 | One of the most obvious short-term effects of buying on credit is that quality of life will be improved. In the past, only the rich could afford luxury items such as cars, washing machines, or computers. Now, however, these items can be purchased by almost anyone. This has many obvious benefits. If, for example, parents want to help their child's education by purchasing a computer, then they can do so regardless of how much money they have in the bank. |
| Topic sentence #2 | Despite this positive short-term effect, there are also some more negative long-term effects, the most important of which is that buying on credit can lead people into a life of debt. Although some people may claim that credit gives much convenience to the consumer, it must be remembered that they pay for this convenience in the form of high interest rates. They will consequently pay much more for the products than if they had saved up and bought them, and it will thus take them much longer to pay for them. Furthermore, the ease with which credit cards can be obtained and used may lead to reckless spending. Credit card users will later be faced with monthly bills, which will use up much of their income and take them years or even a whole lifetime to pay off. |
| Summary | In conclusion, although buying on credit has positive short-term benefits, such as improved quality of life, it also has many negative long-term effects, the most important of which is the possibility of a life of debt. While advertising makes us all want to buy the newest, fastest, smallest product, it would be wise for consumers who plan to buy on credit to consider the long-term consequences before they purchase. |
| Final comment | |

## Appendix 2: **Answers**

b) What method of organisation has been used? I.e. what type of essay is this?

The essay topics are short-term effects and long-term effect. The method of organisation appears to be **effect**, i.e. it is a cause & effect essay (Unit 3), but considering only the effects, not the causes.

c) Use the following table to record the *controlling ideas* as they appear in the *thesis*, the *topic sentences* and the *summary*.

| Thesis | Topic sentences | Summary |
| --- | --- | --- |
| an improved quality of life | quality of life will be improved | improved quality of life |
| the possibility of life-long debt | can lead people into a life of debt | the possibility of a life of debt |

d) What do you notice about the language in b) above? Are the *exact* same phrases used each time? If not, how are they different? Why do you think that is?

The exact same phrases are **not** used each time. There is variation. Some are the same (e.g. 'improved quality of life' in the thesis and summary), some have the order changed (e.g. 'quality of life will be improved' in the first topic sentence), some have word form changes (the adjective 'life-long' in the thesis becomes a noun phrase 'a life of' in the topic sentence and summary).

Repeating words and phrases in the thesis, topic sentences and summary helps build cohesion. However, there should be some variation rather than using the exact same phrases, since variation of expression makes for better writing.

e) Study the following paragraph again. Identify different types of *support* which are used.

One of the most obvious short-term effects of buying on credit is that quality of life will be improved.

**Fact**
In the past, only the rich could afford luxury items such as cars, washing machines, or computers.

**Fact**
Now, however, these items can be purchased by almost anyone. This has many obvious benefits.

**Example (of a benefit)**
If, for example, parents want to help their child's education by purchasing a computer, then they can

do so regardless of how much money they have in the bank.

# Academic Writing Genres — Sheldon Smith

## Unit 1, Exercise 3: Introductions

- identify which part is the *background*;
- identify which part is the **thesis statement**;

---

**1**

Number of paragraphs: __3__

Controlling ideas:
(1) language learning environment;
(2) improved employment prospects;
(3) high cost.

Method of organisation:
The essay topics are *benefits* (paragraphs 1 and 2) and *disadvantage* (paragraph 3). It is therefore an **advantage and disadvantage** (i.e. discussion) essay (see Unit 7).

*Background:* Most people spend around fifteen years of their life in education, from primary school to university study. In the past, students only had the opportunity to study in their own country. Nowadays, however, it is increasingly easy to study overseas, especially at tertiary level. Tertiary education, also called post-secondary education, is the period of study spent at university. As the final aspect of schooling before a person begins their working life, it is arguably the most important stage of their education.

**Thesis statement:** While there are some undoubted benefits of this trend, such as the language environment and improved employment prospects, there is also a significant disadvantage, namely the high cost.

---

**2**

Number of paragraphs: __4__

Controlling ideas:
(1) unsought products;
(2) convenience products;
(3) shopping products;
(4) specialty products.

Method of organisation:
The essay is a *classification* essay (Unit 5).

*Background:* Products that are bought by the end user are called consumer products. They include electric razors, sandwiches, cars, stereos, magazines, and houses. Marketers must know how consumers view the types of consumer product their companies sell so that they can design the marketing mix to appeal to the selected target market. To help them define target markets, marketers classify consumer products by the amount of effort needed to acquire them.

**Thesis statement:** The four major categories under this classification are unsought products, convenience products, shopping products, and specialty products.

---

**3**

Number of paragraphs: __3__

Controlling ideas:
(1) general form (of communication);
(2) speed (of communication);
(3) range of tools available (for communication).

Method of organisation:
The essay looks at how the means of communicating now and in the past are *similar* and how they *differ*. It is therefore a **compare & contrast** essay (Unit 2).

*Background:* Before the advent of computers and modern technology, people communicating over long distances used traditional means such as letters and the telephone. Nowadays there is a vast array of communication tools which can complete this task, ranging from email to instant messaging and video calls.

**Thesis statement:** While the present and previous means of communication are similar in their general form, they differ in regard to their speed and the range of tools available.

# Appendix 2: **Answers**

## Unit 1, Exercise 4: **Identifying topic and supporting sentences**

Study the following paragraphs. The sentences need to be rearranged into the correct order to form the completed paragraph. In each case, you should, you should:
- decide which sentence is the *topic sentence* and label it **TS**;
- decide on the order of the supporting sentences (SS), and label them **1, 2**, etc.;
- highlight any transition words or phrases which helped you to order the sentences.

### Paragraph 1

| | |
|---|---|
| 1 | **Some organisms**, like sea sponges, lack a true nervous system. |
| 3 | The insect nervous system is **more complex** but also fairly decentralized |
| TS | Nervous systems throughout the animal kingdom vary in **structure and complexity**, as illustrated by the variety of animals shown in Figure 35.2. |
| 2 | **Others**, like jellyfish, lack a true brain and instead have a system of separate but connected nerve cells (neurons) called a nerve net. |
| 4 | Octopi may have **the most complicated** of invertebrate nervous systems—they have neurons that are organized in specialized lobes and eyes that are structurally similar to vertebrate species. |

*The paragraph is organised from the simplest to the most complex. **1** uses 'Some organisms', while **2** contrasts this by using the transition signal 'Others', meaning that this sentence should follow the preceding one. **3** and **4** used 'more' and 'most' respectively.*

### Paragraph 2

| | |
|---|---|
| 4 | **In this case**, although exclusivity can provide an initial motivation for going global, managers must realize that competitors will eventually catch up. |
| 1 | Perhaps **the most urgent reason is** to earn additional **profits**. |
| 3 | **In other situations**, management may have exclusive market information about foreign customers, marketplaces, or market situations. |
| TS | Companies decide to go global for a number of **reasons**. |
| 2 | If a firm has a unique product or technological advantage not available to other international competitors, this advantage should result in major **financial success** abroad. |
| 5 | **Finally**, saturated domestic markets, excess capacity, and potential for cost savings can also be motivators to expand into international markets. |

*The support begins by presenting 'the most urgent reason' which relates to 'profits' in **1**. **2** gives further details of this and links to the idea of profits with the phrase 'financial success'. The second idea, in **3**, is introduced via 'In other situations', while the final reason, in **5**, is introduced by 'Finally'.*

# Academic Writing Genres                                    Sheldon Smith

**Paragraph 3**

| 2  | **Taiwan and South Korea** have long had an embargo against Japanese cars for political reasons and to help domestic automakers. |
|----|---|
| 4  | **In another example**, when the environmentally conscious Green movement challenged the biotechnology research conducted by BASF, a major German chemical and drug manufacturer, BASF moved its cancer and immune-system research to Cambridge, Massachusetts. |
| TS | Large multinationals have several **advantages** over other companies. |
| 1  | **For instance**, multinationals can often overcome trade problems. |
| 3  | **Despite this fact,** Honda USA, a Japanese-owned company based in the United States, sends Accords to **Taiwan and South Korea**. |

*1 gives an example of an advantage. It is not clear that 2 follows this sentence. However it is clear that 3 is connected to 2 (by repeating 'Taiwan and South Korea'), and that it should come afterwards. 4 then presents 'another example'.*

## Unit 1, Exercise 5: **Identifying the parts of a topic sentence**

b) Do you notice any pattern in the order of topic and controlling idea?
*The topic usually appears first, the controlling idea second, though the order can be reversed.*

                    *c.i.*                    *t.*
i) There are several important reasons for the collapse of the Roman Empire.

        *t.*                      *c.i.*
ii) Obtaining nutrition and energy from food is a multistep process.*

       *t.*                *c.i.*
iii) The final step in digestion is the elimination of waste products.*

       *t.*              *c.i.*
iv) The amount of sleep we get varies across the lifespan.**

                 *t.*                                  *c.i.*
v) One similarity between current and previous methods of communication relates to the form.

       *c.i.*                *t.*
vi) There are number of factors which affect our body weight.**

    *t.*                          *c.i.*
vii) Sleep debt has significant negative psychological and physiological consequences.**

          *t.*                      *c.i.*
viii) Other theorists believe that intelligence should be defined in more practical terms.**

             *t.*                                  *c.i.*
ix) In order for a memory to go into long-term memory, it has to pass through three distinct stages.**

    *t.*          *c.i.*
x) The second distortion error is suggestibility.**

# Appendix 2: Answers

# Unit 2: Compare & Contrast Essays

## Unit 2, Exercise 1: Comprehension

1. What are the two types of comparison and contrast essay structure?
   - block (also called subject-by-subject)
   - point-by-point

2. What is the difference between the two types of structure? What are the advantages of each?

   **block structure**
   - has all of the information about one of the objects being compared or contrasted first, and all of the information about the other object listed afterwards
   - easier to write
   - suitable for short essays

   **point-by-point structure**
   - each similarity (or difference) for one object is followed immediately by the similarity (or difference) for the other
   - clearer
   - similarities and differences easier to follow

3. What are *criteria* for comparison and contrast? Why it is important to be clear about the criteria which are used?
   - Criteria for comparison/contrast are the aspects that are being compared or contrasted (also called *basis for comparison*)
   - If the criteria are not clear, the comparison/contrast may not be appropriate

4. Study the following transitions. Put them in the correct place in the table.

|  | Comparison | Contrast |
| --- | --- | --- |
| **Sentence connectors** | similarly<br>likewise<br>in the same way | however<br>in contrast<br>in comparison |
| **Clause connectors** | just as<br>both... and...<br>not only... but also... | while<br>whereas<br>but |
| **Other** | just like<br>to be similar to<br>to be the same as | to be different from<br>to be dissimilar to<br>in contrast to |

327

# Academic Writing Genres — Sheldon Smith

## Unit 2, Exercise 2: **Example essay**

a) What type of structure has been used?  point-by-point

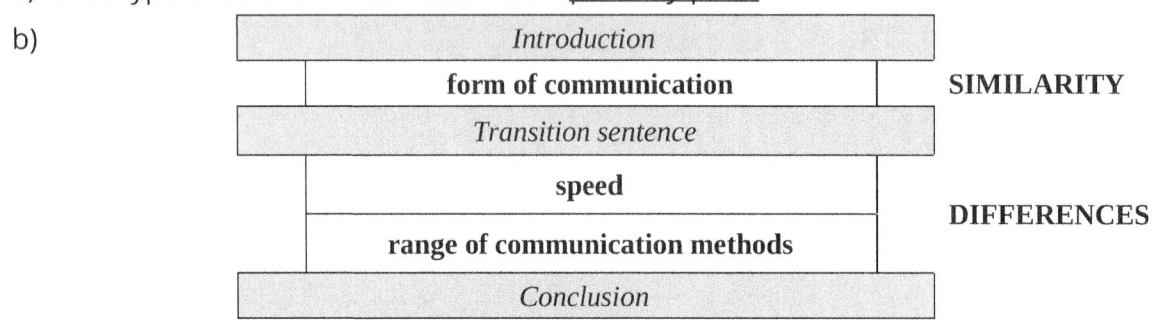

b)

| Introduction | |
| --- | --- |
| form of communication | SIMILARITY |
| Transition sentence | |
| speed | DIFFERENCES |
| range of communication methods | |
| Conclusion | |

c) Study the example essay and highlight the following:
- **language for comparison and contrast**;
- the main ideas listed in: (a) the thesis; (b) the topic sentences; (c) the summary.

Before the advent of computers and modern technology, people communicating over long distances used traditional means such as letters and the telephone. Nowadays there is a vast array of communication tools which can complete this task, ranging from email to instant messaging and video calls. While the present and previous means of communication **are similar** in their general form, they **differ** in regard to their speed and the range of tools available.

One similarity between current and previous methods of communication relates to the form of communication. In the past, written forms such as letters were frequently used, in addition to oral forms such as telephone calls. **Similarly**, people nowadays use both of these forms. **Just as** in the past, written forms of communication are prevalent, for example via email and text messaging. In addition, oral forms are **still** used, including the telephone, mobile phone, and voice messages via instant messaging services.

**However**, there are clearly many differences in the way we communicate over long distances, the most notable of which is speed. This is most evident in relation to written forms of communication. In the past, letters would take days to arrive at their destination. **In contrast**, an email arrives almost instantaneously and can be read seconds after it was sent. In the past, if it was necessary to send a short message, for example at work, a memo could be passed around the office, which would take some time to circulate. This **is different from** the current situation, in which a text message can be sent immediately.

Another significant difference is the range of communication methods. Fifty years ago, the tools available for communicating over long distances were primarily the telephone and the letter. **By comparison**, there is a vast array of communication methods available today. These include not only the telephone, letter, email and text messages already mentioned, but also video conferences via software such as Skype or mobile phone apps such as WeChat and WhatsApp, and social media such as Facebook and Twitter.

In conclusion, methods of communication have greatly advanced over the past fifty years, and while there are some similarities, such as the forms of communication, there are significant differences, chiefly in relation to the speed of communication and the range of communication tools available. There is no doubt that technology will continue to progress in future, and the advanced tools which we use today may one day also become outdated.

# Appendix 2: Answers

d) Study this main body and highlight the following:
- transition phrases for comparison and contrast;
- **the 'reminder' phrases used in the second paragraph**.

[None in first paragraph]

**Just as in the past**, written forms of communication are prevalent today, for example email and text messaging. In addition, oral forms are still used, including the telephone, mobile phone, and voice messages via instant messaging services. In contrast to the past, however, **when written communication could take several days to arrive**, an email arrives almost instantaneously and can be read seconds after it is sent. In comparison to **the limited forms of communication in the past**, nowadays there is a vast array of communication methods available. These include not only the telephone, letter, email and text messages already mentioned, but also video conferences via software such as Skype or mobile phone Apps such as WeChat and WhatsApp, and social media such as Facebook and Twitter.

## Unit 2, Exercise 3: Language for comparison and contrast #1

**1)** Mainland China \_\_\_\_b)\_\_\_\_ Hong Kong in the Confucian aspects of its culture.
 a) compares to  **b) is similar to**  c) is alike

**2)** Mainland China \_\_\_\_a)\_\_\_\_ Hong Kong in the form of written Chinese, as it uses simplified rather than complex characters.
 **a) differs from**  b) different from  c) whereas

**3)** The UK has important trade relations with the USA. \_\_\_\_c)\_\_\_\_ , trade is an important part of the relationship between China and the USA.
 a) The same as  b) Just like  **c) Likewise**

**4)** \_\_\_\_a)\_\_\_\_ to the UK, China does not have close military ties to the USA.
 **a) In contrast**  b) Dissimilar  c) On the other hand

**5)** France and the UK \_\_\_\_c)\_\_\_\_ in their reliance on nuclear energy as a clean energy source.
 a) also  b) both  **c) are alike**

**6)** Nuclear energy accounts for almost 40% of the energy produced in France. \_\_\_\_a)\_\_\_\_ , it is only around 20% of the energy produced in the UK.
 **a) In contrast**  b) While  c) On the contrary

**7)** China is \_\_\_c) *not only*\_\_\_ a Communist country \_\_\_c) *but also*\_\_\_ a rapidly developing country with many free market principles.
 a) both... but also  b) neither... and  **c) not only... but also**

**8)** Although China operates under some free market principles, it \_\_\_\_a)\_\_\_\_ true free market economies in many aspects.
 **a) is unlike**  b) be different from  c) dissimilar to

**9)** \_\_\_\_b)\_\_\_\_ Mexico, Chile is a Spanish-speaking country.
 a) The same as  **b) Just like**  c) Similarly

**10)** Mexico \_\_\_\_b)\_\_\_\_ Chile in the size of its population, which is almost ten times as large.
 a) dissimilar to  **b) is different from**  c) while

# Unit 2, Exercise 4: **Language for comparison and contrast #2**

**1. Likewise**
- A presentation has a clear structure, with introduction, main body and conclusion.
- An essay has a clear structure, with introduction, main body and conclusion.

A presentation has a clear structure, with an introduction, main body and conclusion. **Likewise**, an essay has a clear structure, with an introduction, main body and conclusion.

**2. to differ from**
- A presentation uses semi-formal language.
- An essay uses formal language.

A presentation **differs from** an essay since it uses semi-formal language, rather than formal language.

**3. both... and...**
- A presentation uses transition phrases.
- An essay uses transition phrases.

**Both** a presentation **and** an essay use transition phrases.
[Note: Because the subject is now plural, the verb should be 'use' not 'uses'.]

**4. in contrast to**
- A presentation uses text and visuals.
- An essay uses only text.

**In contrast to** an essay, which uses only text, a presentation uses text and visuals.

**5. In contrast**
- A presentation concludes with a Q&A section.
- An essay concludes with a reference section.

A presentation concludes with a Q&A section. **In contrast**, an essay concludes with the references section.

# Appendix 2: **Answers**

## Unit 2, Exercise 5: **Criteria for comparison and contrast**

a) Identify the *criteria* used to make **comparisons** and **contrasts**.

*Topic: What are the structural and functional similarities and differences between mitochondria and chloroplasts?*

*Mitochondria (singular = mitochondrion) are oval-shaped, double membrane organelles that have their own ribosomes and DNA. They are often called the "powerhouses" or "energy factories" of a cell because they are responsible for making adenosine triphosphate (ATP), the cell's main energy-carrying molecule. ATP represents the short-term stored energy of the cell.*

*Like the mitochondria, chloroplasts* **have their own DNA and ribosomes**, *but chloroplasts have an entirely* different function. *Chloroplasts are plant cell organelles that carry out photosynthesis. Photosynthesis is the series of reactions that use carbon dioxide, water, and light energy to make glucose and oxygen. This is a major difference between plants and animals; plants (autotrophs) are able to make their own food, like sugars, while animals (heterotrophs) must ingest their food.*

*Like mitochondria, chloroplasts* **have a double membrane**. The contents of the inner membrane, *however, are quite different. Within the space enclosed by a chloroplast's inner membrane is a set of interconnected and stacked fluid-filled membrane sacs called thylakoids. Each stack of thylakoids is called a granum (plural = grana). The fluid enclosed by the inner membrane that surrounds the grana is called the stroma.*

Adapted from *Biology 2e* by OpenStax. Download for free at https://openstax.org/details/books/biology-2e.

b) Complete the gaps by identifying appropriate *criteria*.
   i. Dogs and cats differ in terms of their **independence**. Dogs rely very much on their owners, for example to feed them and take them for a walk. In contrast, cats, can be let out to wander the neighbourhood and can even catch food such as mice or small birds.
   ii. One difference between alligators and crocodiles is the **length and width** of their snout. An alligator's snout is shorter and wider than that of a crocodile.
   iii. A second difference between alligators and crocodiles relates to the **visibility** of their teeth with the mouth closed. A crocodile's teeth can be seen protruding from their bottom jaw when its mouth is closed. In contrast, when an alligator's mouth is shut, none of its teeth are visible.
   iv. One similarity between China and India is **population size**. China had 1.39 billion people in 2018. Likewise, India had over 1 billion people in 2018, totalling 1.34 billion. By contrast, the USA, in third place, had only 300,000 in the same year.
   v. One difference between China and India, however, is **population growth**. The population in China is increasing by 1.5% per year, while that of China is only increasing by 0.7% per year, which is only half as much.

**Note: The answer 'population' for *iv* might seem correct, but it is too broad. The ideas are about 'population *size*'.**

# Academic Writing Genres — Sheldon Smith

## Unit 2, Exercise 6: **Using a Venn Diagram**

Essays and presentations are similar in many regards. One similarity is their **clear structure**. Essays have an introduction, main body and conclusion. A presentation, likewise, begins with an introduction, moves on to the main body, and ends with a conclusion.

A second similarity is the use of **transition phrases**. Essay writers use words such as '*However*', '*On the other hand*', and '*In conclusion*' to link ideas together and make their connection clear to the reader. Presenters, likewise, use transition phrases, for example '*Turning now to the next section*', '*OK, let's now look at*' and '*In conclusion*' to link ideas and make their connection clear to the listener.

Essays and presentations, however, have many differences. One of these relates to formality of language. Essays use **formal** language, while presentations use **semi-formal language**. Another difference concerns the ending. A researched essay will conclude with a **reference section** (also called a Works Cited list). In contrast, a presentation concludes with the **Q&A section**. A third difference relates to amount of text. An essay is **text only**, while a presentation combines text with **visuals**.

› Appendix 2: **Answers**

# Unit 3: Cause & Effect Essays

## Unit 3, Exercise 1: **Comprehension**

1 What are the two types of cause and effect essay structure?
   - block
   - chain

2 What is the difference between the two types of structure? What are the advantages of each?

   **Block**
   - lists all causes first, then all effects;
   - generally clearer, especially for short essays.

   **Chain**
   - has one cause, then one effect; each effect may become the cause of the next effect;
   - ensures effects relate directly to causes.

3 Match the following pairs of words, and decide whether they are types of *cause* or types of *effect*. [Note: *immediate* is included twice, as it is both a type of cause and a type of effect.]

   - primary — main [*causes*]
   - delayed — long-term [*effect*]
   - short-term — immediate [*effects*]
   - contributing — remote [*causes*]
   - immediate — secondary [*effects*]

4 Study the paragraph. Try to identify *at least one* example of each of the cause and effect types given in Q3 above. [Note: Each cause and each effect could be more than one type.]

| Causes | Type |
|---|---|
| drinking (alcohol) | contributing, remote |
| checking message on phone | main, immediate |
| **Effects** | **Type** |
| vehicles severely damaged | immediate |
| broken wrist | immediate, short-term |
| speaking in a confused manner | delayed, short-term |
| coma | delayed, short-term |
| blood clot on brain | delayed, primary |
| paralysis | long-term, secondary |
| spending remainder of life in a wheelchair | long-term, secondary |

# Academic Writing Genres

**Sheldon Smith**

## Unit 3, Exercise 2: **Example essay**

a) What type of structure has been used? *block*

b) Complete the following diagram, summarising the main ideas of the essay.

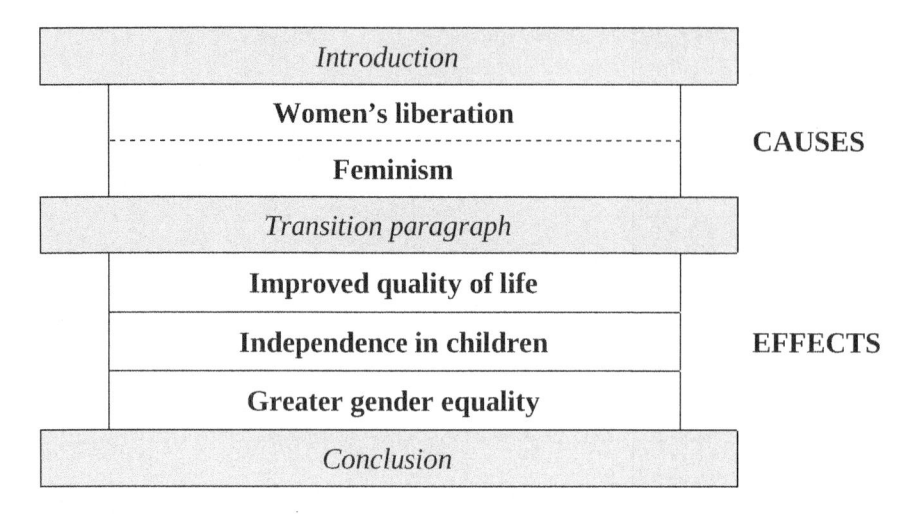

|   |
|---|
| *Introduction* |
| **Women's liberation** |
| **Feminism** |
| *Transition paragraph* |
| **Improved quality of life** |
| **Independence in children** |
| **Greater gender equality** |
| *Conclusion* |

CAUSES (Women's liberation, Feminism)
EFFECTS (Improved quality of life, Independence in children, Greater gender equality)

c) Complete the missing words in the flowchart below to show the chain of cause-effect.

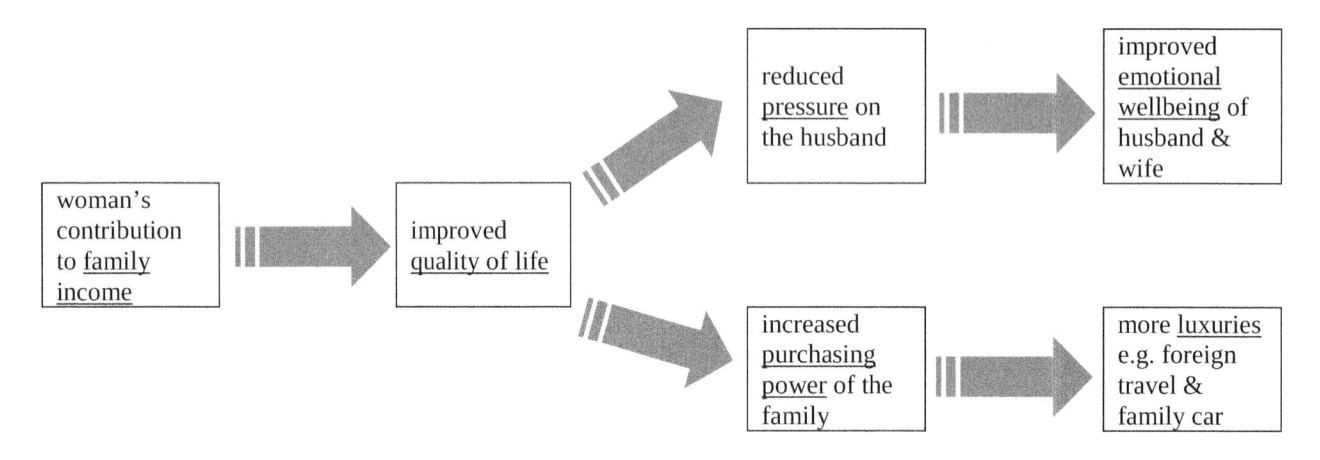

woman's contribution to <u>family income</u> → improved <u>quality of life</u> →
- reduced <u>pressure</u> on the husband → improved <u>emotional wellbeing</u> of husband & wife
- increased <u>purchasing power</u> of the family → more <u>luxuries</u> e.g. foreign travel & family car

*Below is the paragraph from the essay, with the missing words in **bold**.*

> Although the earning capacity of a woman in her lifetime is generally much less than that of a man, she can nevertheless make a significant contribution to the **family income**. The most important consequence of this is an improved **quality of life**. By helping to maintain a steady income for the family, the **pressure** on the husband is considerably reduced, hence improving both the husband's and the wife's **emotional wellbeing**. Additionally, the **purchasing power** of the family will also be raised. This means that the family can afford more **luxuries** such as foreign travel and a family car.

# Appendix 2: Answers

d) Study the example essay and highlight the following:
- **language for cause and effect**;
- the main ideas listed in: (a) the thesis; (b) the topic sentences; (c) the summary.

In the past, most women stayed at home to take care of domestic chores such as cooking or cleaning. Women's liberation and feminism **have meant that** this situation has been transformed and in contemporary society women are playing an almost equal role to men in terms of work. This **has had significant consequences**, both in terms of the family, for example by improving quality of life and increasing children's sense of independence, and also for society itself with greater gender equality.

**The main reasons behind** the increase of women in the workplace are women's liberation and feminism. The women's liberation movement originated in the 1960s and was popularised by authors such as Simone de Beauvoir. **As a consequence of** this, new legislation emerged, granting women equal rights to men in many fields, in particular employment. **Because of** feminist ideas, men have taken up roles which were previously seen as being for women only, most importantly those related to child rearing. **As a result of** this, women have more time to pursue their own careers and interests. These **have led to some significant effects**, both to family life and to society as a whole.

Although the earning capacity of a woman in her lifetime is generally much less than that of a man, she can nevertheless make a significant contribution to the family income. **The most important consequence of** this is an improved quality of life. By helping to maintain a steady income for the family, the pressure on the husband is considerably reduced, **hence** improving both the husband's and the wife's emotional wellbeing. Additionally, the purchasing power of the family will also be raised. This **means that** the family can afford more luxuries such as foreign travel and a family car.

**A further effect** on the family is the promotion of independence in the children. Some might argue that having both parents working might be damaging to the children because of a lack of parental attention. However, such children have to learn to look after themselves at an earlier age, and their parents often rely on them to help with the housework. This **therefore** teaches them important life skills.

As regards society, **the most significant impact of** women going to work is greater gender equality. There are an increasing number of women who are becoming politicians, lawyers, and even CEOs and company managers. This in turn **has led to** greater equality for women in all areas of life, not just employment. For example, women today have much stronger legal rights to protect themselves against domestic violence and sexual discrimination in the workplace.

In conclusion, women's liberation and feminism **have led to** an increasing number of women at work, which in turn **has brought about** some important changes to family life, including improved quality of life and increased independence for children, as well as **affecting** society itself. It is clear that the sexes are still a long way from being equal in all areas of life, however, and perhaps the challenge for the present century is to ensure that this takes place.

**Academic Writing Genres**  **Sheldon Smith**

## Unit 3, Exercise 3: **Language for cause and effect #1**

**1)** \_\_\_\_**a)**\_\_\_\_ increased emissions of pollutants, the Green House effect is accelerating.
    **a) As a result of**    b) As a result    c) Since

**2)** \_\_\_\_**b)**\_\_\_\_ extreme weather incidents are increasing.
    a) As a result of    **b) As a result**    c) Since

**3)** \_\_\_\_**a)**\_\_\_\_ her hard work, her spoken English made great improvement.
    **a) As a consequence of**    b) As a consequence    c) Causes

**4)** She also worked extremely hard on her writing. \_\_\_\_**b)**\_\_\_\_ , her grades for her assignments went up considerably.
    a) As a consequence of    **b) As a consequence**    c) Results in

**5)** A lack of understanding of referencing conventions can \_\_\_\_**c)**\_\_\_\_ plagiarism.
    a) result from    b) be the result of    **c) result in**

**6)** \_\_\_\_**c)**\_\_\_\_ a lack of funding, the research department had to close down.
    a) Results from    b) Consequently    **c) Owing to**

**7)** The sharp increase in immigrants since January \_\_\_\_**b)**\_\_\_\_ the violent unrest in a neighbouring country.
    a) results in    **b) is due to**    c) affects

**8)** Stimulants such as caffeine are substances which \_\_\_\_**a)**\_\_\_\_ the body, leading to increased alertness and difficulty in getting to sleep.
    **a) have an effect on**    b) cause    c) result from

**9)** The increased use of stimulants \_\_\_\_**b)**\_\_\_\_ sleep disorders such as insomnia.
    a) is a consequence of    **b) is one of the causes of**    c) effects

**10)** Although free trade provides overall benefits, increasing imports can hurt domestic industries. \_\_\_\_**b)**\_\_\_\_ , barriers to trade continue to exist.
    a) Because    **b) Consequently**    c) Consequence

# Appendix 2: Answers

## Unit 3, Exercise 4: Language for cause and effect #2

i) Urbanisation has increased in many countries as a result [in / from / **of**] industrialisation.

ii) The increased use of green energy results [**in** / from / of] a reduction of carbon dioxide emissions.

iii) Carbon emissions that result [in / **from** / of] burning fossil fuels are likely to decrease in future.

iv) The harmful effects [**of** / for / on] smoking are well known.

v) Smoking can have an effect [of / for / **on**] not only the lungs but also the heart, brain, stomach and other organs.

vi) The increase in temperature was the cause [**of** / to / by] the increased rate of reaction.

vii) The increased rate of reaction was caused [of / to / **by**] the increase in temperature.

viii) There are several reasons [to / **for** / why] this change.

ix) There are several reasons [to / for / **why**] this change is necessary.

x) There is no reason [**to** / for / why] believe that reduction in fossil fuels will be harmful to the environment.

337

# Unit 3, Exercise 5: Language for cause and effect #3

**1.** People who are <u>stressed often have a haggard look</u> [E]. A pioneering study from 2004 suggests that **the reason is** that <u>stress can accelerate the cell biology of aging</u> [C].*
*Language note*: <u>sentence connector (+ that)</u>

**2. Because of** <u>the existence of stable isotopes</u> [C], <u>we must take special care when quoting the mass of an element</u> [E].**
*Language note*: <u>Because of + sth (noun)</u>

**3.** <u>The patient recently suffered a stroke in the front portion of her right hemisphere</u> [C]. **As a result**, <u>she has great difficulty moving her left leg</u> [E].*
*Language note*: <u>sentence connector</u>

**4.** Dr. Tom Steitz is the Sterling Professor of Biochemistry and Biophysics at Yale University. **As a result of** <u>his lifetime of work</u> [C], <u>he won the Nobel Prize in Chemistry in 2009</u> [E].*
*Language note*: <u>As a result of + sth (noun)</u>

**5.** <u>Prader-Willi Syndrome (PWS)</u> [C], a rare genetic disorder, **results in** <u>persistent feelings of intense hunger and reduced rates of metabolism</u> [E].*
*Language note*: <u>sth + to result in + sth (noun)</u>

**6.** <u>Our body weight</u> [C] **is affected by** <u>a number of factors, including gene-environment interactions, and the number of calories we consume versus the number of calories we burn in daily activity</u> [E].*
*Language note*: <u>sth + to be affected by + sth</u>

# Appendix 2: **Answers**

b) Study the following sentences and do the following.
- Identify which is the cause and label it **C**.
- Identify which is the effect and label it **E**.
- Link the sentences, using the given transition. These are the same transitions as a) Be careful with sentence structure (you will need to rewrite some of the sentences).

## 1. Because of
_C_ There is a growing number of people from ethnically diverse backgrounds.
_E_ There is a need for therapists and psychologists to develop knowledge and skills to become culturally competent.*

**Because of** the growing number of people from ethnically diverse backgrounds, there is a need for therapists and psychologists to develop knowledge and skills to become culturally competent.

## 2. As a result
_C_ We are more active during the night-time hours than our ancestors were.
_E_ Many of us sleep less than 7 hours a night and accrue a sleep debt.*

We are more active during the night-time hours than our ancestors were. **As a result,** many of us sleep less than 7 hours a night and accrue a sleep debt.*

## 3. As a result of
_E_ Amnesia, the loss of long-term memory, occurs.
_C_ There is disease, physical trauma, or psychological trauma.*

Amnesia, the loss of long-term memory, occurs **as a result of** disease, physical trauma, or psychological trauma.

## 4. Results in
_C_ Rheumatoid arthritis is an autoimmune disease that affects the joints.
_E_ There are joint pain, stiffness, and loss of function.*

Rheumatoid arthritis, an autoimmune disease that affects the joints, **results in** joint pain, stiffness, and loss of function.

## 5. To be affected by
_E_ Our body weight.
_C_ Our genes and the amount of energy we consume.*

Our body weight **is affected by** our genes and the amount of energy we consume.

**Academic Writing Genres**  Sheldon Smith

# Unit 4: Problem-Solution Essays

## Unit 4, Exercise 1: **Comprehension**

1 In what way are problem-solution essays similar to cause and effect essays?

   They have the same structure (block, chain).

   They are likely to include causes and effects (of the problem).

2 Problem-solution essays are a sub-type of SPSE essays. What do letters SPSE stand for?
   - Situation
   - Problem
   - Solution
   - Evaluation

3 In which stage of the essay will *causes* of the problem most likely be seen? In which stage is it most likely to see *effect*? Why?

   The Situation stage is likely to outline the causes of the problem, since this gives background to the problem.
   The Problem stage is likely to consider the effects of the problem, since it is often the effects which make the situation problematic.

4 What happens in the 'E' stage?

   The Evaluation considers how effective each of the solutions will be.

5 Where might you find the first 'S' stage and the 'E' stage in *short* essays?

   The Situation stage might be part of the introduction, while the Evaluation stage might be part of the conclusion.

6 Give examples of different ways that the problem can be viewed.

   From different aspects, e.g. economic vs. social vs. political.
   From the point of view of different actors, e.g. students vs. teachers vs. parents.

7 The following are some model verbs which can be used to present solutions. Number them in order of strength, from **1** (strongest) to **5** (weakest).

| should 3 | must 1 | might 5 | can 4 | need to 2 |

# Appendix 2: **Answers**

## Unit 4, Exercise 2: **Example essay**

a) What type of structure has been used?  <u>block</u>

b) Complete the following diagram, summarising the main ideas of the essay.

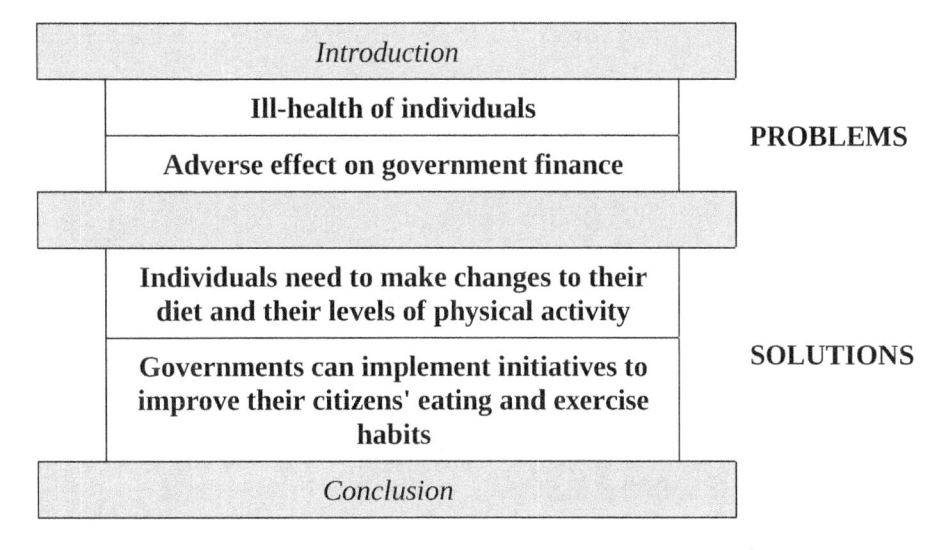

```
┌─────────────────────────────────────────┐
│              Introduction                │
└─────────────────────────────────────────┘
   ┌──────────────────────────────────┐
   │     Ill-health of individuals    │
   ├──────────────────────────────────┤    PROBLEMS
   │ Adverse effect on government finance │
   └──────────────────────────────────┘
┌─────────────────────────────────────────┐
│                                         │
└─────────────────────────────────────────┘
   ┌──────────────────────────────────┐
   │ Individuals need to make changes │
   │ to their diet and their levels   │
   │ of physical activity             │
   ├──────────────────────────────────┤
   │ Governments can implement        │    SOLUTIONS
   │ initiatives to improve their     │
   │ citizens' eating and exercise    │
   │ habits                           │
   └──────────────────────────────────┘
┌─────────────────────────────────────────┐
│              Conclusion                  │
└─────────────────────────────────────────┘
```

c) How has the problem been viewed in the essay (i.e. from whose viewpoint)?

<u>From the viewpoint of individuals and governments (i.e. different actors).</u>

d) The following is a summary of the *situation* given in the introduction. Complete the summary by adding missing words from the text.

> People are eating more **i)** <u>processed</u> and **ii)** <u>convenience</u> foods nowadays. They are also using the **iii)** <u>car</u> more and indulging in habits such as **iv)** <u>watching television</u> and **v)** <u>surfing the internet</u>, both of which mean that people are getting much less **vi)** <u>exercise</u> than in the past, which in turn decreases their amount of **vii)** <u>fitness</u>. Although this is more of a problem in **viii)** <u>developed</u> countries, it is also a growing problem in **ix)** <u>developing nations</u>. It is therefore a **x)** <u>global</u> situation.

d) What is the writer's *evaluation*?

<u>Actions made by individuals are likely to have more impact</u>
<u>However, a concerted effort with the government is essential for success.</u>

# Academic Writing Genres — Sheldon Smith

e) The unit lists the following type of solutions. Which ones have been used in the essay?
- ☐ to provide funding (or resources)
- ☑ to educate — *Classes about healthy eating*
- ☑ to create or enforce laws or rules — *Law to increase vehicle taxes*
- ☑ to change something (which isn't working) — *Individuals need to change their diet/activity*
- ☑ to create something new — *Cycle lanes*

f) Study the example essay and highlight the following:
- **language for presenting solutions (including *modal verbs*)**;
- **language for cause and effect**;
- the main ideas listed in: (a) the thesis; (b) the topic sentences; (c) the summary.

Modern lifestyles have led us to become increasingly reliant on processed and convenience foods. At the same time, our dependence on the car, as well as modern pastimes such as watching television and surfing the internet, have **led to** a decrease in general levels of exercise, and therefore a decrease in fitness levels. While this kind of lifestyle is more pronounced in developed countries, it is increasingly common in developing nations, and should be considered a global phenomenon. This has **led to** significant health problems for individuals, as well as rising costs for governments. To tackle these problems, it is important for individuals to change their diet and levels of activity, and for governments to do more to raise awareness of the issues and promote healthy living initiatives.

One of the problems caused by unhealthy modern lifestyles is ill-health of individuals. It is well known that regular exercise can reduce the risk of heart disease and stroke, which **means that** those with poor fitness levels are at an increased risk of suffering from those problems. Additionally, the worsening of the average diet has been matched by an increase in the number of people who are overweight or obese. In some countries, especially industrialized ones, the number of obese people can amount to one third of the population. This is significant as overweight and obese people are more likely to have serious illnesses such as diabetes and heart disease, which can **lead to** an increase in the number of sick days, increase in unemployment, or shortened lifespan.

Unhealthy modern lifestyles also adversely affect government finance. In countries such as the UK, where there is a national health service, the cost of treatment for illnesses such as diabetes and heart disease must be borne by the government. Loss of productivity through increased sick days or unemployment also **affects** the economy and **therefore** government finances.

**To tackle this problem**, individuals *need to* make changes to their diet and their levels of physical activity. There is a reliance today on the consumption of processed foods, which have a high fat and sugar content. By preparing their own foods, and consuming more fruit and vegetables, people *could* ensure that their diets are healthier and more balanced, which *could* **lead to** a reduction in obesity levels. In order to improve fitness levels, people *could* choose to walk or cycle to work or to the shops rather than taking the car. They *could* also choose to walk upstairs instead of taking the lift. These simple changes *could* **lead to** a significant improvement in health and fitness levels.

Governments *could* also implement initiatives to improve their citizens' eating and exercise habits. This *could* be done through education, for example by adding classes to the curriculum about healthy diet and lifestyles. Governments *could* also do more to encourage their citizens to walk or cycle instead of taking the car, for instance by building more cycle lanes or increasing vehicle taxes. While some might argue that increased taxes are a unreasonable way to solve the problem, it is no different from the high taxes imposed on cigarettes to reduce cigarette consumption.

# Appendix 2: Answers

In short, obesity and poor fitness are a significant problem in modern life, **leading to** ill health and rising costs for governments. Individuals and governments *can* work together **to tackle this problem** and so improve diet and fitness. Of the solutions suggested, those made by individuals themselves are likely to have more impact, though it is clear that a concerted effort with the government is essential for success. With obesity levels in industrialized and industrializing countries continuing to rise, **it is essential that** we take action now.

*Note: The summary does not specifically state the solutions. It states them in general terms, i.e. in terms of the actors (individuals and governments).*

## Unit 4, Exercise 3: **Language for problem-solution**

*There are many possible answers to these questions. However, some suggestions are given below.*

**i)** To deal with the problem of overuse of mobile phones by children, <u>parents should be educated about the dangers that mobile phones can cause.</u>
*Note: A logical actor here is 'parents', though others are possible, e.g. governments.*

**ii)** In order to address the issue of air pollution in cities, <u>governments need to put stricter controls on the number and type of vehicle allowed on the city streets.</u>
*Note: A logical actor here is 'governments' (which could be local governments).*

**iii)** If countries with child labour problems are going to reverse this trend, <u>the governments of those countries need to create and implement strict laws which ban such labour.</u>
*Note: A logical actor here is 'governments', though others are possible, e.g. parents.*

**iv)** To reduce the number of teenage pregnancies, <u>schools should improve their sex education programmes.</u>
*Note: A logical actor here is 'schools', though others are possible, e.g. parents, teachers.*

**v)** In order to tackle the problem of species extinction, <u>governments need to provide funding to animal welfare organisations to help preserve the most endangered species.</u>
*Note: A logical actor here is 'governments', though others are possible.*

Academic Writing Genres — Sheldon Smith

# Unit 5: Classification Essays

## Unit 5, Exercise 1: **Comprehension**

**1** Explain the meaning of the following terms.

- classify     <u>to arrange into groups of categories</u>
- criterion     <u>the basis according to which something is categorised</u>
- sub-divide     <u>to divide something that has already been divided</u>

**2** Complete the diagram classifying ways to organise classification essays.

> Classification essays can be classified according to whether there is a **criterion** or not. Single-**criterion** essays can be sub-divided according to whether or not there are sub-**categories**.

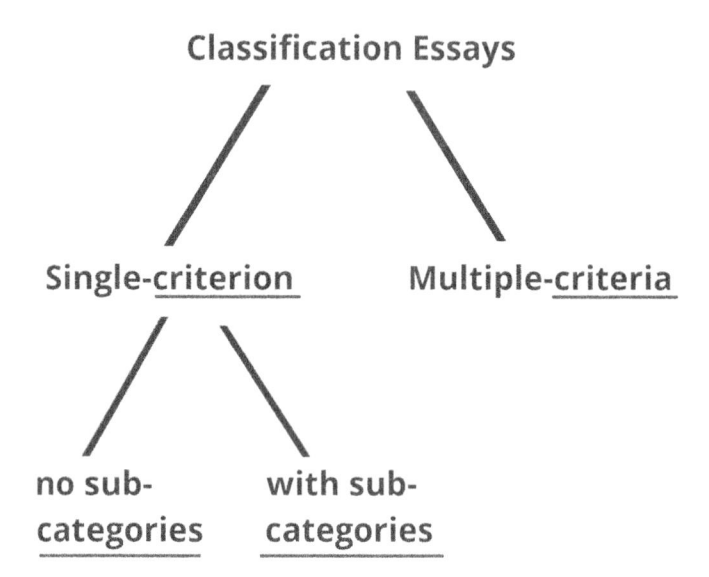

**Classification Essays**
- Single-<u>criterion</u>
  - no sub-<u>categories</u>
  - with sub-<u>categories</u>
- Multiple-<u>criteria</u>

**3** Decide which type of essay (from **2** above) the following statements describe.

- the essay paragraphs describe the *criteria*     <u>multiple-criteria</u>
- the essay paragraphs describe the *categories*     <u>single-criterion</u>
- the criterion should be given in the introduction     <u>single-criterion</u>
- one possible purpose is to justify the method of classification     <u>single-criterion</u>
- one possible purpose is to justify the criteria for classification     <u>multiple-criteria</u>

… Appendix 2: **Answers**

## Unit 5, Exercise 2: **Example essay**

Study the example essay (earlier in this unit) and answer the following questions.

a) What type of structure has been used? Single criterion

b) Complete the following table showing details of the essay.

| Topic | Consumer products |
|---|---|
| **Definition of topic** | Products that are bought by the end user |
| **Why topic is important** | Allows marketers to design marketing mix to appeal to the target market |
| **Criterion for classification** | Amount of effort needed to acquire the product |

|  | Name | Characteristics | Examples |
|---|---|---|---|
| **Category 1** | Unsought products | • Unplanned<br>• Require no effort | Life insurance, burial plots |
| **Category 2** | Convenience products | • Inexpensive<br>• Require little effort | Soft drinks, candy bars, milk, bread, small hardware items |
| **Category 3** | Shopping products | • Brand-to-brand and store-to-store comparisons<br>• May require months or years of search/evaluation | Furniture, automobiles, vacations, some clothing |
| **Category 4** | Specialty products | • Require long and hard search (much time and effort)<br>• Consumer will not accept substitutes | Expensive jewellery, designer clothing, state-of-the-art stereo, limited production automobiles, gourmet restaurants |

# Academic Writing Genres — Sheldon Smith

c) Study the essay and highlight the following.

| | | |
|---|---|---|
| **Language for classification**. | Products that are bought by the end user are called consumer products. They include electric razors, sandwiches, cars, stereos, magazines, and houses. Marketers must know how consumers view the types of consumer product their companies sell so that they can design the marketing mix to appeal to the selected target market. To help them define target markets, marketers **classify** consumer products **by the amount of effort needed to acquire them**. **The four major categories under this classification are** unsought products, convenience products, shopping products, and specialty products. | The criterion in: (a) the **introduction**. |
| | | The four types listed in: (a) the **thesis**. |
| **Transition signals** to introduce the different types. | **The first type** of consumer products, unsought products, are products unplanned by the potential buyer or known products that the buyer does not actively seek. These may require no effort on the part of the consumer, for example life insurance, or considerable effort, such as burial plots. | |
| | **The second type**, convenience products, are relatively inexpensive items that require little shopping effort. Soft drinks, candy bars, milk, bread, and small hardware items are examples. Consumers buy them routinely without much planning. | The four types listed in: (b) the **topic** sentences. |
| | In contrast to convenience products, **the third type**, shopping products, are bought only after a brand-to-brand and store-to-store comparison of price, suitability, and style. Examples are furniture, automobiles, a vacation in Europe, and some items of clothing. While convenience products are bought with little planning, shopping products may be purchased after months or even years of search and evaluation. | |
| | **The final type**, specialty products, are products for which consumers search long and hard and for which they refuse to accept substitutes. Expensive jewellery, designer clothing, state-of-the-art stereo equipment, limited-production automobiles, and gourmet restaurants fall into this category. Because consumers are willing to spend much time and effort to find specialty products, distribution is often limited to one or two sellers in a given region. | |
| The criterion in: (b) the **conclusion**. | In conclusion, consumer products **can be classified according to** the effort required to obtain them, **leading to four categories**, namely unsought products, convenience products, shopping products, and specialty products. Although not the only way to categorise consumer products, these categories greatly assist marketers in appealing to the selected target market. | **Language for classification**. |
| | | The four types listed in: (c) the **summary**. |

d) New introduction (suggested answer)

Products that are bought by the end user are called consumer products. They include electric razors, sandwiches, cars, stereos, magazines, and houses. Marketers must know how consumers view the types of consumer product their companies sell so that they can design the marketing mix to appeal to the selected target market. <u>To help them define target markets, marketers classify consumer products in two ways: by the amount of effort needed to acquire them, and by durability.</u>

Note

The original introduction shows the criterion (*amount of effort needed to acquire them*) and the categories. As this is a multiple-criteria structure, the sentence showing the criterion is no longer background, but becomes part of the thesis, with the second criterion added. The categories are *not* shown in this thesis statement.

## Unit 5, Exercise 3: **Language for classification**

1) Languages _____c)_____ according to their structural characteristics.
   a) on the basis of     b) consist of     **c) can be classified**
2) Languages may also _____c)_____ on the basis of their genetic relationship.
   a) classify     b) comprise     **c) be grouped**
3) Linguists _____a)_____ languages in two ways: according to structure and according to genetics.
   **a) classify**     b) comprise     c) be grouped
4) Countries can be classified _____b)_____ three kinds: low-, middle- and high-income.
   a) by     **b) into**     c) of
5) Animals _____a)_____ invertebrates (without a backbone) and vertebrates (having a backbone).
   **a) may be grouped as**     b) are classified by     c) classify into
6) Animals _____b)_____ invertebrates (without a backbone) and vertebrates (having a backbone).
   a) consist     **b) comprise**     c) are grouped
7) Animals can be classified according to _____b)_____ they have a backbone or not.
   a) where     **b) whether**     c) are
8) Computer systems _____a)_____ of hardware and software.
   **a) consist**     b) comprise     c) are grouped

LANGUAGE NOTE: *consist* is followed by *of*, whereas *comprise* is not.

9) Consumer products _____b)_____ durability.
   a) classify     **b) may be classified by**     c) are grouped into
10) _____c)_____ durability.
   a) This is classified into     b) These are categorised     **c) One way to classify this is by**

# Unit 5, Exercise 4: **Completing a classification diagram**

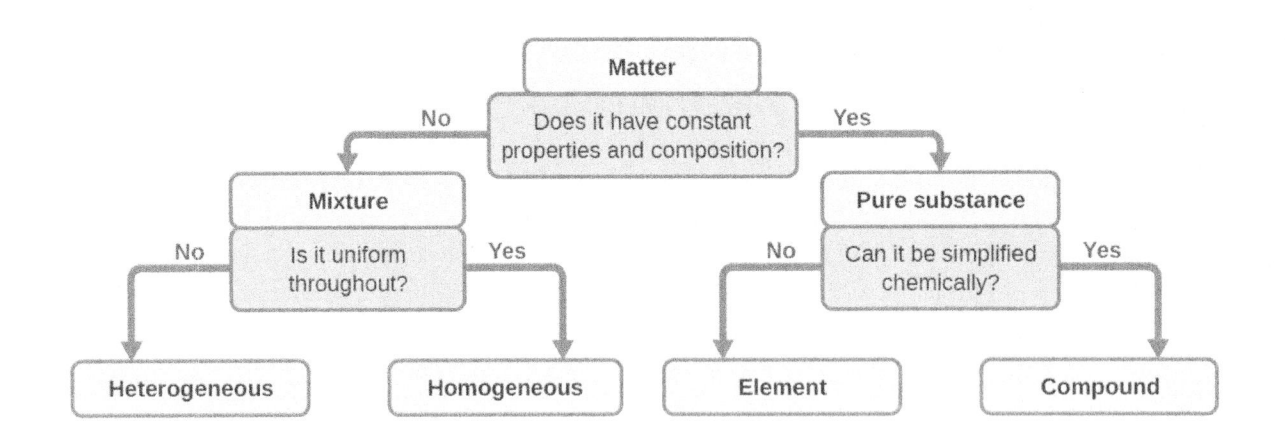

```
                              Matter
                              │
              No   Does it have constant    Yes
          ┌───────  properties and composition?  ───────┐
          ▼                                              ▼
       Mixture                                      Pure substance
          │                                              │
    No  Is it uniform  Yes                   No  Can it be simplified  Yes
   ┌──  throughout?  ──┐                    ┌──   chemically?   ──┐
   ▼                   ▼                    ▼                     ▼
Heterogeneous      Homogeneous           Element              Compound
```

b) Which structure has been used for this classification?

Single-criterion (with sub-categories) structure


c) Use the information in the diagram to complete the following summary.

Matter can be divided into two general categories, namely mixtures and pure substances. A pure substance has a (1) **constant** composition. Pure substances can be (2) **sub**-divided into (3) **two** types, according to whether the substance can chemically simplified or not. Pure substances that (4) **cannot** be broken down into simpler substances are called elements, while those that (5) **can** be broken down are called (6) **compounds**. The second general category, mixtures, can also be (7) **sub**-divided into two types, depending on whether or not they are (9) **uniform** throughout. A mixture which exhibits a (9) **uniform** composition and appears visually the same throughout is called a (110 **homogeneous** mixture, while one which (11) **varies** from point to point is called a heterogeneous mixture.

# Appendix 2: Answers

d) **Highlight** the language which is used to classify or show categories.

---

**Classifying Matter**

Matter ==can be classified into two broad categories==: pure substances and mixtures.

A pure substance has a constant composition. All specimens of a pure substance have exactly the same makeup and properties. Any sample of sucrose (table sugar) consists of 42.1% carbon, 6.5% hydrogen, and 51.4% oxygen by mass. Any sample of sucrose also has the same physical properties, such as melting point, colour, and sweetness, regardless of the source.

==We can divide== pure substances ==into two classes==. Pure substances that cannot be broken down into simpler substances by chemical changes are called elements. Iron, silver, gold, aluminium, sulphur, oxygen, and copper are familiar examples of the more than 100 known elements.

Pure substances that can be broken down by chemical changes are called compounds. This breakdown may produce either elements or other compounds, or both. Mercury(II) oxide, an orange, crystalline solid, can be broken down by heat into the elements mercury and oxygen. When heated in the absence of air, the compound sucrose is broken down into the element carbon and the compound water.

==The second category== of matter is mixtures. A mixture ==is composed of== two or more types of matter that can be present in varying amounts and can be separated by physical changes, such as evaporation.

Mixtures ==can also be broken down into two classes==. A mixture which exhibits a uniform composition and appears visually the same throughout is called a homogeneous mixture. An example of a homogenous mixture is a sports drink, ==consisting of== water, sugar, colouring, flavouring, and electrolytes mixed together uniformly. Other examples include air, maple syrup and gasoline.

---

Matter ==can be divided into two general categories==, namely mixtures and pure substances. A pure substance has constant properties and a constant composition. Pure substances ==can be sub-divided into two types==, ==according to whether== the substance can chemically simplified ==or not==. Pure substances that cannot be broken down into simpler substances are called elements, while those that can be broken down are called compounds. ==The second general category==, mixtures, ==can also be sub-divided into two types==, ==depending on whether or not== they are uniform throughout. A mixture which exhibits a uniform composition and appears visually the same throughout is called a homogeneous mixture, while one which varies from point to point is called a heterogeneous mixture.

## Unit 5, Exercise 5: **Multiple-criteria structure**

| | | | |
|---|---|---|---|
| **Topic** | Joints | | |
| **Definition of topic** | Any place where adjacent bones come together to form a connection | | |

| | Name | Defining feature or characteristics | Categories |
|---|---|---|---|
| **Criteria 1** | Structural | How joints are connected | • fibrous joint<br>• cartilaginous joint<br>• synovial joint |
| **Criteria 2** | Functional | Amount of movement | • immobile<br>• slightly moveable<br>• freely moveable |

## Unit 5, Exercise 6: **Writing a classification essay**

Below is a possible answer to this question. There are other ways to write and present this information. Information taken directly from the table is underlined.

> One way to classify countries is according to per capita GDP per year. Classifying countries in this way allows comparisons to be made between different countries. This classification leads to three categories, namely low-income countries, middle-income countries and high-income countries.
>
> The first category is low-income countries. These are countries with less than $1,045 per capita GDP per year. Although these countries earn 1% of total world income, they represent 12% of the global population. In these countries, 81% of the population is urban. Examples of low-income countries are Myanmar, Ethiopia, and Somalia.
>
> The second category is middle-income countries. These are countries which have a per capita GDP between $1,045 and $12,745 per year. These countries earn 32% of world income and represent 69% of the global population. A total of 62% of the population in these countries is urban. Thailand, China, and Namibia are examples of middle-income countries.
>
> The third and final category is high-income countries. These are countries which have over $12,745 per year per capita income. While these countries earn 67% of world income, they represent only 19% of the global population. A total of 28% of the population of these countries is urban. Countries such as United States, Germany, Canada, and the United Kingdom are examples of high-income countries.
>
> In summary, countries of the world can be divided according to per capita GDP per year into three categories: low-income, middle income and high-income countries.

# Appendix 2: Answers

# Unit 6: Argument Essays

## Unit 6, Exercise 1: Comprehension

1 Explain what an argument essay is. How is it different from a *discussion* essay?

An argument essay looks at one side (rather than both sides), though may consider the other side through counter-argument.

A discussion essay (Unit 7) looks at both sides.

2 How is an *argument* essay different from a *persuasion* essay? Why is argument more common in academic writing that persuasion?

An argument essay presents arguments for (or against) something. It relies on logical reasoning. In contrast, a persuasion essay seeks to convince the reader that the writer's position is the correct one. It relies not only on logical reasoning but also emotional appeals, or asserting the writer's authority.

An argument essay is more common as academic writing is objective, meaning emotional appeals and asserting the writer's authority are not common.

3 What two types of support are especially common/useful for an argument essay?

- *Predicting the consequence*
- *Counter-argument*

4 How are *first* and *second conditional* grammar structures formed?

- First conditional    *If + present tense, will + verb*
- Second conditional    *If + past tense, would + verb*

5 What type of support are *first* and *second conditional* grammar structures used for?

They are used to *predict the consequence.*

6 What, according to the unit, are the three steps in forming a *counter-argument*?

- Understand who the opposition is.
- Consider their view.
- Think of a good response.

# Academic Writing Genres

**Sheldon Smith**

## Unit 6, Exercise 2: **Example essay**

a) What is the position of the writer? Write it in the diagram below.

The writer's position is given in this sentence:
  the technologies that are temporarily making this world a better place to live could well prove to be an ultimate disaster

b) Complete the diagram by summarising the main ideas of the essay.

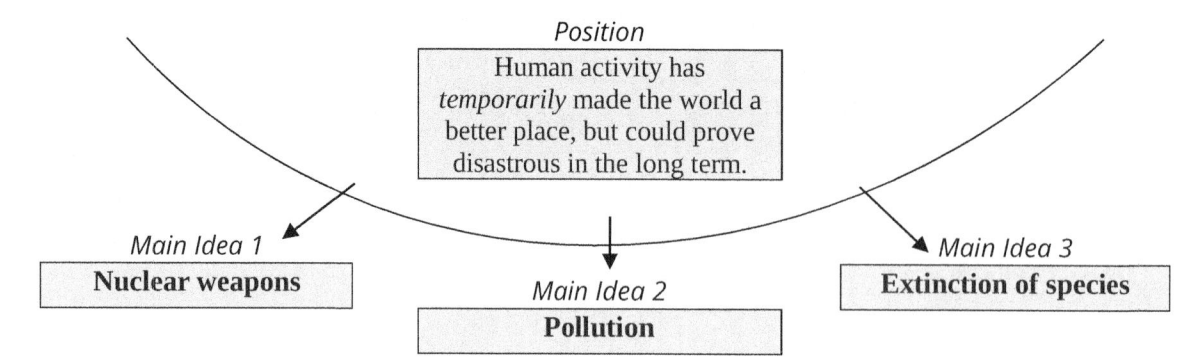

*Position*
Human activity has *temporarily* made the world a better place, but could prove disastrous in the long term.

*Main Idea 1*
**Nuclear weapons**

*Main Idea 2*
**Pollution**

*Main Idea 3*
**Extinction of species**

c) Study the example essay and find (and highlight) examples of each the following:
- **predicting the consequence** [3 examples];
- **counter-argument** [2 examples].

[Introduction – none]

The biggest threat to the earth caused by modern human activity comes from the creation of nuclear weapons. **Although some people claim that countries need these weapons in order to defend themselves, the number and kind of weapons that some countries currently possess are far in excess of what is needed for defence.** If these weapons were used, they could lead to the destruction of the entire planet.

Another harm caused by human activity to this earth is pollution. People have become reliant on modern technology, which can have adverse effects on the environment. For example, reliance on cars causes air and noise pollution. Even seemingly innocent devices, such as computers and mobile phones, use electricity, most of which is produced from coal-burning power stations, which further adds to environmental pollution. **Unless we curb our direct and indirect use of fossil fuels, the harm to the environment may be catastrophic.**

Animals are an important feature of this earth and the past decades have witnessed the extinction of a considerable number of animal species. This is the consequence of human encroachment on wildlife habitats, for example deforestation to expand cities. **Some may argue that such loss of species is natural and has occurred throughout earth's history. However,** the current rate of species loss far exceeds normal levels, and is threatening to become a mass extinction event.

In summary, there is no doubt that human activity has made the world a worse place to live as a result of the creation of nuclear weapons, pollution, and destruction of wildlife. **It is important for us to see not only the short-term effects of our actions, but their long-term effects as well. Otherwise, human activity will be a step towards destruction.**

# Appendix 2: Answers

d) Study the three examples of predicting the consequence identified in c) above and answer the following questions.
- What transition word is used to introduce each example?
- Which tenses are used?
- How does the choice of tense affect the meaning?

Note: The examples have been added to the table for clarity.

| Example | Transition | Tenses used | How choice of tense affects meaning |
|---|---|---|---|
| 1. *If these weapons were used, they could lead to the destruction of the entire planet.* | If | past + could | The past tense makes this an *improbable* action (it is second conditional). It is an outcome the writer does not want. |
| 2. *Unless we curb our direct and indirect use of fossil fuels, the harm to the environment may be catastrophic.* | Unless | present + may | The present tense makes this a *possible* action. It is an outcome the writer wants to happen. |
| 3. *It is important for us to see not only the short-term effects of our actions, but their long-term effects as well. Otherwise, human activity will be a step towards destruction.* | Otherwise | present + future (will) | The present (with future) tense makes this a *possible* result. It is the writer's recommendation, and therefore something the writer wants to happen. |

# Unit 6, Exercise 3: **Predicting the consequence**

*The following are some possible answers to this question. These can be used as further examples. However, there are many possible ways to predict the consequence in each case.*

**i)** If parents smoke cigarettes at home, in front of their children, **they will model behaviour that children might later copy, since parents are their primary role models.**
Note: If + present, will + do

**ii)** Unless individuals change their unhealthy eating habits, **the obesity problem that many countries are facing will continue to worsen.**
Note: Unless + present, will + do

**iii)** Parents need to do more to educate their children about the dangers of social media. Otherwise, **their children may fall victim to online bullying or grooming by paedophiles.**
Note: present, otherwise + may
[In the example, 'may' is used instead of 'will'; other modal verbs are always possible instead of 'will', which is sometimes too strong.]

**iv)** If countries continue to use coal and other fossil fuels as their main source of energy, **we will reach a point of no return for climate change, with the result that major environmental disasters will occur.**
Note: if + present, will + do

**v)** If schools reintroduced rules allowing teachers to hit children, **teachers would be more likely to use physical punishment rather than more psychologically appropriate means, such as discussing problems with students.**
Note: if + past, would + do

# Appendix 2: Answers

## Unit 6, Exercise 4: Counter-argument #1

The following are paragraphs from example essays in other unit. Each paragraph contains a counter-argument. For each paragraph:
- identify and underline the sentence(s) showing counter-argument;
- highlight the language used to show counter-argument.

*From example essay #2 in Unit 1*

Despite this positive short-term effect, there are also some more negative long-term effects, the most important of which is that buying on credit can lead people into a life of debt. **Although some people may claim that** credit gives much convenience to the consumer, it must be remembered that they pay for this convenience in the form of high interest rates. They will consequently pay much more for the products than if they had saved up and bought them, and it will thus take them much longer to pay for them. Furthermore, the ease with which credit cards can be obtained and used may lead to reckless spending. Credit card users will later be faced with monthly bills, which will use up much of their income and take them years or even a whole lifetime to pay off.

*From example essay in Unit 3*

A further effect on the family is the promotion of independence in the children. **Some might argue that** having both parents working might be damaging to the children because of a lack of parental attention. **However**, such children have to learn to look after themselves at an earlier age, and their parents often rely on them to help with the housework. This therefore teaches them important life skills.

*From example essay in Unit 4*

Governments could also implement initiatives to improve their citizens' eating and exercise habits. This could be done through education, for example by adding classes to the curriculum about healthy diet and lifestyles. Governments could also do more to encourage their citizens to walk or cycle instead of taking the car, for instance by building more cycle lanes or increasing vehicle taxes. **While some might argue that** increased taxes are a unreasonable way to solve the problem, it is no different from the high taxes imposed on cigarettes to reduce cigarette consumption.

# Unit 6, Exercise 5: **Counter-argument #2**

*The following are some possible answers to this question. These can be used as further examples. However, there are many possible counter-arguments and ways to structure sentences.*

i) Individuals can do little to tackle climate change.
**While some critics argue that** individuals can do little to tackle climate change, **there are in fact many actions that individuals can take which would make a difference. For example, they can take public transport rather than the private car, thus reducing greenhouse gas emissions.**

ii) Sex education at school might encourage underage children to have sex.
**Although it might seem that** sex education at school might encourage underage children to have sex, **it is more likely that, by being educated and aware of the consequences, they would be less likely to engage in sexual activity.**

iii) Animals should not be used for medical research as they are genetically very different from human being.
**Opponents claim that** animals should not be used for medical research as they are genetically very different from human beings. **However, animals share a significant number of genes with humans. Mice, for examples, which are commonly used in medical research, have 90% of their genes in common with humans.**

iv) Computer games are harmful to children.
**While it may seem that** computer games are harmful to children, **they can in fact teach children many important social skills. For example, many games require players to work together and cooperate in order to succeed, just as people need to do in real life.**

v) Learning a second language is a waste of time.
**It has been suggested that** learning a second language is a waste of time. **However, in an increasingly globalised world, it is all the more important for us to be able to communicate effectively, and even English speakers should make the effort to learn a second language in order to better communicate with others.**

# Appendix 2: Answers

# Unit 7: Discussion Essays

## Unit 7, Exercise 1: **Comprehension**

1 What is a discussion essay?

   A discussion essay examines both sides of a situation, presenting a balanced view.

2 How is a *discussion* essay different from an *argument* essay?

   An argument essay argues for one side of the situation, rather than both.

   Note: An argument essay will still try to present a balanced view, via counter-argument.

3 What elements does the *introduction* to a discussion essay usually contain?

   - General statements
   - Position
   - Definition(s)
   - Thesis statement

4 What elements does the *conclusion* to a discussion essay usually contain?

   - Summary
   - Opinion
   - Recommendation(s)

5 What is the usual order of ideas in the main body?

   Ideas *for* usually come first, then ideas *against*.

   More important ideas usually come before less important ideas.

# Academic Writing Genres

**Sheldon Smith**

## Unit 7, Exercise 2: **Example essay**

a) Study the *Introduction* to the model essay again (below). Identify the different stages.

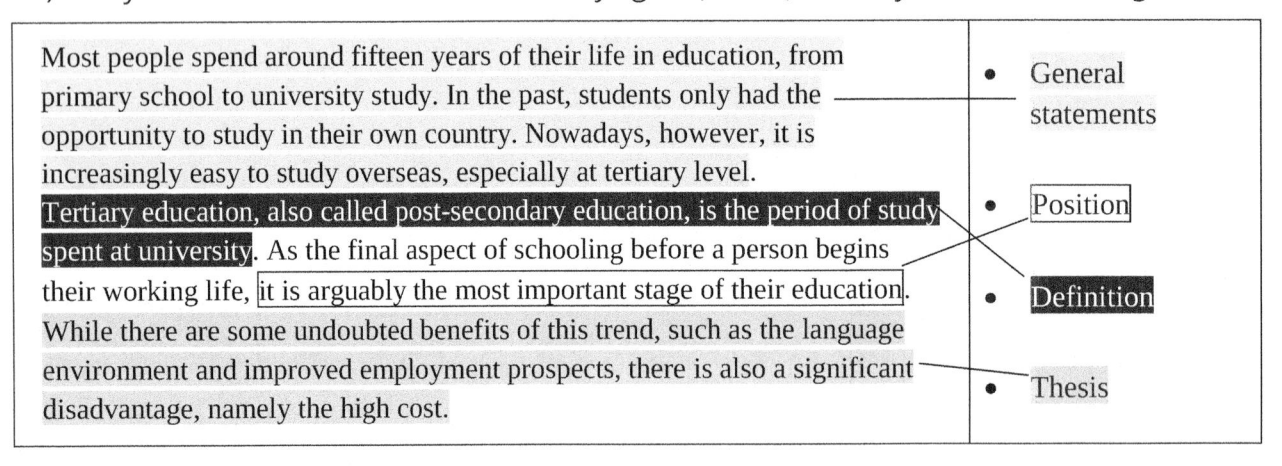

| | |
|---|---|
| Most people spend around fifteen years of their life in education, from primary school to university study. In the past, students only had the opportunity to study in their own country. Nowadays, however, it is increasingly easy to study overseas, especially at tertiary level. Tertiary education, also called post-secondary education, is the period of study spent at university. As the final aspect of schooling before a person begins their working life, it is arguably the most important stage of their education. While there are some undoubted benefits of this trend, such as the language environment and improved employment prospects, there is also a significant disadvantage, namely the high cost. | • General statements<br><br>• Position<br><br>• Definition<br><br>• Thesis |

b) Use the table below to record the main ideas of the essay.

| Arguments for | Arguments against |
|---|---|
| language learning environment | expense |
| employability | X |

c) Study the *Conclusion* to the model essay again (below). Identify the different stages.

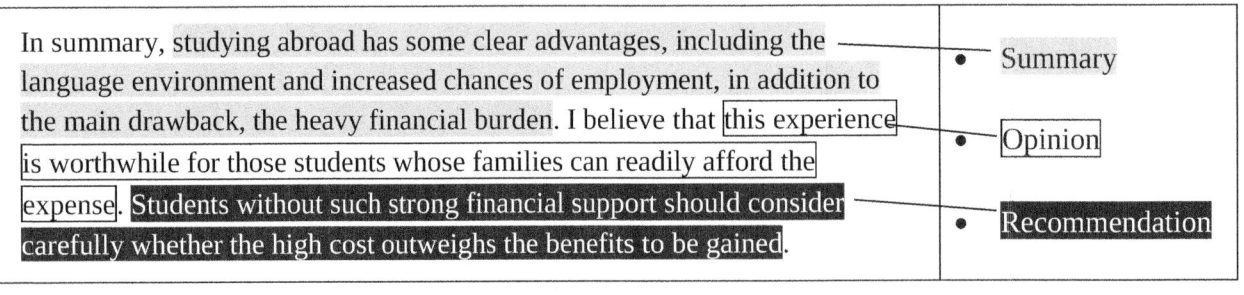

| | |
|---|---|
| In summary, studying abroad has some clear advantages, including the language environment and increased chances of employment, in addition to the main drawback, the heavy financial burden. I believe that this experience is worthwhile for those students whose families can readily afford the expense. Students without such strong financial support should consider carefully whether the high cost outweighs the benefits to be gained. | • Summary<br><br>• Opinion<br><br>• Recommendation |

## Appendix 2: **Answers**

d) Study the essay again and identify the following:
- language to show **order of importance**;
- language to present *the writer's opinion*;
- all occurrences of the words *advantage* and *disadvantage*, or synonyms of these words.

Most people spend around fifteen years of their life in education, from primary school to university study. In the past, students only had the opportunity to study in their own country. Nowadays, however, it is increasingly easy to study overseas, especially at tertiary level. Tertiary education, also called post-secondary education, is the period of study spent at university. As the final aspect of schooling before a person begins their working life, it is arguably the most important stage of their education. While there are some undoubted *benefits* of this trend, such as the language environment and improved employment prospects, there is also a significant *disadvantage*, namely the high cost.

**The first and most important** *advantage* of overseas study is the language learning environment. Students studying overseas will not only have to cope with the local language for their study, but will also have to use it outside the classroom for their everyday life. These factors should make it relatively easy for such students to advance their language abilities.

**Another important** *benefit* is employability. Increasing globalisation means that there are more multinational companies setting up offices in all major countries. These companies will need employees who have a variety of skills, including fluency in more than one language. Students who have studied abroad should find it much easier to obtain a job in this kind of company.

There are, however, some *disadvantages* to overseas study which must be considered, **the most notable of which is** the expense. In addition to the cost of travel, which in itself is not inconsiderable, overseas students are required to pay tuition fees which are usually much higher than those of local students. Added to this is the cost of living, which is often much higher than in the students' own country. Although scholarships may be available for overseas students, there are usually very few of these, most of which will only cover a fraction of the cost. Overseas study therefore constitutes a considerable expense.

In summary, studying abroad has some clear *advantages*, including the language environment and increased chances of employment, in addition to **the main** *drawback*, the heavy financial burden. *I believe that* this experience is worthwhile for those students whose families can readily afford the expense. Students without such strong financial support should consider carefully whether the high cost outweighs the benefits to be gained.

**Academic Writing Genres**  **Sheldon Smith**

## Unit 7, Exercise 3: **Vocabulary extension**

a) Complete the following table, showing different forms of some common words.

| Verb | Noun | Adjective | Adverb |
|---|---|---|---|
| benefit | benefit | beneficial | beneficially |
| X | advantage | advantageous | advantageously |
| X | disadvantage | disadvantageous | disadvantageously |
| X | positive | positive | positively |
| X | negative | negative | negatively |

**Note:** There are other forms of some of these words, e.g. *beneficiary, positivity, negativity*. However, these have special meanings and are unlikely to be used in a *discussion* essay.

b) Use the information in the table to complete the following sentences, using the correct form of the word.

**benefit**
i) Studying overseas is **beneficial** for students in many ways.
ii) Studying overseas can **benefit** students in terms of employability.
iii) Studying overseas is of **benefit** to students in relation to the language learning environment.

**disadvantage**
iv) Studying overseas is **disadvantageous** for students in certain aspects.

**negative**
v) Studying overseas can **negatively** affect students financially.
vi) One **negative** of studying overseas is the expense.

c) Study the sentences in b) above and make a note of the prepositions which are used with some of the words. An example has been done for you.

- beneficial __for__
- to be __of__ benefit __to__
- disadvantageous __for__    Note: Also *advantageous for*
- a negative __of__    Note: Also *a positive of*

360

# Appendix 2: **Answers**

# Unit 8: Definition Essays

## Unit 8, Exercise 1: **Comprehension**

1 The following are possible components of a definition essay. Explain what they mean.

- Etymology — The origin of the word. May also show how the meaning or usage of the word has changed over time.
- Negation — Explaining what it is not (in order to explain what it is).
- Enumeration — Listing each of the characteristics in detail.

2 Give another *three* possible components of a definition essay.
Any *three* of the following *six*.

- Exemplification
- Comparison
- Contrast
- Classification
- Process
- Description

3 What is the usual way to write a formal definition? [Hint: it uses a *wh-* word.]

Word to be defined + verb + category + wh-word + characteristics

4 Which *wh-* words are used with the following?
- People — who
- Places — where
- Time — when
- Objects — which

5 How are definitions given using phrases like 'is concerned with' and 'deals with' different from formal definitions (using the structure in Q3 above)?

These phrases generally do *not* give precise definitions, since the class is usually missing; instead, they are used to list some or all of the characteristics.

# Unit 8, Exercise 2: **Example essay**

Study the example essay earlier in the unit and answer the following questions.

a) What is being defined?

human anatomy

b) Find the formal definition (given in the introduction), then identify following.

The following is the formal definition:
Human anatomy is the branch of science which studies the body's structures.

- category          *branch of science*
- characteristics   *studies the body's structures*

c) The essay introduction uses *exemplification* following the formal definition. What are the examples of?

The body's structures (which are studied in human anatomy)

d) The essay uses *etymology* in the first main body paragraph. What is the *etymology* of the word?

It is from Greek, meaning "to cut apart".

e) The essay uses *classification* in two of the main body paragraphs. In what ways can anatomy be classified?

1) Gross anatomy (also called *macroscopic anatomy*) and microscopic anatomy.

2) Regional anatomy and systemic anatomy.

f) The essay uses *contrast* in the final main body paragraph. What things are being contrasted? What is the difference between them?

Anatomy and physiology.

Anatomy is about structure, while physiology is about function.

# Appendix 2: Answers

## Unit 8, Exercise 3: Writing definitions

a) Complete the following *formal* definitions by adding a category and wh-word. An example has been given.

|    | Word being defined | Verb | Category | Wh-word | Characteristics |
|----|---|---|---|---|---|
| 1. | A pollutant | is | a substance | which | contaminates the water or air or soil. |
| 2. | Lungs | are | organs | which | remove carbon dioxide and provide oxygen to the blood. |
| 3. | A dentist | is | a person | who | deals with the anatomy, development and diseases of teeth. |
| 4. | A battlefield | is | a place | where | battles or other forms of conflict are or have been fought. |
| 5. | An equinox | is | a time | when | the sun crosses the earth's equator and the day and night are of equal length (usually March 21 and September 23). |
| 6. | Steel | is | a metal | which | Is formed by mixing iron with small amounts of carbon. |
| 7. | A celebrity | is | a person | who | is widely known. |
| 8. | Plagiarism | is | writing | which | has been copied from someone else and is presented as being your own original work. |
| 9. | A bee | is | an insect | which | has a hairy body, usually living in a honey-producing hive. |
| 10. | A terminus | is | the place | where | something begins or ends (e.g. a bus route). |

b) Now write formal definitions of the following words. If you are unsure of the meaning, use a dictionary to check – but do *not* just copy from the dictionary.

*The following are some possible answers. Other ways of writing these definitions is possible, depending on characteristics used; but be sure to check correct **category** and **wh- word**.*

- A CEO (chief executive officer): <u>A CEO (chief executive officer) is a person who has the main decision-making power in an organisation or company.</u>
- Biology: <u>Biology is the branch of science which is concerned with the study of living organisms.</u>
- Feminism: <u>Feminism is the belief which holds that women should have the same social, political and economic rights as men.</u>

# Unit 9: Process Essays

## Unit 9, Exercise 1: **Comprehension**

1. Explain what is meant by a process description.
   <u>A process description presents a series of stages to explain how something is or was done or how something happens.</u>

2. The following are the two main types of process description. Explain how they are different.
   - Informational  <u>This type informs the reader so that they can understand the process. The reader is **not** expected to reproduce the process.</u>
   - Directional  <u>This type describes to the reader how they can do something. The reader **is able to reproduce the process**, if they wish.</u>

3. *Informational* process description can be sub-divided into the following two types. Explain the difference between them.
   - Habitual  <u>This type describes how something usually or always happens.</u>
   - Particular  <u>This type describes how something happened.</u>

4. Complete the following summary about the structure of a process essay.

   For the main body of a process essay, a **i) <u>separate</u>** paragraph should be used for each **ii) <u>stage</u>** in the process. These should be presented in **iii) <u>chronological</u>** order. It is important to ensure that the **iv) <u>purpose</u>** of each is clear to the reader. It may be necessary to include **v) <u>definitions</u>** or explanations for any unfamiliar terms or materials. It is common to include a **vi) <u>diagram</u>** to aid understanding. For a **vii)** *<u>directional</u>* process, **viii) <u>optional</u>** steps should be noted, and the reader should be warned of possible **ix) <u>problems</u>** they might encounter. For an *informational (particular)* process, it is common to describe **x) <u>precautions</u>** which were taken to ensure the process was carried out accurately.

5. Complete the following table giving information about language for different process types.

| Type | Language |
| --- | --- |
| Informational (habitual) | Usually uses **i) <u>present simple</u>** tense. |
| Information (particular) | Usually uses **ii) <u>personal</u>** pronouns or **iii) <u>past passive</u>** tense. |
| Directional | Uses **iv) <u>'you'</u>** or **v) <u>imperative</u>**. |

# Appendix 2: **Answers**

## Unit 9. Exercise 2: **Example essay**

Study the example process essay earlier in the unit and answer the following questions.

a) What process is being described?

The nitrogen cycle.

b) What type of process is it? Choose one of the following three.

**i. informational (habitual)**

ii. informational (particular)

iii. directional

c) Highlight all examples of process transitions used in the text.

[*The introduction does not contain any process transitions.*]

**The process** of nitrogen fixation **occurs in three steps** in terrestrial food webs. As shown in Figure 46.17, the nitrogen that enters living systems by nitrogen fixation is successively converted from organic nitrogen back into nitrogen gas by bacteria. **First**, the ammonification process converts nitrogenous waste from living animals or from the remains of dead animals into ammonium ($NH_4^+$) by certain bacteria and fungi. **Second**, through nitrification, the ammonium is converted to nitrites ($NO_2^-$) by nitrifying bacteria, such as Nitrosomonas, which are **in turn** converted to nitrates ($NO_3^-$) by similar organisms. **Third**, the process of denitrification occurs, whereby bacteria, such as Pseudomonas and Clostridium, convert the nitrates into nitrogen gas, allowing it to re-enter the atmosphere.

**A similar process occurs** in the marine nitrogen cycle, where the ammonification, nitrification, and denitrification processes are performed by marine bacteria. Some of this nitrogen falls to the ocean floor as sediments, which can **then** be moved to land in geologic time by uplift of the Earth's surface and thereby incorporated into terrestrial rock. Although the movement of nitrogen from rock directly into living systems has been traditionally seen as insignificant compared with nitrogen fixed from the atmosphere, a recent study showed that this process may indeed be significant and should be included in any study of the global nitrogen cycle.

Human activity can release nitrogen into the environment by two primary means. The first is the combustion of fossil fuels, which releases different nitrogen oxides. Atmospheric nitrogen is associated with several effects on Earth's ecosystems including the production of acid rain (as nitric acid, $HNO_3$) and greenhouse gas (as nitrous oxide, $N_2O$) potentially causing climate change. The second way human activity releases nitrogen is by the use of artificial fertilizers in agriculture, **which are then** washed into lakes, streams, and rivers by surface runoff A major effect from fertilizer runoff is saltwater and freshwater eutrophication, a process whereby nutrient runoff causes the excess growth of microorganisms, depleting dissolved oxygen levels and killing ecosystem fauna.

In short, there are many bacteria which are involved in fixing nitrogen, **which involves three steps** in both terrestrial and marine systems, namely ammonification, nitrification and denitrification. Human activity also contributes to the amount of nitrogen in the environment.

# Academic Writing Genres — Sheldon Smith

d) Complete the following diagram by using information from the example essay.

*The answers are as follows.*

1. Nitrogen (gas)
2. Terrestrial
3. Ammonification
4. fungi
5. Nitrification
6. $NO_3^-$
7. Nitrification
8. Fertilizers
9. Marine
10. sediments

*The following is the original diagram, as it appears in the original source.*

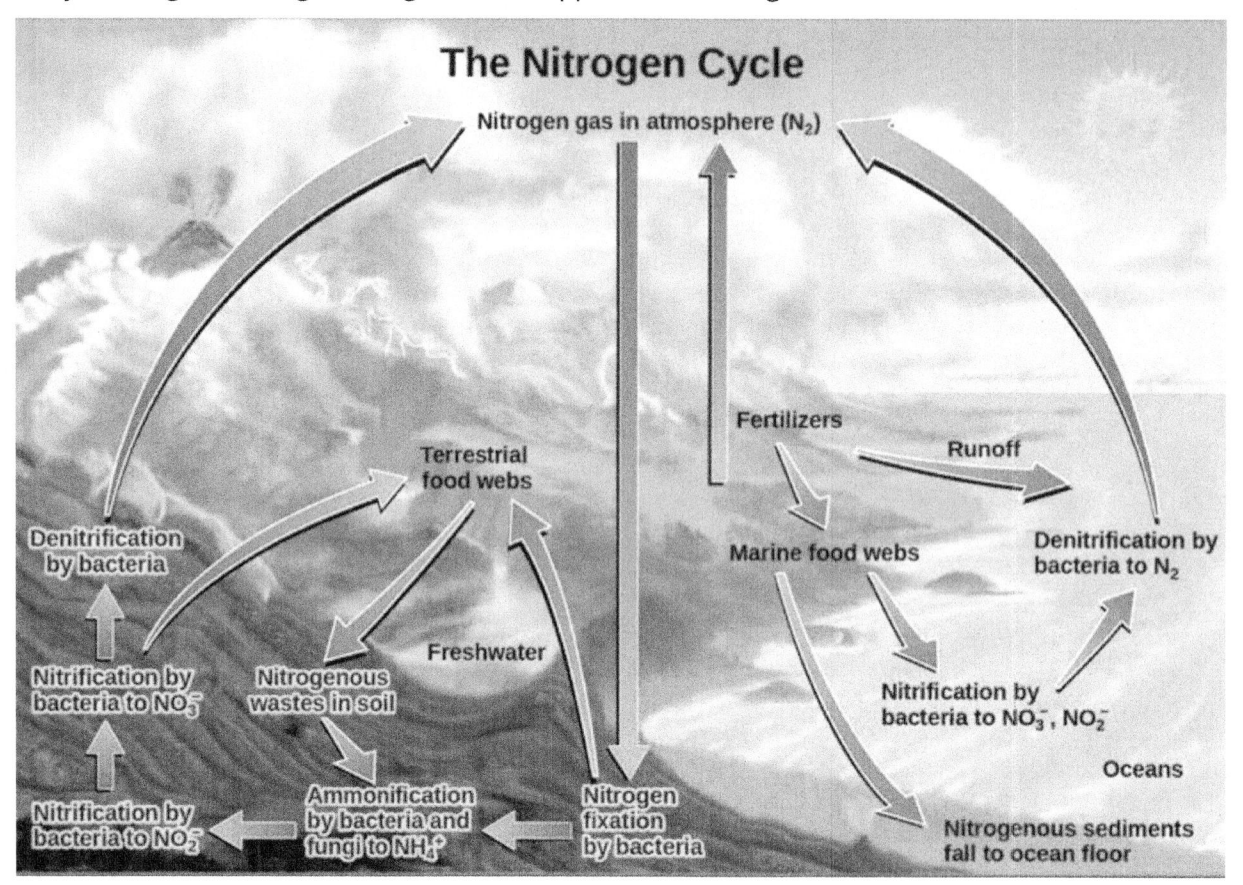

**Figure 46.17.** The Nitrogen Cycle. (credit: modification of work by John M. Evans and Howard Perlman, USGS). Taken from Biology 2e *by OpenStax. Download for free at* https://openstax.org/details/books/biology-2e.

## Unit 9. Exercise 3: **Using a flowchart**

*There are many ways to answer this question. The following is a possible answer. Transition words/phrases are in bold. This is an informational-habitual process, so present tense should be used (mostly present passive, to avoid naming the actor).*

There are several steps involved in the assembly of flat screen televisions. **First**, the chassis is assembled. **After that**, the circuit board is installed. **Subsequently**, the flat screen and the speakers are installed. **This leads to** the final assembly of the television. **The final step of the process** is inspection, including adding an 'Inspected by' sticker to verify that this step has been completed.

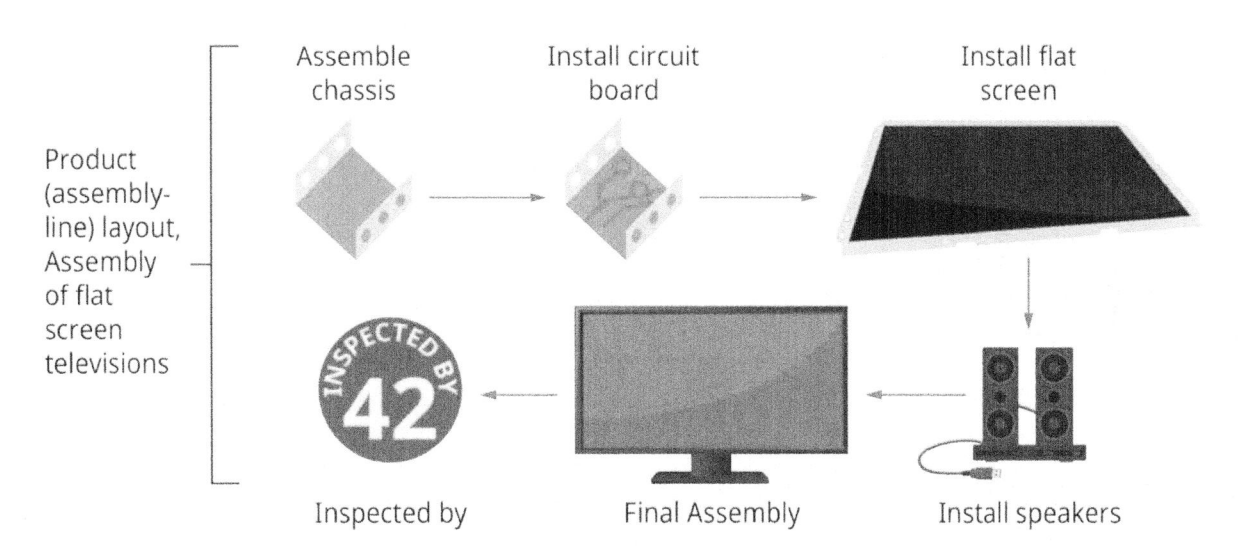

Product (assembly-line) layout, Assembly of flat screen televisions

Assemble chassis → Install circuit board → Install flat screen → Install speakers → Final Assembly → Inspected by

*From* Introduction to Business *by OpenStax. Download for free at https://openstax.org/details/books/Introduction-to-Business.*

# Unit 10: Exemplification Essays

## Unit 10, Exercise 1: **Comprehension**

1  Explain what is meant by exemplification.

   Exemplification means 'showing by giving examples'.

2  The following are ways to structure the main body of an exemplification essay.

   **a)** How many examples are used (single example or multiple examples)?
   **b)** What do the paragraphs in the main body contain?

   - Extended example  *a) Single example (for the whole essay).*
                       *b) Each paragraph has different aspects of the example.*
   - Multiple examples  *a) Multiple examples.*
                        *b) Each paragraph has a different example.*
   - Themed examples  *a) Multiple examples.*
                      *b) Each paragraph also multiple examples linked by a theme.*

3  The unit gives three ways to order the content of the main body. What are the ways? Complete the following gaps (first letter of each missing word has been given).

   - Chronological order
   - Order of importance
   - Order of complexity

4  Which of the three ways given in **Q3** above cannot be reversed? Why?

   Order of complexity cannot be reversed. Going from most to least complex is confusing.

# Appendix 2: Answers

## Unit 10, Exercise 2: Example essay

Study the example exemplification essay earlier in the unit and answer the following questions.

a) What type of structure has been used?

multiple examples

b) Complete the following diagram, summarising the main ideas of the essay.

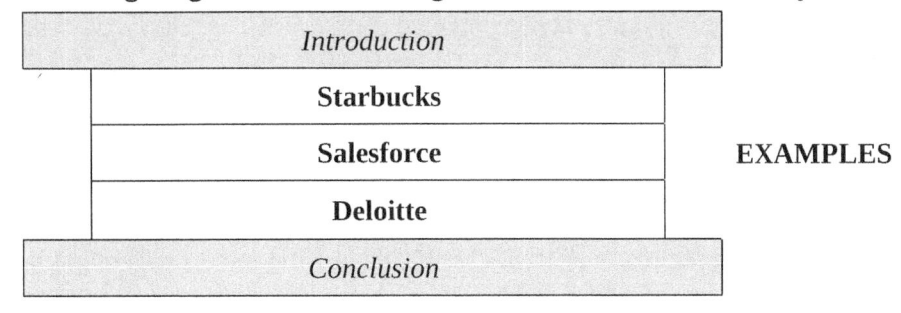

```
┌─────────────────────────────┐
│        Introduction         │
└─────────────────────────────┘
    ┌─────────────────────┐
    │     Starbucks       │
    ├─────────────────────┤
    │     Salesforce      │      EXAMPLES
    ├─────────────────────┤
    │      Deloitte       │
    └─────────────────────┘
┌─────────────────────────────┐
│        Conclusion           │
└─────────────────────────────┘
```

c) The following is a possible paragraph from an essay organised in a different way, namely using **themed examples**. Complete the paragraph by using information from the text.

Another way which is used by many companies to make them socially responsible is encouraging or rewarding employees who take part in **i) volunteer** activities. For instance, Salesforce encourages its employees to take part in activities in the **ii) community**. Employees who participate for **iii) seven** days in a year receive **iv) $1,000** which they can give to any **v) non-profit organisation** they choose. Another example is **vi) Deloitte**. Employees who work for this company can receive pay for as much as **vii) 48 hours** paid volunteer work a year. In 2016, over **viii) 27,000** individuals working for that company took advantage, together working for a total of **ix) 353,000** hours for their communities **x) around the world**.

d) What other *themes* are suggested by the text?
[Hint: Look at the other example paragraph, which is not used in d] above.]

- pay equity
- donating food to food banks
- ethically sourced produce (e.g. coffee)
- donating resources (e.g. trees to farmers)

e) Highlight all examples of exemplification transitions used in:
- the example essay;
- the paragraph in c) above.

### Example essay

Corporate social responsibility (CSR) is the concern of businesses for the welfare of society as a whole. Acting in an ethical manner involves obligations beyond those required by law or union contract. Many companies continue to work hard to make the world a better place to live, with recent data suggesting that Fortune 500 companies spend more than $15 billion annually on CSR activities. **Three examples of** companies which engage in CSR **are** Starbucks, Salesforce and Deloitte.

Starbucks has many initiatives which help it to act in a socially responsible way. **For example**, it has a goal of 100 percent pay equity for gender and race, which it has achieved in the U.S. (Starbucks, 2017). It also donates food to food banks every night. Additionally, it endeavours to ensure its coffee is ethically sourced, with a goal of reaching 100 percent, and currently achieving 99 percent ethically sourced coffee (Starbucks, 2017). A final initiative is donating coffee trees to farmers to replace trees lost to age and disease.

Salesforce **is another example of** a company with an ethical outlook. Salesforce encourages its employees to volunteer in community activities and pays them for doing so. Employees who participate in seven days of volunteerism in one year are given a $1,000 grant by the company to donate to any non-profit organisation the employee chooses (Salesforce, 2018).

**A final example of** a company which engages in CSR **is** Deloitte. Employees who work for Deloitte can get paid for up to 48 hours of volunteer work each year. In 2016, more than 27,000 Deloitte professionals contributed more than 353,000 volunteer hours to their communities around the world (Williams and Marshall, 2019).

In short, many companies are engaging in socially responsible ways, with Starbucks, Salesforce and Deloitte being **three examples**. If more companies can embrace CSR rather than solely pursuing profits, the world will be a better place for all.

### Paragraph from c)

Another way which is used by many companies to make them socially responsible is encouraging or rewarding employees who take part in i) volunteer activities. **For instance**, Salesforce encourages its employees to take part in activities in the ii) community. Employees who participate for iii) seven days in a year receive iv) $1,000 which they can give
to any v) non-profit organisation they choose. **Another example is** vi) Deloitte. Employees who work for this company can receive pay for as much as vii) 48 hours paid volunteer work a year. In 2016, over viii) 27,000 individuals working for that company took advantage,
together working for a total of ix) 353,000 hours for their communities x) around the world.

### Appendix 2: **Answers**

## Unit 10, Exercise 3: **Exemplification transitions**

Complete each sentence by choosing the correct answer to fill the gaps.

All examples adapted from *Chemistry* by OpenStax. Download for free at https://openstax.org/details/books/chemistry.

1) The scientific names of sugars can be recognized by the suffix *-ose* at the end of the name ( __a)__ , fruit sugar is called *fructose* and milk sugar is called *lactose*).
   **a) for instance**    b) is an example of    c) such as

2) Iron typically exhibits a charge of either 2+ or 3+, and the two corresponding compound formulas are $FeCl_2$ and $FeCl_3$. The simplest name, *iron chloride*, will, __a)__ , be ambiguous, as it does not distinguish between these two compounds.
   **a) in this case**    b) to demonstrate    c) such as

3) Group 15 elements __c)__ nitrogen have five valence electrons in the atomic Lewis symbol: one lone pair and three unpaired electrons.
   a) for example    b) is an example of    **c) such as**

4) The formula $H_2O$, which can describe water at either the macroscopic or microscopic levels, __b)__ the symbolic domain.
   a) for example    **b) is an example of**    c) such as

5) As stated in the text, convincing examples that __c)__ the law of conservation of matter outside of the laboratory are few and far between.
   a) is an illustration of    b) illustration    **c) demonstrate**

6) Figure 6.27 __c)__ the traditional way to remember the filling order for orbitals.
   a) such as    b) illustration    **c) illustrates**

7) Extensive properties depend on the amount of matter, **for example**, the mass of gold. Intensive properties do not, __a)__ , the density of gold.
   **a) for example**    b) is an example of    c) such as

8) Heat __b)__ an extensive property, and temperature __b)__ an intensive property.
   a) for example    **b) is an example of**    c) such as

9) Traditionally, the discoverer (or discoverers) of a new element names the element. __a)__ , element 106 is now known as *seaborgium* (Sg) in honour of Glenn Seaborg.
   **a) For example**    b) An example of    c) Such as

10) It is essential to remember that energy must be added to break chemical bonds, whereas forming chemical bonds releases energy. __b)__ $H_2$, the covalent bond is very strong, which means a large amount of energy must be added to break it.
    a) For example    **b) In the case of**    c) Example is

Academic Writing Genres — Sheldon Smith

# Unit 11: Description Essays

## Unit 11, Exercise 1: **Comprehension**

1 The following is a list of aspects, given in the unit, which might form part of the description of a physical object. The first two letters of each is given. Complete the words.
   - we<u>ight</u>
   - si<u>ze</u>
   - co<u>lour</u>
   - sh<u>ape</u>
   - po<u>sition</u>
   - fu<u>nction</u>
   - st<u>ructure</u>
   - pr<u>operties</u>

2 Which of the aspects, given in question 1 above, might appear *first*? Why?
<u>Function, if it is given, might appear first.</u>
<u>This is because it gives purpose to the whole description.</u>

3 Which of the aspects, given in question 1 above, might appear *last*? Why?
<u>Structure and properties might appear last.</u>
<u>This is because they are more complex than basic, physical aspects such as weight, size and so on, and therefore more difficult to understand.</u>

4 What aspects from 1 above might appear in a description of an *organisation*? Which other aspects might be used?

*The following aspects for physical objects also apply to organisations.*
   - **size**
   - **function**
   - **structure**

*The following are further aspects which apply to organisations.*
   - **location**
   - **origin**

5 What tenses are often used in descriptions?
<u>Present simple tense (e.g. to describe physical objects which still exist) or</u>
<u>past simple (e.g. for apparatus used in an experiment, which is past).</u>

# Appendix 2: Answers

## Unit 11, Exercise 2: Example paragraphs

**Example Paragraph 1**

a) What is being described?   The trachea

b) Identify as many of the following aspects of the description as possible.
   The paragraph describes **size, shape, position, function, structure** and **properties**.
   It does NOT describe **weight** or **colour**.

   *See table below for details.*

| | |
|---|---|
| From the nasal cavity, air passes through the pharynx (throat) and the larynx (voice box), as it makes its way to the trachea (Figure 39.7). | |
| The main function of the trachea is to funnel the inhaled air to the lungs and the exhaled air back out of the body. | **function** |
| The human trachea is a cylinder | **shape** |
| about 10 to 12 cm long and 2 cm in diameter | **size** |
| that sits in front of the oesophagus and extends from the larynx into the chest cavity | **position** |
| where it divides into the two primary bronchi at the mid-thorax (Figure 39.8). It is made of incomplete rings of hyaline cartilage and smooth muscle. The trachea is lined with mucus-producing goblet cells and ciliated epithelia. | **structure** |
| The cilia propel foreign particles trapped in the mucus toward the pharynx. The cartilage provides strength and support to the trachea to keep the passage open. The smooth muscle can contract, decreasing the trachea's diameter, which causes expired air to rush upwards from the lungs at a great force. The forced exhalation helps expel mucus when we cough. Smooth muscle can contract or relax, depending on stimuli from the external environment or the body's nervous system. | **properties** |

c) Highlight **useful words or phrases** related to the above aspects.

| Aspect | Useful words/phrases from text (in bold) |
|---|---|
| function | *The main function of the trachea is to funnel…* |
| shape | *cylinder* |
| size | *about 10 to 12 cm long and 2 cm in diameter* |
| position | *sits in front of the oesophagus and extends from the larynx into the chest* |
| structure | *divides into the two primary bronchi at the mid-thorax (Figure 39.8). It is made of incomplete rings of hyaline cartilage and smooth muscle. The trachea is lined with mucus-producing goblet cells and ciliated epithelia* |
| properties | *The cilia propel foreign particles trapped in the mucus toward the pharynx. The cartilage provides strength and support to the trachea to keep the passage open. The smooth muscle can contract, decreasing the trachea's diameter, which causes expired air to rush upwards from the lungs at a great force. The forced exhalation helps expel mucus when we cough. Smooth muscle can contract or relax, depending on stimuli from the external environment or the body's nervous system.* |

d) Label the missing words in the diagrams.

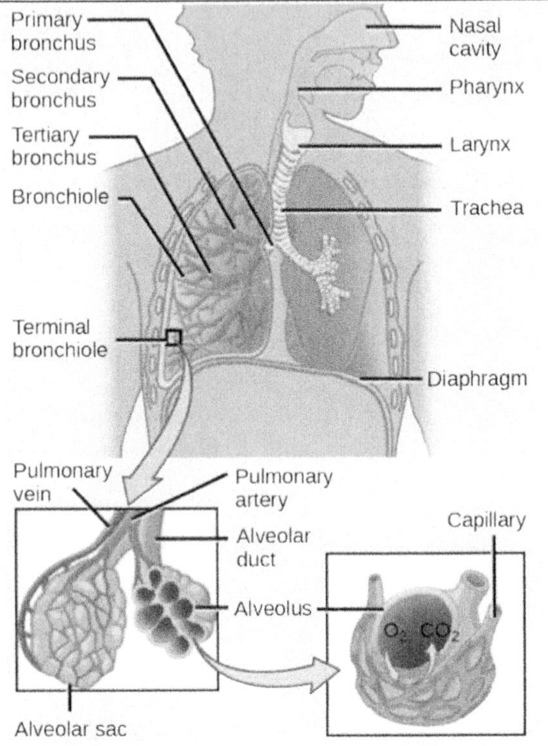


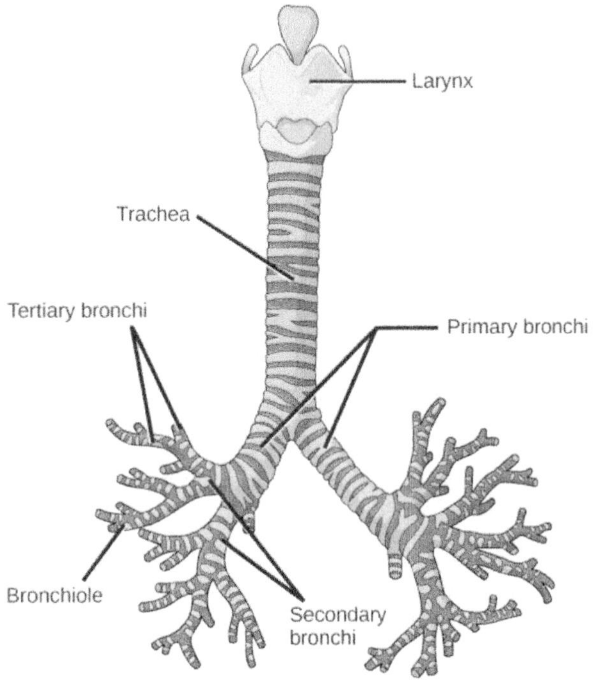


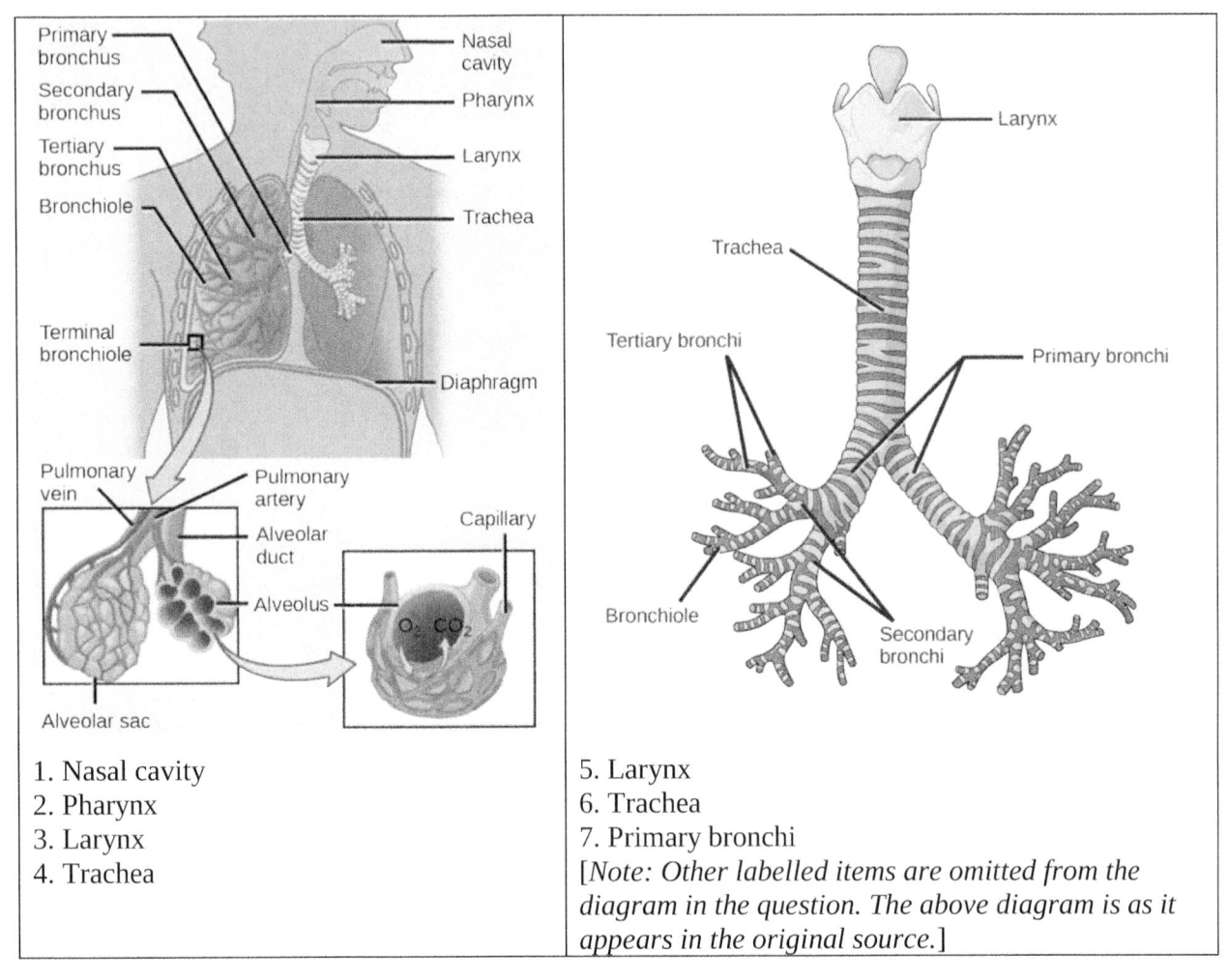

| | |
|---|---|
| 1. Nasal cavity<br>2. Pharynx<br>3. Larynx<br>4. Trachea | 5. Larynx<br>6. Trachea<br>7. Primary bronchi<br>[*Note: Other labelled items are omitted from the diagram in the question. The above diagram is as it appears in the original source.*] |

# Appendix 2: Answers

## Example Paragraph 2

e) What is being described?   The company Guidance Software

f) Identify as many of the following aspects in the description as possible:
   The paragraph describes **size, location, function** and **origin**.
   It does NOT describe **structure**.

   See table below for details.

| | |
|---|---|
| The leader in cybercrimes technology is Guidance Software, | |
| founded in 1997 | origin |
| to develop solutions that search, identify, recover, and deliver digital information in a forensically sound and cost-effective manner. | function |
| Headquartered in Pasadena, California, | location |
| the company employs 391 people | size (number of employees) |
| at offices and training facilities in Chicago, Illinois; Washington, DC; San Francisco, California; Houston, Texas; New York City; and Brazil, England, and Singapore. | location |
| The company's more than 20,000 high-profile clients include leading police agencies, government investigation and law enforcement agencies, and Fortune 1000 corporations in the financial service, insurance, high-tech and consulting, health care, and utility industries. | size (number of clients) |

g) Highlight **useful words or phrases** related to the above aspects.

| Aspect | Useful words/phrases from text (in bold) |
|---|---|
| origin | **founded in** 1997 |
| function | **to** develop solutions that search, identify, recover, and deliver digital information in a forensically sound and cost-effective manner. |
| location | **Headquartered in** Pasadena, California, |
| size | the company **employs** 391 **people** |
| location | **at offices and training facilities in** Chicago, Illinois; Washington, DC; San Francisco, California; Houston, Texas; New York City; and Brazil, England, and Singapore. |
| size | The company's **more than 20,000** high-profile **clients** include leading police agencies, government investigation and law enforcement agencies, and Fortune 1000 corporations in the financial service, insurance, high-tech and consulting, health care, and utility industries. |

# Unit 11, Exercise 3: **Language for description**

Study the following phrases. Identify:
   a) identify the aspects that they are associated with.
   b) **highlight** the words/phrases used for description;
An example has been done for you.

## Physical object

| Sentence | Aspect |
|---|---|
| The human small intestine is over 6m **long**. | size |
| The human small intestine **is divided into** three parts: the duodenum, the jejunum, and the ileum. | structure |
| The inner the ear **consists of** the cochlea and the vestibular system. | structure |
| The iris, which is the coloured part of the eye, is a **circular** muscular ring. | shape |
| The iris **lies between** the lens and cornea. | position |
| The **role of** the iris **is to** regular the amount of light entering the eye. | function |
| Some dinosaurs were nearly 40 **meters** (130 **feet**) **in length**. | size |
| Some dinosaurs **weighed** at least 80,000 kg (88 tons). | weight |
| The algae contain phycoerythrins, accessory photopigments that are **red in colour** and obscure the **green tint** of chlorophyll in some species | colour |

## Organisation

| Sentence | Aspect |
|---|---|
| NASDAQ **was founded in** 1971. | origin |
| It **has** about **3,600 companies**. | size |
| NASDAQ is a sophisticated telecommunications network **that** links dealers throughout the United States. | function |
| NASDAQ lists **more companies than** the NYSE, but the NYSE still leads in total market capitalization, making it the **second largest in the world**. | size |
| Like the NYSE, it **is located in** New York City. | location |
| An average of **1.6 billion shares** were exchanged **daily** in 2016 through NASDAQ. | size |
| It **provides** up-to-date bid and ask prices on about **3,700** of the most active **OTC securities**. | function / size |
| The NASDAQ Stock Market **has three different market tiers**: Capital Market (small cap); Global Market (mid cap); and Global Select Market. | structure |

*Sentences adapted from* Introduction to Business Studies *by OpenStax. Download for free at https://openstax.org/details/books/Introduction-to-Business.*

# Appendix 2: Answers

# Unit 12: About the Report Genre

## Unit 12, Exercise 1: Comprehension

1 What is a report?
A report is a very structured form of writing which presents and analyses information clearly and briefly for a particular audience.

2 Match the following report types with their description.

| Report type | | Description |
|---|---|---|
| i. Laboratory report | i-b | b. This type of report explains and analyses the results of an experiment. |
| ii. Business report | ii-d | d. This analyses a situation and uses theory to provide solutions or recommendations. |
| iii. Research report | iii-f | f. This reports the results of research which has been conducted, for example through surveys (using questionnaires or interviews). |
| iv. Project report | iv-i | i. This reports on work which has been done or is planned. |
| v. Case study report | v-a | a. This examines a real-world situation and analyses it using appropriate theory. |
| vi. Progress report | vi-g | g. This informs a supervisor or customer about progress that has been made on a project over a certain period of time. |
| vii. Field report | vii-c | c. This combines theory and practice by describing an observed person, place or event and analysing the observation. |
| viii. Technical report | viii-e | e. This report is written by engineers and describes technical research. |
| ix. Design report | ix-h | h. This report describes and evaluates a design used to solve a particular problem. |

3 What information will usually go in the Introduction to a report?
There should be some background information on the topic area.
You may need to give definitions of key terms and classify information.
Laboratory reports (see Unit 13) will contain essential theory.
The aims should also be stated.

4 What is an Appendix? What kind of information will go here? What is the plural of this word?
An appendix is used to provide any detailed information which your readers may need for reference, but which do not contain key information.
Information such as a questionnaire used in a survey or a letter of consent for interview participants may appear in the Appendices.
The plural of *appendix* is *appendices*.

# Academic Writing Genres — Sheldon Smith

**5** Study the following sentences. Decide if each one is a feature of a **report**, an **essay**, or **both**.

| | | | |
|---|---|---|---|
| E.g. | Has different types such as *laboratory, business, case study* and *field*. | **report** essay both |
| i. | Allows information to be found quickly in specific sections. | **report** essay both |
| ii. | Demonstrates ability to support an argument (thesis) through knowledge and understanding of the topic. | report **essay** both |
| iii. | Requires good writing skills, such as the ability to construct paragraphs with clear topic sentences. | report essay **both** |
| iv. | Has clearly defined sections, each with a different function. | **report** essay both |
| v. | Uses headings and sub-headings. | **report** essay both |
| vi. | Requires accurate use of vocabulary and grammar. | report essay **both** |
| vii. | Will often include a Contents page. | **report** essay both |
| viii. | Does not usually include graphics such as tables, graphs, charts. | report **essay** both |
| ix. | Generally only includes secondary research (e.g. citations from books or journals). | report **essay** both |
| x. | May include appendices with additional information. | **report** essay both |

**6** The following are typical components or sections of a report.

Recommendations **7**   Main body **5**   Title page **1**   Reference section **8**
Appendices **9**   Conclusion **6**   Abstract **2**   Contents page **3**
Introduction **4**

**7** The following are extracts from reports.

| | Extract | Section |
|---|---|---|
| i. | It is recommended that the company implement measures to reduce the high turnover of staff. | Recommendations |
| ii. | The aim of this report is to investigate whether class size has an effect on learning outcomes. | Introduction [*could also be in the* Abstract] |
| iii. | As can be seen from the graph, the average GDP increased significantly during the five year period. | Main body |
| iv. | Spielman (2017) defines the fundamental attribution error as the tendency to assume that the behaviour of a person is the result of their personality, failing to recognise the effect of the situation on their behaviour. | Introduction [*could also be* Main body] |
| v. | Spielman, R.M. (2017) *Psychology*. Houston: OpenStax. | Reference section |
| vi. | This report has shown that having diabetes increases the risk of heart disease. | Conclusion |

# Appendix 2: Answers

## Unit 12, Exercise 2: Example report

a) What type of report is this? How do you know?
It is a *research report*. It uses research gained from a survey (questionnaire) as primary data.

b) The report contains answers to the following questions.

| Question | Section(s) | Answer |
|---|---|---|
| 1. What is the topic of the report? | Title | Newly qualified doctors' views about whether their medical school had trained them well. |
| 2. How was data gathered? | Title, Abstract, Method | Questionnaire (survey) |
| 3. What percentage of newly trained doctors felt well prepared in: 2000/2001, 2003 and 2005? | Abstract, Results, Discussion | 2000/2001  36.2%<br>2003  50.3%<br>2005  58.5% |
| 4. What may have been responsible for changes in preparedness? | Abstract, Discussion | Changes in medical school courses [Note: the answers 'course changes' and 'curricular changes' are also correct.] |
| 5. Do the writers feel that doctors are more prepared now than in the past? | Abstract, Conclusion | Yes |
| 6. What further studies are recommended by the writers? | Recommendations | 1) To explore the relationship between subjective and objective measures of preparedness<br>2) To follow up the long-term impact of the course changes |
| 7. What is the source of the following statement: 'Lack of preparedness has been linked to stress in junior doctors [5]'? | References | Paice E, Rutter H, Wetherell M, Winder B, McManus IC: **Stressful incidents, stress and coping strategies in the pre-registration house officer year.** *Med Educ* 2002, **36**:56-65. |
| 8. What are the limitations of the study? | Discussion | The major limitation to this study is the use of a subjective outcome measure (there is no good evidence that those who feel more prepared are in fact more prepared). |
| 9. What are the aims of the study? | Introduction | *Aim 1:* To report on the views of newly qualified doctors in 2003 and 2005, compared with those in 2000/2001, about their preparation for their first year of clinical work.<br>*Aim 2:* To begin to investigate whether the increased attention to preparedness for practice has resulted in improvements in the way newly qualified doctors feel. |
| 10. How long after graduation were questionnaires sent? | Method | Approximately 9 months after their graduation. |

c) Study the report again and find examples of *language phrases* for all of the following:

**stating aims;**
- **Our main aim in this study is to** report on the views of newly qualified doctors in 2003 and 2005, compared with those in 2000/2001, about their preparation for their first year of clinical work. **A secondary aim is to** begin to investigate whether the increased attention to preparedness for practice, manifested through curricular changes at UK medical schools, has resulted in improvements in the way newly qualified doctors feel.

**referring to tables or graphs;**
- The proportion of doctors who agreed, partly agreed, or disagreed with the statement *'My experience at medical school prepared me well for the jobs I have undertaken so far'* **is shown in Table 1**.
- **Figure 1 shows** the percentage of respondents from schools using the old course and the new course who felt well prepared in the year under study.
- In the 2000/2001 cohort, 36.3% strongly agreed or agreed, in the 2003 cohort, the corresponding percentage was 50.3% and in the 2005 cohort, it was 58.5% (**see Table 1**).
- **Figure 1 shows that**, within each cohort, a statistically significantly higher percentage of the respondents from schools with new courses felt well prepared.

**two uses of the pronoun 'we', and one use of the pronoun 'our';**
- **We** report on how preparedness has changed since then... [Abstract]
- **Our** main aim in this study is to *report on the views of newly qualified doctors...* [Aim]
- **We** have grouped the 2000 and 2001 cohorts... [Method]
  Note: Method often uses past passive *to avoid use of 'We'. However, there are differences between disciplines, and the insistence of pass passive is slowly changing.*

**stating limitations;**
- **The major limitation to this study is** the use of a subjective outcome measure.

**giving conclusions.**
- **In conclusion, this paper provides evidence that** doctors feel more prepared for their first year of medical work.

d) What is the difference between the two phrases (in c) above) which refer to **Figure 1**?
- **Figure 1 shows** the percentage of respondents from schools using the old course and the new course who felt well prepared in the year under study.

<u>This phrase introduces a sentence which says what the figure shows (percentage of respondents). There is no interpretation in the sentence.</u>

- **Figure 1 shows that**, within each cohort, a statistically significantly higher percentage of the respondents from schools with new courses felt well prepared.

<u>This phrase introduces a sentence which interprets the information (i.e. that a higher percentage of respondents felt well prepared).</u>

# Appendix 2: **Answers**

# Unit 13: Laboratory Reports

## Unit 13, Exercise 1: **Comprehension**

1. What is a laboratory report?
   A laboratory report explains the results of an experiment.

2. The following show the usual components or sections of a laboratory report. The first letter of each is given. Complete the word(s). Note: some answers are *two* words.

   - Title page
   - Abstract
   - Contents page
   - Introduction
     - Background
     - Theory
     - Aims
   - Method
   - Results
   - Discussion
   - Conclusion
   - Reference section
   - Appendices

3. What may be contained in the 'T' section (see Q2 above) of a laboratory report? Where would you find this section? What other name might it have?
   The *Theory* section may contain equations or definitions of key terms.
   It is usually part of the Introduction.
   It may also be called Theoretical Background.

4. Why are calculations part of the 'D' section, rather than the section before?
   The Results section is primarily concerned with description, while the Discussion section is concerned with analysis. Calculations are analysis of information.

5. Apart from analysis (and calculations), what else may be contained in the 'D' section?
   The Discussion will often include figures (graphs or other visual material).
   The Discussion section may consider how the results compare to the expected values.
   It should also consider any possible sources of error, and how these could be overcome.
   Suggested improvements, in the apparatus or method, should also be given.

**6** The following are extracts from laboratory reports. Decide which section they are likely to go in, based on the language and content.

| | Extract | Section |
|---|---|---|
| i. | The test apparatus consisted of a 50 cm long and 6 cm wide metal bar with two cube-shaped opaque PVC boxes with a side length of 5.5 cm attached to it at a distance of 22 cm from each other.** | Method (Apparatus) |
| ii. | These results are in line with the hypothesis that fruit odour in *C. macrocarpa* and *L. cymosa* is an evolved signal to seed-dispersing primates and/or other contemporary or extinct frugivores.** | Discussion Conclusion |
| iii. | The aim of this preliminary study was to compare the effectiveness of the extraction of bioactive components from poplar propolis (phenolics, flavones/flavonols and flavanones/dihydroflavonols) using the maceration method, MAE and UE.* | Introduction (Aims) |
| iv. | MAE of bioactive phenolics and flavonoids from poplar type propolis was found to be a very fast extraction method, compared to maceration and even UE.* | Discussion Conclusion |
| v. | Different extraction methods of biologically active components from propolis: a preliminary study* | Title |
| vi. | The use of propolis as a remedy has a long history [1]. In addition, preparations, as well as food and beverage additives containing propolis extracts can be found on the market in numerous countries [2].* | Introduction (Background) |
| vii. | The sample was placed in an Erlenmayer flask with the corresponding amount of solvent and was treated with ultrasound at 25°C for a given duration.* | Method |
| viii. | The results demonstrate that the use of ultrasound and of microwave extractions greatly reduce the extraction time.* | Discussion |
| ix. | MAE (microwave assisted extraction) is the process of using microwave energy to heat solvents in contact with a sample in order to partition some chemical components from the matrix into the solvent.* | Introduction (Theory) |
| x. | Three extraction methods were employed in order to obtain the biologically active components of poplar type (European) propolis. The results are summarized in Table 1.* | Results |

\* Adapted from *Different extraction methods of biologically active components from propolis: a preliminary study*, by Boryana Trusheva, Dorina Trunkova and Vassya Bankova. Available from https://bmcchem.biomedcentral.com/articles/10.1186/1752-153X-1-13.

\*\* Adapted from *Chemical recognition of fruit ripeness in spider monkeys (Ateles geoffroyi)*, by Nevo, Omer *et al*. Available from https://www.nature.com/articles/srep14895

# Appendix 2: Answers

## Unit 13, Exercise 2: Example report

Study the example report on *determination of g* (earlier in this unit) and answer the following questions.

a) The report contains answers to the following questions.

| Question | Section(s) | Answer |
|---|---|---|
| 1. What was the value of $g$ obtained in the experiment? | Abstract Discussion Conclusion | 9.71 ms$^{-2}$ |
| 2. When did Galileo conduct experiments studying the pendulum? | Introduction (Background) | The early 17th century |
| 3. What apparatus was used in the experiment? | Method | A string, a metal bob of mass 500g, a support stand with a clamp, and a stopwatch. |
| 4. What two sources of error are given? | Discussion | (1) The reaction time of the experimenter. (2) Error in measuring the length of the string. |
| 5. What do $T$, $l$ and $g$ represent in the follow equation? $T = 2\pi\sqrt{(l/g)}$ | Introduction (Theory) | $T$ is the period, $l$ is the length of the pendulum and $g$ is acceleration due to gravity. |
| 6. Why was the time for ten oscillations measured, rather than the time for a single oscillation? | Method | In order to reduce the error in measuring the time. |
| 7. What was the time for 10 oscillations when the length was 1.2m? | Results Discussion | 22.0s |
| 8. How could the experiment be improved? | Abstract Discussion Conclusion | By using a photogate timer, or by increasing the number of trials and using the average value of T at each length. |
| 9. What was the aim of the experiment? | Introduction (Aims) | The aim of the experiment was to measure acceleration due to gravity in Guangzhou, China by using a simple pendulum. |
| 10. What is the equation for the line of best fit (of the graph)? | Discussion | y=0.02463x + 0.0083 |

b) Study the report again and find examples of *language phrases* for all of the following:

**stating aims;**
- **The aim of the experiment was to** measure acceleration due to gravity in Guangzhou, China by...

**referring to tables or graphs;**
- The apparatus, **shown in Figure 1**, comprised a string, a metal bob of mass 500g, a support stand...
- Excel was used to plot this data on a graph of pendulum length against period squared (**Figure 2**).
- The results of the eight measurements **are shown in Table 1. Column 1 shows** the length of the pendulum, measured in metres, **while column 2 shows** the time for ten oscillations, measured in seconds.
- The time for one oscillation at each length, and the square of this value, were calculated from the data above (**see Table 2**).

**listing the apparatus;**
- **The apparatus**, shown in Figure 1, **comprised** a string, a metal bob of mass 500g, a support stand...

**giving improvements.**
- **The experiment could be improved with** more precise timing of the period. This could be achieved by using a photogate timer. Additionally, **an improved result could be obtained by** repeating the experiment for the same lengths and the average value of T could be used.

c) The following table has extracts from the report. Complete the table.

| Section | Function | Tense(s) | Example |
|---|---|---|---|
| Introduction (Background) | To describe past events | Past simple | In the early 17th century, Galileo **(i) conducted** experiments on pendulums and **(ii) discovered** that two pendulums of equal length **(iii) kept** time together, regardless of the arc of their swing. |
| Introduction (Theory) | To give theory | Present simple | A simple pendulum **(iv) consists** of a light string, fixed at one end, with a mass *m* suspended from the other end. The mass **(v) swings** back and forth with a period *T*. |
| Introduction (Aim) | To state the aim | Past simple | The aim of the experiment **(vi) was** to measure acceleration due to gravity. |
| Method | To show the equipment | Past simple | The apparatus, shown in Figure 1, **(vii) comprised** a string, a metal bob of mass 500g, a support stand with a clamp, and a stopwatch. |
| Method | To give the method | Past simple passive | The metal bob **(viii) was attached** to one end of the string, while the other end of the string **(ix) was attached** to the stand. An initial length of 0.6m **(x) was used**. |
| Results | To describe graphs | Present simple passive + Present simple | The results of the eight measurements **(xi) are shown** in Table 1. Column 1 **(xii) shows** the length of the pendulum, measured in metres |
| Discussion | Showing results of calculations | Present simple | Multiplying the gradient by $4\pi^2$ to calculate *g* **(xiii) gives** a value of 9.71 ms$^{-2}$, which **(xiv) is** close to the accepted value of 9.79 ms$^{-2}$. |
| Discussion | Showing sources of error | Present simple | There **(xv) are** various possible sources of error. |
| Conclusion | To state conclusion | Present perfect passive | Using a simple pendulum, a value of $g = 9.71$ ms$^{-2}$ **(xvi) has been obtained** as the value of gravity in Guangzhou, which is close to the accepted value. |

# Appendix 2: Answers

# Unit 14: Business Reports

## Unit 14, Exercise 1: **Comprehension**

1 What is a business report?

<u>A business report is a report which is written in order to help an organisation achieve an objective, for example to increase sales of a particular product or to improve its financial situation.</u>

2 What are some of the key skills involved in writing a business report?

<u>Key skills in business report writing are the ability (1) to apply business theory to real world situations, (2) to identify problems, (3) to suggest solutions, (4) to interpret information and (5) to make recommendations.</u>

3 The following shows common components or sections of a business report. The first letter of each is given. Complete the word(s). Note: some answers are *more than one* word. Some examples have been done.

- Title Page
- Letter of Transmittal
- Executive Summary
- Contents page
- Introduction
- Literature Review
- Methodology
- Findings
- Discussion
- Conclusion
- Recommendations
- Reference section
- Appendices

4 What is a *Letter of transmittal*?

<u>A brief cover letter to the person who requested the report, with information such as scope of the report and the problems which the report addresses. Not usually used at university.</u>

**5** What is an *Executive summary*? How long should it be? How is it usually formatted?

An Executive Summary gives the main points of the report (e.g. purpose, scope, main findings, conclusions and recommendations).

It should be around 10-15% the length of the report (between one and three paragraphs).

It should be on a separate (single) page.

**6** What elements may be contained in the *Introduction* section of a business report?
- Background (e.g. events leading to the problem, context such as company size)
- Purpose
- Scope (what aspects will be covered)
- Report structure
- Definition of key terms

**7** What is the difference between the *Findings* and the *Discussion* section?

The Findings section is factual, i.e. it does not contain opinion.

The Discussion section is where you analyse the facts, giving your 'expert' opinions

**8** Give examples of some business tools which could be used to structure the *Discussion* section of the text.

PESTEL (Political, Economic, Social, Technological, Environmental, Legal)

PEST

SWOT (Strengths, Weaknesses, Opportunities, Threats)

STP (Segmentation, Targeting, Positioning)

Target Market Analysis

**9** Which sections of a business report are sometimes combined?

It is possible to combine the Discussion and Findings section (called *Findings and discussion*, or just *Findings*).

It is also possible to combine the Conclusions and Recommendations.

**10** Why is the audience especially important for a business report?

This is especially important for a business report since there are many possible people the report might be intended for (e.g. finance personnel, marketing staff, the CEO).

# Appendix 2: Answers

## Unit 14, Exercise 2: Example report

Study the example report on *ratio analysis of Tesco Plc* (earlier in this unit) and answer the following questions.

a) The following shows a *Table of contents* for the report. Some headings are missing. Complete the missing headings by referring to the report.

1. Introduction ..................................................................1
    1.1 Ratio analysis...........................................................1
    1.2 **(i)** Tesco Plc........................................................1
    1.3 Aim......................................................................1
2. Methodology ....................................................................2
3. Findings and discussion........................................................2
    3.1 **(ii)** Profitability ratios..........................................2
        3.1.1 Return on capital employed......................................2
        3.1.2 **(iii)** Net profit margin....................................3
    3.2 **(iv)** Efficiency ratios.............................................4
        3.2.1 Asset turnover ratio............................................4
    3.3 **(v)** Liquidity ratios...............................................5
        3.3.1 **(vi)** Current ratio.........................................5
        3.3.2 **(vii)** Acid-test (quick) ratio..............................5
        3.3.3 Net working capital.............................................5
    3.4 Financial ratios ........................................................5
        3.4.1 **(viii)** Gearing ratio.......................................5
        3.4.2 Interest coverage ratio.........................................5
    3.5 Shareholders ratios .....................................................6
        3.5.1 **(ix)** Price/earnings ratio..................................6
        3.5.2 Dividend cover...................................................6
4. Conclusion and recommendations...............................................6
**(x)** References................................................................6
Appendices ........................................................................6

b) Complete the following summary of the report, by using the *Executive Summary*.

The report gives an analysis of the **(i)** financial performance of **(ii)** Tesco Plc between 2010 and **(iii)** 2014 by comparing it to the performance of **(iv)** Morrisons and **(v)** Sainsbury. The performance of the company was **(vi)** unsatisfactory when compared to those other companies. The recommendation is for Tesco to move carefully as it expands into **(vii)** international markets, by first making sure it has a relatively strong position in the **(viii)** UK market.

c) The report contains answers to the following questions.

| Question | Section(s) | Answer |
|---|---|---|
| 1. In which year was Tesco's net profit margin at its lowest? What was the value in that year? | 3.1.2 Net Profit Margin | 2013<br>3.02% |
| 2. What action for the future does the author recommend? | - Executive Summary<br>- 4. Conclusion and Recommendations | The author recommends that Tesco proceed with caution with its international expansion, first ensuring it has a strong position in relation to its competitors in its core UK market base. |
| 3. What is the source of the financial data? | - Executive Summary<br>- 2. Methodology | The data was taken from publicly available financial statements. |
| 4. Which two companies was Tesco compared with in the report? | *This answer is in the title, as well as all sections.* | Sainsbury and Morrisons |
| 5. What is the equation for *asset turnover ratio*? | 3.2.1. Asset Turnover Ratio | $\text{Asset Turnover Ratio} = \dfrac{\text{Revenue}}{\text{Average total assets}}$ |
| 6. In section 3.2.1, the author cites Bodie, Kane and Marcus (2004). What is the name of the book the author has read for this citation? | References | *Essentials of Investments* |
| 7. How many people work for Tesco Plc in the UK, and how many people work for the company worldwide? | 1.2 Tesco Plc | 300,000 in the UK<br>440,000 worldwide |
| 8. What is the overall performance of Tesco Plc from 2010-2014? | - Executive Summary<br>- Conclusion and Recommendations | The company performance between was unsatisfactory when compared to other companies in the same industry |
| 9. What is ratio analysis? | 1.1 Ratio analysis | A method of assessing the condition and performance of a company by using the company's financial statements. |
| 10. Which company had the highest ROCE in 2014? | 3.1.1 Return on Capital Employed | Sainsbury |

## Appendix 2: Answers

d) Study the report again and find examples of *language phrases* for all of the following:

stating the aim;
- **The aim of this report is to** assess the performance of Tesco Plc between 2010 and 2014 by comparing it to two of its closest rivals.

referring to tables or graphs;
- **As shown in Figure 1**, Tesco is the leading supermarket in the UK…
- **Table 1 shows** the ROCE for Tesco from 2010 to 2014.
- **Figure 2 shows** the ROCE of Tesco in comparison to its rivals (full data given in Appendix 1
- Net profit margin for Tesco over this period **is shown in Table 2**.
- **Figure 3 compares** Tesco's performance with that of Morrisons and Sainsbury (for full data, see Appendix 1).
- **As shown in Table 3**, Tesco's asset turnover ratio increased over the period, from 2.17 in 2010 to 2.66 in 2014.
- **Figure 4**, however, **indicates** that Sainsbury performed better than Tesco with regard to its asset turnover ratio in the period under review.

giving recommendations.
- **It is recommended that** Tesco **proceed** with caution with its international expansion, first ensuring it has a strong position in relation to its competitors in its core UK market base.

# Unit 15: Other Report Types

There are no exercises requiring answers in Unit 15.

# Unit 16: Posters

## Unit 16, Exercise 1: **Comprehension**

**1** How is a poster similar to and how is it different from a presentation visual aid?

<u>**Similar**</u>: <u>information must be presented clearly, succinctly and with visual impact.</u>

<u>**Different**</u>: <u>A poster must be self-contained, takes more time to prepare and costs more to make.</u>

**2** What are the benefits of a poster for:
- the viewer    <u>it offers them choice</u>
- the presenter    <u>it gives you more personal contact with those who are interested</u>

**3** Complete the following flowchart, showing the process of planning a poster.

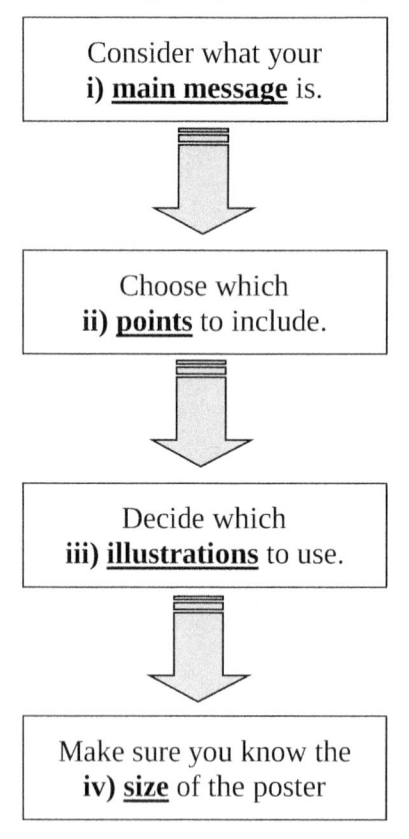

```
┌─────────────────────────┐
│   Consider what your    │
│   i) main message is.   │
└─────────────────────────┘
             ↓
┌─────────────────────────┐
│      Choose which       │
│   ii) points to include.│
└─────────────────────────┘
             ↓
┌─────────────────────────┐
│      Decide which       │
│ iii) illustrations to use.│
└─────────────────────────┘
             ↓
┌─────────────────────────┐
│  Make sure you know the │
│  iv) size of the poster │
└─────────────────────────┘
```

## Appendix 2: **Answers**

4 The following is a list of aspects, given in the unit, which you should consider when you **design the poster**. The first letter of each is given. Complete the words.
- C<u>olour</u>
- I<u>llustrations</u>
- L<u>ayout</u>
- W<u>hite</u> space
- F<u>ont</u> size
- F<u>ont</u>

5 What information is given in the unit about the size of the following aspects of text?
- Title — <u>largest of all text on the poster</u>
- Headings — <u>large font, smaller than title</u>
- Main text — <u>can be read from 1-2m away, at least 18pt, up to 30pt</u>

6 Which type of font is recommended for text on a poster: *serif* or *sans serif*? Why? Give some common examples of the recommended font.

<u>Sans serif font is recommended, because it is simple and easy to read.</u>

<u>Common examples are Arial and Helvetica.</u>

7 Give **two** reasons why bullet points are helpful for a poster.

<u>They help to keep the text simple.</u>

<u>They increase the amount of white space.</u>

8 What is the function of the poster's headings? Is it essential to use the same headings as the paper that the poster is based on (e.g. IMRAD)?

<u>They show the flow of information.</u>

<u>They do **not** have to follow the headings used in the paper, though those can be used as a fall-back if you are unsure what headings to use.</u>

9 What can you do to compensate for the lack of detail in your poster?

<u>You can prepare a handout with additional points, or give out a copy of your whole paper.</u>

10 How much information should be included in the poster? What problems are you likely to encounter with the amount of information if you are starting from a paper already written?

<u>All the relevant information required to achieve your main message should be included.</u>

<u>If you are starting from a paper you have already written, you are more likely to include too much information without enough editing.</u>

# Unit 16, Exercise 2: **Example posers**

a) Compare and contrast the two example posters earlier in the unit. How are they similar? How do they differ? Record your answers in the Venn diagram below.

**Poster #1**
- portrait
- 2 columns
- Section: Conclusion and future work
- figures have captions
- bullet points
- san serif font
- no graphs etc

**same**
- size
- University (of Lincoln)
- Sections: Introduction, Method Discussion, References
- clear title and headings
- short sentences/paragraphs
- 1 (or 2) fonts used
- uses photos

**Poster #2**
- landscape
- 3 columns
- Sections: Motivation, Screening Pathway, Aim
- no captions for figures
- no bullets
- serif font
- has a bar chart & flowchart

# Appendix 2: Answers

# Unit 17: Reflective Writing

## Unit 17, Exercise 1: Comprehension

1. What is the purpose of reflection?
   To make sense of a practical experience and continue to develop.

2. Give examples of reflective assignments you might encounter at university.
   - Reflective essay
   - Learning log
   - Learning portfolio

3. Complete the four stages of Kolb's learning cycle as shown in the diagram.

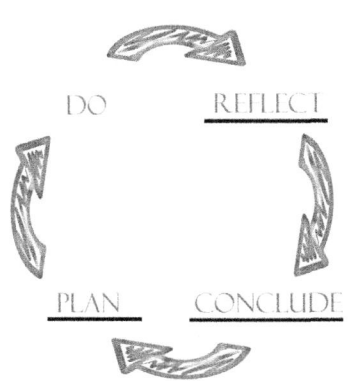

   DO — REFLECT — CONCLUDE — PLAN

   **The Kolb Learning Cycle**

4. The following shows the different areas of Johns' model of structured reflection. Match each area with the correct description (right).

| Area | Description (what it relates to) |
| --- | --- |
| Descriptive | Relates to the final reflection on the experience. |
| Aesthetic | Relates to your reactions and motivation. |
| Personal | Relates to how your actions match the way you want to act. |
| Ethical | Relates to description of the experience. |
| Empirical | Relates to concrete actions (in the here and now). |
| Reflexive | Relates to how you use your knowledge. |

Matches:
- Descriptive → Relates to description of the experience.
- Aesthetic → Relates to concrete actions (in the here and now).
- Personal → Relates to your reactions and motivation.
- Ethical → Relates to how your actions match the way you want to act.
- Empirical → Relates to how you use your knowledge.
- Reflexive → Relates to the final reflection on the experience.

5. Which of the areas above do the following questions relate to?
   - How did my actions match with my beliefs?  ethical
   - How did I feel in this situation?  personal
   - Why did I respond as I did?  aesthetic
   - Could I handle this better in similar situations?  reflexive
   - What knowledge did or should have informed me?  empirical

**6** Complete the following flowchart, showing the stages of the Gibbs reflective cycle.

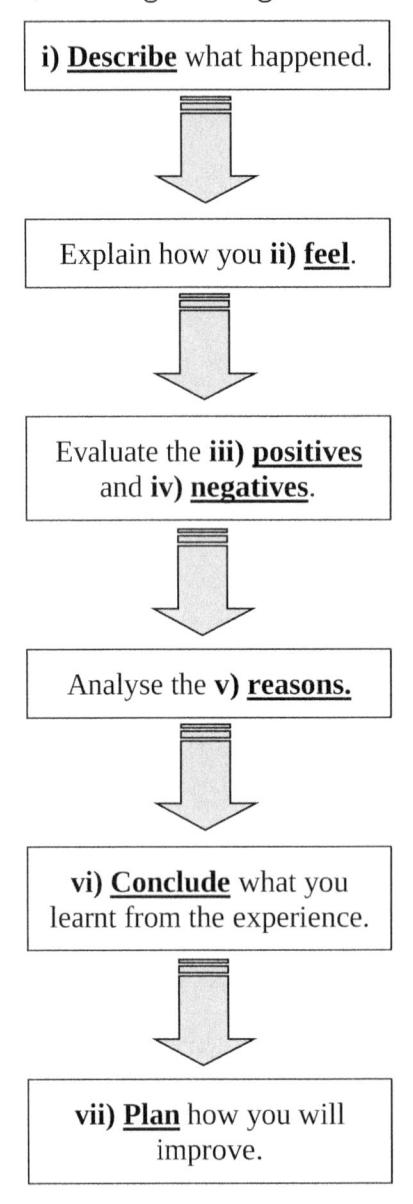

```
i) Describe what happened.
          ↓
Explain how you ii) feel.
          ↓
Evaluate the iii) positives and iv) negatives.
          ↓
Analyse the v) reasons.
          ↓
vi) Conclude what you learnt from the experience.
          ↓
vii) Plan how you will improve.
```

**7** How is reflective writing different from regular academic writing? How is it similar?

|  | **Reflective writing** | **Regular academic writing** |
|---|---|---|
| *Differences* | <ul><li>Common to use first person 'I'</li><li>Uses more informal language</li><li>Less structured</li><li>Subjective</li></ul> | <ul><li>Rarely uses first person</li><li>Uses formal language</li><li>Very structured</li><li>Objective</li></ul> |
| *Similarities* | May refer to academic literature to support points. ||

# Appendix 2: Answers

## Unit 17, Exercise 2: Example reflection

The reflection follows the Gibbs reflective cycle. Identify each of the stages.

| | |
|---|---|
| My students are getting ready to submit a reflective assignment. I have seen some of their drafts and can see that they have a general understanding of how to reflect, but tend to be too descriptive, without thinking deeply enough. This is not surprising since they have not, in their prior studies, had to engage in reflective practice. Boud, Keogh and Walker (2013) observe that reflection is easily neglected since it is both unique to the learner and impossible to observe directly. They cite Duley (1981, p.611) in pointing out that reflection is 'The skill of experiential learning in which people tend to be the most deficient'. I decided to add information to a learning website I use to help my students with their studies. Although I had several handouts from which I could get information, I felt they were rather too simple. I therefore searched for more information about the learning cycle and reflection in text books and online. | **Description** |
| I was initially quite confused at the different models, none of which quite matched the one I was used to. I was a little worried that I had been teaching students in the wrong way. However, I found the different models and ideas stimulating, and liked the fact that the information challenged what I already knew and made me think more deeply. | **Feeling** |
| After reading more about the topic I felt I already had a good understanding of what reflection means, but I had problems deciding how to present the information in a useful way on the learning website. | **Evaluation** |
| This is partly because of the many different models, which I felt would confuse my students. It is also because the website information needs to be fairly brief, but at the same time needs to be accurate and useful. In a lesson, I can help students by adding explanations and working individually with them, but on the website, I cannot do this. I discussed the information with colleagues, which helped to clarify my ideas. I also asked them to look at an initial version of the page on the website and give me some feedback, which also helped to improve the content. | **Analysis** |
| I came to the conclusion that it would be best to use a single model. According to Hilsdon (2005), the reflective models of Gibbs (1988) and Johns (1993, 1998) are commonly used since they 'offer structured approaches to reflection', in the form of headings in a cycle for the former and a series of questions for the latter. Although Hilsdon cautions that reflection 'needs to involve more than simply thinking about and describing our own actions according to models such as that of Gibbs or Johns', and needs to involve a 'recognition of how our identity and subject position may be structured in the discourse forms we use', he is talking about native speakers on graduate courses. In the case the undergraduate ESL learners I teach, who are just beginning their reflective journey, these structured models provide the best next step. I decided that the Gibbs reflective cycle would be most suitable for my students, since it is based on the Kolb cycle I had previously been using, but it has more structure, with a clearer set of stages and questions to help students reflect. As mentioned above, my students' reflections tend to be too descriptive. One advantage of using the Gibbs reflective cycle is that it shows students they have made a useful beginning (by describing), but that this is only a first step towards reflection, and they need to go further by explaining how they feel, by evaluating, analysing, concluding and planning. | **Conclusion** |
| Once the information is on the website and I have used it to guide students in their reflection, I will examine how well students use this information to reflect, and consider how it can be improved to help other students in the future. | **Plan** |

Academic Writing Genres        Sheldon Smith

# Unit 18: Book Reviews

## Unit 18, Exercise 1: **Comprehension**

1. What features does a book review share with other kinds of review (e.g. film review, review of TV programmes)?
    - It offers a description of the main points.
    - It considers the strengths and weaknesses.
    - It gives an overall evaluation.
    - The allows someone to decide whether or not it will be of interest to them.

2. How long is a typical book review?

    Typically around 500-750 words (rarely exceeds 1000 words).

3. How is a book *review* different from a book *report*?

    A book review is a critical evaluation, used in university courses or academic journals.

    A book report is purely descriptive, common in high school. It is shorter than a review.

4. Explain, with examples, what *bibliographic details* are. Where you would normally find them?

    Bibliographic details are details about the book, such as the name of the book, the name(s) of the author(s), the publisher, date and place of publication, the format, the edition, the number of pages, the price, the ISBN.

    Bibliographic details usually go at the start of the book review.

5. Explain the following terms.
    - The thesis of the *book*.    Its specific contribution (to the field).
    - The thesis of the *review*.   The initial appraisal of the work and key observations.

6. Which is more important, *description* or *evaluation*? Which part is usually longer? Why?

    Evaluation is more important.

    The description is usually longer (half or two thirds of the content of the main body), in order to lay the foundation for the evaluation.

## Appendix 2: **Answers**

7 Complete the missing words in the table below (first column).

| Area | Key questions |
|---|---|
| (i) **Content** of the book | Is everything included? Is there too much information? Is anything essential left out? |
| The author's (ii) **purpose** | Has the author succeeded? |
| The intended (iii) **audience** | Is the book appropriate for them? Why (not)? Who else might benefit from reading it? |
| The author's (iv) **arguments** and (v) **themes** | How valid or effective are they? Do you agree with the author's opinions? Why (not)? |
| (vi) **Sources** used in the book | How strong are they? Are there enough? |
| How the book is (vii) **organised** | Is it logical or useful? Are there any problems? Is the book clear and easy to use? |

8 What may be achieved in the introduction to a book review?
- Give an anecdote or quotation which captures the main idea of the book.
- Identify the author and title.
- Specify the type of book.
- State the book's subject matter.
- Give further background to place the book in context.

9 Give examples of the kind of background that may be given in the introduction.
- Previous work by the author in the same field.
- Previous work by other writers in the same field.
- Information about the book series (if the book is part of a series).

10 The following are some positive adjectives which could be used to describe a book. However, the letters are mixed up. Unscramble them to form the adjective.
- relac ⇨ clear
- prechenomvies ⇨ comprehensive
- noccies ⇨ concise
- verimfation ⇨ informative
- nittinegers ⇨ interesting
- bealared ⇨ readable
- lusstibanta ⇨ substantial
- hugothor ⇨ thorough
- poutated ⇨ up-to-date
- gellowdranies ⇨ well-organised

# Unit 18, Exercise 2: **Example book review**

a) The *Introduction* to the example book review is copied below. Identify the different elements (shown to the right).

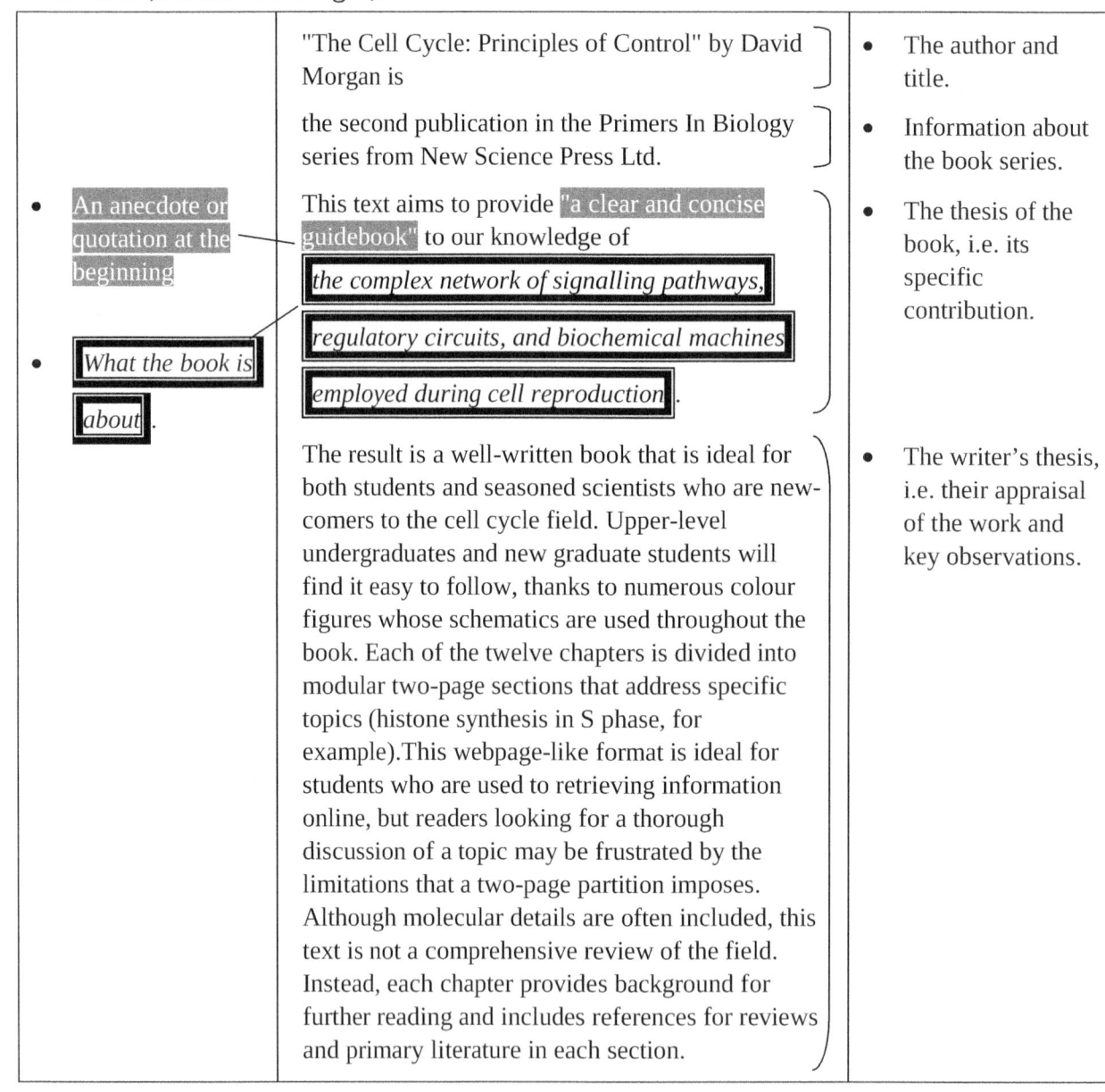

| | | |
|---|---|---|
| | "The Cell Cycle: Principles of Control" by David Morgan is | • The author and title. |
| | the second publication in the Primers In Biology series from New Science Press Ltd. | • Information about the book series. |
| • An anecdote or quotation at the beginning<br><br>• What the book is about. | This text aims to provide "a clear and concise guidebook" to our knowledge of the complex network of signalling pathways, regulatory circuits, and biochemical machines employed during cell reproduction. | • The thesis of the book, i.e. its specific contribution. |
| | The result is a well-written book that is ideal for both students and seasoned scientists who are newcomers to the cell cycle field. Upper-level undergraduates and new graduate students will find it easy to follow, thanks to numerous colour figures whose schematics are used throughout the book. Each of the twelve chapters is divided into modular two-page sections that address specific topics (histone synthesis in S phase, for example).This webpage-like format is ideal for students who are used to retrieving information online, but readers looking for a thorough discussion of a topic may be frustrated by the limitations that a two-page partition imposes. Although molecular details are often included, this text is not a comprehensive review of the field. Instead, each chapter provides background for further reading and includes references for reviews and primary literature in each section. | • The writer's thesis, i.e. their appraisal of the work and key observations. |

# Appendix 2: Answers

b) How is the book review organised: description then evaluation, or the two combined?
The two are combined.

c) How many chapters are contained in the book? ___12___

d) Who does the writer suggest would be a suitable audience for the book?
Students and seasoned scientists who are new-comers to the cell cycle field. [*Introduction*]
Upper-level undergraduates and new graduate students. [*Introduction*]

e) How does the writer organise the description of the content of the book (e.g. by theme, by chapter, other)? It is organised by chapter.

f) How is the book organised (i.e. what is the layout of the book)?
Each of the twelve chapters is divided into modular two-page sections (webpage-like format).

g) Give an example of a weakness of the book. [Hint: It is given in the Introduction]
Readers looking for a thorough discussion of a topic may be frustrated by the limitations that a two-page partition imposes. Although molecular details are often included, this text is not a comprehensive review of the field.

h) Which area does the following paragraph of the review consider? What does it tell you about the book?
It considers the content of the book.
It shows that the content is complete (in fact, more than complete).

i) Is the review positive or negative? How do you know? Find examples of adjectives or phrases to support your opinion.
It is positive.
*The following are some examples of positive adjectives/phrases (highlighted).*
- The result is a **well-written** book that is **ideal for** both…
- This webpage-like format is **ideal for**…
- **A welcome aspect**…
- This is **especially helpful for**…
- This allows Morgan to **address seamlessly**…
- this approach gives the reader **a more fluid view** of …
- A **thorough** introduction …
- Morgan's **excellent** description of …
- Overall, this book offers an **excellent** portrait of …
- I believe this book would be an **ideal** text **for** …

# Unit 19: Research Proposals

## Unit 19, Exercise 1: **Comprehension**

1 What is a research proposal?

   A research proposal is an assignment written before research is conducted in order to gain approval or funding for the research.

2 What are the two types of research proposal? What is the difference between them?

   *Approval proposal.* This type of proposal is written before undertaking a final project, dissertation or thesis, and is submitted to your supervisor for approval.

   *Funding proposal.* This type of proposal is submitted to an external organisation in order to seek funding for your research.

3 Which type of proposal is more common for university study?

   An *approval proposal* is more common at university.

4 True or **false**: A research proposal is a formally structured document. Justify your answer.

   **False.** Many research proposals are submitted using an application form, meaning that a formally structured document is not required. A formally structured document is only required if there is no application form.

5 What elements might the *Introduction* contain?
   - Background information.
   - Description of the research area.
   - Motivation for the research.
   - Explanation of its importance.
   - The overall aim of the research.
   - Specific research objectives.
   - Research questions.

## Appendix 2: **Answers**

6 How is the *Literature review* in a research proposal similar to the one in the final document? How is it different?

   **Similar**: This section provides a critical summary of previous research, identifying possible gaps and how your research will fill them.

   **Different**: It is only a preliminary review (it is unlikely to be complete at this stage).

7 What tense is usually used to describe the method? Why is this tense used? How and why is this different from the tense used in the final document?

   Future tense.
   This tense is used because the research has not yet been conducted.
   In the final document, the method will use past (passive) tense.

8 What elements might the *Methodology* contain?
   - Information on how your research will be conducted.
   - The kind of data which will be obtained (e.g. quantitative or qualitative).
   - The source of data.
   - The research methodology.
   - Why this approach has been chosen.
   - Ethical and safety issues.
   - Required resources.

9 The proposal should include a *timeline*. Give *brief* answers to the following questions about the timeline.
   - Why is it important?   It will help you finish the research within the allotted time.
   - What should it contain?   When important aspects of the research will start/finish.

   How can it be formatted?   As a table, a list, or a GANTT chart.

10 What other sections could a research proposal contain?
   - Expected results.
   - Expected chapter outline.
   - Supervision.
   - Dissemination of results.

# Unit 20: Theses/Dissertations

## Unit 20, Exercise 1: **Comprehension**

1. What is the difference between a *thesis* and a *dissertation*?
   <u>A thesis is written at the end of a PhD (UK), Master's (USA), or both (Australia).</u>
   <u>A dissertation is written at the end of a Master's degree (UK) or PhD (USA).</u>

2. How long (number of words) is a typical thesis/dissertation?
   <u>A thesis/dissertation for a Master's is around 15,000-20,000 words.</u>
   <u>A thesis/dissertation for a PhD is up to 80,000 words.</u>

3. Give examples of assignments that might be part of a Master's or PhD programme that might help you prepare to write a thesis/dissertation.
   - <u>Research proposal</u>
   - <u>Literature review</u>
   - <u>Pilot studies</u>
   - <u>Learning journals</u>

4. Give examples of requirements you should consider before writing your thesis/dissertation.
   - <u>Word limits</u>
   - <u>Required chapters/content</u>
   - <u>Content of appendices</u>

5. The following are the components of a typical thesis/dissertation. Number them (from 1-13).
   - Abstract — 2
   - Acknowledgements — 3
   - Appendices — 13
   - Conclusion — 10
   - Contents page — 4
   - Discussion — 9
   - Findings — 8
   - Introduction — 5
   - Literature Review — 6
   - Methodology — 7
   - Recommendations — 11
   - Reference section — 12
   - Title page — 1

## Appendix 2: Answers

**6** What elements of a thesis/dissertation are *not* usually found in reports?

Acknowledgements

List of illustrations, List of tables, and List of abbreviations (in the Contents).

**7** Why might it be best to write the Abstract *last*?

Because it summarises the whole document, and you may not be able to write a good summary until the document is finished.

**8** What is the purpose of the Introduction? What should it contain?

The purpose of the Introduction is to enable the reader to understand the main body of the thesis/dissertation.

The Introduction should show the context of the research, why the subject is important, the aim and objectives of the research, and how the thesis/dissertation is organized.

**9** How might the following types of data be represented in the *Results* chapter?

- Quantitative data    Graphs and pie charts.
- Qualitative data    Tables, along with quoted excerpts.

**10** What problems might you encounter when preparing the *Reference section* for a thesis/dissertation? How can you overcome these problems?

The extensive writing process means it is easy to omit one or more references, or include one or more which are not cited (they may have been in an earlier draft, then deleted).

You should check carefully (when proofreading the final draft).

# Unit 21: Abstracts

## Unit 21, Exercise 1: **Comprehension**

**1** What is an abstract? What is the purpose of an abstract?
An abstract is a shortened version of an academic paper, appearing before the paper. Its purpose is to provide concise information to the reader so they can decide whether to read the article in detail.

**2** How are an *abstract* and an *executive summary* similar? How are they different?
**Similar**: both present a summary of the document.
**Differences**: an *abstract* is for expert audience, to help them decide whether to read the whole; an *executive summary* is for a non-expert audience, more detailed and longer than an abstract, for management personnel, so they do not need to read the whole.

**3** What are the two types of abstract? Which one is most commonly used?
- **Informative** (*most common type*)
- **Descriptive**

**4** How long is a typical abstract? How long is an executive summary?
An abstract is 5% to 10% (100 to 200 words for a short document).
A descriptive abstract may be shorter, up to 100 words.
An executive summary is longer than an abstract, typically 10% to 20%.

**5** Complete the following summary of language for abstracts, using words from the box.
In order to convey information effectively, abstracts usually use a) **simple** sentences and b) **active** statements. c) **Non-standard** abbreviations should be avoided. The verb d) **tense** often differs according to the type of abstract, for example e) **present** for *descriptive* abstracts and f) **past** for *informative* ones. *Descriptive* abstracts usually use g) **general** words and phrases, while *informative* abstracts tend to use more h) **precise** language.

## Unit 21, Exercise 2: **Example abstracts**

a) Which abstract is *informative* and which is *descriptive*? How do you know?
Abstract 1 is *descriptive*. The information is very general, e.g.:
- *ways of addressing the issues are examined*; (What are the ways? They are not listed.)
- *the phenomenographic process is analysed*; (What is the process? It is not stated.)
- *and suggestions are made*. (What are the suggestions? They are not given.)

Abstract 2 is *informative*. The information is specific, e.g.:
- *Exposure to adverts for e-cigarettes does not seem to increase the appeal of tobacco smoking in children.* (This is a specific finding.)

The tenses also give an indication (see b) below).

# Appendix 2: Answers

b) What tense is most common in each abstract? In each one, find examples of:
- **present** tense [this is most common in **1**, the *descriptive* abstract]
- **past** tense [this is most common in **2**, the *informative* abstract]

In this paper the author **considers** issues of quality in phenomenographic research. Research rigor, which **is** traditionally evaluated by validity and reliability criteria, **ensures** that research findings reflect the object of study. Quality in research **subsumes** rigor and **extends** considerably beyond satisfying the criteria for rigor. A piece of research **has** to convince readers of its quality when evaluated against criteria that have been developed through contributions and agreements within the research community. This paper **tackles** the quality issue in phenomenographic research in three steps. First, criteria for quality in qualitative research **are discussed**. Second and drawing on the literature, related issues when the criteria **are applied** to phenomenographic studies and the ways of addressing the issues **are examined**. Finally, the phenomenographic process **is analyzed** and suggestions **are made** for enhancing quality at each stage of the process. New phenomenographic researchers especially will find this paper as a useful guide.

There **are** concerns that the marketing of e-cigarettes may increase the appeal of tobacco smoking in children. We **examined** this concern by assessing the impact on appeal of tobacco smoking after exposure to advertisements for e-cigarettes with and without candy-like flavours, such as bubble gum and milk chocolate. We **assigned** 598 English school children (aged 11–16 years) to 1 of 3 different conditions corresponding to the adverts to which they were exposed: adverts for flavoured e-cigarettes, adverts for non-flavoured e-cigarettes or a control condition in which no adverts were shown. The primary endpoint **was** appeal of tobacco smoking. Secondary endpoints **were**: appeal of using e-cigarettes, susceptibility to tobacco smoking, perceived harm of tobacco, appeal of e-cigarette adverts and interest in buying and trying e-cigarettes. Tobacco smokers and e-cigarette users **were** excluded from analyses (final sample=471). Exposure to either set of adverts **did** not increase the appeal of tobacco smoking, the appeal of using e-cigarettes, or susceptibility to tobacco smoking. Also, it **did** not reduce the perceived harm of tobacco smoking, which was high. Flavoured e-cigarette adverts **were**, however, more appealing than adverts for non-flavoured e-cigarettes and elicited greater interest in buying and trying e-cigarettes. Exposure to adverts for e-cigarettes **does** not seem to increase the appeal of tobacco smoking in children. Flavoured, compared with non-flavoured, e-cigarette adverts **did**, however, elicit greater appeal and interest in buying and trying e-cigarettes. Further studies extending the current research **are needed** to elucidate the impact of flavoured and non-flavoured e-cigarette adverts.

c) Study the second extract again (copied below). Identify and label the following elements:
- Background
- Methods
- Results
- Conclusions

Below are the sections. This is how the abstract was presented in the original journal. It is an increasing trend for journals to require headings for sections of abstracts.

> **Background** There are concerns that the marketing of e-cigarettes may increase the appeal of tobacco smoking in children. We examined this concern by assessing the impact on appeal of tobacco smoking after exposure to advertisements for e-cigarettes with and without candy-like flavours, such as bubble gum and milk chocolate.
>
> **Methods** We assigned 598 English school children (aged 11–16 years) to 1 of 3 different conditions corresponding to the adverts to which they were exposed: adverts for flavoured e-cigarettes, adverts for non-flavoured e-cigarettes or a control condition in which no adverts were shown. The primary endpoint was appeal of tobacco smoking. Secondary endpoints were: appeal of using e-cigarettes, susceptibility to tobacco smoking, perceived harm of tobacco, appeal of e-cigarette adverts and interest in buying and trying e-cigarettes.
>
> **Results** Tobacco smokers and e-cigarette users were excluded from analyses (final sample=471). Exposure to either set of adverts did not increase the appeal of tobacco smoking, the appeal of using e-cigarettes, or susceptibility to tobacco smoking. Also, it did not reduce the perceived harm of tobacco smoking, which was high. Flavoured e-cigarette adverts were, however, more appealing than adverts for non-flavoured e-cigarettes and elicited greater interest in buying and trying e-cigarettes.
>
> **Conclusions** Exposure to adverts for e-cigarettes does not seem to increase the appeal of tobacco smoking in children. Flavoured, compared with non-flavoured, e-cigarette adverts did, however, elicit greater appeal and interest in buying and trying e-cigarettes. Further studies extending the current research are needed to elucidate the impact of flavoured and non-flavoured e-cigarette adverts.
>
> Abstract adapted from *Vasiljevic M, Petrescu DC, Marteau TM (2016) 'Impact of advertisements promoting candy-like flavoured e-cigarettes on appeal of tobacco smoking among children: an experimental study'*, Tobacco Control, 2016;25:e107-e112.

# Appendix 2: Answers

# Unit 22: Literature Reviews

## Unit 22, Exercise 1: Comprehension

1. What is a literature review? What is its purpose?
   <u>A literature review gives a critical summary of the existing research in the field.</u>
   <u>Its purpose is to identify gaps and create a starting point for your own research.</u>

2. True or **false**: A literature review is a stand-alone piece of writing. Explain your answer.
   **False**. <u>Literature reviews may be stand-alone pieces of writing (written before the research).</u>
   <u>They often form part of larger pieces of writing such as theses, dissertations and reports.</u>

3. What do you need to do in the introduction to a literature review?
   - <u>outline the topic or issue (in order to provide context for the review)</u>
   - <u>give key concepts or terms</u>
   - <u>give an overview of the method of organisation of the main body of the review</u>
   - <u>give the scope (why certain literature is included while other literature is excluded)</u>

4. What do you need to do in the conclusion to a literature review?
   - <u>summarise the most significant findings of the studies you have reviewed</u>
   - <u>identify gaps in knowledge</u>
   - <u>identify areas for future study</u>
   - <u>identify methods relevant to your study</u>

5. What are the organising principles given in the text?
   - <u>Chronology</u>
   - <u>Theme</u>
   - <u>Conclusions</u>
   - <u>Methodology</u>

6. When reviewing a particular study, how can you demonstrate its importance?
   <u>The more important you feel a particular study is, the more space it should take up in the</u>
   <u>literature review (space equals significance).</u>

7. Complete the following summary of writing guidelines for literature reviews.

   When writing the review, you should use a) **evidence** from specific b) **writers** or studies to support your points. You should be c) **selective** and include only the most important points. It is important for the literature to be d) **relevant** to the focus of your review. It is also important to be e) **brief**, which means summarising information rather than using f) **quotations**. If more than one writer says the same thing, you should g) **synthesise** the information, in other words, link the sources together. Finally it is important to be h) **cautious** in how you report findings, and not overstate the claims made in the findings.

# Unit 22, Exercise 2: Example literature review

a) Complete the following summary of the *background* of the article.

Job satisfaction and burnout in the **i) nursing** industry are of **ii) global** importance for two reasons: first, because of their effect on quality and **iii) safety** of patient care; and second, because low **iv) job satisfaction** can lead to nurses leaving their job. Shifts of **v) 12 h** or longer have become increasingly common in Europe, mainly because of managers' ideas of improved **vi) efficiency**. Longer shifts may be beneficial to nurses because they lead to fewer **vii) work days** and more **viii) days off-work**. This in turn means lower **ix) commuting costs** and greater **x) flexibility**. However, **xi) previous studies** in Europe have not shown evidence of nurses working fewer days in a week. The trend for longer shifts for nurses has not been based on **xii) research evidence** of improved benefits for nurses and a lack of **xiii) harm** to patients.

b) The following four sources are all listed in the literature review (only the first two have names used in the review): **16. Stimpfel, 18. Estabrooks et al., 19,** and **20**. Which of the sources are associated with the following findings?

| Findings | Source(s) |
| --- | --- |
| **a)** Nurses working extended shifts were more satisfied with their *work schedules* or *work-life balance*. | 16. Stimpfel<br>20 |
| **b)** Nurses working longer shifts were more likely to experience *burnout*. | 16. Stimpfel<br>19<br>20 |
| **c)** Nurses working longer shifts were more likely to experience *job dissatisfaction*. | 16. Stimpfel<br>19 |
| **d)** Nurses working longer shifts were more likely to *leave their job*. | 19 |
| **e)** There was not enough evidence that shift length affected nurse job satisfaction and burnout. | 18. Estabrooks *et al.* |

# Appendix 2: **Answers**

c) Study the example literature review to answer the questions.

| Section | Item | Questions | Answers |
|---|---|---|---|
| **Context** | The introduction gives an outline of the topic or issue. | 1. What is the topic or issue covered in the literature review? | The effects of nurses working long shifts (12 h or more). |
| **Scope** | The scope is given (what literature is included/excluded). | 2. What is the scope of the research paper? | The scope of the research paper is European hospitals. |
| | | 3. How is the scope of the literature review *different from the research paper*? | The scope of the review is broader, since it includes US and European hospitals |
| | | 4. What problem does the writer identify with using this broader scope for the literature review? | The US research cannot be generalised since regulations in US hospitals are different from European hospitals. |
| | | 5. How might this problem help to justify the writer's own research? | Since the US research cannot be generalised to European hospitals, new research to verify them in European hospitals would need to be conducted. |
| **Organising principle** | Literature is grouped appropriately (by *chronology, theme, conclusions,* or *methodology*). | 6. How is the literature review organised? | The organising principle is conclusions. The sources are linked according to what they found out (the 'outcomes'). Note: There is some mention of chronology ('a more recent systematic review' and 'A recent study') but this is not the main way the review is organised. |
| **Sub-headings** | Main body uses sub-headings, if necessary (long reviews only). | 7. Are sub-headings used? Why (not)? | No. Since it is a very short review, they are not needed. |
| **Evidence** | Specific writers or studies are referred to, to support points. | 8. How many writers or studies are referred to in the review? | Eight (sources numbered 14-21) |
| **Brevity** | Main ideas of writers/studies are summarised (rather than paraphrased or quoted). | 9. How many quotations are used in the review? | None. The writer summarises the information. |
| **Importance** | More important findings take up more space. | 10. *Which* two *sources are most important, i.e. which ones take up most space?* | Source 20 occupies the most space. Source 16 (Stimpfel) occupies the second most amount of space. |
| **Comparison/ contrast** | Similarities/ differences between findings are highlighted. | 11. Identify at least one transition signal to show comparison *and at least* one *to show* contrast. | ..., **while** *a more recent systematic review reported*... **Similarly**, *Stimpfel[16] reported that*... |
| **Synthesis** | Sources are linked together if they say the same thing. | 12. Give examples of sources which are linked in (i) the background and (ii) the review. | (i) Sources 1-2, 5-6, 7-8, 11-12, and 9, 13, 14 are linked in the background. (ii) Sources 14-17 are linked in the first sentence of the review. |

# Appendix 3 | Transitions signals

The following is an explanation of transition signals, and also a list by different type. The majority of these are taken from units earlier in the book.

## Overview

Transition signals are used to show relationships between ideas in writing. They allow the ideas to 'cohere' or stick together, thereby creating cohesion. For example, the transition signal 'for example' is used to give examples, while the word 'while' is used to show a contrast. In addition, there are phrases like 'in addition' for adding new ideas. Likewise, there are words such as 'likewise' to connect similar ideas.

## Grammar of transition signals

Broadly speaking, transition signals can be divided into three types:
- sentence connectors;
- clause connectors;
- other connectors.

*Sentence connectors* are used to connect two sentences together. They are joined by a full-stop (period) or semi-colon, and are followed by a comma. The following are examples of sentence connectors.
- Transition signals are very useful. **However**, they should not be used to begin every sentence.
- Transition signals are very useful; **however**, they should not be used to begin every sentence.
- Contrast signals are one type of transition signals. **In addition**, there are others such as compare signals and addition signals.
- There are three main ways to improve cohesion in your writing. **First**, you can use transition signals.

*Clause connectors* are used to connect two independent clauses together to form one sentence. They are joined by a comma. The following are examples of clause connectors.
- Transition signals are very useful, **but** they should not be used to begin every sentence.
- **Although** transition signals are very useful, they should not be used to begin every sentence.
- Contrast signals are one type of transition signal, **and** there are others such as compare signals and addition signals.

*Other* connectors follow different grammar patterns. Many are followed by noun phrases. Some are verbs and should therefore be used as verbs in a sentence. The following are examples of other connectors.

- **Despite** their importance in achieving cohesion, transition signals should not be used to begin every sentence.
- Good cohesion **is the result of** using repeated words, reference words, and transition signals.
- **It is clear that** careful use of transition signals will improve the cohesion in your writing.
- Contrast signals are one type of transition signal. **Another** type is comparison signals.

# Types of transition signal

Below are examples of different types of transition signals. They are divided by type, and sub-divided according to grammar.

## Comparison

| Sentence connectors | Clause connectors | Other |
|---|---|---|
| - Similarly<br>- Likewise<br>- Also<br>- In the same way | - as<br>- just as<br>- both... and...<br>- not only... but also...<br>- neither... nor...<br>- in the same way as | - like<br>- just like<br>- to be similar to<br>- to be similar in (+ similarity)<br>- to be comparable to<br>- to be the same as<br>- alike<br>- to be alike in (+ similarity)<br>- to compare (to/with) |

## Contrast

| Sentence connectors | Clause connectors | Other |
|---|---|---|
| - However<br>- In contrast<br>- In comparison<br>- By comparison<br>- On the other hand | - while<br>- whereas<br>- but | - to differ from<br>- to be different (from/to)<br>- to be dissimilar to<br>- (to be) unlike<br>- in contrast to |

## Concession

| Sentence connectors | Clause connectors | Other |
|---|---|---|
| - However<br>- Nevertheless<br>- Nonetheless<br>- Still | - although<br>- even though<br>- though<br>- but<br>- yet | - despite<br>- in spite of |

# Appendix 3: Transition signals

## Cause and effect

Below are some common cause and effect transition signals. They are presented in the same way as in the cause and effect unit. [C] is used to indicate a cause, while [E] is used to indicate the effect. Those in the 'other' group are sub-divided according to the main word used in the transition signal (e.g. *reason, cause, result, effect*).

**Sentence connectors**

| [C]. | As a result,<br>As a consequence,<br>Consequently,<br>Therefore,<br>Thus,<br>Hence, | [E] |
|---|---|---|

**Clause connectors**

| [E] | because<br>since<br>as | [C] |
|---|---|---|
| Because<br>As | [C], [E] | |

**Other**

*reason (n)*
- [C] is the reason for [E]
- [E]. The reason is [C]

*cause (n)*
- [C] is the cause of [E]
- [C] is one of the causes of [E]
- The cause of [E] is [C]

*cause (v)*
- [C] causes [E]
- [E] is caused by [C]

*lead to (v)*
- [C] leads to [E]

*because of (conj)*
- Because of [C], [E]
- [E] is because of [C]

*due to (conj)*
- Due to [C], [E]
- [E] is due to [C]

*owing to (conj)*
- Owing to [C], [E]
- [E] is owing to [C]

*explain (v)*
- [C] explains why [E]

*explanation (n)*
- [C] is the explanation for [E]

*result (n)*
- [C]. The result is [E]
- As a result of [C], [E]
- The result of [C] is [E]
- [E] is the result of [C]

*result (v)*
- [C] results in [E]
- [E] results from [C]

*effect (n)*
- The effect of [C] is [E]
- [C] has an effect on [E]
- [E] is the effect of [C]
- [E] is one of the effects of [C]

*affect (v)*
- [C] affects [E]
- [E] is affected by [C]

*consequence (n)*
- As a consequence of [C], [E]
- The consequence of [C] is [E]
- [E] is a consequence of [C]
- [E] is the consequence of [C]

# Examples

| Sentence connectors | Clause connectors | Other |
|---|---|---|
| • For example<br>• For instance<br>• In this case | like* | • such as<br>• (to be) an example of<br>• one example of this (is)<br>• take the case of<br>• to demonstrate<br>• to illustrate |

*Informal

# Additional ideas

| Sentence connectors | Clause connectors | Other |
|---|---|---|
| • Also<br>• Besides<br>• Furthermore<br>• In addition<br>• Moreover<br>• Additionally | • and<br>• nor | • another<br>• an additional |

# Chronological order

| Sentence connectors | Clause connectors | Other |
|---|---|---|
| • First<br>• First of all<br>• Second<br>• Third<br>• Next<br>• Now<br>• Soon<br>• Last<br>• Finally<br>• Previously<br>• Meanwhile<br>• Gradually<br>• After that<br>• Since | • as<br>• as soon as<br>• before*<br>• after*<br>• since*<br>• until<br>• when<br>• while | • the first<br>• the second<br>• the next<br>• the last<br>• the final<br>• before* (lunch etc.)<br>• after* (the war etc.)<br>• since* (1970 etc.)<br>• in the year (2000 etc.) |

\* These can be both *clause connectors* or *other*, depending on usage, e.g.:
  - **After** the water was placed in the beaker, the reagent was added.
  - **After** placing the water in the beaker, the reagent was added.

# Appendix 3: Transition signals

## Order of importance

| Sentence connectors | Clause connectors | Other |
|---|---|---|
| - Above all<br>- First and foremost<br>- More importantly<br>- Most importantly<br>- Primarily | | - a more important<br>- the most important<br>- the second most significant<br>- the primary |

## Alternative ideas

| Sentence connectors | Clause connectors | Other |
|---|---|---|
| - Alternatively<br>- Otherwise | - or<br>- if<br>- unless | |

## To identify/clarify

| Sentence connectors | Clause connectors | Other |
|---|---|---|
| - That is<br>- In other words<br>- Specifically | | - namely<br>- i.e. |

## To reinforce

| Sentence connectors | Clause connectors | Other |
|---|---|---|
| - In fact<br>- Indeed<br>- Of course<br>- Clearly | | |

## To conclude

| Sentence connectors | Clause connectors | Other |
|---|---|---|
| - All in all<br>- In brief<br>- In conclusion<br>- In short<br>- In summary | | - to summarise<br>- to conclude<br>- It is clear that...<br>- We can see that...<br>- The evidence suggests...<br>- These examples show... |

# Appendix 4 | Essay Topics

The following are some possible topics for writing different types of essay. They can also be found in the exercises for the respective units, but are copied here for convenience.

## Unit 2: Comparison & Contrast

The following topics can be compared and contrasted. Choose one to write a *comparison and contrast* essay.

1. One aspect of two cultures (e.g. education, family life, entertainment).
2. One aspect of your country today compared to 20 years ago (e.g. education, family life, technology).
3. Two historical periods or events (e.g. Roman Empire vs. Egyptian Empire, World War I vs. World War II).
4. Two religions.
5. Two forms of government (or governments in two different countries).
6. Online learning vs. traditional classroom-based learning.
7. Secondary (i.e. high school) education and education at tertiary (i.e. university) level.
8. One aspect of two languages (e.g. vocabulary, grammar, writing).
9. Two famous people from the same field (e.g. two writers, two actors).
10. Two famous creative works (e.g. two paintings, two novels, two films).

## Unit 3: Cause & Effect

The following topics can be used to write a *cause and effect* essay.

1. Global warming.
2. Air pollution.
3. Increased life expectancy.
4. Plagiarism.
5. Computer game addiction.
6. Increase in online shopping.
7. Increased demand for fast food.
8. Sleep debt (not getting enough sleep).
9. Increased urbanisation (i.e. people moving out of rural areas and into cities).
10. Refugees (people who leave their country to go to a safer foreign country).
11. Increased use of mobile phones.
12. Stress.
13. Poverty.
14. Unemployment.
15. Inflation.
16. Homelessness.
17. High crime rates in certain countries.
18. Racism.
19. Bullying (physical and/or online i.e. cyber-bullying).
20. A historical topic you know well (e.g. World War II, the American Civil War).

# Academic Writing Genres — Sheldon Smith

## Unit 4: **Problem-Solution**

The following topics can be used to write a *problem-solution* essay.

1. Children are using mobile phones and computers from an earlier age and for longer hours than in the past. What problems does this cause? What are some possible solutions?
2. Civil wars and natural disasters are increasing the number of immigrants to certain nations. What problems does this cause? What solutions are there?
3. What problems are caused by high rate of teenage pregnancy in some countries and communities? How can these problems be addressed?
4. In some countries, students need to pay for university tuition using student loans, often building up huge debts in the process. Why is this a problem? How can this be improved?
5. In some countries, child labour exists. Why is this problematic? How can it be solved?
6. In many countries, divorce rates are increasing. What are the problems and solutions?
7. Many cities in the world have high levels of air pollution. What problems does this cause? How can these problems be tackled?
8. It is increasingly difficult for working people to find a good work-life balance, with the result that many people are overworked. What problems does this cause? How can these be resolved?
9. Why is the growing extinction of animal species a problem? How can it be solved?
10. Some people are unable to afford computers or access to the internet, leading to an 'digital divide'. What are the problems this leads to, and how can these be solved?

## Unit 5: **Classification**

The following topics can be classified and used to write a *classification* essay.

1. Types of energy.
2. Different groups of countries in World War II.
3. Written assignments at university.
4. Types of mobile applications.
5. Types of smart device.
6. Online learning resources.
7. Online communication tools.

## Unit 6: **Argument**

The following topics can be used to write an *argument* essay.

1. It is essential to use animals for research in order to produce medicines and cosmetics which are safe for human use.
2. Students learn best in same sex schools.
3. Sex education is an important part of the curriculum and should be taught when students reach the age of 12.
4. Military spending is essential for national defence.
5. It is important for everyone to learn a second language.
6. Violent computer games lead to violent behaviour and should be banned for under-18s.
7. Governments should spend a large portion of their national budget on tackling climate change.
8. Developed nations need to offer much more financial support to poorer, developing nations.
9. Eating meat is inhumane and everyone should become vegetarian.
10. All schools should have free internet access.

# Appendix 4: Essay topics

## Unit 7: Discussion

The following topics can be used to write a *discussion* essay.
1. Some teachers argue that students learn more effectively when they study in groups. Others believe that students learn best by studying on their own. Discuss the benefits of both, and decide which opinion you agree with.
2. In order to tackle climate change, governments need to work together. Discuss.
3. In the modern world, access to the internet is essential for students' education. Discuss.
4. Some people believe that computers and mobile phones are harmful to children's development. Others, however, believe they offer benefits. Discuss both these views.
5. Many people live far from their workplace and spend much time and money travelling to work each day. What are the advantages and disadvantages of this situation?
6. Cloning is to the benefit of mankind. Discuss.
7. In some countries, governments are encouraging industries and businesses to move out of large cities and into less populated areas. What are the pros and cons of this development?
8. Some countries restrict news content in order to protect their citizens. Others, however, allow complete freedom of the press. What are the advantages of these two approaches?
9. Examine the arguments for and against capital punishment.
10. What are the advantages and disadvantages of technology in the classroom?

## Unit 8: Definition

The following topics can be defined and used to write a *definition* essay.
- A subject you are familiar with (e.g. mathematics, economics, business studies, literature).
- An important term in your field of study (e.g. *homeostasis* in biology, *scarcity* in economics, *cognition* in psychology).
- Cyberbullying.
- Language.
- Intelligence.

## Unit 9: Process

The following topics can be used to write a *process* essay.
- Essay writing is often described as a process. Write about the process of writing an essay, from understanding the title to proofreading the final draft. [Note: For more about the writing process, see https://www.eapfoundation.com/writing/process/.]
- How to find source material for a researched essay.
- How to improve your writing when you have received feedback (from a peer or from your teacher).
- How to prepare for an exam.
- How to start a business.
- How bad habits develop.
- How to prepare for an interview.

## Unit 10: Exemplification

The following topics can be used to write an *exemplification* essay.
- Describe, with examples, the types of writing that students may be required to produce at university.
- Explain, with examples, how technology can be beneficial for education.
- Give examples of types of energy.
- In what ways can technology be harmful to social relationships? Give examples.
- How society has changed over the past twenty years. Give examples.
- Which modern historical figure has had the biggest impact on your country? Justify your answer with examples.
- Choose a field of study (e.g. economics, biology, psychology) and gives examples of how this field is important to the modern world.
- Choose a field of study and give examples of some of the skills required to be successful in that field.

## Unit 11: Description

The following topics can be used to write a *description* essay or paragraph.
- Write a description of a physical object which is important or commonly used in your field of study. Try to describe as many aspects as you can (e.g. size, shape, function).
- Describe an organisation which you know about or which is important in your field of study (e.g. WTO, IMF, WWF, UN, EU, OPEC, UNESCO). Try to describe as many aspects as you can (e.g. size, function, origin), researching online if necessary.

*Note: Because this essay type is more commonly encountered at paragraph rather than essay level, the above can be written as a paragraph rather than a whole essay, though a whole essay is also possible.*

# Appendix 5 | Essay Grid

**Title:**

Write the **introduction** to the essay here. →
You should include:
- general statements;
- definition(s), if needed;
- position, if appropriate;
- thesis statement.

Write the **first main body paragraph** here. →
You should include:
- a topic sentence;
- examples, reasons, facts, statistics, etc. to support your ideas;
- citations, if you have any.

# Academic Writing Genres

**Sheldon Smith**

Write the **second main body paragraph** here. →
You should include:
- a topic sentence;
- examples, reasons, facts, statistics, etc. to support your ideas;
- citations, if you have any.

Write the **third main body paragraph** here. →
You should include:
- a topic sentence;
- examples, reasons, facts, statistics, etc. to support your ideas;
- citations, if you have any.

## Appendix 5: **Essay grid**

Write the **conclusion** here. →

You should include:
- a summary;
- a final comment;
- recommendation (if appropriate).

---

If you have referred to outside sources, write the **references** (or works cited) here. →

References

# Index

abstract .................................................. 296
abstract type
    descriptive ........................................ 297
    informative ........................................ 297
AIMRAD ................................................ 166
appendices ............................................ 166
block (structure) ....................... 35, 54, 69
book review .......................................... 260
cause
    immediate/remote ............................. 53
    main/contributing .............................. 53
chain (structure) ............................. 54, 69
characteristics (for classification) .......... 80
checklist
    abstract ............................................... 299
    argument essay ................................. 100
    book review ....................................... 263
    business report ................................. 205
    cause and effect essay ...................... 57
    classification essay ............................. 84
    comparison and contrast essay ........ 40
    definition essay ................................. 122
    description essay .............................. 152
    discussion essay ................................ 112
    essay (general) .................................... 22
    exemplification essay ....................... 142
    laboratory report .............................. 188
    literature review ............................... 309
    poster ................................................. 238
    problem-solution essay ..................... 71
    process essay .................................... 132
    reflection (Gibbs) .............................. 252
    reflection (Johns) .............................. 253
    report (general) ................................. 169
    research proposal ............................. 275
    thesis/dissertation ............................ 287
concluding sentence ............................. 19
conclusion .............................................. 20

contents page ...................................... 165
controlling idea ...................................... 17
counter-argument .................................. 97
criteria
    for classification .................................. 80
    for comparison/contrast .................... 40
discussion section (report) .................. 183
dissertation ............. *See* thesis/dissertation
division .................................................... 80
effect
    immediate/delayed ............................ 53
    primary/secondary ............................. 53
    short-term/long-term ........................ 53
end matter ........................................... 166
enumeration ......................................... 120
essay
    overview .............................................. 14
    structure ............................................. 21
essay grid ............................................. 421
essay type
    argument ............................................ 96
    cause and effect ................................. 52
    classification ....................................... 80
    comparison and contrast ................... 34
    definition .......................................... 120
    description ....................................... 150
    discussion ......................................... 110
    exemplification ................................. 140
    problem-solution ............................... 68
    process .............................................. 130
etymology ............................................ 120
evaluation .............................................. 68
executive summary .............................. 296
final comment ........................................ 20
first conditional ..................................... 98
general statements ............................... 15
Gibbs (reflective cycle) ......................... 248

# Index

IMRAD .................................................. 166
introduction ........................................... 15
Johns' (model of structured reflection) 249
Kolb (learning cycle) ............................. 248
laboratory report
    language ......................................... 185
    structure ......................................... 181
language (phrases) ... *See* transition signals
learning cycle ....................................... 248
letter of transmittal .............................. 202
literature review ................................... 306
main body ............................................. 17
method section (report) ...................... 182
modal verbs .......................................... 70
multiple criteria (structure) .................. 81
negation ............................................... 120
persuasion ............................................ 97
point-by-point (structure) .................... 35
predicting the consequence ................. 97
preliminaries ........................................ 165
primary research .................................. 163
process
    directional ...................................... 130
    habitual ........................................... 130
    informational .................................. 130
    particular ........................................ 130
reflective writing .................................. 248
relative clause ...................................... 121
report
    language ......................................... 168
    structure ......................................... 164
report type
    business report .............................. 200
    case study report ........................... 221
    design report ................................. 224
    field report ..................................... 225
    laboratory report ........................... 180
    progress report .............................. 222
    project report ................................. 223
    research report .............................. 220
    technical report ............................. 226
reports .................................................. 162
reports vs. essays ................................. 163
research proposal
    approval proposal .......................... 272
    funding proposal ............................ 272
results section (report) ........................ 182
second conditional ............................... 98
single criterion (structure) .................... 81
situation ............................................... 68
SPSE essay ........................................... 68
summary .............................................. 20
supporting sentences .......................... 18
thesis statement .................................. 16
thesis/dissertation
    difference ....................................... 282
    structure ......................................... 283
title page .............................................. 165
topic ..................................................... 17
topic sentence ..................................... 17
transition signals/language
    book review .................................... 262
    cause and effect ............................. 55
    classification (criterion) ................. 82
    classification (result) ..................... 82
    comparison .................................... 36
    concluding ...................................... 19
    contrast ........................................... 38
    counter-argument ......................... 99
    description ..................................... 151
    exemplification .............................. 141
    process ........................................... 131
    reflective writing ............................ 251
    sub-division .................................... 83
Venn diagram ....................................... 48
white space .......................................... 235

Printed in Great Britain
by Amazon